FAMILY LAW

This text is dedicated to
the memory of our co-author

Hilary E. Walpole

1957–2001

FAMILY LAW

General Editor
Geoffrey Shannon

 BLACKSTONE
PRESS LIMITED

Published by
Blackstone Press Limited
Aldine Place
London
W12 8AA
United Kingdom

Sales enquiries and orders
Telephone +44-(0)-20-8740-2277
Facsimile +44-(0)-20-8743-2292
e-mail: sales@blackstone.demon.co.uk
website: www.blackstonepress.com

ISBN 1-84174-180-9
© Law Society of Ireland 2001
First published 2001

British Library Cataloguing in Publication Data
A catalogue record for this book is available from the British Library

Typeset in 10/12pt Meridien by Hewer Text Ltd, Edinburgh
Printed and bound in Great Britain by M & A Thomson Litho Ltd, East Kilbride

AUTHORS

David Bergin is a solicitor and partner in O'Connor & Bergin. He is Chairman of the Law Society of Ireland's Family Law and Civil Legal Aid Committee. He is co-author of *The Law of Divorce in Ireland* (Jordans, 1997) and *Irish Family Legislation* (Jordans, 1999).

Stephanie Coggans is a Solicitor in Charge with the Legal Aid Board. She is a contributor to *Family Law Practitioner* (Round Hall, 2000), *The Divorce Act in Practice* (Round Hall, 1999) and is co-author of *The Family Law (Divorce) Act 1996* (Round Hall, 1998).

Louise Crowley is a solicitor who is a full-time lecturer in the Law Department of National University of Ireland, Cork. She was previously in private practice. Louise completed an LL.M. in National University of Ireland, Cork in 1997, which incorporated a thesis on the financial implications of the Family Law (Divorce) Act 1996.

Eugene Davy is principal in the Dublin firm Eugene Davy, Solicitors. He is a former Chairman of the Law Society of Ireland's Family Law and Civil Legal Aid Committee and is a member of the editorial board of the *Irish Journal of Family Law* (Round Hall).

Sarah Farrell is a practising barrister. She has a particular interest in child abduction and has contributed to the chapter entitled 'Child Abduction'.

Brian Gallagher is a practising solicitor and managing partner of Gallagher Shatter. He is Chairman of the Law Society of Ireland's Conveyancing Committee. Brian has published widely in the family law area and is author of *Powers of Attorney Act 1996* (Round Hall, 1998).

Rosemary Horgan is a solicitor in private practice. She is a partner and head of the family law department in Ronan Daly Jermyn. She is a former Chairman of the Law Society of Ireland's Family Law and Civil Legal Aid Committee. Rosemary is a member of the editorial board of the *Irish Journal of Family Law* and is a contributor to both *Family Law Practitioner* and *The Divorce Act in Practice*.

Conor Power is a practising family law barrister. He is a member of the editorial board of the *Irish Journal of Family Law* and is general editor of *Family Legislation Service* (Round Hall, 2000).

Geoffrey Shannon is a solicitor and Deputy Director of Education in the Law Society of Ireland. He is editor of the *Irish Journal of Family Law*, *The Divorce Act in Practice* and *Family Law Practitioner*. Geoffrey is a member of the Law Society of Ireland's Family Law and Civil Legal Aid Committee and has written extensively on family law issues in various legal journals.

The late **Hilary Walpole** was a solicitor who specialised in revenue law. She was a director with PricewaterhouseCoopers and an associate of the Institute of Taxation. Hilary lectured on taxation to students of professional bodies. In recent years, she carried out detailed research into the tax legislation affecting marital breakdown and lobbied successfully for a number of changes in this legislation. She was a contributor to *The Divorce Act in Practice* and *Family Law Practitioner*. and wrote extensively on issues of taxation and family law.

PREFACE

This manual is emerging at a time when the volume as well as the increasing complexity of legislation in the area of family law, coupled with the *in camera* nature of family law proceedings, have resulted in a clamour for guidance by practitioners. The pension adjustment provision contained in the Family Law Act 1995 and the Family Law (Divorce) Act 1996 along with recent statutory innovations for the giving of child evidence in the Children Act 1997 clearly illustrate this trend. In fact, the Children Act 1997 brings about a fundamental revolution in the law relating to children and will continue to influence law and practice for many years to come.

While the manual will serve the particular needs of apprentice solicitors, it is hoped that the text will provide assistance to all practitioners in the growing and developing area of family law. It draws on the hands-on experience of Ireland's leading family lawyers and their everyday experience of working with legislation to provide a full understanding of family law and its practical applications.

I am indebted to a large number of people who have contributed to this project. I would like to thank the contributors whose work, unstinting patience, guidance and support have assisted in bringing the project to completion. In particular, I would like to acknowledge the contribution of Hilary Walpole, who wrote the chapter on 'Taxation Implications of Marriage Breakdown' but, sadly, did not live to see it published. In addition, I would like to acknowledge the assistance afforded by Bríd Moriarty and Sinéad Conneely, who both expended a great amount of time in reading and commenting on a draft of this text.

While every effort has been made to ensure that the text is accurate, the authors would be very grateful to learn of any errors or omissions. Indeed, as editor, I would be pleased to receive any comments on the material included in this work and invite suggestions as to any material which might be included in future editions.

When commencing this project the primary objective was to focus attention on the main areas of family law of relevance to apprentice solicitors and to provide a user-friendly resource to practice in the area. My hope is that this work has, in some way, achieved this.

Geoffrey Shannon
February 2001

CONTENTS

CONTENTS

CONTENTS

CONTENTS

TABLES OF LEGISLATION

ARTICLES OF THE CONSTITUTION

TABLE OF STATUTES

TABLE OF RULES AND REGULATIONS

TABLE OF TREATIES AND CONVENTIONS

LIST OF CASES

CHAPTER 1

TAKING INSTRUCTIONS IN FAMILY LAW

1.1   Family Law is Different

Family law is different from other areas of practice. In the first place the lawyer must be particularly sensitive to the welfare needs of children as well as to the emotional and psychological trauma experienced by clients involved in conflictual family law litigation. Secondly, in other areas of practice the court must reach objective decisions about past facts and events and determine the legal rights, which have accrued to the litigants when determining the case. In family law cases the court must also exercise a wide judicial discretion when determining choices about current and future behaviour, needs and responsibilities of the family members. The court is not bound by 'who owns which asset' but rather must decide 'to whom should it be given' in the context of separation or divorce. The task of the family lawyer is to bring a working knowledge of the law to bear on the specific client's problem in a professional and planned way.

The first interview with the client should achieve the following goals:

(a)   identify the facts;

(b)   identify the legal issues involved;

(c)   identify the legal or non-legal solutions;

(d)   identify the corroborative evidence;

(e)   evaluate the solutions and then advise the client of the most appropriate solutions; and

(f)   deal with the requirements of the Solicitors (Amendment) Act 1994, s. 68.

Each of these goals will be examined in turn in this chapter.

The Practice Management Guidelines of the Law Society of Ireland recommend the adoption of a procedure designed to achieve these goals in a consistent manner:

'At the outset of the case a practice should establish a procedure for taking instructions (B3.1) which will ensure that fee earners:

a. agree and record:

i.   the client's instructions,

ii.   advice given,

iii.   action to be taken by the practice,

iv.   terms of business,

v.   the basis of charging and the likely cost (or if this cannot be estimated, such information about costs should be given),

vi.   who will be responsible for the conduct of the case;

    b. confirm these with the client (where appropriate, in writing);

    c. provide information to the client about how queries, problems and complaints are resolved by the practice;

    d. identify key dates in the matter and record these in the file and in the back up system.'

Case management is an essential part of good client care. It is well worth examining the specific goals and tasks essential to the first interview with the client.

1.2 Identification of Facts

1.2.1 CLIENT CONSULTATION

The first consultation with the client is extremely important. It is important to obtain enough client information to open a file (name, address, address for correspondence, telephone number, etc.). It is also important to establish relevant dates, for example the date of marriage, dates of birth of the children, date of desertion/separation/adultery, details of other orders obtained or sought to date, as well as a basic history of the conflict to date. If the solicitor adopts a standard format for the interview then it is more likely that all of the necessary basic information will be obtained, and that the solicitor will not become lost in the detail of the particular facts of the case. It is important to establish enough information at the outset to avoid having to revert to the client for the information later.

In family law cases clients are frequently upset and ill at ease. It is essential that the style of interview employed by the solicitor facilitates the full identification of all of the facts in a sensitive manner. It is not only legal knowledge that is relevant, but also the solicitor's ability to set the client at ease, to communicate easily and to obtain the relevant information from the client. It may be acutely embarrassing, for example, for a client to admit to negative conduct on their part if they feel that the lawyer is judging them. Thoughtful and sensitive questioning is essential to elicit a frank response.

It is important to adopt a professional but client-centred approach to the first interview. It is also very important to allow adequate time for the first interview. It is sometimes very difficult to obtain instructions from a client. Difficult clients are a fact of life and it is important to develop strategies to avoid some of the more obvious problems.

1.2.1.1 The passive client

The client may present as passive, seeking the solicitor to take the initiative and decide what course of action is to be followed. Frequently, this type of client is afraid of their spouse/partner and is reluctant to take responsibility for the action needed to achieve a solution to their problem. The solicitor must explain the legal position and the range of options available to them, as well as the best option available. The passive client wants a particular solution but would prefer to blame the solicitor for the action needed to achieve it. While it is important to explore the client's needs, fears and expectations, it is very important for the client to be clear of his or her decision on how best to proceed. This client may need to be referred on to counselling before taking a decision.

1.2.1.2 The tearful client

When a client presents as distraught and tearful throughout the interview, it is essential that he or she be referred on to counselling to deal with the emotional aspect of the problem. Solicitors are only equipped to deal with the legal issues. Solicitors are not, and should never become, social workers or counsellors. It is important in this type of situation to deal with the role and competence of the solicitor at the very outset. Family law problems can be very personal and it is impossible for clients to make any informed decisions until they have dealt with the emotional and psychological aspects of their problem. That is not to say that tearful or distraught clients should not receive legal advice. What is important is that they are assured that their solicitor empathises with their distress, which is perfectly understandable and normal, but that the solicitor's role is as an impartial legal adviser. It may be wise for them to defer a decision on what solution to pursue until they have had an opportunity to consider the matter very calmly.

1.2.1.3 The client who comes with a 'friend'

Sometimes a client will be accompanied by 'a friend', who may wish to do most of the talking. This situation must be handled with great sensitivity. It is very important to acknowledge the need of the client for support; however it is also important to be sure that the instructions are coming from the client and not the friend. The friend may not know all of the facts and the client may be embarrassed to outline them in the presence of the friend. In the first instance the client should be offered tissues and water or some refreshment so that he or she can regain some composure before the consultation continues. The friend can then be asked to step outside for a portion of the consultation where personal details are elicited. This is quite ethical, and, for example, if the friend is a potential witness, it is perfectly in order to ask the friend to absent him or herself for legal ethical reasons. Sometimes the client will indicate that he or she does not require this, but this is generally indicated out of politeness to the friend. It is usually sufficient to indicate that it is the solicitor's practice, or the practice of the firm, to proceed in this manner at least for some of the consultation. The client can be assured that he or she can consult with the 'friend' before any decision is taken. It is an opportunity for the solicitor to explain his or her role and the importance of the solicitor/client confidential relationship.

1.2.1.4 The adversarial client

The client who presents wanting immediate court action and disputatious correspondence to be written at the outset can be very difficult for the family lawyer. This client has made his or her mind up, possibly on the erroneous basis of what they think the law is. It is important to outline clearly to this client what the law is and how it is likely to be applied on the facts presented by them. The Code of Conduct for Family Lawyers produced by the Law Society can be very useful in dealing with such a client. If child-care issues are involved it is absolutely essential that this client is advised to take a child-centred approach to the resolution of the issue. They can be advised of the approach that a court is likely to adopt in such circumstances. It is also quite useful to address with them the issue of legal costs in order to encourage a more realistic attitude to the problem. It is important for the solicitor to be quite clear that, although he or she will act on the instructions of the client, it is his or her duty to conduct the case in an ethical manner in accordance with the law as it is and not as the client perceives it to be.

1.2.1.5 The quick-fix client

This type of client wants an immediate short-term solution to their problem. For example: 'I will agree to leave the family home and my spouse can keep it provided I get custody and can get him/her out of my life'. This type of client frequently re-appears some months or years later to achieve the solution they should have pursued in the first place. If they have entered into a mediated separation agreement they will be bound by the agreement and may find it very difficult to renegotiate, even on divorce. It is very important with this type of client that they are fully advised on the range of options and solutions open to them to achieve a long-term solution to their legal problem. It is, of course, equally important to acknowledge the autonomy of the client in the decision-making process, as long as they make an informed decision.

1.2.1.6   The professional client

It is important to deal with the professional client in a very clear and sensitive manner. Even if the client is a fellow professional it is equally important to explain the advice in relation to the facts of their case. Anyone involved in a family law problem is likely to be under stress. A solicitor is being engaged for professional expertise.

1.3   Identification of Legal Issues Involved

This should be straightforward, provided the investigation of the facts has been sufficiently thorough. Identification of the legal issues involved cannot be achieved without a full investigation of the facts.

For example, a hasty first consultation on the issue of domestic violence may not give enough information to determine whether nullity of the marriage is an issue. It must also be sufficiently thorough to enable the solicitor to determine eligibility under the various headings of entitlement to relief in the context of maintenance proceedings or separation/ divorce proceedings.

1.4   Identification of Legal and Non-legal Solutions

In family law cases it is not enough to identify the legal solutions to the problem. In private child law cases, separation and divorce cases it is a statutory responsibility to discuss with the client the non-legal solutions of reconciliation, mediation and negotiated agreement through solicitors.

It is essential in domestic violence cases, for example, to have an awareness of the particular dynamic of domestic violence. Counselling advised in this context should take into account the background of domestic violence, as to do otherwise might endanger the client. It is important for the solicitor to be aware of the various services available in his or her locality, such as: parenting courses; personal development groups, Men Overcoming Violent Emotions (MOVE); domestic violence project groups; domestic violence support groups; anger management therapy; mediation, both public and private; marriage guidance counselling; family therapy; and rape crisis centres.

Many of these groups will be well-known and professionally based, others less so. It is important to ensure that the client is being referred to an accredited organisation. A list is available in a booklet prepared by the Department of Health, Social and Family Affairs. The local Bar Association will often also have a list.

1.5   Identification of Corroborative Evidence

It is very important to identify the potential corroborative evidence at an early stage, as the potential for success may be significantly affected by its presence or absence. For example:

(a)   Is there medical evidence to support the allegation of assault or ground an application under the Domestic Violence Act 1996?

(b)   Were the Garda Síochána called to this incident or in the past and has any complaint been made?

(c)   What does the information grounding the application for the protection/interim barring order under the Domestic Violence Act 1996 disclose in relation to the facts?

(d)   Can a fault-based separation under the 1989 Act, s. 2(1)(a), (b) or (c) be established?

    (e)   Have the parties lived separately for four out of the previous five years to establish the threshold criteria for divorce?

    (f)   Are the children attending school regularly?

    (g)   Does the Health Board know the family?

    (h)   How is the property held?

    (i)   What evidence of earnings or income is available?

If there is corroborative evidence available from any source it is important to identify this at the outset.

1.6   Evaluation of Solutions and Advice to Client

It is very important to advise the client on the various solutions to the problem presented. For example, the client may have a classic case to institute nullity proceedings, but that remedy could completely militate against obtaining substantive matrimonial relief. A safety order may be more appropriate on the facts than a barring order or perhaps more suitable to the objective which the client wishes to achieve. The client may be unable to institute divorce proceedings but only separation proceedings. A separation agreement may achieve a consensual solution but may not be enough to secure, for example, the pension security needs of a client.

Solicitors are required to consider non-legal solutions. In the case of proceedings under the Guardianship of Infants Act 1964 (as amended), the Judicial Separation and Family Law Reform Act 1989, the Family Law Act 1995 and the Family Law (Divorce) Act 1996 solicitors have a legal obligation to discuss them with the client, and to write to the client subsequently advising them in writing of the names and addresses of organisations and persons qualified to assist them in pursuing the matter through the non-legal medium. In other cases a good solicitor will always bear in mind the non-legal solution in addition to the legal solution.

Advice at the end of the first interview may well be tentative and it is important to say so. It is very important that advice reflects what is achievable and does not foreclose other potential solutions. A common mistake for the young lawyer is to endeavour to impress the client with legal knowledge and use a lot of legal jargon. In reality this approach is counterproductive. It is important to record the advice given (for example advice on reconciliation, mediation and separation agreements). A pro forma prompt sheet for the taking of instructions is very helpful in this regard. It is usually helpful if the solicitor follows up the first consultation by advice on the alternatives in writing. This clarifies the facts and the legal possibilities for the client and enables them to consider the best solution for them.

1.7   Solicitors Act Requirements

1.7.1   GENERAL

Costs are a very important issue in the eyes of the client and also for the legal practice. Clients always want to know how much it will cost them, and this is very difficult to be accurate about in the early stages in family law cases. The basis of charging depends upon the following matters:

    (a)   whether the matter is contentious or non contentious;

    (b)   the time spent on the case (most firms have a minimum hourly rate and time may either be recorded manually or by a computer system);

(c)   the complexity of the issues involved and the degree of skill needed;

(d)   the number of documents prepared, or reviewed;

(e)   where money or property is involved, its amount or value; and

(f)   the urgency of the matter.

The rules on costs are set out in the Solicitors (Amendment) Act 1994, s. 68, and in the Rules of the Superior Courts, Appendix W (SI 15/1986). In the Circuit Court, the issue of costs is set out in the Circuit Court Rules 1965 (SI 202/1965). Solicitors acting as advocates without counsel are entitled to charge a separate advocacy fee (Ord. 55, r. 32). In the District Court, solicitors' costs including appearance are prescribed by the District Court (Costs) Rules 1982 (SI 218/1982). Where the court awards costs and the parties cannot agree on the level of same, the quantum is measured in the High Court by the Taxing Master of the High Court, and in the Circuit Court by the County Registrar. Costs awarded in the District Court are usually measured at the conclusion of the case.

In general, work in connection with court proceedings is contentious and can be charged as such. Family law is generally taxed on solicitors' own client basis. The client is responsible for the solicitor's costs for the work performed, expenses paid and disbursements made on his behalf in the proceedings. It is important to keep attendance notes which should record the time, whether it is by telephone or an office attendance, what was discussed, what action was to be taken as a result, and who was in attendance. Time recording is important to record such detail, including time spent on research, preparation of documentation, perusal of documentation, etc. However, although time is an extremely important element in charging, it is not the only element. Clients must be informed of the rate of charge and the other matters to be taken into account in assessing the solicitor/client costs.

In family law cases, costs do not automatically follow the action, and are at the discretion of the court, so that even if the client is successful he or she may not secure their costs against the other side. On the other hand clients must be advised that, should they lose, they may be obliged to pay the costs incurred by the other side at the discretion of the court.

Section 68 of the Solicitors (Amendment) Act 1994 requires the solicitor to appraise the client of the likely charges at the very outset of and during the case. This can only be done on an approximate basis in family law matters, as much depends upon the variable factors set out above. The client must be informed in writing of the estimated fees or of the basis upon which fees are to be charged. Failure to comply with this requirement amounts to unprofessional conduct and the costs may not be recovered from the client where s. 68 has not been complied with.

1.7.2   LEGALLY-AIDED PARTIES

Civil legal aid may be granted to either or both parties subject to the litigants' statutory eligibility being determined by the Legal Aid Board. The granting of legal aid to one party to litigation can place the unaided party at a severe disadvantage. Costs are equally important to the legally-aided party however. They may not be on the minimum legal aid contribution of £23 and may be paying a substantial amount for their legal services. If they are awarded money or property, at the end of the day the Legal Aid Board may seek to recoup the costs of the provision of the legal aid service out of the money or property they are awarded. There is a mandatory waiver of the Board's 'call' over any money or other property in certain situations. In addition, the legally-aided client may be subject to the 'statutory charge'. The statutory charge provisions appear to be mandatory, unless one of the exceptions provided by the Civil Legal Aid Act 1995 applies. One example of an exception is where the charge relates to property or money recovered which consists of a house or portion thereof being 'the normal place of residence' of the recipient of legal aid or advice. This example would, however, not appear to cover a situation where the court proceedings secured a property adjustment order in respect of other property in order to provide accommodation for the legally-aided recipient.

Where the unsuccessful party is in receipt of civil legal aid, the Legal Aid Board does not discharge the legal costs of the losing legally-aided party. However, where a successful unaided litigant submits a bill of costs to the Board, the Board may make an *ex gratia* payment towards such costs of such amount as it considers appropriate, where it considers that:

(a)   the proceedings were instituted by the unsuccessful litigant;

(b)   the successful litigant has taken all reasonable steps to recover costs from the other litigant;

(c)   the successful litigant will suffer severe financial hardship unless an *ex gratia* payment is made;

(d)   the amount of the *ex gratia* payment will not exceed the amount payable after taxation on a party-and-party basis; and

(e)   the case has been finally determined.

Both private and legal aid clients must be informed of the basis of charge by virtue of the Solicitors (Amendment) Act 1994, s. 68. If a solicitor fails to comply with this section they may not be able to recover their professional fee and, in addition, failure to comply with s. 68 is unprofessional conduct and may be treated as such by the Law Society.

CHAPTER 2

NULLITY

2.1 Introduction

Traditionally, applications to declare marriages null and void have had a special position in Irish family law. This was due to the absence of divorce until 1995. The introduction of divorce has had an effect on the number of nullity decrees sought. There are, however, fundamental ideological and practical differences between the two decrees that must be clarified. The law of nullity is concerned with the legal validity of a marriage at its inception. A marriage can be declared a nullity where some vital component, e.g. the consent to marry, is missing. On the other hand, a divorce dissolves an existing and valid marital tie between the spouses. When a marriage is declared null and void, a court is declaring that the couple were never legally married to one another and they are thus legally free to remarry. While a divorce also leaves the couple free to remarry, the previous marriage is not legally erased and will continue to be a legal reality in the lives of the couple. Finally, the ground upon which an annulment is sought must exist at the date of the marriage, while divorce usually involves a deteriorating matrimonial relationship.

Practical examples of this include the continuing financial and other obligations that may emanate from a divorce by reason of the ancillary orders available. There are no such orders available consequent upon a decree of nullity. This may in some part account for the enduring use of the nullity jurisdiction in appropriate cases. The lack of such provision also demonstrates the absence of statutory reform to the law of nullity, which is still based on common law principles.

Historically, the jurisdiction to declare a marriage null and void was vested in the ecclesiastical courts. With the disestablishment of the Church of Ireland in 1870, jurisdiction was given to the civil courts. The transfer was on the basis of the Matrimonial Causes and Marriage Law (Ireland) Amendment Act 1870, s. 13, which provides:

> In all suits and proceedings the said Court for Matrimonial Causes and Matters shall proceed and act and give relief on principles and rules which, in the opinion of the said Court, shall be as nearly as may be conformable to the principles and rules on which the ecclesiastical courts of Ireland have heretofore acted and given relief but subject to the provisions herein contained, and to the rules and orders to be made by the said Court under this Act.

While the courts are still bound by this statutory provision, they have tended to give it a broad reading in recent years so that the law of nullity has not stagnated but has developed to take account of modern knowledge. The jurisdiction to grant decrees of nullity was assigned exclusively to the High Court until 1996, but s. 38(2) of the Family Law Act 1995 (which came into force on 1 August 1996) gave the Circuit Family Court concurrent jurisdiction in nullity matters. This has made the decree more accessible and affordable to many couples.

The Irish courts have jurisdiction under the Family Law Act 1995, s. 38 to grant annulments if, but only if, one of the following requirements is satisfied:

(a)   either of the spouses concerned was domiciled in the State on the date of the institution of the proceedings concerned;

(b)   either of the spouses was ordinarily resident in the State throughout the period of one year ending on that date; and

(c)   either of the spouses died before that date and

    (i)   was at the time of death domiciled in the State, or

    (ii)   had been ordinarily resident in the State throughout the period of one year ending on that date.

In the Circuit Family Court the decree can be sought in the Circuit where either the petitioner or the respondent ordinarily resides or carries on a business, profession or occupation.

It should also be noted there is often confusion between church nullity and State nullity. Each church is entitled to set requirements regarding marriage according to its own rites. They are accordingly entitled to annul marriages for failure to comply with such rules, but this in no way affects the marriage in the civil law, and care must be taken to fully distinguish between the two. Only a State nullity declares a marriage of no legal effect and entitles a person to remarry in law.

2.2   Void and Voidable Marriages

The grounds upon which a marriage can be declared null and void mirror the legal requirements for a valid marriage and the nature of marriage in Ireland. Where those requirements have not been matched, any subsequent marriage will be of no effect and will be classed as either void or voidable. There are some important differences between these two categories of nullity actions, the basis for which reflects the ground being used. (It should be noted that often more generic phrases are used, e.g. that a marriage is 'null and void', or even that it is 'void' without actually using the terms in a technical sense.)

There are three broad grounds upon which a marriage can be declared void:

(a)   non-observance of formalities;

(b)   lack of capacity;

(c)   lack of consent.

When void for one of these reasons, the marriage never legally existed at all; it was void *ab initio*. In theory, therefore, there is no legal requirement for a court decree, though one should be sought for the sake of clarity, even if it is of declaratory effect only. These grounds reflect public policy considerations for valid marriages (as opposed to matters private to the parties) and thus a declaration that a marriage is void can be sought by interested persons other than the parties to the marriage. A decree can also be sought after the parties have died.

A decree in respect of a marriage that is voidable can only be sought by the parties to the marriage and cannot be instituted after the death of one of the parties. This reflects the personal nature of the grounds for having a marriage decreed voidable, which are:

(i)   impotence;

(ii)   inability to enter and sustain a normal marital relationship.

Voidable marriages are valid until a decree has been granted by a competent court. However, once a decree has been granted, the marriage is retrospectively invalidated *ab initio* and is then seen as having never legally occurred. Thus, e.g., a marriage contracted subsequent to a voidable marriage is bigamous until the first has been annulled, but it thereafter becomes valid from the date of its solemnisation (see *F.M.L. and A.L. v An tArd Chláraitheoir* [1984] ILRM 667). There are other differences between void and voidable marriages that will be dealt with below. It ought to be noted that some cases involve facts that cannot be neatly categorised into one ground or another and that there will be some crossover between the different grounds.

2.3   Void Marriages

Of the three grounds rendering a marriage void mentioned above, the most important is the absence of consent. The vast majority of marriages declared void are so declared on that ground. Before considering the different circumstances that affect the validity of consent, the other two grounds ought to be explored.

2.3.1   NON-OBSERVANCE OF FORMALITIES

The formal requirements for contracting a valid marriage are complex, confused and antiquated, and have been dealt with elsewhere. Non-observance of formalities does not normally affect the validity of a marriage, but where certain formalities have not been observed the marriage will be void if the parties knowingly and wilfully contract the marriage contrary to the requirements: see *I.E. v W.E.* [1985] ILRM 691 and *D.C. v N.M.* [1997] 2 IR 218.

Nowadays, the most important formality is the requirement under the Family Law Act 1995, s. 32 to give at least three months' notice in writing to the Registrar of Marriages for the relevant district of an intention to marry, unless a judicial exemption has been obtained before the marriage. The 1995 Act states that this requirement is a substantive requirement for marriages solemnised within the State.

2.3.2   LACK OF CAPACITY

The capacity to enter a valid marriage is dependent on the common law definition of marriage, being the voluntary union for life of one man and one woman to the exclusion of all others. Therefore, where these elements are not present, the marriage is void and lack of capacity will occur if:

(a)   either party is already validly married to another person;

(b)   the parties are of the same sex;

(c)   they are within the prohibited degrees of relationship;

(d)   either party is under 18 years of age.

The latter requirement was introduced by the Family Law Act 1995, s. 31, and is declared a substantive requirement applying to marriages either solemnised within the State or between parties ordinarily resident within the State. A marriage will not be void for nonage where judicial exemption from the requirement has been obtained under the 1995 Act, s. 33, before the marriage occurs.

2.3.3   LACK OF CONSENT

Under this heading the voluntary nature of the marriage contract is examined to ensure that the parties have willingly become husband and wife. If the consent is vitiated by some factor the marriage is void. The courts seek to establish whether the consent was real or only apparent. This aspect of the law of nullity has seen some considerable development in recent years, caused by the relatively high number of annulments sought on this basis. The ground encompasses a variety of issues that may render consent invalid and reflects the nature of marriage as a contract between the parties, albeit a special one. Thus, Finlay CJ in *N (otherwise K) v K* [1985] IR 733 said, at p. 742:

> 'The entry into a valid marriage is not only the making of a contract but is also, in law, the acquisition of a status. Consent to the taking of such a step must therefore, if the marriage is to be valid, be a fully free exercise of the independent will of the parties.'

The possible bases for lack of consent include:

(a)   mental incapacity;

(b)   intoxication;

(c)   fraud, mistake and misrepresentation;

(d)   duress and undue influence;

(e)   limited purpose marriages.

2.3.3.1   Mental incapacity

There are several aspects to this heading, which is concerned with the parties' mental ability to give consent. (To this extent, there is a crossover with the ground of inability to enter and sustain a normal marital relationship, see below.) Of central concern is the degree of competence necessary to have the capacity to enter a marriage, though there is neither a statutory nor a common law definition of this capacity. However, given that people in general are presumed sane, and that marriages are presumed valid, there should also be a presumption that people have the capacity to contract a marriage. This is supported by the existence of the unenumerated Constitutional right to marry, see *Ryan v Attorney General* [1965] IR 294. It is thus for the party alleging incapacity to prove it. There are several grounds upon which this may be done.

First, where a person has been certified a 'lunatic' by inquisition or declared a 'lunatic or person under a frenzy', whose person and estate have been committed to the care and custody of trustees, their marriage is void under the Marriage of Lunatics Act 1811, even if contracted during a lucid interval. Of wider scope is the common law rule that a marriage is void if either party lacks the mental ability to understand the nature and responsibilities of marriage. This is not the same as proving that a person suffered from a mental illness at the time of marriage, as the focus here is on the understanding of the party. It has been held that since marriage is a simple contract, the law does not require a high degree of intelligence to understand it, see *Re Park* [1954] P 89.

A recent authority is *M.E. v A.E.* [1987] IR 147, where the respondent, a Roman Catholic priest, had married the petitioner following some traumatic events in his life. He gave evidence that he considered the marriage as an effort to get him over those problems, and saw it as a temporary arrangement. Evidence was also given that he suffered from paranoid schizophrenia, which would have affected his ability to understand the marriage contract. O'Hanlon J held that the marriage was void due to the respondent's inability to give a full, free and informed consent to marriage.

2.3.3.2   Intoxication

There are few cases on the point, but it is clear that where a party is so intoxicated as to be incapable of consenting the marriage is void. This is treated in a similar manner to mental incapacity, in that the free will of the party must be absent by reason of intoxication.

2.3.3.3 Fraud, mistake and misrepresentation

Traditionally these vitiating factors were interpreted in a very restrictive manner. Thus in *Swift v Kelly* (1835) 12 ER 648, Lord Brougham said: 'no marriage shall be held void merely upon proof that it had been contracted upon false representations and that, but for such contrivances, consent would never have been obtained.' This restrictive view has been eclipsed by developments as regards the reality of consent in several recent cases and may no longer apply. The Supreme Court, although dealing with matters concerning duress, has signaled a broad and subjective approach to consent in *N (otherwise K) v K* [1985] IR 733 which, coupled with other recent cases, provides more scope for annulment on this ground.

It has always been accepted that a mistake as to the nature and effects of the ceremony will render the marriage invalid. In *Ford v Stier* [1896] P 1 a man was induced to go through a ceremony of marriage, although he believed it to be a betrothal only. The marriage was void. Similarly, mistake as to the identity of the other person will render the marriage invalid, and thus, for example, if William, masquerading as Donncha, marries Nicola, who in turn believes she is marrying Donncha, the marriage is void.

An important limitation in the past was that mistake as to the character of a person did not impact on the validity of the marriage. In *Moss v Moss* [1897] P 263 a concealed pregnancy by another man was not recognised as a ground for annulment. This would also cover other mistaken attributes, e.g. marrying a pauper believing him or her to be wealthy. However, recent cases have shown a willingness to annul marriages where some important attribute has been concealed. In *F v F* [1991] 1 IR 348 the respondent concealed his homosexuality (which he continued to practise after the marriage) from the petitioner by tricks and lies. The petitioner would not have married him if she had known of this, and Barron J held, declaring the marriage void, that her consent to marriage was apparent only and not a real consent.

This was since expanded upon by the Supreme Court in *M.O'M. v B.O'C.* [1996] 1 IR 208. The respondent had not told the petitioner that he had been in psychiatric therapy before the marriage. The petitioner gave evidence that she would not have married him if she had known this. The marriage was declared void because the undisclosed information concerned a matter of substance which would legitimately affect the petitioner's decision. The failure to disclose meant she did not have adequate knowledge to give proper informed consent.

The Supreme Court has more recently signalled a retrenchment of nullity law on this ground. In *P.F. v G.D.M.* (unreported, 28 November 2000, Supreme Ct) the court refused a decree of nullity to a petitioner who claimed that had he known his wife was having an affair during their engagement he would not have consented to marrying her. The court stated that to grant a nullity for such concealment would bring uncertainty to a wide variety of marriages.

Another development in this regard is the dictum of Kenny J in *S v S* (unreported, 1 July 1976, Supreme Ct). This case concerned impotence, but Kenny J held that the unilateral and concealed determination of the husband at the time of marriage not to engage in sexual intercourse rendered the wife's consent to marriage invalid, and the marriage was void as a consequence. Commentators have tended to generalise this finding, to say that fraud in relation to a fundamental feature of marriage may render a marriage void for lack of consent. This innovative judgment appears not to have formed the basis for such a ruling to date, though it represents an important development of principle.

2.3.3.4 Duress and undue influence

In practice, this is probably the most important ground upon which a marriage can be declared void for lack of consent. The law has again changed from a restrictive approach to a broader one that takes a subjective approach to the issue of consent. The courts are now anxious to ensure that consent is real and not apparent, and that it is an exercise of the free will of the parties. Thus many factors will be relevant, including age and maturity at marriage, pressure from the other party or whether there were outside pressures, either from third parties or even from events themselves. Many of the cases have revolved around pregnancy at the time of marriage, as this caused a considerable stigma in the past.

The old approach was to annul marriages only where duress was proved, not on the broader ground of undue influence. The traditional view was that duress amounting to an unlawful threat to life or liberty had to be exerted. This is well illustrated by the case of *Griffith v Griffith* [1944] IR 35 where the petitioner and the respondent met and were intimate in the Dublin mountains. The respondent later became pregnant. The petitioner was told to marry her or the Gardaí would be told of the unlawful carnal knowledge (the respondent was then 17). They married, but did not live together after the wedding. When the child was born, the parties began living together and it was only then that the petitioner became familiar with the facts of life. He also realised, for obvious reasons, that the child was not his. Haugh J held that the mix of fraud and duress rendered the marriage invalid, but only because the fear they caused in the petitioner's mind was improperly imposed. It appears that had the petitioner been the father there would be no duress, the pressure not being improper.

A change is detectable from the mid-1970s. In *B v D* (unreported, 20 June 1973, High Ct, Murnaghan J) the parties were 27 and 34 when married. Both parties were teachers, but had little else in common. The husband frightened the petitioner and took money belonging to her. They married under his duress in that she found herself in a situation from which she could not extract herself. The marriage was declared void as the court held that her free will was overborne.

In *S v O'S* (unreported, 11 November 1978, High Ct, Finlay J) the husband was a medical student who knew the petitioner for about a year and a half. They had planned to marry after his studies were complete. On one occasion the petitioner went to a dance without the respondent and this had a marked effect upon him. He developed Munchausen's Syndrome, which caused him to project bizarre illnesses, and he demanded her constant presence, together with an early marriage. He also threatened to kill himself if this did not occur. The couple did marry, but it was held invalid by the High Court on the basis that:

> 'a person in the emotional bondage of another person could not consciously have the freedom of will to marry'.

In *M.K. v F.McC.* [1982] ILRM 277 O'Hanlon J described these two as cases of undue influence rather than duress. In this case the wife, who was 19, became pregnant and both parties came under very strong pressure to marry from their respective parents. They married six weeks after discovering the pregnancy, though neither played an active role in the preparation for the wedding. The wife had a miscarriage two weeks later; the couple separated three years later. O'Hanlon J rejected the *Griffith* test in favour of the more lenient approach, and held the marriage void as the will of both parties was overborne and they had entered the marriage unwillingly. It should also be noted that the pressure to marry in this case came from third parties, and not one of the parties themselves as occurred in previous cases.

There was no universal acceptance by the High Court of this broader approach at once, and most notably there was a series of judgments from Barron J where the older approach was adhered to. See e.g. *A.C.L. v R.L.* (unreported, October 1982, High Ct) and *E.P. v M.C.* [1985] 5 ILRM 34. There were other judgments in favour of the broad approach.

However, the broad approach was accepted by the Supreme Court in the important case of *N (otherwise K) v K* [1986] 6 ILRM 75, where the petitioner was 19 and the respondent was 20. She became pregnant in 1978, which caused considerable difficulties with her parents. The parties agreed to marry, but they took little interest in each other. The marriage was arranged by their parents, without any great involvement by the parties. During the marriage they had a checkered history of living together and apart. The petitioner claimed that her father forced her into marriage (which he denied) by giving her the choice between that and abortion. The High Court refused a decree, holding that although they would not have married but for the pregnancy and that the parties were immature, the pressure did not amount to duress. The Supreme Court reversed this on appeal.

Finlay CJ held that consent to marriage must be a fully free exercise of the independent will of the parties, and the question was whether the consent was real or apparent. The Chief Justice said that there was no question of the pressure being proper or improper, and that if the decision to marry was caused by external pressure or influence, whether falsely or honestly applied, so as to lose the character of being a free act of a person's will, the marriage was invalid. In addition, the Chief Justice stated that defined concepts such as duress and undue influence 'must remain subservient to the ultimate objective of ascertaining whether the consent of the petitioning party was real or apparent.' McCarthy J, at p. 93, stressed the need for:

'a true voluntary consent based upon adequate knowledge and freed from vitiating factors commonly described as undue influence or duress, particularly those emanating from third parties.'

The Supreme Court's decision was important also for applying a subjective as opposed to an objective approach to the issue of consent. As Shatter remarked: 'It also clearly required trial judges in future to base their determination on one central question: did each party to the marriage genuinely freely consent to marry?' (See Shatter, *Family Law* (4th edn, 1997), para 5.61.)

That the pressure need not emanate from a person but can stem from events was considered in *B v O'R* [1991] 1 IR 289. The parties married in 1966, when the petitioner was 16 and the respondent 26. The petitioner had been raised in an orphanage, and at the age of 15 went to work in a café. She met the respondent and had sexual intercourse with him. Soon after, she went to reside with her parents, but they sent her back to the orphanage when she discovered her pregnancy. The sister in charge contacted the respondent and arranged for them to be married. The petitioner was described as being in a dazed state at the time. The couple stayed together for many years, having four children before the petition was presented in 1987.

The High Court (Carroll J) held that the pressure causing duress or undue influence must come from a person, and not from events, in this case an unwanted pregnancy, or from fear of having nowhere to live, or being on one's own, and refused a decree. This decision was reversed by the Supreme Court. The court accepted that the petitioner was immature and unassertive at the time, and did not have her will overborne by any person. However, from the facts as found by the High Court, it was held that the petitioner was not in a position to give a consent to marriage that was real and that given by her at the time was apparent only. It should be noted that in the Supreme Court the case was argued on the basis of the capacity of the petitioner to give a valid consent and not duress as such.

That decision is a recognition that events can combine to deprive a person of the ability to give an informed consent without the meddling of a third party, and confirms the approach advocated by Finlay CJ in *N (otherwise K) v K* that the core focus is on the reality of consent, not the categorisation of the underlying fault. A similar approach can also be seen in *O.B. v R* [2000] ILRM 306 where it was held that a crisis pregnancy of a young girl who had no sex education and was cut off by her family meant she could not give proper consent to marriage. In 1970, when she was 18, she went through a ceremony of marriage with the respondent. She had been seeing the respondent for several weeks and was pregnant at the time. She had never received sexual education and got no practical support from her parents. It was clear to her that the only way she could keep the child was if she married. Both parties were very distant and ill-informed when entering the marriage. The respondent was a heavy drinker and had affairs with other women, by whom he had children. They lived together for about two years, by which time the petitioner had saved enough money to leave.

There also seems to be an acceptance of economic duress, for example in *W v C* [1989] IR 696 where a marriage was entered on the petitioner's request, despite the respondent having verbally and sexually abused her. She had become pregnant and was told by the principal of the school she would lose her job if she did not marry. There was also pressure to marry from her father. Barron J said the decision to marry was brought about by the strain of the circumstances and declared the marriage void, as the consent was a sham.

Although unwanted pregnancies are involved in many of the cases, the fact of pregnancy alone is not enough. Some other factor of external or third party pressure has always been involved where a decree has been granted. This was recognised by Geoghegan J in *D.C. v N.M.* [1997] 2 IR 218 where the petitioner claimed the marriage was void because he was forced to marry in 1978 by reason of the respondent's pregnancy. The couple had been in a relationship for some time and had a long-term plan to marry. The pregnancy accelerated those plans. Geoghegan J held, in refusing a decree, that were he to grant it, no marriage arising from an unwanted pregnancy could be upheld. He said that this was not a case involving an immature couple unable to withstand external pressure, which he found not to have existed in any case.

2.3.3.5 Limited purpose marriages

These are marriages that are entered for purposes other than those seen as legitimate (an idea which must itself be wide). A good example is marriage in order to gain tax advantages or citizenship. This latter arose in *Kelly v Ireland* [1996] 2 ILRM 364 where the applicant, who was Sudanese, moved to England in 1977. She had a daughter at the time and lived with the father of the child. She married David Kelly, an Irish citizen, in London in 1984 and received an Irish passport (at the time there was some ongoing fraud in relation to issuing such in London). Later she left the UK and on her attempted re-entry the passport was seized. The embassy refused another and the Minister for Foreign Affairs declared her not to be an Irish citizen. She sought to reverse that decision, part of which involved establishing a valid marriage. It was argued that the parties did not have the capacity to marry since the purpose was to circumvent the UK's immigration law. Barron J commented that entering a sham marriage raised the issue of consent to marriage as opposed to capacity.

The judge noted two views, firstly that once the formalities are complied with and the couple have capacity, the marriage is valid. The second is that the surrounding circumstances can be looked at to see if it is a sham to achieve some other end. In effect the judge seemed to take the latter approach because he examined the intentions of the parties and found that there was a relationship before the marriage but that she ultimately married for the passport. Barron J said that people marry for a wide variety of reasons and accepted the dictum of Barrington J in *R.S.J. v J.S.J.* [1982] ILRM 263, where he said that 'one could not say that a marriage is void merely because one party did not love or had not the capacity to love the other'. The judge said the onus was on the State to show the marriage a sham and that the couple did not enter the ceremony to become man and wife, but merely to prevent deportation. It failed to prove this and the marriage was valid.

2.4 Voidable Marriages

There are two grounds on which a marriage can be declared voidable. The first is impotence and the second is the inability to enter and sustain a normal marital relationship. The latter is a new ground that has only developed over the last two decades by analogy with the older ground of impotence. This new ground is one of the most frequently used for seeking annulment.

2.4.1 IMPOTENCE

Impotence has always been a ground for annulling a marriage. Impotence is not a reference to fertility or the inability to procreate, but rather to the inability to have sexual intercourse or to consummate the marriage. This may seem peculiar, given that the traditional rationale of impotence as a ground for nullity is the importance of procreation to marriage. However, older commentaries also focus on marriage as the refuge of the lawful indulgence of the passions and a protection from illicit intercourse.

When intercourse has occurred, even once, the marriage is consummated and is valid. Intercourse in this regard has been described as comprising 'ordinary and complete' sexual intercourse following the solemnisation of the marriage. 'Ordinary and complete' intercourse should be seen in comparison to partial or imperfect intercourse in an effort to determine whether a person is capable of natural coitus, with the issues revolving around the practical possibility of full penetration by the male into the female. In *W v W* [1967] 3 All ER 178 the husband could penetrate his wife, but thereafter his erection collapsed and he was found impotent. The issue of fertility is not at issue, and thus the use of contraceptives is irrelevant (see *Baxter v Baxter* [1948] AC 274) as is the ability to ejaculate. In *M v M* (unreported, 19 December 1985, High Ct, McMahon J) a decree was refused where the husband was incapable of emission, though capable of erection and penetration. Finally, the use of artificial insemination cannot amount to full and ordinary intercourse.

The onus of proof is said to be a high one to prove impotence, which must continue to exist at the date of the hearing. It must be shown that full penetration is not possible, or only possible under conditions which are unreasonable to expect the party affected to go through, e.g., a serious operation. In other words it must not be reasonably curable. With advances in medication and other treatments this may become more difficult to show, e.g. would a refusal to take Viagra be unreasonable?

The impotence can result from physical or psychological reasons. There are a variety of causes, from a lack of the necessary organs to physical malformation, or psychological illness such as repugnance to the sexual act resulting in paralysis of the will or other illnesses leading to conditions such as vaginismus (see Casey and Creaven, *Psychiatry and the Law* (Oak Tree Press, 1999) Chapters 10 and 11).

Impotence need not be general, it can be towards a specific partner, i.e. *quod hanc* or *quod hunc*. In *R (otherwise W) v W* (unreported, 1 February 1980, High Ct, Finlay J) the couple had sex before marriage but afterwards the wife was unable to as she developed a psychological block in relation to her husband. She was capable of having sex with others as she began a relationship with another man, by whom she had a child. A decree was granted.

It is important to differentiate between psychological impotence and wilful refusal to consummate; the latter is not impotence and will not result in an annulment. The distinction between the two is not easy to establish however. In *McK v McK* [1936] IR 177 repeated attempts by the husband to engage in intercourse were refused by his wife. On examination she was found physically capable of engaging in sexual intercourse and no claim of psychological inhibition was made. Hanna J refused a decree as he concluded that the wife was not impotent, but rather had resolved not to have children.

Wilful refusal could be a ground for nullity under Kenny J's dictum in *S v S* (unreported, 1 July 1976, Supreme Ct), cited previously at para **2.3.3.3**, a case that also involved impotence. Here the couple engaged in sexual intercourse before the marriage, but did not during their honeymoon or their return home. The marriage only lasted six months, after which the husband, who had told his wife that it was a mistake and that she made him sick, left to live with another woman. The wife petitioned for nullity, which was granted by the Supreme Court, with the majority basing the ruling on his impotence toward her, i.e. *quod hanc*. In his judgment Kenny J held the husband not to be impotent, but held that he had unilaterally formed the intention at the time of marriage not to have intercourse with his wife. Since Kenny J regarded this as a repudiation of a fundamental feature of the marriage

16

contract without the agreement of the wife and that it vitiated her consent to marry, the marriage was therefore void (see also *M. O'M. v B. O'C.* [1996] 1 IR 208). Such a dictum could not apply where the other spouse knew of the determination at the time of marriage and consented to it.

It is open to argument that a repugnance to the sexual act may give rise to issues of incapacity to enter and sustain a normal marital relationship. See *A.B. v E.B.* [1996] IFLR 75, where this argument was rejected on the facts of the case. Such an argument could also be made regarding willful refusal.

A petitioner can rely on his or her own impotence. However, it appears that before doing so the respondent must have repudiated the marriage in some way. This was a traditional requirement, but has been put in doubt recently. An example of repudiation can be seen in *R (otherwise W) v W*, above, where a decree was granted on the basis of the petitioner's impotence. The respondent was deemed to have repudiated the marriage by having sought a church annulment. In *E.C. v K.M.* [1991] 2 IR 192, Barr J granted an annulment to an impotent petitioner. He characterised the need for repudiation as some conduct on the part of the respondent which prevents him or her denying the just cause of the petition, which in this case consisted of participation in church nullity proceedings instituted by the petitioner.

The confusion surrounding the need for repudiation comes from *obiter* comments of O'Hanlon J in *P.C. v V.C.* (unreported, 7 July 1989, High Ct) where it was suggested that a decree should not be refused to a petitioner relying on his or her own impotence where that person was unaware of the impotence at the time of entering the marriage. This is also a view supported by Shatter, *Family Law* (4th edn, 1997) para 5.93.

As a means of gathering evidence, a court can appoint a medical inspector, under Ord. 72 r. 32 of the Rules of the Superior Courts 1986 in the High Court, and Ord. 78 r. 24 of the Circuit Court Rules, to examine each of the parties and report to the court. This is not essential, and need not be done where other evidence is available. If the court is to appoint one, a rota system is used to determine the doctors to be appointed, though in practice many parties agree the doctors, e.g. one that has already treated a party. A party is free to refuse inspection, but this may raise an inference of impotence where the parties have cohabited for some time and the other party is willing to engage in sexual intercourse. A social report under the Family Law Act 1995, s. 47 can also be sought in nullity cases. In *P.McG. v A.F.* (unreported, 28 January 2000, High Ct, Budd J) it was held that the appointment of a medical inspector was not a bar to making an order under s. 47, which would provide a wider range of information to the court.

2.4.2 INABILITY TO ENTER AND SUSTAIN NORMAL MARITAL RELATIONSHIP

This ground, which has various appellations, first appeared in law in 1982 and has since become one of the principal grounds upon which a marriage can be annulled. The possibility of this ground was accepted in *R.S.J. v J.S.J.* [1982] ILRM 263, where Barrington J said that if a petitioner through illness lacked the capacity to form a caring or considerate relationship with the spouse, ground for annulment was established. This was approved in *D v C* [1984] ILRM 173, where Costello J said there was more to marriage than physical consummation and that there was also a need for the creation and maintenance of an emotional and psychological relationship. Here, the husband suffered manic depression at the time of, and after, the marriage, and because of his mood swings the relationship that should have developed between the parties failed to occur. He was also a drug addict and an alcoholic. This was the first case in which an annulment was granted on the new ground. It was also recognised that this ground rendered a marriage voidable, which allowed its development to proceed by analogy with impotence.

The inability can be inherent in either or both parties and can exist generally or in relation to each other. A range of conditions can be relied upon to ground an application on this basis, including an involuntary characteristic of a party, so long as this renders a spouse incapable of entering or sustaining a marital relationship. Suffering from a condition simpliciter will not suffice. The incapacity must exist at the time of entering the marriage, and although evidence of post-marital behaviour will be introduced, this is only relevant to demonstrate the position as of the time of marriage. In *W v P* (unreported, 7 June 1984, High Ct) Barrington J referred to the lifelong nature of marriage, meaning that each party should have the capacity to live in society with the other. There have been cases where an annulment has been granted because of psychiatric illness, such as paranoid schizophrenia and depression, lack of maturity and homosexuality.

The latter was recognised by the Supreme Court in the leading case of *U.F. (otherwise C) v J.C.* [1991] 2 IR 330. In that case the High Court (Keane J) questioned the basis of the new ground and felt that, because of the Matrimonial Causes and Marriage Law (Ireland) Amendment Act 1870, s. 13, any development should be left to the legislature. The petitioner had sought an annulment on the basis that her husband was a homosexual, and as a result lacked the capacity to maintain a matrimonial relationship. She did not know of his homosexuality at the time of marriage. The parties had sexual relations before and after marriage, and had a child. Throughout the marriage the respondent continued his homosexual affairs. Finlay CJ confirmed that inability to enter a normal marital relationship was a ground for nullity and said the incapacity could arise:

> 'from psychiatric or mental illness so recognised or defined but also in cases where it arose from some inherent quality or characteristic of an individual's nature or personality which could not be said to be voluntary or self-induced'.

Thus, there are two possible reasons for the incapacity: (a) mental illness; and (b) some involuntary characteristic. In developing these, the court took cognisance of developments in psychiatry, which allowed the courts to develop the law of nullity, which was largely based on the common law at any rate. Homosexuality has been used to ground petitions in numerous cases.

Immaturity and incompatibility (which would fall into Finlay CJ's second category for establishing the ground) have also been recognised as grounds for a decree, though the Supreme Court in *H.S. v J.S.* [1992] 2 Fam LJ 33 said this will only be the case where they arise from a psychiatric disorder (in which case the marriage will be void for lack of consent) or where it affects the capacity to enter and sustain a normal marital relationship. This relational incapacity was used in *P.C. v V.C.* (unreported, 7 July 1989, High Ct, O'Hanlon J) where it was held that immaturity in the character and temperament of both parties, and their inability to compromise and adjust to the emotional needs of each other rendered the marriage voidable.

It appears that the petitioner may rely on his or her own incapacity in seeking a decree, but with the same limitation as applies to impotence, i.e., that the respondent must have repudiated the marriage in some way.

There have been fears expressed that the determinations in these cases involve an overly subjective analysis by judges, or an over-reliance on psychiatric evidence, which is adduced almost as a matter of course in these cases. There were also fears that the examination of the post-marital situation likened this ground to divorce. That however is not the case as the characteristic or condition must exist at the time of marriage, see the Supreme Court decision in *K.T. v D.T.* [1996] IFLR 82, and evidence of post-marital behaviour is of relevance to demonstrate this, especially as the claim by definition involves some degree of hindsight.

That the illness must exist at the date of marriage was demonstrated in *S.C. v P.D.* (unreported, March 1996, High Ct, McCracken J) where the idea of latent illness was rejected. Here the respondent suffered a manic depressive illness which had not manifested itself at the time of marriage. It was held that the onset of the illness was only triggered by a post-marital event, pregnancy in this case. A decree was refused as the illness was latent, which did not affect the respondent's ability to enter the marriage, as at that time it may affect the ability to sustain the marriage only. McCracken J likened this situation to one involving epilepsy or even a brain tumour.

The use of psychiatric evidence was considered by Laffoy J in *P.C. v C.M.* (unreported, 11 January 1996, High Ct) where the respondent had a child by another man before marriage to the petitioner. After the marriage she resumed that relationship, and had an affair with a counsellor. The psychiatrist giving evidence for the petitioner believed she suffered from an immature personality disorder and lacked the empathy to form a mature relationship. The psychiatrist for the respondent gave evidence to the contrary, i.e. that she did not suffer a personality disorder. Laffoy J said the issue was whether the respondent was capable of entering and sustaining a life-long union because of some inherent, involuntary, characteristic. Thus, it was unnecessary to decide which of the psychiatrists was correct, as, while such evidence is useful for providing an insight into the personalities and attitude of the parties, the decision was ultimately for the court. Such evidence would be more important in cases involving mental illnesses. Laffoy J refused a decree as the conduct of the respondent was held to have been wilful and voluntary, and as such the facts showed a marriage that had broken down.

In *O'R v B* [1995] 2 ILRM 57, Kinlen J also stated that the issues were for the court to determine, not expert witnesses. He also felt an independent *amicus curiae*, or a contradictor in uncontested cases, should be involved to give independent evidence relating to the marriage. As in the case of impotence, a medical inspector can be appointed to examine the parties. Although the inspection envisaged by Ord. 72, r. 32 of the Rules of the Superior Courts 1986, appears to cover physical inspection only, the court forms for appointment have been amended by the central office to cater for psychological inspection; this appears to have been accepted as a practice in *P.McG. v A.F.* (unreported, 28 January 2000, High Ct, Budd J). Order 78, r. 24 of the Circuit Court Rules makes explicit reference to psychiatric inspection. A report can also be commissioned under the Family Law Act 1995, s. 47, which may provide a wider range of evidence to the court.

2.5   Burden of Proof

The onus of proof is always on the petitioner to establish the ground upon which the marriage can be annulled, as there is a presumption of validity towards marriage. There has been some question regarding the correct standard of proof to be applied in nullity cases. In older cases a high standard was required, for example, in *McK v McK* [1936] IR 177 it was said that the petition was to be established 'clearly, unequivocally and beyond reasonable doubt'. However, more recently, there has been a trend toward the balance of probabilities standard. This was mentioned by McCarthy J in *U.F. (otherwise C) v J.C.,* above, and Kinlen J in *O'R v B* (para **2.4.2** above) who, after analysing the relevant authorities, also came to that conclusion. However, in so doing, he also said that there was a heavy burden to show that the marriage was invalid. It appears that clear evidence to prove the marriage invalid on the balance of probabilities is required, and in *E.P. v M.C.* [1985] 5 ILRM 34 a decree was refused in an undefended case because the judge felt that the case may have appeared differently if the respondent had given evidence.

Many kinds of evidence have been used by courts, from expert witnesses to evidence of the demeanour of parties at the ceremony, including wedding photographs. Third party evidence regarding the attitude of the parties, including their participation in preparing the ceremony, has also been considered. Courts are wary of uncorroborated evidence, which will weigh on the assessment of the facts. See also the comments of McCarthy J in *N (otherwise K) v K*, where he commented on the need for a *legitimus contradictor* in such cases.

2.6 Bars to Relief

There are some grounds on which a decree of nullity can be refused in relation to voidable marriages. If the ground applies, the court has a discretion to refuse an annulment.

2.6.1 APPROBATION

A petitioner may be refused a decree if it is felt that he or she has accepted the marriage in some way, as approbation is conduct by which the petitioner has clearly accepted that marriage as valid, at a time when he or she knew of the entitlement to a decree. In effect, approbation acts as a kind of estoppel as there is a principle against taking both the benefit and avoiding the burden. In *W v W* [1952] P 152 the respondent was impotent. The petitioner knew this and they adopted a child together, which was held to constitute approbation, and a decree was refused.

Before there is approbation the petitioner must be aware of the right to set the marriage aside, i.e. be aware of the facts and that the facts entitle a decree. In *D v C* [1984] ILRM 173 the marriage was celebrated in 1974, but the petition was only presented in 1983. This was because the wife did not know of the psychiatric illness that was her basis for seeking the annulment until several years after the marriage, nor that it entitled her to a decree. Costello J rejected a defence based on approbation, which he said, at p. 191:

> 'can only succeed where it is shown that the petitioner acted not only with knowledge of the facts which entitled her to a nullity decree but also with knowledge that those facts would, as a matter of law, have entitled her to the right she now seeks to enforce.'

This clearly applied here as the ground for nullity based on incapacity did not even exist in 1974. It would still apply to a person who was factually aware of a problem, but unaware of the entitlement to nullity on that basis.

If, prior to presenting a petition, the petitioner applied for other matrimonial reliefs, this will not usually amount to approbation if the validity of the marriage was not at issue in that previous application. In *D v C* the petitioner had previously sought a barring order and custody order, and the respondent claimed that *res judicata* applied to prevent an annulment. That failed as there was no determination regarding the validity of the marriage in the earlier proceedings, the marriage being assumed valid. If the relief is sought at a time when the petitioner knows of the entitlement to a decree, then an annulment may be refused, see the comments of Morris J in *R.McG. v K.N.* [1995] Fam LJ 101.

2.6.2 DELAY

This can lead to a finding of approbation, but can also be a reason in itself. It is not an absolute bar, though there ought to be a good reason given for it, and the longer the delay the harder this is. In practice, decrees have been granted in cases involving long delays, e.g. in *C.M. v E.L.* (unreported, 27 July 1994, High Ct, Barr J) a decree was granted in relation to a 23-year old marriage as the petitioner was not aware that psychiatric illness could found a ground for relief, and in *O'R v B* (para **2.4.2** above) a decree was made concerning a marriage 13 years prior to the decision. Again, it appears that for relief to be denied the petitioner must be aware of the availability of a decree.

2.6.3 RATIFICATION OF VOID MARRIAGES

In theory a void marriage cannot be ratified as such because it was never valid in law and a court order is declaratory only. However, there have been some judicial comments to the effect that a decree may be refused in some circumstances; see *Ussher v Ussher* [1912] 2 IR 455 and *N (otherwise K) v K* [1985] IR 733, where Henchy J said that requirements of basic fairness or natural justice may preclude a decree. This has not yet formed the basis of a refusal. One matter to note is the Marriages Act 1972, which validated marriages solemnised in France which were void until the passing of the Act.

2.6.4 COLLUSION

Collusion has been defined as 'an agreement between the parties so that the true case is not presented to the court'; see Barron J in *E.P. v M.C.* [1985] 5 ILRM 34. A court can refuse a decree on this basis, which, again, seems peculiar in relation to void marriages. The rule is an effort to ensure that couples do not use the nullity jurisdiction to effect a divorce. This was more likely before the introduction of divorce, but may still occur if the parties cannot satisfy the criteria for a divorce.

The rules of court demand that the parties in their affidavits grounding the petition and answer state that there has been no collusion or connivance between them. It is now clear that a judge must have clear evidence of collusion before refusing a decree on that basis: see *M v M* [1979] ILRM 160. However, despite rejecting collusion in *E.P. v M.C.* (above), Barron J refused a decree as he feared that, had the respondent given evidence, a different case would be presented, and thus the petitioner failed to establish that there were no grounds for thinking the true case had not been presented to court. This seems a difficult conclusion to sustain given the earlier case of *M v M*, which was not cited in the judgment.

2.7 Consequences of the Decree

Where the marriage is void, it never legally existed and therefore no legal consequences flow from it. The same is true of voidable marriages, as once a decree is obtained, the marriage is void *ab initio*. Thus, the couple are not spouses under any of the family law statutes. No maintenance is payable between the couple, and there is no provision for the ancillary relief available after, e.g., a divorce. The one payment that can be ordered is alimony *pendente lite*, or pending the trial. This maintenance ceases once a decree is made.

The issue of property rights between spouses falls back on the ordinary concepts of the law of property and equity. In theory any previous agreement in relation to property, most notably a separation agreement, is void for mistake, but how much of such an agreement would be unraveled by a court is another matter. In *C.M. v E.L.* (unreported, 27 July 1994, High Ct, Barr J) it was said that the decree was not intended to upset the provisions of a separation agreement. This may also occur if the agreement specifically states that an annulment is not to affect its operation.

As between children and their parents, the position is different. In the past a nullity decree rendered the children illegitimate, as it was then known, and consequently all the disabilities that flowed from that status were imposed on the children. This included the absence of a proper legal relationship with their father. That situation was substantially reformed with the passing of the Status of Children Act 1987.

Nowadays, the fathers of children of annulled marriages remain their guardians under s. 2 of the Guardianship of Infants Act 1964, as amended by the Children Act 1997. This provides that the father falls within the definition of same if he and the mother contracted a voidable marriage and the child was born before the decree was granted, or within the ten months after the decree was granted. This is also true for a void marriage which the father reasonably believed to be valid, where the ceremony occurred before the birth of the child, or at some time during the period of ten months before that birth, or where the ceremony occurred after the birth of the child, at the time of that ceremony. There is a presumption that the father did have the belief referred to.

Thereafter, the relationship between the parents and children can be regulated by orders under the 1964 Act in the case of dispute, e.g. over custody and access or maintenance payable in respect of the children. Finally, s. 46 of the Family Law Act 1995 provides that where a decree is made, the court may declare one parent unfit to have custody of a child on the death of the other parent.

2.8 Practice and Procedure

In the High Court the proceedings are governed by Ord. 70 of the Rules of the Superior Courts. This provides that nullity cases are initiated by a petition, accompanied by grounding affidavit that verifies the facts of which the petitioner has knowledge and the truth of the other facts alleged. It must also state that no collusion or connivance exists between the petitioner and the respondent. The petitioner must also exact a citation, to be served on the respondent with the petition, with a certificate of service to be filed in the central office.

The petitioner cannot proceed unless the respondent enters an appearance, or until he or she, on affidavit, swears that the citation was served and that no appearance was entered. Otherwise, the respondent must file an answer, together with a grounding affidavit.

In the Circuit Family Court, proceedings are governed by Ord. 78 of the Circuit Court Rules 1997. Rule 5 states that nullity proceedings shall proceed by way of Family Law Civil Bill. The respondent must file a defence, with possible counterclaim where appropriate. Finally, under the Family Law Act 1995, s. 29, a court can grant a declaration of marital status. Under s. 29(7), where it is alleged that a marriage is void or voidable, the court can treat an application for such a declaration as an application for a decree of nullity and postpone the application for a declaration.

CHAPTER 3

SEPARATION AGREEMENTS

3.1   Introduction

A separation agreement is a document that may be drawn up and executed by the parties to a marriage, where that marriage has broken down, and where they do not wish to have recourse to the courts for the purpose of agreeing the terms of the breakdown. The Dublin Solicitors' Bar Association draft deed of separation sets out all of the various terms that may be incorporated into a deed of separation, depending on the circumstances of the parties concerned. Usually, any deed of separation will contain a clause agreeing to live apart, and will thereafter make provision for custody, access to children, maintenance, division of matrimonial property, reference to Succession Act rights, and, if necessary, may contain a non-molestation clause. The terms will be committed to writing and signed by both parties.

Parties wishing to do so may negotiate the terms of a separation agreement with the assistance of either a mediator or a solicitor representing each spouse independently. Sections 5 and 6 of the Judicial Separation and Family Law Reform Act 1989 oblige the solicitor acting for an applicant or a respondent, prior to instituting or defending judicial separation proceedings, to:

(a)   discuss with the client the possibility of reconciliation and supply the names and addresses of persons qualified to help effect a reconciliation;

(b)   discuss the possibility of engaging in mediation to help effect a separation on an agreed basis and supply the names and addresses of persons qualified to provide a mediation service; and

(c)   discuss the possibility of effecting a separation by way of a separation deed or written agreement.

Similar provisions are contained in the Family Law (Divorce) Act 1996, ss. 5 and 6 in relation to divorce proceedings: see also **4.2.5.2**.

We will first of all look at the contents of a deed of separation, and then examine the issue of enforcement of its terms.

3.2   Terms of a Separation Agreement

A fundamental provision of almost every separation agreement is an agreement that the parties will live apart, and the spouses are thereby released from the duty of cohabiting with one another. It is prudent for the separation agreement to outline the date on which the parties began living apart, so that this will be clear in the event of either spouse wishing to obtain a divorce.

It is also common to incorporate what is referred to as a 'non-molestation clause' in a deed of separation. This is generally a term that neither spouse will 'molest, annoy, disturb or interfere with the other'. Any breach of the non-molestation clause must be dealt with by an application for injunctive relief, or, where the behaviour which has breached the molestation clause demands further action, application may be made to the court pursuant to the provisions of the Domestic Violence Act 1996.

3.3 Guardianship and Custody of Children

In circumstances where there are children under the age of 18 years, all arrangements regarding the children may be detailed in the deed of separation. Married spouses remain joint guardians of their children, and the issue of custody is usually referred to, whether sole custody to one party or another, or joint custody to both spouses. The issue of access is usually referred to, and detailed arrangements for access may also be set out. Where the parties have managed to separate in a relatively amicable fashion, the agreement may deal with the issue of access by including a clause which refers to the taking into account of the wishes of the children, and which also refers to access taking place at 'dates and times to be agreed between the parties'. It is prudent, within the confines of this particular clause, to refer to the issue of passports for the children, and the agreement may detail the fact that passports are to be obtained for the children and by whom those passports shall be held. The issue of travel abroad or removal of the children from the jurisdiction may also be dealt with in this clause.

Maintenance which is to be paid by one spouse to another, or by one spouse in respect of dependent family members, can be detailed in a clause set out in this regard. The amount of maintenance to be paid will usually have been agreed in prior negotiations. Reference should also be made to the duration of time during which maintenance is to be paid, and also how the maintenance is to be paid, e.g. whether it is to be paid weekly, or through the District Court Office. If maintenance is to be paid through the District Court Clerk's Office, the agreement should be made a rule of court pursuant to the Family Law (Maintenance of Spouses and Children) Act 1976, s. 8. It is also usual to include a clause in relation to variation of maintenance in the future, for example, by keeping the amount payable in line with the Consumer Price Index: see also **5.10**. The execution of a separation agreement does not preclude a spouse having recourse to court by seeking a maintenance order under the Family Law (Maintenance of Spouses and Children) Act 1976, but presumably, in those circumstances, the court would be requested by the paying spouse to take into account the terms of the separation agreement. This is an issue which frequently arises in the course of conducting negotiations on the terms of a separation agreement. While provisions set out in a separation agreement cannot exclude a court from hearing and determining an application for maintenance under the 1976 Act, the court will probably take account of the circumstances in which a clause was signed which precluded the spouse from seeking maintenance in the future. For example, where a spouse who signed a term confirming that they would not seek maintenance in the future was independently legally advised, the court may take the view, in the absence of a change of circumstances, that that spouse understood what he or she was signing and the circumstances in which he or she agreed not to seek maintenance in the future.

3.4 Property and Succession

The agreement of the parties in relation to matrimonial property may also be set out in the terms of the separation agreement, and will obviously vary from case to case, depending on the circumstances concerned. Frequently, it is agreed between the parties that one of them will be permitted to remain in the family home, for example, until the younger child has reached the age of 18, whereupon the family home will be sold and the proceeds distributed between the parties in an agreed manner. In the alternative, the parties may agree that subject to the payment by one of them to the other of a lump sum, the receiving party will surrender the entire of their legal and beneficial interest in the family home, and the property will thereafter be transferred into the name of the paying spouse. It is also usual for separation agreements to contain a clause containing a general consent to the sale or other disposal of any interest in the family home at any future date for the purposes of the Family Home Protection Act 1976. This will obviate the need for former spouses to contact one another for the purposes of the execution of Family Home Protection Act Declarations in the future.

In relation to other matrimonial assets, a separation agreement may specify, for example, what is to happen with the family business, and on what terms it is to be wound up, or indeed continued as a growing concern. All matrimonial property may be dealt with in the separation agreement.

The issue of succession rights may be referred to in an agreement by the inclusion of a clause by the spouses to renounce their respective rights under the Succession Act 1965, to a share in the estate of the other. Any such renunciation will not prevent the parties making application to court if they seek a divorce, and consequently, an order pursuant to the provisions of the Family Law (Divorce) Act 1996, s. 18(1). However, the 1996 Act, s. 18(10) enables the court, on granting a decree of divorce or at any time thereafter, on the application of either of the spouses during the lifetime of the other, to make an order that the other spouse shall not be entitled to apply for an order under s. 18. A relevant and instructive case is *J.C.N. v R.T.N.* (unreported, 15 January 1999, High Ct). It must be clearly noted that a spouse who renounces his/her rights to succession in a separation agreement retains no right to apply for a share from the estate of the deceased spouse pursuant to the Family Law Act 1995, s. 15(a).

There is no provision for agreeing an adjustment to a pension scheme of which either of the spouses is a member. However, a separated spouse remains a widow(er) for the purposes of a 'contingent benefit' under a pension scheme. If it is felt that a pension adjustment order is required, then the terms of such an order may be agreed between the parties, and application made on consent for an ancillary order pursuant to a decree of judicial separation. In those circumstances, a separation agreement will not be executed: see Chapter 7: Pensions on Separation and Divorce.

The issue of income tax is one which should also be dealt with in a separation agreement in the event that maintenance is being paid by one spouse to the other. The provisions of the Taxes Consolidation Act 1997, ss. 1025 and 1026 apply to maintenance payments, and direct that maintenance is to be deducted from the paying spouse's gross earnings prior to their being assessed for income tax. Because of this, the receiving spouse must then pay income tax in respect of the maintenance payments which he/she receives. In most circumstances, the spouses opt to be assessed as single persons for income tax reasons. However, pursuant to the Taxes Consolidation Act 1997, s. 1026, separated spouses may elect for joint assessment income tax, provided that they are resident in the State for income tax purposes, and also provided that legally enforceable maintenance payments are being made by one spouse to the other. An election to joint assessment must be made directly to the Revenue Commissioners in writing. This enables one of the parties to obtain the benefit of Full Married Person's Tax Allowance and double tax bands. All other aspects of taxation may also be agreed between the parties, and the terms incorporated in the agreement. It should be noted that maintenance which is specifically designated for the support of children is not taxable in the hands of the custodial parent to whom it is paid: see para **9.3**.

Finally, most separation agreements contain a detailed indemnification clause, which seeks to have the effect of indemnifying both spouses from all future debts which are incurred by either of them.

This is not an exhaustive list of the terms which may be incorporated in a separation agreement, but should rather be used a guide.

3.5 Family Law (Maintenance of Spouses and Children) Act 1976, s. 8

It is possible to have an executed separation agreement made a rule of court, in either the Circuit or High Court, provided the agreement contains a provision relating to the payment of one spouse to the other of maintenance payments for their own benefit or for the benefit of dependent family members, or a provision which governs the rights and liabilities of spouses in relation to the making or securing of payments or the disposition or use of any property.

If an agreement is made a rule of court, it affords to the spouse receiving maintenance payments the right to have that maintenance paid through the District Court Clerk, with consequent implications for the recovery of maintenance arrears. In addition, the ruling of the agreement also provides the recipient spouse with the remedy of contempt of court where breach of the agreement occurs.

However, if a maintenance agreement is comprised in a separation agreement which is then ruled pursuant to s. 8, recourse may not be had to court for the purpose of varying the maintenance terms, but simply for the purpose of payment and enforcement. See also para **5.10**.

3.6 Separation Agreements and Future Proceedings

The most important judicial development in the law on separation agreements is the decision of the Supreme Court in *P.O'D. v A.O'D* [1998] 1 ILRM 543. In this case the parties married in 1961 and the marriage broke down in 1969 due to the husband's alcoholism and loss of employment leading to indebtedness. In April 1969 the husband transferred the family home to his wife's sole name. A separation agreement was entered into between the parties on 16 January 1979. The agreement was in the usual form and there was a specific recital in the agreement recognising that the husband had paid all the mortgage instalments on the family home up until April 1969 and thereafter the wife had taken sole responsibility for the mortgage.

Keane J, delivering the judgment of the Supreme Court, stated that a separation agreement amounts in law to a binding contract and, as such, is a bar to subsequent proceedings for judicial separation under the Judicial Separation and Family Law Reform Act 1989. Citing the dicta of Blayney J in *F v F* [1995] 2 IR 354, Keane J justified the bar, not only because the parties to a binding agreement should not be permitted to go behind it, but also because the parties, by agreeing to live separate and apart, had rendered superfluous the granting of a decree of judicial separation. He stated:

> 'First, where the agreement provides, as it invariably does, that the parties are to live separate and apart, the granting of such a decree would be superfluous. Secondly, where parties have entered into a binding contract to dispose of differences that have arisen between them as husband and wife it would be unjust to allow one party unilaterally to repudiate that agreement irrespective of whether it took the form of a compromise of proceedings actually instituted.'

The above passage should be brought to the notice of all parties in negotiating the terms of a separation agreement as a spouse precluded from seeking a decree of judicial separation cannot seek the extensive range of financial and property reliefs available under Part II of the Family Law Act 1995 (which repealed Part II of the 1989 Act). In particular, the obtaining of a judicial separation decree is an essential prerequisite to invoking the court's jurisdiction to grant a pension adjustment order: see Chapter 7: Pensions on Separation and Divorce.

It should be noted that a separation agreement does not act as a bar to divorce proceedings under the 1996 Act since s. 20(3) of that Act merely requires the court, in determining what provision should be made for spouses and dependent children in divorce proceedings, to have regard to the terms of any separation agreement which has been entered into by the spouses and is still in force. Further, a separation agreement cannot act as a bar to a spouse who is party to a separation agreement either instituting maintenance proceedings under the Family Law (Maintenance of Spouses and Children) Act 1976 (see *H.D. v P.D.* unreported, 8 May 1978, Supreme Ct, and the dicta of Denham J in *F v F* [1995] 2 IR 354), or bringing proceedings under the Guardianship of Infants Act 1964 to vary guardianship, custody or access arrangements previously agreed.

CHAPTER 4

JUDICIAL SEPARATION AND DIVORCE

4.1 Introduction

4.1.1 GENERAL

Marriage is a legally binding contract entered into by a man and a woman which, in general terms, attracts the same rules of law as any other type of contract. However, unlike other contracts, the marriage contract can be terminated on the granting of a decree of judicial separation or divorce. Once the contract has been entered into both parties acquire certain rights and responsibilities which are enshrined in the law.

4.1.2 THE IRISH CONSTITUTION 1937

The contract of marriage is accorded a special status by the State.

Article 41.3.1 of the Constitution states:

The State pledges itself to guard with special care the institution of Marriage on which the Family is founded and to protect it against attack.

The Constitution also provides at Article 41.1.1 that:

The State recognises the Family as the natural primary and fundamental unit group of Society and as a moral institution possessing inalienable and imprescriptible rights, antecedent and superior to all positive law.

The State, therefore, guarantees to protect the Family in its constitution and authority as the necessary basis of social order and as indispensable to the welfare of the Nation and the State.

4.1.3 FORMALITIES

For a marriage to be recognised as valid the following formalities must be complied with:

- (a) each party must have the required age and mental capacity;

- (b) the parties must not be within the prohibited degrees of relationship, either of blood or affinity;

- (c) neither party must be a party to a prior subsisting marriage;

- (d) the parties must understand the nature, purpose and consequences of marriage and must fully and freely consent to the marriage;

- (e) certain procedural formalities must be observed.

Any marriage solemnised between persons who are under the age of 18 years shall not be valid: Family Law Act 1995, s. 31(1)(a). This provision applies to all marriages solemnised in the State and marriages solemnised outside the State between persons either or both of whom are ordinarily resident in this State.

The persons involved in a marriage must give at least three months prior notice to the Registrar in writing of their intention to marry: Family Law Act 1995, s. 31(1)(b). It is possible in certain circumstances to obtain an exemption from the three-month notice requirement but a special application must be made to court in this regard: Family Law Act 1995, s. 33. In most cases where an application is made the court will exempt the couple from the notice requirement. Such applications are dealt with in camera and on an informal basis. In Dublin they are usually dealt with prior to the call-over of cases without lawyers and without any court fees.

There is no legal obligation on couples to attend a pre-marriage course prior to the ceremony.

If one or other of the parties has obtained a decree of divorce in another jurisdiction then difficulties may arise in satisfying the Registrar as to the ability of the parties to enter into a legally enforceable marriage contract. This matter will be considered subsequently.

4.2 Judicial Separation

4.2.1 INTRODUCTION

It is sometimes forgotten that until 1989 family law in Ireland was, to a large degree, fairly primitive. When a couple separated either party could bring an application for a decree of divorce *a mensa et thoro*. This decree was simply a divorce 'from bed and board'. It did not allow a couple to remarry and could only be obtained on the grounds of adultery, cruelty or 'unnatural practices'. At no stage did either the legislature or the courts define what 'unnatural practices' were. This remedy has now been abolished. All it did was to relieve one spouse from the duty of cohabiting with the other spouse. It was also open to an applicant to make application to court for orders in relation to property under the Partition Acts, maintenance applications and orders in relation to custody and access but very little else.

The Judicial Separation and Family Law Reform Act 1989 (the '1989 Act') dramatically widened and increased the power of the court to make ancillary orders either before or at the same time as the granting of the decree of judicial separation. For the first time the courts were in a position to grant exclusion orders, property adjustment orders, lump sum orders etc.

The Family Law Act 1995 (the '1995 Act') further extended the powers of the court in making ancillary relief orders. The 1995 Act allowed the court to make financial compensation orders and pension adjustment orders for the first time. All of these ancillary reliefs will be considered later.

The Family Law (Divorce) Act 1996 (the '1996 Act') gave the court the power to dissolve a marriage contract and allowed parties to one marriage ceremony to remarry after the granting of a decree of divorce.

4.2.2 JUDICIAL SEPARATION VERSUS DIVORCE

It is interesting to compare the grounds for the granting of a decree of judicial separation with the grounds for the granting of a decree of divorce. The element of 'fault' is still very relevant insofar as the granting of a decree of judicial separation is concerned whilst, in relation to divorce, it is of no relevance.

It is important to consider the grounds for the granting of a decree of judicial separation because there are still many applications for such decrees being made. This will continue to be the case.

4.2.3   STATISTICS

From 27 February 1997 to July 2000 there have been approximately 8,500 applications for divorce. Prior to the referendum on divorce it was estimated that there were some 80,000 to 85,000 people in the State whose marriages had been broken down for many years, and it was expected that the courts would be inundated with divorce applications. However, only ten per cent of persons who could have applied for a decree of divorce did in fact do so.

When divorce became available in both Italy and Spain for the first time, the percentage of applications made by those whose marriages had been broken down for some time was far greater than in Ireland.

Prior to the referendum, it had been argued by many opponents of divorce that men would be the first to make applications for decrees of divorce in an attempt, in many cases, to 'impoverish their spouses'. It is interesting to note that the latest statistics published in February 2000 show that women outnumber men by two to one in seeking divorces. For the year ending December 1999 there were 3,240 divorce applications and 2,475 decrees of divorce were granted. Of this figure, 1,611 of the applications were made by the wife whilst only 864 were made by the husband.

The number of applications for decrees of judicial separation and nullity decrees has remained constant over the last three years, despite the introduction of divorce. There are at present approximately 1,500 to 1,600 such applications per year.

The reasons for the slow uptake of the remedy of divorce are many and varied.

In some instances applicants are wary of the powers available to the courts under the Family Law (Divorce) Act 1996 to interfere with pre-existing arrangements, and have been waiting to see what trends will develop in the courts.

Another reason for the small number of applications to date is that a very high percentage of divorce applications are brought by solicitors in the employment of the Legal Aid Board. As there are very long delays in obtaining legal aid, this has led to a slowdown in the making of divorce applications, which are not treated as emergency relief and are not given priority.

There are various reasons why the number of applications for decrees of judicial separation have not decreased, including:

(a)   a couple may have separated but not have lived apart for the requisite period of four out of the last five years and still wish to regularise their affairs without delay; and

(b)   it is not uncommon for couples to refrain from applying for a decree of divorce, even if they are legally entitled to do so, for personal or religious reasons.

4.2.4   GROUNDS FOR JUDICIAL SEPARATION

Section 1 of the 1989 Act created a new 'Circuit Family Court'. All applications for decrees of judicial separation must be made in either the Circuit or the High Court in the first instance.

The 1989 Act specifies six grounds upon which the court may grant a decree of judicial separation. Such a decree can be granted on one or more of the said grounds, which must be proved 'on the balance of probabilities': 1989 Act, s. 3(1).

It is important to note that unless an applicant satisfies the court that he or she should be granted a decree of judicial separation or a divorce, as the case may be, they cannot avail of many of the ancillary relief orders now in existence.

The following are the six grounds for the granting of a decree of judicial separation.

4.2.4.1 The respondent has committed adultery

This was already one of the grounds for the granting of a decree of divorce *a mensa et thoro* (the others being cruelty and 'unnatural practices'). Adultery can be difficult to prove but it can be inferred from the circumstances. 'Adultery is presumed if it is proved that a married man goes to and spends the night with a woman in a brothel or if he spends the night with a woman other than his wife in a hotel bedroom': *J.M.H. v J.P.H.* (unreported, January 1983, High Ct, Ellis J).

The 1989 Act purported to abolish collusion, condonation, and recrimination as bars to relief (1989 Act, s. 44).

4.2.4.2 The respondent has behaved in such a way that the applicant cannot reasonably be expected to live with the respondent

The behaviour in this section includes cruelty, both mental and physical. The test is an objective one. The court will decide whether or not an individual can 'reasonably be expected' to put up with the behaviour of his or her spouse. What is 'cruelty' depends on the facts of each case. The character of the conduct must be 'grave and weighty'. It must have been such as to render the continued performance of the obligations of marriage impossible: *E.D. v F.D.* (unreported, 16 December 1981, High Ct, Butler J).

The conduct itself need not necessarily consist of one or two major acts of violence but can consist of a large number of lesser acts of aggression or violence which, when taken on their own, would not be sufficient grounds for the granting of a decree but when taken together are.

Mental or psychological cruelty is covered under the 1989 Act, s. 2(1)(b). It is somewhat more difficult to prove mental or psychological cruelty in the courts than it is to prove physical cruelty. Costello J in the case of *McA v McA* [1981] 1 ILRM 361 (High Ct) stated that the test to be applied in determining whether conduct constituted cruelty or not was whether the conduct alleged 'renders the cohabitation unsafe or makes it likely that cohabitation will be attended by injury to the person or health of the party'.

If a couple continue cohabiting for a period of six months or less after the 'last incident of violence or cruelty' and an application is made under s. 2(1)(b) of the 1989 Act then 'such cohabitation shall be disregarded in reaching a decision as to whether or not a decree should be granted' (1989 Act, s. 4(2)).

4.2.4.3 There has been desertion by the respondent of the applicant for a continuous period of at least one year immediately preceding the date of the application

For this ground (under the 1989 Act, s. 2(1)(c)) to succeed the desertion must be 'continuous'. In considering whether or not the period is continuous no account is to be taken of one or more periods totalling six months when the parties have resumed living together. The parties must however be living apart at the date of application to court for the granting of the decree.

'Desertion' also includes 'constructive desertion'. This involves conduct on the part of one

JUDICIAL SEPARATION AND DIVORCE

spouse that results in the other spouse, with just cause, leaving and living apart from that
other spouse (1989 Act, s. 2(3)(b)).

In deciding whether or not constructive desertion exists in a particular case the court will
use the same criteria as is availed of in deciding whether or not there has been constructive
desertion in a maintenance application.

Habitual drunkenness, violence, adultery, constant threats, abusing children and mental
cruelty have, in practice, all been regarded as sufficient grounds for a spouse's departure.

Kenny J, in the case of *J.C. v J.H.C.* (unreported, August 1982, High Ct, Kenny J) stated that
a wife was justified in leaving the family home because of the husband's 'occasional
outbursts of violence'.

The issue of constructive desertion was considered in detail in the case of *Counihan v
Counihan* (unreported, July 1973, High Ct, Kenny J) wherein Kenny J stated that an
intention to disrupt the marriage or bring the cohabitation to an end must be shown.
However, the probable consequences of the conduct of a spouse can give rise to a
presumption of such an intention. In the *Counihan* case Kenny J held that the husband's
irresponsibility in financial matters, his recklessness in contracting large debts, and his
taking a job which meant he could be at home only at weekends did not constitute cruelty
or conduct which would justify a claim of constructive desertion.

4.2.4.4 The spouses have lived apart from one another for a continuous period of at least one year immediately preceding the date of the application and the respondent consents to a decree being granted

The 'date of the application' referred to in the 1989 Act, s. 2(1)(d), refers to the date of the
actual court hearing itself and not the date of the issuing of proceedings.

Again, the period of one year must be 'continuous', and no account is to be taken of any
periods less than a total of six months in deciding whether or not the period is continuous.
The reasons for the commencement of the living apart by the couple are not relevant. The
issue of consent is only relevant to the granting of the decree and not to the fact of living
apart.

4.2.4.5 The spouses have lived apart from one another for a continuous period of at least three years immediately preceding the date of the application

In the 1989 Act, s. 2(1)(e), the onus of proof is on the applicant and there is no need to
show that the respondent was at fault in any way for the breakdown of the marriage. This
section is relevant where the respondent spouse will not consent to the granting of a decree.
Again the rules relating to the continuity of the period and the six-month period are the
same as in earlier sections.

4.2.4.6 The marriage has broken down to the extent that the court is satisfied in all the circumstances that a normal marital relationship has not existed between the spouses for a period of at least one year immediately preceding the date of the application

Section 2(1)(f) of the 1989 Act forms the basis for the granting of the vast majority of
decrees of judicial separation.

There is no definition of what a 'normal marital relationship' is, in the Act or indeed in any
subsequent legislation. What one individual or what one judge thinks is a normal marital
relationship may well be considered by another individual or judge to be entirely the
opposite.

The court need not satisfy itself that the marriage has *irretrievably* broken down. The court must simply satisfy itself that the marriage has in fact broken down. 'Fault' is not a prerequisite for the granting of a decree under this subsection and there would appear to be nothing to prevent an applicant relying on his or her own actions such as adultery or cruelty in order to obtain a decree (see *T.F. v Ireland* [1995] 1 IR 321).

For the court to be satisfied that a normal marital relationship has not existed for a period of at least 12 months, what is required, according to Murphy J, is to prove the 'loss of an essential ingredient of the marriage' (*T.F. v Ireland* [1995] 1 IR 321 at p. 341). He stated that 'such an essential ingredient includes the consent of either party because the implacable opposition of one or other of the spouses to the continuation of the marriage however unjust or unreasonable must destroy the fundamental relationship.'

The Supreme Court upheld the views of the High Court.

The grounds referred to in the 1989 Act, ss. 2(1)(a) to (e) (see **4.2.4.1** to **4.2.4.5** above) could all be incorporated under the 1989 Act s. 2(1)(f). However the advantage of making an application under s. 2(1)(a) and s. 2(1)(b) is that the applicant spouse may obtain a decree on the grounds of adultery or cruelty without having to wait for one year before issuing proceedings.

The grounds upon which a decree of judicial separation is granted can of course affect the level of ancillary relief orders which will be made subsequently.

The criteria for the making of ancillary relief orders pursuant to the provisions of the 1989 Act were originally contained in s. 20(2) which said section was subsequently replaced by the 1995 Act, s. 16(2).

One of the criteria contained in the said section is the conduct of the parties. If a decree of judicial separation is granted on the grounds of adultery or cruelty then such behaviour can be taken into account by a court when deciding the level of periodical payment orders or the type of property adjustment order to be made.

In the case of *M.M. v C.M.* (unreported, July 1993, High Ct, O'Hanlon J) the court decided that both spouses had committed adultery. Despite criticising the behaviour of the parties in some detail the court granted the decree pursuant to the 1989 Act, s. 2(1)(f) as it felt that there would be no point in the circumstances in blaming either party for the breakdown.

In the course of her judgment in the case of *A.F. v E.F.* (unreported, May 1995, Circuit Ct) McGuinness J granted a decree of judicial separation on the grounds set out in the 1989 Act, s. 2(1)(a) and (f). She stated that, where alternative grounds exist, the court must always retain a degree of discretion as to the grounds on which the decree should be granted. In this particular case the husband had been unaware of the wife's adulterous affair which had gone on for many years prior to the final breakdown of the marriage. McGuinness J stated that 'there is a crucial difference between the adultery in this case and those cases where a second relationship is entered into after the breakdown of the marriage'.

In the majority of cases the court prefers to grant a decree pursuant to the provisions of the 1989 Act, s. 2(1)(f) as this tends to lessen the conflict between the parties.

In addition, the amount of evidence which needs to be presented to a court is reduced if the behaviour of the parties is not dealt with in any detail.

4.2.5 GRANTING OF DECREE OF JUDICIAL SEPARATION AND MATTERS RELATING TO WELFARE OF CHILDREN

Section 3(1) of the 1989 Act states that if any of the six grounds outlined above are proven on the balance of probabilities the court shall grant a decree of judicial separation on condition that it is satisfied that:

    (a)   the welfare of any dependent children of the marriage is properly catered for; and

    (b)   both the solicitor for the applicant and the solicitor for the respondent have complied with the obligations imposed on them by the 1989 Act, ss. 5 and 6.

4.2.5.1   Welfare of children

Section 3(2)(a) of the 1989 Act states:

> *where there are in respect of the spouses concerned any dependent children of the family, the court shall not grant a decree of judicial separation unless the court:*
>
>   *(i)   is satisfied that such provision has been made; or*
>
>   *(ii)   intends by order upon the granting of the decree to make such provision for the welfare of the children as is proper in the circumstances.*

Section 3(2)(b) then goes on define 'dependent children of the family' and 'welfare'. Under the provisions of the 1989 Act, the court must satisfy itself that proper provision has been made for the children before granting a decree of judicial separation.

A 'dependent child' is defined in the 1989 Act, s. 10. Such child must either be aged under 16 years, or if he or she has attained that age is under the age of 21 years and receiving or undergoing a full-time course of education at an educational establishment, or is suffering from a mental or physical disability to such extent that it is not reasonably possible for him or her to maintain himself or herself fully.

'Welfare' under the 1989 Act comprises, as it does under the Guardianship of Infants Act 1964, the religious, moral, intellectual, physical and social welfare of the child or children concerned. Section 3(2)(a) of the 1989 Act was considered in detail in the case of *V.S. v R.S.* [1992] 2 Fam LJ 52. The fundamental issue in this case was whether or not a decree of judicial separation could be granted at all but Lynch J, inter alia, discussed the 1989 Act, s. 3(2), and categorically stated that unless the court is satisfied, on the balance of probabilities, that it can make provision for the dependent children of the marriage pursuant to the 1989 Act, s. 3(2), it is precluded from granting a decree of judicial separation. In the instant case, he stated that he was in a position to make such provision and then proceeded to set out detailed access arrangements and granted custody of the younger child to the plaintiff wife and custody of the older child to the defendant husband.

It is also clear that the courts can vary existing orders or agreements relating to children's custody, access or general welfare. The court can impose conditions on the exercising of custody or access as it feels necessary.

4.2.5.2   Duties and obligations of solicitors in applications for decrees of judicial separation

In 1989 this was a novel concept. For the first time, lawyers were directed by the legislature as to how to advise their clients in a marital breakdown situation.

These provisions in the 1989 Act, ss. 5 and 6, *must* be complied with by practitioners representing both the applicant and the respondent.

Before making an application to court for a decree of judicial separation or before defending such an application the lawyer for both the applicant and the respondent must:

    (a)   discuss reconciliation; *and*

    (b)   discuss and advise on mediation; *and*

    (c)   discuss the possible negotiation and conclusion of a separation deed or agreement.

The solicitors concerned must also provide the names and addresses of persons or organisations who are qualified to provide services such as marriage counselling, mediation, etc.

Not only must the lawyers for both parties discuss such matters but they must also sign a separate certificate stating that they have complied with the provisions of the 1989 Act, s. 5 or s. 6 as the case may be. If no certificate is available then the court *may* adjourn the proceedings until such a discussion has taken place.

Most family law practitioners, at the initial consultation (unless it is inappropriate), furnish to their clients a printed document pointing to the possibilities of mediation, marriage counselling, etc., and provide a typed list of agencies that could be of assistance.

Where an application is made to court for a decree of judicial separation the court *must* give consideration to the possibility of a reconciliation (1989 Act, s. 7(1) as amended by 1996 Act, s. 45). If both spouses so wish the court may adjourn a hearing to facilitate the negotiation of a separation agreement if reconciliation is not possible. The court can also advise spouses involved in matrimonial proceedings to seek the assistance of a third party (1989 Act, s. 7(6) as amended by 1996 Act, s. 45). However, the court cannot *order* the spouses to do so. Any communication by the spouses with any third party such as a marriage counsellor or mediator is not admissible subsequently in evidence.

4.2.6 EFFECT OF DECREE OF JUDICIAL SEPARATION

Where a court grants a decree of judicial separation it is no longer obligatory for the spouses who are the parties to such proceedings to cohabit (1989 Act, s. 8(1)).

When a decree is granted, indeed, the parties cannot continue living together, without negating the fundamental reason for granting the decree in the first place.

The granting of a decree of judicial separation permits the court, as already indicated, to make various ancillary relief orders pursuant to Part II of the Family Law Act 1995 as amended by the Family Law (Divorce) Act 1996. These will be discussed later.

The court may also, when granting a decree of judicial separation, declare either spouse to be unfit to have custody of any dependent child of the family (1989 Act, s. 41(2)).

4.3 Divorce

4.3.1 INTRODUCTION

It is often forgotten that from 1922 to 1937 there was no specific prohibition on the granting of divorce decrees in Ireland. The 1922 Constitution, which remained in force until 1937, did not make any reference to divorce at all. The Oireachtas, which was established in 1922, could have enacted legislation enabling divorce decrees to be granted but did not do so.

Prior to 1922, the Matrimonial Causes Act 1857 created a divorce jurisdiction in England but did not extend this Act to Ireland. Between 1857 and 1922 the only method of obtaining a decree of divorce was by way of a private Act of Parliament which was extremely difficult to arrange.

Article 41.3.2 of the 1937 Constitution stated that 'no law shall be enacted providing for the grant of a dissolution of marriage' and it was only with the passing of the Family Law (Divorce) Act 1996 that this power was returned to the Oireachtas.

Following the referendum of 24 November 1995, the Fifteenth Amendment of the Constitution Act 1995 was passed. As a result, Article 41.3.2 of the Constitution was replaced by the following Article:

A court designated by law may grant a dissolution of marriage where, but only where, it is satisfied that:

(i) at the date of the institution of the proceedings the spouses have lived apart from one another for a period of, or periods amounting to, at least four years during the previous five years;

(ii) there is no reasonable prospect of reconciliation between the spouses;

(iii) such provision as the court considers proper having regard to the circumstances exists or will be made for the spouses, any children of either or both of them and any other person prescribed by law; and

(iv) any further conditions prescribed by law are complied with.

Subsequently, on 27 November 1996 the Family Law (Divorce) Act 1996 was passed and came into operation three months thereafter, on 27 February 1997. For information and statistics see paras **4.2.1** to **4.2.3** above.

4.3.2   JURISDICTION

The Family Law (Divorce) Act 1996 made provision for the exercise by the courts of the jurisdiction conferred by the Constitution, pursuant to the Amendment, to grant decrees of divorce and to make various other related orders. Both the Circuit Court and the High Court have an original concurrent jurisdiction to hear divorce applications (1996 Act, s. 38(1)).

The court may grant a decree of divorce if:

(a)   either of the spouses concerned is domiciled in the State on the date of the institution of the proceedings concerned; or

(b)   either of the spouses was ordinarily resident in the State throughout the period of one year ending on that date (1996 Act, s. 39(1)).

The definition of 'domiciled' is the same as that used in considering the validity of foreign divorces pursuant to the Domicile and Recognition of Foreign Divorces Act 1986, i.e. 'living in a place with the *intention* of residing in that place permanently'.

The Circuit Court has jurisdiction only to deal with cases where the property concerned has a rateable valuation of less than £200. If ancillary relief orders can be made by a court in relation to land where the rateable valuation of same exceeds £200 the court must transfer the proceedings to the High Court if an application for such a transfer is made to it 'by any person having an interest in the proceedings' (1996 Act, s. 38(2)). Any order made prior to such application to transfer will be valid unless discharged or varied by the High Court. It would appear therefore that both parties may consent to the Circuit Court having jurisdiction to deal with applications for ancillary relief orders, even where relevant properties exceed a rateable valuation of £200.

Section 38(3) of the 1996 Act states that 'the jurisdiction conferred on the Circuit Family Court by this Act may be exercised by the Judge of the Circuit in which any of the parties to the proceedings ordinarily resides or carries on any business, profession or occupation'. If the application has been made on the basis of either spouse being domiciled in Ireland, but not ordinarily resident in, or engaged in any business, profession or occupation in the State, then such application must be made in the High Court.

4.3.3   GROUNDS FOR DIVORCE

Section 5(1) of the 1996 Act sets out the grounds upon which a court will grant a decree of divorce on application by either spouse. These grounds are as follows:

(a)   at the date of the institution of the proceedings, the spouses have lived apart from one another for a period of, or periods amounting to, at least four years during the previous five years;

(b)   there is no reasonable prospect of reconciliation between the spouses;

(c)   such provision as the court considers proper having regard to the circumstances exist or will be made for the spouses and any dependent members of the family.

All of these grounds must be satisfied before a decree can be granted.

4.3.3.1   Absence of fault

The White Paper on marital breakdown suggested five possible approaches to a constitutional amendment. Some of these approaches suggested that a decree of divorce could be granted on a 'no fault' basis. Others contained detailed examples of behaviour, such as adultery, desertion, etc., which could be used as grounds for the granting of a decree.

When we consider the grounds on which a decree of judicial separation can be granted in Ireland and indeed the grounds upon which a decree of divorce can currently be granted in England, it is perhaps surprising that the grounds for a divorce in Ireland do not include any reference to the conduct or behaviour of the parties. The question of responsibility for the break-up of the marriage is entirely irrelevant insofar as the granting of the decree itself is concerned. It may be relevant, however, when a court is making ancillary relief orders and is one of the factors to be taken into account under s. 20 of the 1996 Act by a court when making such orders.

4.3.3.2   'Living apart' for a period of at least four years

Definition of 'living apart'

Before a court can grant a decree of divorce, the applicant spouse must prove that he or she has lived apart from the other spouse for the relevant period 'at the date of the institution of the proceedings'. The four-year period, therefore, must have expired prior to the actual issuing and serving of a grounding summons. This contrasts with the requirement under s. 2 of the 1989 Act (see above).

It is clear that an individual can be living apart from his or her spouse whilst still residing under the same roof.

There is no attempt to define 'living apart' in the 1996 Act but the 1989 Act, s. 2(3), states that: 'spouses shall be treated as living apart from each other unless they are living with each other in the same household, and references to spouses living with each other shall be construed as references to their living with each other in the same household'. The use of the word 'household' instead of 'house' is most important and is relevant to the consideration of this issue in the context of the 1996 Act.

The vast majority of applications for divorce involve couples who have lived apart in different homes for a period in excess of four years. If a spouse is to argue that he or she has lived apart from the other spouse whilst still under the same roof then detailed evidence will have to be furnished to a court in order to obtain a decree. The court will have to satisfy itself that, although the spouses have continued to reside in the same home, they have led separate lives.

In such circumstances it is necessary for the spouses to give evidence as to their sleeping arrangements, preparation of meals, caring for the children (if any), holidays, payment of bills and organisation of the finances.

English case law on 'living apart'

There are a number of examples in English case law where the courts have held that a couple can be living apart from one another while residing under the same roof. These cases have already been considered by the Irish courts and will continue to be of relevance in relation to this issue.

The legal concept of 'living apart' does not require a change of address. It is not 'the withdrawal from a place, but from a state of things' (*Pulford v Pulford* [1923] P 18). Spouses will be considered to be 'living apart' when, although each is living in the family home, they have ceased 'to be one household and become two households' (*Hopes v Hopes* [1948] 2 All ER 920).

Another helpful English case is that of *Holmes v Mitchell* [1991] STC 25. This was an income tax appeal and there was a detailed consideration of the definition of 'living apart under the same roof'. Following this case the English Inspector of Taxes has issued guidelines insofar as the questions which should be asked in an effort to ascertain whether or not a couple are 'living apart under the one roof':

(a) How is the house divided up and what are the arrangements for using kitchen and bathroom facilities?

(b) What services do the couple provide for each other, for example, cooking, cleaning, etc.?

(c) What financial arrangements have been made in relation to the alleged separation?

(d) What do the husband and the wife do to avoid meeting each other in the house?

The Irish courts, when deciding whether or not the parties have been 'living apart' for a period of four years, will take into account all relevant evidence when making a decision. It is therefore important for practitioners, when drawing up deeds of separation and other matrimonial agreements, to clearly state the date on which the couple commenced living apart (see Walls and Bergin, *The Law of Divorce in Ireland* (Jordans, 1997) p. 13).

It is of course possible for spouses to live physically apart from each other for in excess of four years and still not be entitled to obtain a decree of divorce. If, for instance, one spouse is hospitalised for a lengthy period or if one spouse works abroad with the consent of the other spouse then it is clear that a decree of divorce cannot be granted. Again, however, each case will depend on its own facts.

As can be seen from detailed consideration of the case of *M.McA. v X.McA.* (unreported, 21 January 2000, High Ct, McCracken J), the intention of the parties is of great importance. It is extremely difficult to ascertain the 'intention' of the parties to a divorce application and, as will be seen, this intention can only be ascertained from a detailed consideration of the facts of each particular case. If such an argument is made by one or other of the parties to a divorce application, then it will be necessary for the court to consider in great detail the ups and downs of the marriage relationship between the husband and wife.

Irish case law on 'living apart'

The High Court considered this issue in some detail in the case of *M.McA v X.McA* (unreported, 21 January 2000, High Ct, McCracken J).

The facts

The husband and the wife were married on 7 October 1968 and had two children, neither of whom were dependants at the time of the hearing. The applicant wife applied for a decree of judicial separation and the respondent husband counterclaimed for a decree of divorce. The applicant disputed this claim. She stated that the couple had not been living apart for a period of four years. The respondent husband stated that although he and his wife were living under the same roof they were certainly not living together as spouses for a lengthy period, therefore they satisfied the four-year rule.

In 1988 the applicant wife discovered that the respondent was having an affair and confronted him in September of that year. The husband left the family home and continued the affair for some time. In 1991 the respondent husband ended his relationship and returned to live in the family home. The applicant stated in evidence that she was 'glad to have him come back' and said that she had never really accepted that the marriage had ended. The respondent husband said that he came home simply to maintain his relationship with his children.

Over the next few years the parties slept in separate bedrooms and never resumed sexual relations. They did on several occasions go away on holidays with the children but again slept in separate bedrooms whilst on holidays. They were polite to each other and if both were present at mealtimes would take their meals together. When he was at home (which was not very often) the respondent would tend to go to bed or at least to his room early and watch television. He also had a separate telephone line installed in his bedroom.

The couple were 'important people in their town' and attended a number of functions together.

Following the return of the husband in 1991 he agreed to pay his wife a sum of £750 per month in cash and later increased this sum to £1,000 per month. He also discharged the cost of the wife's car and motoring expenses.

In 1995, whilst the husband and the wife were still living together in the same house ('but not as a couple'), the applicant wife entered into a relationship, including a sexual relationship, with another gentleman and in 1996 the respondent husband entered into a relationship with a lady with whom he is now living.

The law

McCracken J considered the law on 'living apart'. He pointed out that the Act does not attempt to provide any definition or explanation of the meaning of the words 'living apart from one another'. The court considered the various English authorities and in particular the judgment of Sachs J in the case of *Santos v Santos* [1972] 2 All ER 246 wherein he stated:

> 'living apart . . . is a state of affairs to establish which it is in the vast generality of cases arising under those heads necessary to prove something more than that the husband and the wife are physically separated That involves considering attitudes of mind and naturally the difficulty of judicially determining that attitude in a particular case may on occasions be great'.

In the *McA* case the court held that the 'intention of the parties is a very relevant matter in determining issues such as whether they live apart or whether there has been desertion'. It was argued by the husband's lawyers that once the parties started to live apart they continued to live apart in the legal sense, even after the respondent husband returned to the family home, because there was no true reconciliation between the parties. The court did not accept this particular argument.

McCracken J subsequently stated that

> 'marriage is not primarily concerned about where the spouses live or whether they live under the same roof and indeed there can be a number of circumstances in which the matrimonial relationship continues even though the parties are not living under the same roof as, for example, where one party is in hospital or an institution of some kind or is obliged to spend a great deal of time away from home in the course of his or her employment. Such separations do not necessarily constitute the persons as living apart from one another. Clearly there must be something more than mere physical separation and the mental or intellectual attitudes of the parties are also of considerable relevance.'

The judgment

McCracken J held that parties who live under the same roof may be living apart from one another and commented: 'Whether this is so is a matter which can only be determined in the light of the facts of any particular case'.

He further stated that 'marriage involves mutuality and it is my view on the evidence that when the respondent husband returned in 1991 he did not intend to return to a marriage but rather that he wanted to have a better relationship with his children'. From the time the husband first left in 1988 he considered the marriage to be at an end. The court accepted that the applicant wife did not want the marriage to end and hoped that when the husband returned in 1991 it would lead to a normal marital relationship.

McCracken J pointed out that the proceedings in this case for divorce were issued on 16 August 1999 and, although the husband had returned in 1991, the wife became involved in another relationship in 1995. The court felt that this was 'evidence of the mental attitude of the applicant to the marriage in 1995, whatever she may have hoped for in 1991 when the respondent returned.'

McCracken J therefore granted a decree of divorce as he was satisfied that:

'the respondent never considered himself to be living together with the applicant in a marriage and, certainly in the last four years of the marriage the applicant did not consider herself to be living together with the respondent in that same sense'.

4.3.3.3 'Four years during the previous five years'

When applying for a decree of divorce the spouses must have lived apart from one another for a minimum period of four years during the five years preceding the institution of divorce proceedings. Where spouses have lived apart from one another for four years during a five-year period, the fact that during that time they lived together for brief periods or indeed for longer periods will not prevent either spouse being granted a decree of divorce. This allows the couple to make efforts to reconcile or sort out their differences during the relevant periods.

4.3.3.4 No reasonable prospect of reconciliation between the spouses

Before granting a decree of divorce the court must also be satisfied that there is no reasonable prospect of a reconciliation between the spouses (1996 Act, s. 5(1)(b)). It is therefore possible, although it has not happened as yet, for a court to refuse to grant a decree of divorce because in the court's own view the couple may have a chance of saving their marriage and may reconcile.

Section 8(1) of the 1996 Act states that:

'where an application is made to the court for the grant of a decree of divorce, the court shall give consideration to the possibility of reconciliation between the spouses concerned and, accordingly may adjourn the proceedings at any time for the purpose of enabling attempts to be made by the spouses if they both so wish, to effect such a reconciliation with or without the assistance of a third party.'

The important words here are 'if they both so wish'. The interpretation of this section would appear to be somewhat different from the interpretation of the 1996 Act, s. 5(1)(b). There it would appear that the court can interfere of its own volition. Under the 1996 Act, s. 8(1), if both the husband and the wife wish to attempt to reconcile, then the court *may* adjourn the proceedings to enable this to be done. It would be inappropriate for a court to force the hearing in such circumstances to go ahead against the wishes of the parties.

This contrasts greatly with the situation in civil cases where adjournments prior to a hearing are generally extremely difficult to obtain and are almost unheard of once the hearing has actually started. The legislature quite rightly accepts that matrimonial cases must be dealt with in a different way from ordinary civil cases.

Section 8(1) refers to the possible assistance of a third party in effecting a reconciliation. Section 43 provides that the cost of such services 'shall be in the discretion of the court', presumably as between the parties, as certainly the State will not contribute, except in certain cases, indirectly, through the legal aid scheme.

If a case is adjourned to enable the parties to attempt to reconcile, a regular source of concern of both parties is the use to which any documents produced or comments made to such third parties is put thereafter. This is dealt with in the 1996 Act, s. 9, which states that:

> *an oral or written communication between either of the spouses concerned and a third party made for the purpose of seeking assistance to effect a reconciliation or to reach agreement between them on some or all of the terms of a separation or a divorce (whether or not made in the presence or with the knowledge of the other spouse), and any record of such communication, made or caused to be made by either of the spouses concerned or such a third party, shall not be admissible as evidence in any court.*

This section also operates even if such communications were made *prior* to the issuing of proceedings. Some efforts have been made by practitioners to subpoena records relating to such confidential communications, but without success.

4.3.3.5 Proper provision for the spouse and dependent members of the family

The court must be satisfied that such provision as the court considers proper, having regard to the circumstances, exists or will be made for the spouses, any dependent members of the family and any person prescribed by law (1996 Act, s. 5(1)(c)).

Definition of 'dependent member'

In order to determine whether proper provision has been made, it is necessary to understand what is meant by 'dependent member of the family'. Section 2(1) of the 1996 Act defines such dependent member of the family, in relation to a spouse, or the spouses concerned, as being any child of:

(a)   both spouses or adopted by both spouses under the Adoption Acts 1952–1991 or in relation to where both spouses are *in loco parentis*; or

(b)   of either spouse or adopted by either spouse under those Acts or in relation to where either spouse is *in loco parentis* where the other spouse, being aware that he or she is not the parent of the child, has treated the child as a member of the family, who is under the age of 18 years or if the child has attained that age;

  (i)   is or will be or, if an order were made under this Act providing for a periodical payment order for the benefit of the child or for the provision of a lump sum for the child, would be receiving full-time education or instruction at any university, college, school or other educational establishment, and is under the age of 23 years; or

  (ii)   has a mental or physical disability to such extent that it is not reasonably possible for the child to maintain himself or herself fully.

Therefore it can be seen that a dependent member of the family includes children born to both spouses, or one spouse if adopted by both spouses or by one spouse, or to whom either spouse is *in loco parentis*.

Definition of 'spouse' and 'family'

A reference to a 'spouse' includes a reference to a person who is a party to a marriage which has been dissolved under the 1996 Act, s. 2(2)(c) and a reference to a 'family' includes a reference to a family as respects which the marriage of the spouses concerned has been dissolved under the 1996 Act, s. 2(2)(d).

Pursuant to the 1996 Act, s. 5(1)(c), an applicant cannot simply state to a court that he or she will make proper provision for the dependent members of the family or the other spouse in the future at some undefined time. The provisions must have already been made or must be made by the court.

4.3.4 CASE LAW

In *R.C. v C.C.* [1997] 1 FLR 1 (High Ct), Barron J granted the first decree of divorce in Ireland pursuant to the provisions of the Constitution on 17 January 1997. He did so notwithstanding the fact that the 1996 Act had not yet come into force at that time.

The application was made by the husband, with the cooperation of the wife, as he was suffering from a terminal illness (and indeed died before the 1996 Act came into operation).

All financial issues in dispute between the parties were resolved by agreement prior to the divorce hearing.

The court considered the various matters which needed to be addressed under the Constitution prior to granting the decree of divorce. In particular, Barron J pointed out that the provisions of Clause 3 of Article 41.2.3 of the Constitution differ from the corresponding statutory provision (1996 Act, s. 5(1)(c)) insofar as children are concerned. The former requires 'such provision as the Court considers proper having regard to the circumstances exist or will be made for the spouses, any *children* of either or both of them and any other person prescribed by law . . .'; whereas the latter provides for 'such provision as the court considers proper having regard to the circumstances exists or will be made for the spouses and *any dependent members of the family*'.

As already mentioned, the definition of a 'dependent member of the family' includes children up to a maximum age of 23 years (whilst still undergoing a full-time course of education). It would seem, however, that if an application is made for a decree of divorce pursuant to the provisions of the Constitution, the court will have to satisfy itself that the welfare of *all* the children, regardless of age, is protected.

If the application for a decree of divorce is made pursuant to the 1996 Act, the court will only have to consider the welfare of children up to the maximum age of 23 years (see Walls and Bergin, *The Law of Divorce in Ireland* (Jordans, 1997) p. 17).

In the course of his judgment, Barron J stated:

> 'while I do not purport to determine that non-dependent children should necessarily have provision made for them, I am satisfied that in the particular circumstances of the present case it is proper that certainly the two daughters of the marriage should have provision made for them in the interests of the family as a whole'.

In this case both daughters were over the age of 23 and in employment. There was no evidence that either of the children had any special needs or any special requirements for their welfare. The court, however, felt that it must satisfy itself that proper provision had been made for them in any event.

4.3.5 THE EFFECTS OF A DECREE OF DIVORCE

(a) Where a decree of divorce is granted, the marriage, the subject of the decree, is dissolved and either party to that marriage may remarry (1996 Act, s. 10(1)).

(b) The granting of a decree of divorce shall not affect the right of the father and mother of an infant to continue to be joint guardians of any relevant children (1996 Act, s. 10(2)). The court, however may declare either of the parties unfit to have custody of any minor child and if it does so that party is not entitled to the right to custody of that minor on the death of the other party (1996 Act, s. 41).

(c) A divorced party ceases to be a 'spouse' for the purposes of the Succession Act 1965 and the Family Home Protection Act 1976 but does retain his or her rights to bring proceedings under the Domestic Violence Act 1996 against a former spouse.

(d) There are consequences for liability to tax, as to which see Chapter 9 of this text.

(e)   The granting of a decree of divorce does not deprive a spouse of his or her right to claim a widow or widower's pension, the one parent family payment or the right to continue to receive Deserted Wife's Allowance or Benefits.

4.3.6   SOLICITORS' OBLIGATIONS

Solicitors are obliged to file s. 6 or s. 7 certificates. These certificates are precisely the same as those certificates which must be filed by solicitors representing the applicants and respondents in applications for decrees of judicial separation. The s. 6 certificate is signed and lodged in court by the applicant's solicitor, and the s. 7 certificate is signed and filed in court by the respondent's solicitor.

Before filing an application to court for a decree of divorce or before defending such an application, the lawyers for both the applicant and the respondent must:

(a)   discuss the possibility of reconciliation and give to his or her client the names and addresses of persons qualified to help to effect such a reconciliation;

(b)   discuss the possibility of mediation and again provide the names and addresses of qualified mediators; and

(c)   discuss the possibility of effecting a separation by means of a deed or agreement in writing, rather than the issuing of court proceedings.

The lawyers must also ensure that the applicant or respondent, as the case may be, is aware of the remedy of judicial separation as an alternative to divorce.

The s. 6 certificate or the s. 7 certificate, as the case may be, must accompany the originating summons or the defence when same is served and filed in court. If this is not done, then the court may adjourn the proceedings for a reasonable period to enable the solicitor to carry out his or her duties pursuant to the provisions of ss. 6 and 7 of the Act.

CHAPTER 5

MAINTENANCE

5.1   Introduction

There is a general duty on each of the spouses to maintain each other and their children according to the Social Welfare (Consolidation) Act 1993, s. 285 (the '1993 Act'). At common law the duty was on the husband to maintain his wife and children, but there was no effective way of enforcing this. The wife was not under a corresponding duty. It ought to be noted that family law is concerned with private law, not social welfare law as such. This reflects the nature of the support obligation: it is essentially private, with the State only making payments where the family cannot maintain itself. Indeed, if one of the spouses or children is in receipt of social welfare, the duty of the other spouse is not discharged. In fact he or she becomes liable to repay the State if that can be afforded, under what is known as the liable relative scheme (see 1993 Act, Part IX).

The primary concern is the obligation to maintain in the context of marital breakdown. Traditionally, maintenance was payable for different reasons and under different provisions. For example, alimony was payable after a decree of divorce *a mensa et thoro* (the precursor to judicial separation). An affiliation order could be made in relation to an illegitimate child. The Guardianship of Infants Act 1964 still contains provisions relating to the maintenance of children. Periodic payment orders are available following a judicial separation or divorce.

5.2   Family Law (Maintenance of Spouses and Children) Act 1976

The principal statute is the Family Law (Maintenance of Spouses and Children) Act 1976 (the '1976 Act'). This Act governs the grant of maintenance orders for the benefit of spouses and dependent children of the family. A maintenance order is basically an order that one spouse make periodic payments to the other of such amount and frequency as the court directs. The recipient is called the maintenance creditor and the payer is called the maintenance debtor.

A 'dependent child of the family' is the phrase used to describe children for whom a maintenance order can be sought from a spouse. It has a wider meaning than just children of the marriage and is defined as meaning any dependent child:

(a)   of both spouses, or adopted by both spouses under the Adoption Acts, or in relation to whom both spouses are *in loco parentis*; or

(b)   of either spouse, or adopted by either spouse under the Adoption Acts, or in relation to whom either spouse is *in loco parentis*, where the other spouse, being aware that he is not the parent of the child, has treated the child as a member of the family.

In this context, and for other purposes of the Act, a 'dependent child' means any child (including a child whose parents are not married to each other) who is under the age of 18 years, or, if he has attained that age:

(a) is or will be or, if an order were made under this Act providing for periodical payments for his support, would be receiving full-time education or instruction at any university, college, school or other educational establishment, and is under the age of 23 years; or

(b) is suffering from mental or physical disability to such extent that it is not reasonably possible for him to maintain himself fully.

These two phrases 'dependent child of the family' and 'dependent child' are used with reference to different applications under the Act. The former is used in reference to the children who must be maintained by the spouse of the applicant. The latter is used in relation to maintenance applications against a parent of a non-marital child under the 1976 Act, s. 5A (as inserted by the Status of Children Act 1987).

Applications under the 1976 Act are sometimes referred to as maintenance applications simpliciter, in that the only relief being sought is maintenance. When first enacted, this Act was only concerned with maintenance between spouses and the children of marriage. The 1976 Act was amended to cover the maintenance of non-marital children by the Status of Children Act 1987, which abolished the old method of an affiliation order and introduced a maintenance application instead. Apart from that instance, the Act only applies between spouses; there is no provision for cohabitees, nor for those who have a decree of nullity or a divorce, to recover maintenance under this Act.

It ought to be remembered that maintenance can also be ordered as ancillary relief subsequent to a judicial separation and a divorce. In these cases it is called an order for periodic payments. Although governed by different statutes it has been held that similar principles apply to orders for periodic payments as apply in maintenance applications simpliciter; see *B.F. v V.F.* (unreported, 20 May 1993, High Ct, Lynch J). However, when such an order is made following a separation or divorce it will usually form part of an overall property settlement between the couple which may introduce different factors into the equation.

5.3 The Maintenance Order

A maintenance order is one that compels a spouse to make periodic payments to the other of such amount and at such times as the court directs. The centrepiece of the 1976 Act is s. 5, which basically makes need the basis for the grant. It provides in part:

> where it appears to the court, on application to it by a spouse, that the other spouse has failed to provide such maintenance for the applicant spouse and any dependent children of the family as is proper in the circumstances, the court may make an order (in this Act referred to as a maintenance order) that the other spouse make to the applicant spouse periodical payments, for the support of the applicant spouse and of each of the dependent children of the family, for such period during the lifetime of the applicant spouse, of such amount and at such times, as the court may consider proper.

The applicant under s. 5 must be a spouse, though there is a provision that where one parent is dead or missing or is living separately and apart from the other spouse and the other is not maintaining the dependent children of the family, then any person can apply for an order in respect of them (see 1976 Act, s. 5(1)(b)). It should be noted that there is no requirement that the couple be living apart, and so the order can be made and enforced while an otherwise normal relationship subsists.

Under the 1976 Act, s. 5(4), a maintenance order shall specify each part of a payment under the order that is for the support of a dependent child and may specify the period during the lifetime of the person applying for the order for which so much of a payment under the order as is for the support of a dependent child shall be made.

Once an order is made it becomes enforceable, though there can be problems with enforcement. Also, the order can be varied at any time. A maintenance order can also be discharged one year after its making, so long as the maintenance creditor would not be prejudiced by that, e.g. where there is a good record of payment. It is also discharged when a dependent member of the family ceases to be such, or where it is proper to do so in the light of new evidence.

An interim maintenance order is available under the 1976 Act, s. 7 to cover the period between the application and the full hearing. This may be ordered where it appears to the court proper to do so having regard to the needs of the applicant and any children and the other circumstances of the case. The interim order is for a definite and specified period or until the application is adjudicated upon by the court.

5.4   Basis of Assessment

5.4.1   GENERALLY

It will also be seen from the 1976 Act, s. 5(1)(a) that the applicant spouse must establish that the other spouse has failed to provide such maintenance as is proper in the circumstances. The court decides what maintenance is proper in the circumstances. If a respondent has not failed to provide such maintenance, an order should not be granted against him or her.

The basic criteria governing the granting of an order are set down in s. 5(4) of the Act, whereby the court is to have regard to all the circumstances of the case, but in particular to the following:

    (a)   the income, earning capacity (if any), property and other financial resources of:

        (i)   the spouses and any dependent children of the family, and

        (ii)   any other dependent children of whom either spouse is a parent, including income or benefits to which either spouse or any such children are entitled by or under statute, with the exception of a benefit or allowance or any increase in such benefit or allowance in respect of any dependent children granted to either parent of such children; and

    (b)   the financial and other responsibilities of:

        (i)   the spouses towards each other and towards any dependent children of the family, and

        (ii)   each spouse as a parent towards any other dependent children, and the needs of any such children, including the need for care and attention;

    (c)   the conduct of each of the spouses, if that conduct is such that in the opinion of the court it would in all the circumstances be repugnant to justice to disregard it.

In general, it is a mix between the needs of the applicant spouse and children and the resources of the respondent spouse. All relevant resources and expenses are taken into account. Included is any expense of maintaining children other than the children of the family. The overall object is to provide 'proper provision' in the circumstances. Unfortunately those circumstances are often difficult and in fact the real basis is the need of the applicant. It is well recognised that following the break-up of a marriage each spouse has fewer resources, and the approach of the courts to maintenance has sometimes been to apply hardship equally between the couple. Duncan and Scully used the phrase 'equal misery' in *Marriage Breakdown in Ireland* (Butterworths, 1990); see also *R.F. v J.F.* [1996] IFLR 12 where no award of maintenance was made as both spouses were on social welfare.

The Act is not meant to compensate for past income losses attributable to marriage. Thus, in *R.S.J. v J.S.J.* [1982] ILRM 263, the wife sought compensation for giving up her job on marriage and because she could not return to the same position. That claim was rejected.

The reference to 'proper in the circumstances' does introduce a subjective element into the definition of need. In *L.B. v H.B.* (unreported, July 1980, High Ct), where the couple were wealthy, the court made an order in favour of the applicant for £300 per week, a record at the time. This is not a typical case and most involve the division of very scarce resources. But it does demonstrate another feature of the maintenance regime: the very wide discretion that is vested in the court in deciding the amount of maintenance.

5.4.2　CRITERIA

The leading case concerning the criteria to be considered when making an award is *R.H. v N.H.* [1986] ILRM 352. Here, Finlay CJ set out the five governing principles to factor into the making of a maintenance order:

  (a) Have regard to the fact that after separation there are two households, which raises expenses and lowers the couple's living standard.

  (b) The court must find the minimum reasonable requirements of the dependent spouse and children.

  (c) The court must then ascertain the income and/or earning capacity of the dependent spouse.

  (d) The court must ascertain the net income of the respondent.

  (e) The court must ascertain the respondent's minimum requirement for living.

The first point is self-evident, but also the most significant. It leads to a sharing of the 'equal misery' and is a factor seen as vital by the courts. This consideration should also guard against unrealistic expectations, which one spouse often has of the maintenance-paying ability of the other. The court will also have regard to spendthrift behaviour of a spouse and will demand that the financial needs of the family come first.

As regards the second, the standard is subjective. In *R.K. v M.K.* (unreported, 24 October 1978, High Ct), the applicant wife required more maintenance because of an illness and this was granted. Generally, the court aims to find the minimum reasonable requirement, because in most cases there will only be enough income to cover this, though if the couple are wealthy higher maintenance can be ordered.

Given that in most cases the applicant is the wife, who may also be looking after children on a full-time basis, it is often unrealistic to speak of an earning capacity. If the children are in her care and are young, she will have little time for work. When children are older, she may not have been earning for years and may require re-training. In *B.F. v V.F.* (unreported, 20 May 1993, High Ct, Lynch J) Lynch J did not expect the wife to work outside the home as there were young children. As society and the economy change more might be expected from women in this regard, especially as children get older. It should be remembered that a husband applicant could make similar arguments if he was caring for the children. If the applicant has assets these will be taken into consideration and he or she may be expected to sell these to generate income.

On the fourth point, the net income is counted from all sources. If there are capital assets generating little income, the court will order these to be sold, e.g. antiques in *C.P. v D.P.* [1983] ILRM 380. In *J.C. v J.H.C.* (unreported, 4 August 1982, High Ct, Keane J) Keane J ordered the husband to pay £82 per week from an income of £97 because the court said he had assets to cover this sum.

The fifth point is significant, because most couples have ordinary incomes that will not stretch very far. The most important consideration is the actual ability of the respondent to pay the maintenance. The courts have said the object is not to make the respondent destitute (if for no other reason, than that he or she may give up his or her job!) and thus the courts must be realistic about income and not overestimate it, see *R.H. v N.H.* [1986] ILRM 352 where overtime was possible, but not a fact, and thus was not counted.

5.5 Relationships with Third Parties

The issue here is whether the income or expense of a second relationship should be taken into account. The case law thus far has focused on adulterous relationships, as most second relationships were in the absence of divorce. Divorce brings a new dimension to the problem. Firstly, the couple are no longer spouses and thus cannot apply under the 1976 Act. Instead there will have been a periodic payments order made, if necessary, when the divorce was granted. It should be noted that for the purposes of the reliefs available after divorce, the couple continue to be regarded as spouses, since there is no 'clean break' under Irish law (see Power 'Maintenance: No Clean Break With the Past' [1998] 1 IJFL 15). However, if the maintenance debtor remarries, and his or her second spouse seeks maintenance, the maintenance payable to the former spouse and children must be taken into account in assessing the respondent's income.

Other, non-marital, relationships are different, as these do not attract the constitutional protection of marriage. The courts have taken different approaches on these. In *O'K v O'K* (unreported, November 1982, High Ct, Barron J) it was stated by Barron J that the income of a new partner should not be considered, but when setting the amount of maintenance he appeared to do just that. In *McG v McG* (unreported, 8 February 1985, High Ct, Barron J) Barron J said the relationship ought to be considered, but when calculating the amount he seemed to ignore it. The better view now is that such relationships are taken into account.

5.6 Spousal Conduct

The basis for maintenance is need, not the behaviour of the parties. Nevertheless, conduct is still relevant. Under the 1976 Act as originally drafted, desertion was an absolute bar to relief and adultery was a discretionary bar. (Desertion includes constructive desertion, whereby if one spouse was forced to leave because of the actions of the other, the abusive spouse is deemed to be in desertion.) A change was introduced in the Judicial Separation and Family Law Reform Act 1989, and desertion is now only a discretionary bar to relief while adultery was removed as a bar. There is now a general provision that the court is to have regard to the conduct of a spouse where it is repugnant to justice to disregard it. It appears that this will only apply to serious misconduct.

If the spouse cannot get a maintenance order because of his or her conduct, he or she will still be able to get one in respect of his or her children. In *P v P* (unreported, March 1980, High Ct) the couple were young, and the wife had little interest in the marriage. She left a number of times and eventually would not let the husband see the child. She was held to be in desertion and was, at the time, absolutely barred from maintenance, but did get an order in respect of the child. Of course the child cannot really be looked at in isolation, and the maintenance order did in fact include a portion for the wife as carer.

5.7   Non-Marital Children

Section 5A was inserted into the 1976 Act by the Status of Children Act 1987, and caters for maintenance in respect of children born outside marriage, called 'dependent children' in the 1976 Act. This section allows one parent to apply for maintenance against the other in respect of the child. The law governing such applications is substantially similar to that governing maintenance under the 1976 Act, s. 5, and the criteria are also similar, with some alterations to take account of the different circumstances.

Other payments can also be ordered in respect of non-marital children, e.g., under the 1976 Act, s. 21A (as inserted by the Status of Children Act 1987) the court can order the payment of up to £750 each for birth and funeral expenses.

Section 15 of the 1987 Act caters for situations where the parentage of a child is in dispute and provides that where, in any proceedings before a court relating to the maintenance of a child or the payment of a lump sum in respect of the expenses for the birth or funeral of a child, the making of an order depends on a finding that a person is a parent of the child, the court shall not in those proceedings make any such order unless it is proved on the balance of probabilities that the person is a parent of the child.

5.8   Variation

Section 6 of the 1976 Act provides for the variation of orders, and a change in the amount can be made if there is a change of circumstances, of which there must be evidence. In *K v K* (unreported, 13 February 1992, Supreme Ct) it was said that on an application for variation the court cannot begin the case *de novo*, but should merely ascertain whether the circumstances had changed since the order was made so as to warrant an increase or decrease. In this case the court took judicial notice of inflation, i.e. there was no need to prove it by evidence, and increased the amount payable. It also accepted 'as a matter of probability' that it becomes more costly to maintain children as they become older.

As noted above, a maintenance debtor can apply for the discharge of an order after one year so long as the maintenance creditor would not be prejudiced. It will be automatically discharged when a dependent child reaches the age of 18 or 23, as appropriate. An application for discharge can be made where such a child ceases to be dependent for other reasons, or where a divorce means the maintenance creditor is no longer a spouse, or where it is proper to do so in the light of new evidence.

5.9   Lump Sum Payments

Section 42 of the Family Law Act 1995 provides for the making of lump sum payments. These can be ordered where in proceedings under any Act an order providing for the periodical payments in respect of spouses or dependent children of the family can be made. In such cases the court may, in addition to or instead of such an order, make an order providing for the making by the respondent to the applicant of a lump sum payment or lump sums of such amount or amounts and at such time or times as may be specified.

This order can be in substitution for or in addition to any maintenance order. The section applies to proceedings concerning all periodic payments orders, including maintenance applications and interim applications. When making the order the court is to have regard to the amount that is or would be payable under a periodic payments order. The maximum amount that can be ordered by the District Court is £5,000.

5.10 Maintenance Agreements

The parties often reach agreement on the amount of payment to be made. This can relate solely to maintenance, or be part of a more comprehensive separation agreement. This raises a number of concerns. Firstly, if the agreement contains provision for a lump sum can the parties agree a 'clean break', i.e. that that is the end of their financial obligations to each other?

In other words, can they agree not to go back to court? The short answer is no. This is prohibited by the 1976 Act, s. 27, which provides that any agreement that attempts to exclude or limit the operation of the Act is void. The Supreme Court reiterated this in *H.D. v P.D.* (unreported, 8 May 1978, Supreme Ct) where it said that the spouses cannot contract out of their rights to go to court.

If the spouses agree maintenance, and one then goes back to court to seek a variation, the court will have regard to the agreement in deciding the claim under the Act; a maintenance agreement and maintenance order can work together.

Section 8 of the 1976 Act provides a mechanism whereby the agreement can be made a rule of court, the primary reason being to facilitate the use of the enforcement mechanisms under the Act. The test for making it a rule of court is whether it is 'fair and reasonable'.

One problem in particular has occupied the court in this regard. This concerns a situation where there is no variation clause in the agreement. (This affects only a maintenance debtor because the agreement can always be supplemented upwards by an additional maintenance order.) In theory, as a contract, the agreement is unalterable. Thus, if the debtor cannot pay there is a breach of contract. More importantly, if it has been made a rule of court the debtor is in breach of the Act. But, in the absence of a variation clause, if his circumstances change the amount of payment cannot be reduced under the agreement. The courts have consistently said that the 1976 Act, s. 6, cannot be used to vary an agreement, because that section does not apply to agreements. In *J.D. v B.D.* [1985] ILRM 688 an agreement did not contain a variation clause, and later the husband's financial position worsened. Carroll J refused to make it a rule of court because she said that without such a clause it was not fair and reasonable. (In effect the agreement will not then be enforced.) However, some agreements do slip through without a variation clause.

In *D v D* [1989] 2 IR 361, Barron J held that a maintenance agreement could be varied under the 1976 Act, s. 6, but this is now seen as incorrect (see *P.J. v J.J.* [1992] ILRM 273). However, he also said that if he was bound to strictly adhere to the agreement, he could balance the situation by making a small maintenance order in the payer's favour. See also *J.H. v R.H.* [1996] IFLR 23.

5.11 Jurisdiction

The District Court can make orders up to £200 per week per spouse and £60 per week per child. The Circuit Family Court can also grant orders and has an unlimited jurisdiction. However, on appeal to the Circuit Family Court from the District Court, the Circuit Court is limited to the jurisdiction of the District Court. An appeal from the District Court to the Circuit Family Court is in the nature of a re-hearing.

Under the 1976 Act, s. 23(3), each spouse is to provide such details of his or her property and income as may be reasonably required for the purpose of the proceedings. If there is a refusal to provide these details, an application can be made to court to compel compliance. Section 25 of the 1976 Act provides that proceedings are to be conducted in a summary manner and be heard otherwise than in public.

5.12 Enforcement

The basic rule contained in s. 9 of the 1976 Act is that maintenance payments will be transmitted through the District Court Clerk. If the application is being made to the Circuit Family Court, the Circuit Family Court can direct the payments to be made through the District Court Office. The main advantage in having the payments made this way is that there will be a proper record of all payments and the District Court Clerk will be in a position to give evidence in relation to arrears. Where there is default in payment, the Clerk can take reasonable steps to recover payments, when requested by the maintenance creditor. The creditor can also pursue other enforcement remedies against the debtor. There are a number of these, and they will be considered in turn.

5.12.1 SECURED PAYMENTS

Section 41 of the Family Law Act 1995 provides that where, in proceedings under any Act, the court makes or has made an order providing for the payment either:

(a) by a spouse to the other spouse of periodical payments for the support or maintenance of that other spouse; or

(b) by a parent to the other parent or to another person specified in the order of periodical payments for the support or maintenance of a child of the family

then the court may in those proceedings or subsequently order the spouse or parent liable to make the payments under the order to secure them to the other spouse or parent or the other person specified in the order to the satisfaction of the court.

This provision applies to all periodic payments orders. Essentially, this provision is a means of enforcement, but it could also be used to put in place methods of payment to suit different cases.

5.12.2 ATTACHMENT OF EARNINGS ORDER

If the maintenance debtor is an employee then the maintenance creditor may obtain an attachment of earnings order under the 1976 Act, s. 10 (as amended by the Family Law Act 1995). This is an order directing the maintenance debtor's employers to deduct a specified sum from the debtor's wages. Before the enactment of the Family Law Act 1995 an attachment of earnings order could not be made unless the maintenance debtor failed to comply with the maintenance order. The application would then be made to the court which made the antecedent maintenance order. (However, if the High Court or Circuit Family Court directed the payments to be made through the District Court Clerk's Office then an application could be made to the District Court.)

The 1995 Act amended the 1976 Act, s. 10 to provide that an attachment of earnings order will be automatically granted when a maintenance order is made, unless the maintenance creditor proves to the satisfaction of the court that he or she would make payments without the necessity for such an order.

When a court makes an attachment of earnings order it must specify the normal deduction rate and the protected earnings rate. The normal deduction rate is the amount to be deducted and paid over to the maintenance creditor. The protected earnings rate is the rate beneath which the debtor's income will not fall and is designed to match the reasonable needs and expenses of the debtor. The courts have no interest in setting this too low, as the debtor may be tempted to cease employment altogether. It has been shown that the use of an attachment of earnings order substantially increases the rate of compliance with maintenance orders: see Ward, *Financial Consequences of Marital Breakdown* (1990).

5.12.3 ENFORCEMENT OF COURT ORDERS ACT 1940

Another method of enforcing maintenance orders is pursuant to the Enforcement of Court Orders Act 1940, s. 8 (as amended by the 1995 Act, s. 22). Either the maintenance creditor, or District Court Clerk where maintenance payments are made through the District Court Clerk's Office, must swear an information before a District Justice. The information sets out the amount of arrears owing. The District Court can either issue a summons against the maintenance debtor or issue a warrant (where there is a long history of default) for the debtor's arrest. When the maintenance debtor eventually comes before the court the District Justice can, if the debtor has no defence, imprison him or her for a maximum period of three months. The District Court can also order the distress of goods, which will then be sold.

The above procedure can only be used if the antecedent order was made in the District Court, or if the High Court or Circuit Family Court directed the payments to be made to the District Court Clerk's Office. Otherwise, committal proceedings against the maintenance debtor for contempt of court can be issued in the High Court or Circuit Family Court.

It should be noted that under the 1976 Act and under the Enforcement of Court Orders Act 1940 the creditor is limited to claiming a maximum six months' arrears. It is, however, open to the creditor to issue ordinary debt collection proceedings for the recovery of arrears going back further than six months.

5.12.4 INTERNATIONAL ENFORCEMENT

There are special problems concerning the enforcement in Ireland of maintenance orders made abroad, though this may be of vital importance to the maintenance creditor. At common law, foreign monetary awards could only be enforced in Ireland if the sum payable was final and conclusive. It was thought that this precluded the enforcement of maintenance, which by definition is an ongoing and potentially variable obligation. However, it was held in *G v G* [1984] IR 368 that each payment could be considered final when it fell due and arrears could thus be enforced. At any rate there have been a number of measures introduced to facilitate the enforcement of such orders.

5.12.4.1 Maintenance Orders Act 1974

Under this Act maintenance orders made in the UK can be enforced in Ireland and orders made in Ireland can be enforced in the UK. The Act confers jurisdiction on the Master of the High Court at first instance to make an enforcement order. If and when the Master makes an enforcement order the District Court acquires jurisdiction to hear enforcement proceedings against a maintenance debtor for arrears of maintenance in the same way as maintenance orders made in the State.

5.12.4.2 Jurisdiction of Courts and Enforcement of Judgments Act 1998

This Act incorporates into Irish law the Brussels Convention and Lugano Convention relating to the jurisdiction and enforcement of judgments in civil and commercial matters. These provide inter alia for the enforcement of maintenance orders throughout the European Union and EFTA countries respectively.

5.12.4.3 Maintenance Act 1994

This Act brings two international conventions, the Rome Convention and the New York Convention, into Irish law. The Rome Convention applies throughout EU member states, and operates together with the provisions of the Brussels Convention. A Central Authority was established in each member state to assist the enforcement of maintenance orders made in other member states. The New York Convention provides a similar mechanism of enforcement, but it covers a wider range of countries than the Rome Convention.

CHAPTER 6

ANCILLARY ORDERS, PROCEDURE AND DISCOVERY ON JUDICIAL SEPARATION AND DIVORCE

6.1 Ancillary Relief on Judicial Separation and Divorce

6.1.1 INTRODUCTION

Prior to the introduction of the Judicial Separation and Family Law Reform Act 1989 (the '1989 Act'), the regulation by couples of matters ancillary to separation had to be dealt with by orders made pursuant to a number of different pieces of legislation, such as the Married Women's Status Act 1957 or the Guardianship of Infants Act 1964. Alternatively, the parties could regulate all matters in a deed of separation, if terms could be agreed between them. The 1989 Act not only transformed the basis upon which separation decrees could be granted by the court but it also considerably extended the court's powers to make ancillary orders under Part II of same. Part II of the 1989 Act was repealed and replaced by Part II of the Family Law Act 1995 (the '1995 Act') which came into force on 1 August 1996. The provisions of the Family Law Act 1995 must therefore be applied in all judicial separation cases instituted on or after that date.

Part III of the Family Law (Divorce) Act 1996 (the '1996 Act') sets out the court's powers to make preliminary and ancillary relief orders in divorce proceedings instituted under that Act. The provisions of the 1995 and 1996 Acts amended, extended and enhanced the pre-existing range of financial, property and other ancillary reliefs previously set out in Part II of the 1989 Act. The legislature sought in the enactment of the two later Acts to fill gaps and remedy omissions which had come to light and developed since the 1989 Act.

The 1995 Act was enacted during the period of preparation for the referendum on divorce which was held on 24 November 1995. It was the intention of the Government that the 1995 Act would cater for all financial consequences on marital breakdown, and that the sole remaining issue to be determined was the issue of the right to remarry. It can therefore be seen that the 1995 Act not only re-enacted most of the provisions of the 1989 Act, but also introduced provisions for the making of ancillary orders consequent on the obtaining of a foreign decree of divorce or legal separation which would be recognised in this State. Essentially, the 1995 Act contains provisions enabling the court to grant a comprehensive range of property and other ancillary orders following the obtaining of a decree of separation or annulment, either from an Irish or foreign court. The issue of pensions was dealt with for the first time by the introduction of a pensions adjustment order, a remedy previously not available to the court in any form.

Part III of the Family Law (Divorce) Act 1996 sets out the preliminary and ancillary orders available in or after proceedings for divorce have been instituted. While the provisions of Part III of the 1996 Act originate in the corresponding provisions of the 1989 and 1995 Acts, it is clear that on the granting of a decree of divorce, the status of the parties as spouses terminates, and the inheritance rights, and, in some cases, pension rights of the former spouses, are automatically terminated. The 1996 Act also effected amendments to the 1995 Act to take account of the introduction of divorce.

6.1.2 FACTORS GOVERNING THE MAKING OF ANCILLARY ORDERS

Section 16 of the 1995 Act sets out the factors to which the court is to have regard in deciding whether to make orders for ancillary relief pursuant to the 1995 Act, ss. 7 to 13, 18 and 25, on the granting of a decree of judicial separation.

Similar criteria are contained in the 1996 Act, s. 20, and, in addition, the court is charged by s. 5(1)(c), on the granting of a decree of divorce, to ensure that 'proper provision' exists and will be made, having regard to the circumstances, for the spouses and any dependent members of the family. These provisions will be examined in more detail.

6.1.3 PRELIMINARY ORDERS ON JUDICIAL SEPARATION AND DIVORCE

Preliminary orders are orders which may be made by the court before the full hearing of an application for judicial separation or divorce. They are designed to provide relief where it is required immediately, and where the full hearing of the application will not take place for some time. The possibility of obtaining a preliminary order avoids the necessity of instituting applications for relief under different pieces of legislation, such as the Guardianship of Infants Act 1964 or the Domestic Violence Act 1996. Preliminary orders cease to have effect once the application for separation or divorce has been determined.

6.1.4 PRELIMINARY ORDERS ON JUDICIAL SEPARATION

Section 6 of the 1995 Act provides for the making of preliminary orders in proceedings for judicial separation. The court may make orders in relation to domestic violence, custody and access proceedings, and orders for the protection of the family home and its contents. Section 6(a) refers to the Family Law (Protection of Spouses and Children) Act 1981, which has been repealed and replaced by the Domestic Violence Act 1996.

6.1.5 PRELIMINARY ORDERS ON DIVORCE

Section 11 of the 1996 Act permits the court to grant preliminary orders where application has been made to it for a decree of divorce, again in relation to domestic violence, custody and access proceedings, and orders for protection of the family home and its contents.

6.1.6 MAINTENANCE PENDING SUIT ORDERS

Another form of preliminary order is a *maintenance pending suit order*, which is provided for in the 1995 Act, s. 7 and the 1996 Act, s. 12. These sections permit the court to make orders for temporary maintenance, which orders will expire on the date of the full hearing of the application. The sections do not provide for retrospective maintenance prior to the date of the institution of proceedings. The court can make orders for *interim periodical payments* or *lump sum payments,* and the enactment of these provisions was intended to cover situations where there may be hardship for one of the spouses pending the determination of proceedings.

The criteria set out in the 1995 Act, s. 16 and the 1996 Act, s. 20 are to be applied by the court in the making of these orders. In addition, the 1995 Act, s. 7(2) and the 1996 Act, s. 12(2) provide that the court may impose terms and conditions on whatever order it chooses to make, which terms and conditions must be specified in the order. For example, the court may direct that a lump sum be paid by one spouse to the other to discharge mortgage arrears, or to pay outstanding school fees.

6.1.7 CUSTODY AND ACCESS DISPUTES ON JUDICIAL SEPARATION AND DIVORCE

As we have already seen, these issues may be dealt with by the court by way of preliminary orders pursuant to the 1995 Act, s. 6 and the 1996 Act, s. 11. If no orders are made prior to the hearing of the action, then the court may make orders pertaining to the welfare of the children pursuant to the 1995 Act, s. 16(1)(g) and the 1996 Act, s. 15(1)(f), and in both cases orders will be made pursuant to the provisions of the Guardianship of Infants Act 1964, s. 11. All orders for custody, access and other matters pertaining to the interests and welfare of children will be made pursuant to these two sections.

In the case of judicial separation, the court may make such an order at the time, or after the decree of judicial separation has been granted. In the case of divorce, the 1996 Act, s. 15(1), specifies that application may be made to it in relation to any of the issues set out in s. 15 at any time after the decree of divorce has been granted. In both cases, such application must be made during the lifetime of the other spouse.

Obviously, parties do not have to seek either judicial separation or divorce in order to avail of the provisions of the 1964 Act. The guiding principle of the 1964 Act, i.e. 'the welfare principle', is applied in the making of orders under judicial separation and divorce.

Section 11 of the Children Act 1997 expressly provides for the making of joint custody orders, pursuant to the 1964 Act, s. 11A (as inserted by the 1997 Act).

The role of 'social reports' in family law proceedings is dealt with in the 1995 Act, s. 47 and the 1996 Act, s. 42, which latter section simply directs that the 1995 Act, s. 47 shall apply to divorce proceedings. The power of the courts to procure such reports was first set out in the 1989 Act, s. 40 and since the introduction of social reports, they have become widely used as tools in the resolution of child-centred disputes. The Probation and Welfare Service provides a limited service in the area of family law, and the virtual loss of this service is regrettable, imposing as it does the need on parties to obtain outside reports from professionals, often at substantial cost. The parties may agree that a social report is necessary to aid in the resolution of a dispute, or the court may, of its own motion, direct that such a report be furnished to it. In deciding whether or not the procurement of such a report is necessary, the court must have regard to submissions made to it by either of the parties, or by 'any other person to whom they relate'. The method of payment and by whom payment should be made may be determined by the court, and the author of the report may give evidence in relation to it, and be cross-examined in relation to same.

6.1.8 DOMESTIC VIOLENCE ON JUDICIAL SEPARATION AND DIVORCE

An applicant for relief against domestic violence may make application to the court in that regard as a preliminary issue, again pursuant to the 1995 Act, s. 6, on judicial separation, and s. 11 of the 1996 Act in relation to divorce. In both cases, applications may be made for a safety order, a barring order, an interim barring order, or a protection order.

On the hearing of an application for a judicial separation or divorce, the court may make orders pursuant to the Domestic Violence Act 1996, under the 1995 Act, s. 10(1)(d) and under the 1996 Act, s. 15(1)(d). Section 52(c) of the 1996 Act amended the Family Law Act 1995 to take account of the introduction of the Domestic Violence Act 1996. Relief pursuant to the Domestic Violence Act 1996 may be sought on judicial separation or divorce, either on behalf of the applicant, or on behalf of a dependent family member. Such orders may be made where the court is of the opinion that there are reasonable grounds for believing that the safety or welfare of the applicant, or any dependent child, requires such orders to be made.

A divorced party remains a spouse for the purposes of relief under the Domestic Violence Act 1996, and such relief may be sought at any time after the granting of the decree of divorce. This is provided for in the Family Law (Divorce) Act 1996, s. 51, the effect of which is to ensure that a former spouse who has obtained a decree of divorce, either in this jurisdiction, or in a foreign jurisdiction, does not lose the protection of the Domestic Violence Act 1996. This is obviously important for people who continue to experience violence at the hands of a former partner, as they would otherwise be barred from relief under the Domestic Violence Act 1996, by the provisions of s. 3 of that Act.

In relation to judicial separation, the case of *A.K. v J.K.* (1996) FLJ 22 is instructive. In that case, an interim barring order was granted to the applicant by way of preliminary relief, notwithstanding the fact that the applicant had left the family home three years prior to the date of the application. McGuinness J did not find the applicant to be barred from seeking relief as a result of delay.

6.1.9   FINANCIAL PROVISION ON MARITAL BREAKDOWN

The issue of how financial provision is made for both parties to a matrimonial dispute will be examined with reference to maintenance, incorporating financial compensation orders and pension adjustment orders, property, and issues pertaining to succession.

6.1.9.1   Maintenance

The common law duty of spouses to maintain one another is preserved in statute and survives throughout, and after the termination of, the marital relationship. This duty can be enforced whether or not the spouses are residing together or have separated, and also survives the execution by parties of a separation agreement, or the granting by a court of an order for judicial separation or divorce. The duty also extends beyond the remarriage of the paying spouse, regardless of any new duties or responsibilities that they may acquire. Liability to maintain a former spouse only terminates when that other spouse dies or remarries, and even in the case of death, a secured maintenance order, made pursuant to the Family Law (Maintenance of Spouses and Children) Act 1976, will ensure that the liability continues.

On the granting of a decree of judicial separation, the court may make an order in respect of maintenance pursuant to the provisions of the 1995 Act, s. 8. It has already been seen how it is possible to obtain maintenance pending suit orders under the 1995 Act, s. 7. A maintenance order may be made pursuant to s. 8 on the application of either of the spouses, or on the application of a person on behalf of a dependent family member. The application must be made during the lifetime of the other spouse.

Three different types of maintenance order can be made under the 1995 Act:

(a)   pursuant to s. 8(1)(a), a *periodical payments order*, either in respect of the other spouse or in respect of a dependent family member;

(b)   pursuant to s. 8(1)(b), a *secured periodical payments order*, again either in respect of the other spouse, or in respect of a dependent family member;

(c)   pursuant to s. 8(1)(c), a *lump sum payment(s) order*, again in respect of the other spouse, or a dependent family member.

While s. 8 does not provide for the making of retrospective maintenance orders to take account of the non-payment of maintenance prior to the institution of the proceedings, s. 8(2) provides that the court may direct that a lump sum be paid by one spouse to the other to discharge any liabilities or expenses 'reasonably incurred' prior to the issuing of the application. These expenses or liabilities will have been incurred by the other spouse in maintaining themselves or the dependent family members, if any.

Pursuant to s. 8(3), the court may order that lump sums be paid by instalments, and that such instalments be secured to the satisfaction of the court.

As has been seen, the application may be made at the time of the granting of the decree of judicial separation, or subsequently at any time during the lifetime of both spouses. However, if a spouse in whose favour an order is made remarries, then that order will cease to have effect insofar as the remarried spouse is concerned, but not insofar as any dependent family members are concerned (1995 Act, s. 8(5)(a)). The issue of enforcement of maintenance orders has always been difficult, often because at the time the original order is made, it may not be apparent that the paying spouse will default. The provisions of s. 8(6) of the 1995 Act were most welcome, introducing as they did a new power to the court to make an attachment of earnings order at the same time as the making of a periodical payments order, without any default in payment having occurred. However, before making such an attachment of earnings order, the court must give the spouse concerned an opportunity to make representations in relation to that aspect of the matter. Obviously, these provisions are of little use if a paying spouse is self-employed or working in the black economy. Orders for periodical payment may also be directed by the court to be paid through the District Court Office, which in effect means that a record of such payments or non-payments will be available in the event of default by the paying spouse. The onus to enforce payments is, however, on the recipient spouse, who must request a summons to be issued seeking enforcement of maintenance arrears. Often, the recipient spouse will be reluctant to do this and the default goes unremedied.

The issue of financial provision is one of the most contentious issues on separation or divorce, as the reality for most ordinary families post-separation means that they will be less financially secure. The calculation of what is appropriate maintenance in each case is ultimately decided by the courts on the facts of each case as it appears before them. In deciding what orders to make, the court will have regard to all pleadings and, in particular, to the statements of means furnished by both parties pursuant to the Circuit Court Rules (No. 1) 1997, SI 84/1997. A properly completed and up-to-date affidavit of means is of invaluable assistance to both practitioners and judges, and, where properly completed, will obviate the necessity for lengthy discovery. However, if there is inadequate information supplied after the affidavit of means has been filed, then it may be necessary to seek either voluntary discovery or discovery by order of the court. In addition, the court is bound by the provisions of s. 16 of the 1995 Act to take into account the matters set out in s. 16(2)(a) to (l) in deciding what order to make. Section 16(1) sets out the guiding principle in relation to all ancillary relief orders which is that the court:

> *shall endeavour to ensure that such provision is made for each spouse concerned and for any dependant member of the family concerned as is adequate and reasonable having regard to all the circumstances of the case.*

The list of items to which the court shall have regard is comprehensive, and includes the length of time during which the spouses lived together, the conduct of the parties, and the rights of any person other than the spouses but including a person to whom either spouse is remarried. In the context of judicial separation, remarriage could have taken place after a recognised foreign divorce had been obtained.

The issue of conduct must be seen as only one of the items to which the courts shall have regard in deciding whether or not to make an order. In general, this is precisely how the courts view the issue of conduct, and, increasingly, they are less likely to listen to protracted arguments concerning the behaviour of the parties. The courts now place emphasis on financial circumstances with a view to removing the focus on fault. Courts tend to realise that neither party will be entirely without blame, and will refer to behaviour or conduct if it has caused an imbalance in the relationship between the parties. Obviously, conduct will not be ignored where it would be 'unjust' to do so, as referred to in both the 1995 and 1996 Acts.

In the case of *J.D. v D.D.* (unreported, 14 May 1997, High Ct, McGuinness J), the court carefully examined the financial background and position of both parties, and applied the provisions of the 1995 Act, and in particular, the provisions of s. 16 of that Act, in deciding what form of financial provision should be made by the applicant wife. The parties in that case had been married for over 30 years, and were quite wealthy. The family assets comprised valuable property, fine arts and antiques, and income from an auctioneering business, directorships, investments, bank deposit interest, and family trusts. During the course of preparation for the trial, it was discovered that the husband had been less than forthcoming with discovery of his financial circumstances, and indeed, monies were transferred out of the jurisdiction prior to the hearing of the action. The court referred in some detail to the issue of whether or not it was possible to obtain finality, or a 'clean break' in cases of this sort. The court referred to the case of *F v F (Judicial Separation)* [1995] 2 IR 354 in which Denham J stated:

'Certainty and finality of litigation are important. Some issues in family law are not capable of a final order by law, e.g. maintenance. However, the fact that some issues in Family Law Courts are not capable of finality does not deprive this area of the law of the important concepts of certainty and finality. Whereas care for dependants requires that there be no finality in some areas, the general law regarding certainty should apply unless excluded by law or justice'.

McGuinness J held that the case of *F v F* could be distinguished as it had been decided in the context of the 1989 Act, and went on to point out that by the subsequent enactment of the 1995 and 1996 Acts,

'. . . the Oireachtas has made it clear that "a clean break" situation is not to be sought and that, if anything, financial certainty is virtually to be prevented'.

McGuinness J went on to say: 'The statutory policy is, therefore, totally opposed to the concept of the "clean break"'. In the particular case, McGuinness J felt that she could not 'fly in the face of the clear policy of the legislature, and endeavour to create a clean break which cannot in any event be achieved'.

Having applied the provisions of s. 16 of the 1995 Act to the instant case, the court noted that the husband had undertaken to discharge the outstanding costs of the wife's residence, and directed a lump sum payment of £200,000 to be paid by the husband to the wife. A periodical payment order of £20,000 per annum was ordered and any of the husband's pension provisions which would benefit the wife were to be left untouched.

In applying the provisions of s. 16 of the 1995 Act, the court referred to conduct, but in the overall context of the case, it was largely disregarded. The court referred to the length of the marriage, and to the fact that the marriage was:

'a lengthy partnership of complimentary roles and it seems to me that it should result in a reasonably equal division of the accumulated assets'.

It can be seen from this case that the capital assets of both parties will be taken into account in assessing maintenance.

In the case of *S.B. v R.B.* [1996] 1 FLR 220, McGuinness J took into account the fact that the husband had monies available to him which permitted the purchase by him of a large car, and the reduction by him of the mortgage repayments on his new home. The court adjusted the maintenance payments to the wife accordingly. In addition to capital assets, the court will have regard to the total financial resources of both spouses, taking into account actual income and assets, likely future income and assets, and potential income from employment and capital assets. The two main factors to be taken into account by the court are financial need, and the capacity of the paying spouse to pay. Frequently, courts will comment as to the likely future earning power of one of the spouses, and this frequently impacts more on wives, particularly where they have chosen to remain at home to take care of the children.

In looking at financial resources, the court has no power to order a third party, such as a co-habitee, to contribute towards maintenance payments. The fact that any third party may make monies available to either of the spouses may however be relevant in assessing the maintenance payable: *O'K. v O'K.* (unreported, 16 November 1992, High Ct, Barron J).

6.1.9.2 Lump sum payments

One method of achieving a certain degree of finality in a case is to have a lump sum ordered where it is considered that periodical maintenance payments might not be made. In the case of *E.P. v C.P.* (unreported, 27 November 1998, High Ct, McGuinness J), the judge opted to make a lump sum order in proceedings for a decree of judicial separation. The court directed that a lump sum of £40,000 was to be paid by the husband to the wife, being payment of arrears in the sum of £10,000, together with a sum of £30,000 being maintenance for the children of the marriage for a period of four years. She pointed out that the applicant could thereafter apply for further maintenance. McGuinness J made the order in this case in light of the history of non-payment of maintenance by the respondent husband. Practitioners should be aware of the tax implications of such orders: see Chapter 9.

6.1.9.3 The assessment of maintenance by Irish courts

The calculation of how much maintenance is to be paid in any particular case is ultimately a matter for the court to decide, and each case will stand on its own facts. There is no set formula, either in legislation or in case law, as there is in other jurisdictions for determining the amount of maintenance to be paid. The court in each case will attempt to strike a balance in all the circumstances and will also take into account all matters it considers proper. The court is guided in this regard by the provisions of s. 16 of the 1995 Act and s. 20 of the 1996 Act.

The provisions of the 1996 Act state that before a decree of divorce can be granted 'such provision as the court considers proper having regard to the circumstances exists and will be made for the spouses and any dependent members of the family'. In the case of divorce, the court must consider all dependent children of either party. The court on divorce does not have to be satisfied that proper provision has been made in the past, but must be satisfied that it will be so in the future. In practice, however, it will be possible to demonstrate proper provision by the court granting ancillary relief orders. In this regard, the court has the authority to review orders previously made, or the terms of a separation agreement entered into by the parties. This could involve the reassessment and amendment of orders previously made, sometimes to the dissatisfaction of one of the parties.

In the United Kingdom, certain formulae laid down in recent case law are used to calculate maintenance levels, but the existence of these formulae only serves to highlight the fact that each and every case turns on its own facts. It might be preferable if there were differing models to be regarded when deciding what maintenance should be awarded. For example, as in many states in the United States, the issue of compensatory maintenance could be explored, which would allow a spouse to be compensated for losses sustained by him or her during the course of the marriage.

For the moment, case law provides guidance in this regard.

6.1.9.4   Variation and discharge of maintenance orders

The provisions of the 1995 Act, s. 18, apply to maintenance pending suit orders, periodical (and secured) payments orders, and lump sum orders, if paid by instalments. Section 18 permits the variation or discharge of such order on application to the court by a number of parties. Either of the spouses concerned may apply for variation or discharge, or if either of the spouses has died, another person who has a sufficient interest in the matter may also apply. A person on behalf of a dependent family member may also apply for variation or discharge. The court, if it considers it proper to do so, will have regard to any change in the circumstances of the parties, and to any new evidence which there may be. Orders under s. 18 of the 1995 Act may vary, discharge, suspend temporarily or revive the operation of an order previously suspended. Original orders subsequently varied may also be varied.

Section 18(3) of the 1995 Act provides that maintenance payable to a dependent family member shall automatically be discharged when the dependent family member reaches the appropriate age of either 18 or 23 years, or indeed if, on application to it, the court decides that a dependent family member is no longer dependent, it may also order the discharge of the maintenance payment.

Section 18(1)(j) of the 1995 Act provides that any order made under s. 18 may also be varied, thus permitting repeated variation orders.

6.1.9.5   Financial compensation orders

Section 11 of the 1995 Act introduced a practical measure that enables the court to make orders in respect of life assurance for dependent spouses and children. On the granting of a decree of judicial separation or at any time thereafter, the court may make a financial compensation order requiring either or both of the spouses to do one or more of the following:

(a)   effect a life insurance policy for the benefit of the applicant, or any other dependent family member specified in the order;

(b)   assign such a policy in whole or in part to the other spouse or dependent family member;

(c)   continue to discharge the premiums due on a particular policy.

The court is directed by the provisions of s. 11(1)(a) and (b) to consider whether the financial security of either of the spouses or any dependent family member requires the making of such an order or whether they can be compensated by such an order for the loss of a benefit because of the judicial separation. However, the court is also directed, by s. 11(2)(a), to have regard to whether adequate and reasonable provision can be made for the other spouse or dependent family member by orders under ss. 8 to 10 and 12 of the 1995 Act.

Any financial compensation order made ceases to have effect on the remarriage or death of the applicant, and the court shall not make an order granting a financial compensation order if the applicant spouse has already remarried. Note also that the provisions of s. 18 of the 1995 Act apply to s. 11: see **7.1.1**.

6.1.9.6   Pensions

Prior to the enactment of the 1995 Act, the pension as a family asset could not be interfered with on judicial separation. As a valuable matrimonial asset, this was clearly a shortcoming in the legislative provisions governing separation. Sections 12 and 13 of the 1995 Act set out, for the first time, legislative provisions that enable the distribution of pension benefits. In that regard, pensions are to be regarded in the same way as any other asset, although the complexity of s. 12 and the corresponding provision, s. 17 of the 1996 Act, belies the simplicity of this statement.

Prior to the coming into operation of the 1995 Act, parties wishing to adjust a pension had to examine their own individual pension scheme to see whether the entitlements could be apportioned between the parties. However, without the ability of the court to intervene, it was frequently impossible to adjust what was essentially a private contract between the trustees of the pension fund and the member of the pension fund.

If it is required that a pension benefit be adjusted, an application to court must be made for a decree of judicial separation or divorce and consequent relief under ss. 12 and 13. It is not enough simply to reach an agreement and incorporate it in a deed of separation.

A pension adjustment order may be made in relation to:

(a)   a retirement benefit; and/or

(b)   a contingent benefit,

under a scheme of which either of the spouses is a member at the time the order is made. A pension scheme is defined within s. 12 as:

(i)   an occupational pension scheme (as defined by the Pensions Act 1990, s. 2);

(ii)   a retirement annuity contract (or policy for the self-employed), as approved by the Revenue Commissioners under the Income Tax Act 1967;

(iii) a trust (pension) scheme or part of such scheme similarly approved by the Revenue Commissioners;

(iv)   an annuity contract or a buyout policy similarly approved by the Revenue Commissioners;

(v)   Any other pension scheme or arrangement, e.g. a personal pension plan, other than one established under the Social Welfare Acts, which provides benefits for the member on retirement, or on the ceasing of relevant employment, or benefits for the widow, widower or dependants of that member on the death of the member.

6.1.9.7   Who can apply?

Either spouse may apply for a pension adjustment order, either for his or her own benefit or for the benefit of a dependent family member. A third party may also apply for the benefit of a dependent family member.

It should be noted that the 1995 Act, s. 12(23)(a) prohibits the making of an order for the benefit of an applicant who has remarried. Note also that orders made for a dependent family member will cease to be of effect when the dependency ceases. It must also be noted that a contingent benefit can be adjusted in respect of a child, a dependent family member or a spouse, but a similar order cannot be made in respect of a retirement benefit.

It is important to note that the provisions of the 1995 Act, s. 12(23)(b), direct that a pension adjustment order may be made in addition to or in substitution in whole or in part for orders under ss. 8, 9, 10 or 11, and in deciding whether or not to make a pension adjustment order, the court must have regard to whether orders made under these sections could adequately provide reasonable financial provision for the spouse or dependent family members. Once again, the provisions of s. 16 apply and must be taken into account by the court in deciding whether or not to make an order. However, the issue of variation is dealt with in s. 12(26) which enables the court to restrict or exclude the application of s. 18 to a pension adjustment order already made. This does not of course preclude an application for a further pension adjustment order being made on divorce.

If a spouse is a member of more than one pension scheme, then orders must be made in respect of each individual scheme. In addition, separate pension adjustment orders must be made in respect of both the contingent and the retirement benefit.

6.1.9.8 **What is a contingent benefit?**

A contingent benefit is usually referred to as 'a death in service benefit'. It is paid to a widow, widower or dependent child of a pension scheme member who dies while in relevant employment. The member of the scheme must not have attained the normal pensionable age provided for under the rules of his/her particular scheme.

6.1.9.9 **What is a retirement benefit?**

A retirement benefit is payable to a member of a scheme who retires after the attainment of normal pensionable age. This money may also be payable to a widow, widower or dependent child on the death of the retirement member. The retirement benefit could take the form of a weekly or monthly pension payable for life or other specified period, and also perhaps a lump sum.

A retirement benefit may be paid under an occupational pension scheme which has been established by an employer, or a scheme which has been established to make independent provision for a person either in employment or self-employed. There are two different kinds of pension schemes; a *defined contribution scheme*, and a *defined benefit scheme*.

(a) In a defined contribution scheme, a designated percentage of the insured person's salary is paid into the scheme. Usually, the employer also contributes to the scheme, and sometimes the employer alone contributes to the scheme. The insured person alone may also contribute to the scheme where he/she is self-employed. The monies paid are then used by way of investment to provide a contingent and/ or retirement benefit.

(b) In a defined benefit scheme, the amounts payable are calculated by reference to the amount of salary received at the date of retirement of an employee, and the length of their employment. An example of this would be the Teachers' Pension Scheme.

The distinctions between retirement and contingent benefit, and between defined contribution schemes and defined benefit schemes are important because each is treated differently when it comes to the making of a pension adjustment order.

6.1.9.10 **Adjustments to pensions on divorce**

Section 17 of the 1996 Act sets out the law relating to the regulating of pensions as an ancillary relief on divorce. A pension adjustment order may be sought under the 1996 Act, s. 17, by either an applicant spouse, or by a person acting on behalf of a dependent family member. A pension adjustment order may be obtained either at the time the decree of divorce is granted, or, in the case of an application to adjust a retirement benefit, at any time during the lifetime of the spouse who is a member of the pension scheme in question (hereinafter referred to as the member spouse).

However, note that an application to adjust a contingent benefit must be made within 12 months of the granting of the decree of divorce.

Essentially, the effect of an order under the 1996 Act, s. 17, as under the 1995 Act, s. 12, is to provide a spouse or dependent family member with pension entitlements of their own, post-divorce. The effect of an order made under s. 17 will be to disregard the terms of the pension scheme in question, and to direct the distribution of the pension benefits as ordered by the court.

When the power to adjust pensions was first made available to the courts with the advent of the 1995 Act, s. 12, there was a certain amount of reticence on the part of applicants and practitioners to use the new powers. As time goes on, however, it is clear that pension adjustment orders are being more frequently granted due to a growing realisation that the pension is a valuable family asset, adjustment of which can assist in providing proper provision for spouses on retirement. The provisions of the 1996 Act, s. 17(23)(b) should be noted, however, insofar as they direct that the court is to have regard as to whether proper provision can be made for the applicant or dependent family member by making an order under the provisions of the 1996 Act, ss. 13, 14, 15 or 16. Thus the court is being directed to ascertain whether non-pension benefits or assets can be adjusted to provide proper provision while leaving the pension intact.

The provisions of the 1996 Act, s. 17 are largely similar to those of the 1995 Act, s. 12 with the obvious difference that on divorce, 'the status of spouse' terminates, as do any benefits which would have been payable only to a spouse of the member of the pension scheme.

Note also that before deciding whether to make any order under the 1996 Act, s. 17, the court must apply the provisions of the 1996 Act, s. 20 and, in particular, the provisions of s. 20(2)(k) which directs the court to take into account the value to either of the spouses of any benefit which they might lose by virtue of the decree of divorce being granted. A benefit is specifically referred to in the subsection as, for example, a benefit under a pension scheme.

In addition to the foregoing, there is no requirement in the context of divorce legislation for a provision similar to that of the 1995 Act, s. 13.

Because the provisions of s. 17 of the 1996 Act are so similar to those of s. 12 of the 1995 Act, we will concentrate only on highlighting the differences between them. A significant difference in relation to time limits arises in the context of contingent benefits. Any application to vary a contingent benefit must be made either at the time the decree of divorce is granted, or within 12 months of the decree of divorce being granted, and not at any time during the lifetime of the member spouse.

If an applicant spouse seeks a pension adjustment order, having remarried, a court cannot make any form of pension adjustment order pursuant to the provisions of s. 17(23)(a) of the 1996 Act. Any order which is being made in relation to a contingent benefit under s. 17(3) ceases to have effect on the remarriage of the spouse in whose favour the order was made. However, if an order has been made in relation to a retirement benefit, that order does not automatically cease to have effect on remarriage. It is necessary for the member spouse to apply to the court pursuant to the provisions of s. 22 of the 1996 Act to have the pension adjustment order either varied, or discharged altogether, because of the changed circumstances of the recipient spouse. Note also that s. 17 contains a similar provision to s. 12 of the 1995 Act in relation to variation insofar as it specifically provides that an order can be made restricting to a specified extent or excluding the right to vary a pension adjustment order. It has become common for orders under s. 17(26) to be sought once a divorce decree has been granted, thus ensuring some form of certainty for the member spouse.

Other than those set out above, the provisions of s. 17 are almost identical to those of s. 12 of the 1995 Act. See Chapter 7 for a detailed discussion on pensions and judicial commentary on the subject.

6.1.10 THE FAMILY HOME

6.1.10.1 Generally

A dispute in relation to the family home forms a substantial part of almost every application for judicial separation or divorce. Whether the family home is owned by one or both of the parties, or whether it is rented by way of tenancy with a local authority or privately, a dispute as to who continues to live there usually causes a degree of acrimony between the parties.

A family home is defined in the Family Home Protection Act 1976, s. 2(1) (the '1976 Act'). This definition has been adopted in both the 1995 Act and the 1996 Act with some modifications. The definition contained in the 1976 Act, s. 2(1), specifies the family home as:

. . . primarily a dwelling in which a married couple ordinarily reside. The expression comprises, in addition, a dwelling in which a spouse whose protection is in issue ordinarily resides, or if that spouse has left the other spouse, ordinarily resided before so leaving.

Section 54(1)(a) of the 1995 Act defined a dwelling as:

any building or part of a building occupied as a separate dwelling and includes any garden or other land usually occupied with the dwelling, being land that is subsidiary and ancillary to it, is required for amenity or convenience and is not being used or developed primarily for commercial purposes, and includes a structure that is not permanently attached to the ground and a vehicle, or vessel, whether mobile or not, occupied as a separate dwelling.

Section 54(1) amends the 1976 Act, s. 2.

6.1.10.2 Orders in respect of family home

The orders which can be made in respect of the family home, either on separation or divorce, are as follows:

(a) Preliminary orders under the 1995 Act, s. 6(c), and the 1996 Act, s. 11(c), which permit the court to make orders under the 1976 Act, ss. 5 or 9. As with all preliminary orders, if made, such orders remain effective until the hearing of the action.

(b) Property adjustment orders under the 1995 Act, s. 9 and the 1996 Act, s. 14. The provisions of both sections are almost identical, and the court is empowered to make property adjustment orders as follows:

(i) the court may direct that property be transferred from one spouse to another, or to any dependent family member, or to a specified person for the benefit of such a member;

(ii) the court can direct the settlement of any property for the benefit of either spouses, or for a dependent family member;

(iii) the court can direct an order which varies a previously agreed settlement of property (e.g. a separation agreement);

(iv) the court can direct an extinguishment or reduction of any interest held by either of the spouses under any such settlement.

An application for a property adjustment order must be made during the lifetime of the other spouse, but can be made any time after the granting of either a decree of judicial separation or divorce. However, both sections provide that if either spouse remarries, no property adjustment order may be made in favour of the married spouse.

In both sections, provision is made for the signing by the County Registrar of all necessary transfer documentation in the event of default by the transferring spouse.

In both sections, a family home in which following a decree of divorce or judicial separation, either of the spouses concerned, having remarried, ordinarily resides with his/her spouse, is immune from any potential property transfer order.

Both the 1995 and 1996 Acts specify the provision of miscellaneous ancillary orders in connection with the family home. Section 10 of the 1995 Act and s. 15 of the 1996 Act, on judicial separation and divorce respectively, direct that orders can be made providing one of the spouses with a right to reside in the family home for their lifetime (or other period), and also providing for a sale of the family home subject to conditions imposed by the court (if any), and thereafter, providing for the disposal of the proceeds of sale between the spouses, and any other person having an interest therein. Orders can also be obtained pursuant to ss. 10 and 15 under the 1995 Act, s. 36, which section deals with the determination of questions between spouses in relation to property. Finally, orders can also be obtained under the 1995 Act, s. 10, pursuant to the provisions of the Family Home Protection Act 1976, ss. 4, 5, 7 and 9, and on divorce, under the 1976 Act, ss. 5, 7 and 9.

Both the 1995 and 1996 Acts direct the court to take account of the fact that where a decree of judicial separation or divorce is granted, it is no longer possible for the spouses to reside together, and that proper and secure accommodation (where practical) should be provided for a spouse who is wholly or mainly dependent on the other spouse, and for any dependent family member (1995 Act, s. 10(2), 1996 Act, s. 15(2)).

The court can direct the sale of the family home, on judicial separation, pursuant to the provisions of the 1995 Act, s. 15, and on divorce, pursuant to the provisions of the 1996 Act, s. 19. The court in both cases can order the sale of property, including the family home, and the court can attach whatever conditions it considers appropriate to such an order. In both cases, no order can be made directing the sale of a family home in which, following the grant of a decree of judicial separation or divorce, either of the spouses concerned (having remarried) ordinarily resides with their new spouse.

Both on judicial separation and divorce, there is no property adjustment order which can be made in respect of the family home which is not capable of variation, other than an order directing the sale of the family home which order has been complied with and completed. The 1995 Act, s. 18 and the 1996 Act, s. 22 provide for the variation of orders which have previously been made under both pieces of legislation. It is possible to restrict the application of these sections to property adjustment orders which have been made on judicial separation and divorce. If no such restriction has been ordered by the court, then if the court can be convinced that an order previously made is to be varied, it can do so, and this can include varying an order directing that a spouse has an exclusive right to reside in the family home, for life or for another period. In all cases where variation of property adjustment orders is requested, the court would require compelling evidence before doing so.

6.1.10.3   Adjustment orders in respect of property other than family home

It is often assumed that property adjustment orders only refer to the family home. This is not the case, and property adjustment orders can be made in favour of all kinds of property, both movable and immovable, and both real and personal. For example, a property adjustment order may be made on separation or divorce in connection with stocks, shares, art, livestock, businesses, investments, savings, holiday homes, commercial properties, and cars or boats. The court, in both cases, has wide discretionary powers in relation to making such property adjustment orders as it deems necessary in each individual case. In the case of divorce, the court must take into account the terms of any separation agreement which has been entered into by the parties, and also presumably, the terms of any decree of judicial separation previously granted, although this is not specified in the 1996 Act. However, notwithstanding the terms of any such agreement, the court may, under s. 14 of the 1996 Act, set aside such terms.

We have already seen how the provisions of s. 9 and s. 14 can be applied to the family home, and similarly, these provisions can be applied to other properties.

6.1.10.4   Case law

There are very few reported judgments concerning the issue of property transfer orders. In the case of *J.D. v D.D.* (unreported, 14 May 1997, High Ct, McGuinness J) the court referred to the provisions of s. 9 of the 1995 Act, and stated:

'It would therefore appear that there is no limit to the number of occasions on which a spouse can seek and the court can grant, if appropriate, a property adjustment order, save that such an order can only be granted during the lifetime of the other spouse and cannot be granted in favour of a spouse who has remarried'.

In that case, the parties were well off financially, and the family assets comprised of the family home, other property, antiques, art, and a business. The court commented that all of the husband's financial assets would be taken into account, including items categorised as family heirlooms. There was also a family trust in respect of which the husband was a beneficiary.

After an in-depth discussion as to whether or not a 'clean break' was possible, the court concluded that it was not, given the boundaries of the legislation, and the court went on to take into account the guidelines set out in s. 16 of the 1995 Act. (See generally Shannon, *The Divorce Act in Practice* (Round Hall, 1999).) In that case, the wife had already vacated the family home, but the husband undertook to finance a new home for her, and the court directed that she be paid a lump sum of £200,000 having taken into account the length of the marriage, and the contribution the wife had made towards the accumulation of substantial assets by the husband. The court also directed that the husband's pension benefits were to be left in place insofar as they provided any benefit for the wife. Finally, a periodical payments order of £20,000 per annum was made.

In the case of *McA v McA* (unreported, 21 January 2000, High Ct, McCracken J) the court took account of the value of the respondent's business in directing a lump sum payment to be made to the wife, in what was another 'high money case'. It had been agreed between the parties that various properties would be transferred to the wife, and while no direct property adjustment order was made, the value of the applicant wife's shareholding in the family business was measured, and monies directed to be paid to her on that basis.

In the case of *C v C* [1994] 1 Fam LJ 22, Barr J refused to make a property adjustment order in respect of the husband's business premises under s. 15 of the 1989 Act which related to property adjustment orders. The wife had sought an order in respect of her husband's business premises. Barr J commented that the wife had never had any connection with the husband's business premises, and therefore was not entitled to any interest therein. The concept of 'connection' to properties acquired by one of the parties throughout the marriage may be of some guidance to the courts when deciding whether or not to make a property adjustment order.

It should be remembered that, notwithstanding the paucity of written judgments, property adjustment orders are directed by the Circuit Court or the High Court very frequently, and one of the overriding considerations being applied by the courts is the need to provide for the security and welfare of the children in deciding such issues.

6.1.11 SUCCESSION RIGHTS

The Succession Act 1965 ('the 1965 Act') is the principal authority on all aspects of the law of succession in Ireland. While the general principles of succession have remained largely unchanged since its enactment, the provisions of the 1989, 1995 and 1996 Acts have introduced changes to succession consequent on marital disputes.

The 1965 Act provides that by virtue of their status as a spouse, a widow or widower is granted an automatic share in the estate of their deceased spouse. If a testator dies leaving a spouse only, then that spouse is legally entitled to one-half of the estate. If a testator dies leaving a spouse and children, the spouse has a legal right to one-third of the estate. Thus, a spouse was provided for out of the estate of the deceased spouse regardless of the terms of his/her will.

The first variation of those principles appeared in s. 17 of the 1989 Act, which permitted the court, on the application of either spouse, to consider whether it would make an order extinguishing the share to which either spouse would otherwise be entitled in the estate of the other spouse as a legal right or on intestacy under the Succession Act 1965.

As Part II of the 1989 Act was repealed and replaced by Part II of the 1995 Act, s. 14 of that Act now pertains to the issue of orders which are sought on judicial separation seeking to extinguish the succession rights of either of the parties. The court must be satisfied that 'adequate and reasonable' financial provision exists or can be made by way of orders for other ancillary reliefs, such as maintenance, a property adjustment order, etc. The court must also be concerned to ensure that proper provision is made for the spouse concerned 'having regard to all the circumstances', and that the order made is 'in the interests of justice'. The court will not therefore make an order extinguishing inheritance rights where such an order would jeopardise the spouse's future financial security, e.g. where the spouses are elderly (in the case of *P.S. v A.S.* (unreported, July 1996, High Ct).

On divorce, the situation is different. As the spouses have lost their status as spouses, there is no longer any need to have a provision equivalent to s. 14 of the 1995 Act because neither of the spouses is automatically entitled to a share in the estate of his/her divorced spouse as a legal right or on intestacy upon the latter's death. The loss of these inheritance rights is one of the factors which the court must take into account in deciding what other forms of ancillary relief orders to make. The issue of Succession Act rights is dealt with, however, in the 1996 Act, s. 18(1), which provides that, if one of the spouses in respect of whom a decree of divorce has been granted dies, the former spouse may make application to the court (not more than six months after a grant of probate or letters of administration have been extracted) to have provision made for themselves out of the estate of the deceased spouse. The court must consider whether making such an order would be appropriate having regard to the rights of any other person having an interest in the matter, and must be satisfied that proper provision in the circumstances was not made for the applicant spouse during the lifetime of the deceased spouse under any of the other sections granting ancillary relief on divorce. If a spouse has remarried since the granting of the decree of divorce, the court will not make an order under s. 18(1). The court must also take into account any property adjustment order which has been made in favour of the applicant, and also any devise or bequest made to the applicant by the deceased spouse on their death.

Section 18(10) of the 1996 Act makes provision for the granting of what is known as a 'blocking order', i.e. an order directing that the provisions of s. 18(1) shall not be available to one or both of the spouses, post-divorce.

Section 52(g) of the 1996 Act extends this provision to judicial separation, by inserting a new s. 15A in the 1995 Act. The provision extends only to parties whose Succession Act rights have been extinguished by virtue of an order made under s. 14 of the 1995 Act, but not by a spouse whose Succession Act rights have been extinguished pursuant to an order under s. 17 of the 1989 Act.

It is important to note that an application under both sections must be made not more than six months after the representation is granted under the 1965 Act in respect of the estate.

It should be noted that provision which has been made for an applicant out of a deceased's estate by order of the court must not exceed what that applicant would have received if a divorce had not been granted, or, if an order extinguishing the Succession Act rights had not been made under the 1995 Act, s. 14, pursuant to the 1995 Act, s. 15A(4) and the 1996 Act, s. 18(4). The court cannot make an order in favour of a spouse who has remarried, pursuant to the provisions of the 1995 Act, s. 15A(2) and the 1996 Act, s. 18(2).

6.1.12 FACTORS TO BE CONSIDERED BY THE COURT IN MAKING ANCILLARY ORDERS

The court is directed, both on judicial separation and on divorce, to have regard to certain matters in deciding whether or not to make orders for ancillary reliefs in respect of maintenance, pensions, property, ancillary property orders, financial compensation orders, succession rights, or variations of any of those orders. The specific matters to which the court shall in both cases have regard are almost exactly the same, contained in the 1995 Act, s. 16(2)(a) to (l) and the 1996 Act, s. 20(2)(a) to (l). Each factor will be considered in turn.

6.1.12.1　Actual and potential financial resources

(a) The income, earning capacity, property and other financial resources which each of the spouses concerned has or is likely to have in the foreseeable future

This requirement directs attention to the actual and potential financial resources and earnings of each spouse. The significance of the individual facts of every case was highlighted in *J.C. v C.C.* [1994] 1 Fam LJ 22. In *S.B. v R.B.* [1997] 3 Fam LJ 66, McGuinness J stated that the decision of the court in determining the value of the financial order was influenced by the fact of the wife's heart condition, which made it 'at least difficult for her to earn anything substantial outside the home'. Such a disability was not even necessary in the view of Lynch J, who stated in *B.F. v V.F.* (unreported, 20 May 1993, High Ct) that he was 'satisfied that it is reasonable and proper for the wife at present not to seek work outside the home. She provides a home for the three children of the marriage . . . that is a full-time occupation in itself'. Therein, Lynch J, on appeal from the Circuit Court, increased maintenance payments to the applicant wife and ordered a lump sum payment.

6.1.12.2　Financial needs, obligations and responsibilities

(b) The financial needs, obligations and responsibilities which each of the spouses has or is likely to have in the foreseeable future (whether in the case of remarriage or otherwise)

In *S v S* [1977] 1 All ER 56, Ormrod LJ stated that when attention is concentrated primarily on the actual needs of the parties involved, the calculation of financial provision then becomes easier, more logical and constructive. The calculation of what constitutes the reasonable needs of both parties is a matter to be determined in each case. Facts particular to each case may give rise to additional needs that must be provided for, e.g. the poor health of one spouse. In *R.K. v M.K.* (unreported, 24 October 1978, High Ct) Finlay P (as he then was) accepted that a wife who was suffering from motor neurone disease, with resulting depression and anxiety, would require hired help in addition to the other essentials of life.

6.1.12.3　Standard of living

(c) The standard of living enjoyed by the family before the proceedings were instituted or before the spouses separated, as the case may be

One of the practical realities of judicial separation and divorce, in particular where the parties are of limited or average means, is that both parties will inevitably face a reduction in living standards following the grant of the decree. Irish courts have generally held that following a decree of judicial separation/divorce, the standard of living of neither party should be above that which would have existed if the marriage had continued. Where a decree of judicial separation/divorce is granted two houses will be necessary and both spouses will inevitably suffer financially. This has been repeatedly recognised by the courts. In *H.D. v E.D.* (unreported, 11 January 1994, High Ct) Costello J noted that '[a] broken marriage inevitably means a lowering of the living standards of both parties, which can be very considerable in some instances'. Similarly, in *B.F v V.F.* (unreported, 20 May 1993, High Ct) Lynch J stated:

> 'It is inevitable that all parties will suffer a significant diminution in the overall standard of living. The necessity for two separate residences to be maintained and two households to be provided for makes this an inescapable consequence of the separation.'

In some ways this factor is probably more relevant where there are substantial assets involved. In particular, this factor will allow the court to ensure that the dependent spouse of a very wealthy person will not necessarily lose their financial status and can, despite the departure of the affluent spouse, be adequately provided for and continue to enjoy a luxurious lifestyle. In *G.H. v E.H.* (unreported, 9 February 1998, High Ct) Barr J confirmed the applicant's 'right to the benefit of a reasonable lifestyle commensurate with that available to the respondent', and thus affirmed her entitlement to maintenance from the respondent of £200 per week. See also *M.McA. v X.McA.* (unreported, 21 January 2000, High Ct, McCracken J) where the High Court, in granting a divorce, made a maintenance order in the sum of £4,500 per month and a further lump sum payment of £300,000. For further discussion of this case, see **4.3.3.2**.

Essentially, this factor aids the court in determining the type of lifestyle the separated spouses are entitled to lead and the needs that they are likely to have.

6.1.12.4 Age of spouses and length of marriage

(d) The age of each of the spouses and the length of time during which the spouses have lived together

The importance of these factors will vary with the particular facts of each case. In *Gengler v Gengler* [1976] 2 All ER 81, it was held that to attempt to state when a marriage should be classed as short, not very short, long or not very long, is rather like trying to define the length of a piece of string.

6.1.12.5 Disability

(e) Any physical or mental disability of either of the spouses

Where one or other of the parties to the proceedings suffers from a physical or mental disability, the court is likely to regard this as a burden of that spouse, which necessitates greater financial provision. Certainly, a disability which prevents or inhibits a spouse from working will result in the making of a greater periodical payments order in favour of the dependent spouse.

6.1.12.6 Spousal contributions

(f) The contributions which each of the spouses has made or is likely in the foreseeable future to make to the welfare of the family, including any contribution made by each of them to the income, earning capacity, property and financial resources of the other spouse and any contributions made by either of them by looking after the home or caring for the family

This factor represents the growing tendency of the legislature and the courts to look beyond the financial contributions of each spouse. It places an onus on the courts, when making ancillary orders, to distribute the assets on the equitable basis of both financial and non-financial contributions. In the case of *J.D. v D.D.* [1997] 3 IR 64 McGuinness J ordered 'a reasonably equal division of the accumulated assets' as the application for an order of judicial separation followed a 30-year marriage and she so ordered because of the husband's long-term acceptance of their respective traditional roles as financial provider and homemaker. See also *M.Y. v A.Y.* (unreported, 11 December 1995, High Ct, Budd J).

6.1.12.7 Earning capacity

(g) The effect on the earning capacity of each of the spouses of the marital responsibilities assumed by each during the period when they lived together (with one another) and, in particular, the degree to which the future earning capacity of a spouse is impaired by reason of that spouse having relinquished or forgone the opportunity of remunerative activity in order to look after the home or care for the family

This provision clearly authorises the court, in making ancillary orders, to take account of, and to compensate accordingly, a spouse's past and future earnings lost due to his or her assumption of marital and domestic responsibilities.

6.1.12.8 Statutory entitlements

(h) Any income or benefits to which either of the spouses is entitled by or under statute

In order to ensure the making of a fair and appropriate periodical payments or lump sum order, the court is obliged to take all income which is received by both parties into account. This factor includes all social welfare payments as well as children's allowance, old age pension and other benefit payments. This provision, particularly as it deals with social welfare payments, is likely to become relevant in cases where the parties to the proceedings are of limited means.

6.1.12.9 Conduct

(i) The conduct of each of the spouses, if the conduct is such that in the opinion of the court it would in all the circumstances of the case be unjust to disregard it

The Irish court, in making ancillary orders, is now afforded greater scope to take account of misconduct by either spouse. In the case of *E.M. v W.M.* [1994] 3 Fam LJ 93 McGuinness J considered that the respondent husband's behaviour was relevant to her decision. Similarly, in *M.Y. v A.Y.* (unreported, 11 December 1995, High Ct) Budd J approved the approach of Costello J in *E.D. v F.D.* (unreported, 23 October 1980, High Ct) in relation to the issue of misconduct when determining maintenance:

'Where a husband deserts his wife and children, the court should be concerned to ensure that their financial position is protected even if this means causing a drop in the husband's living standards' (*M.Y. v A.Y.* at p. 4; see also *J.D. v D.D.* [1997] 3 IR 64.)

6.1.12.10 Accommodation needs

(j) The accommodation needs of either spouse

In every case in which a decree of judicial separation is granted, two homes are required to replace one. This fact will invariably impact significantly on the financial orders to be made by the court. The needs of both spouses must be considered, which can result in the sale of the family home and the division of the net proceeds. This was deemed by McGuinness J to be both the appropriate and necessary measure in *O'L v O'L* [1996] 2 Fam LJ 63:

'In all the circumstances I am satisfied that common sense and justice require that the family home be sold and that the proceeds of sale be divided so as to provide as far as possible for the purchase by the wife of a smaller house . . . and to provide for the husband something towards a deposit on the purchase by him of suitable accommodation for himself.'

6.1.12.11 Future losses

(k) The value to each of the spouses of any benefit (for example, a benefit under a pension scheme) which by reason of the decree of judicial separation (divorce) concerned that spouse will forfeit the opportunity or possibility of acquiring

This factor requires the court, when making an order for judicial separation/divorce, to take account of the loss of a benefit, such as a pension scheme. As a factor to be considered by the court prior to the making of ancillary orders, it includes benefits not only received by either spouse, but also those that the spouse may possibly acquire in the future. Financial experts will be required to give evidence to the court as to the value of these future losses.

6.1.12.12 Third party rights

(l) The rights of any person other than the spouses but including a person to whom either spouse is remarried

The final factor requires the court to take account of 'the rights of any person other than the spouses but including a person to whom either spouse is remarried'. The remedy of divorce by its very nature permits both parties to remarry once the decree is granted. Consequently, any financial resources or assets that become available to one of the parties to the application by way of a new relationship must be taken into account when granting any ancillary orders. For example, in *J.C.N. v R.T.N.* (unreported, 15 January 1999, High Ct) McGuinness J took cognisance of the husband's commitments to his partner and the two dependent children of their relationship. In particular, the court noted that the husband had built up the pension scheme after separating from his wife 'with a view to a pension being paid to his present partner'.

6.1.12.13 Preliminary considerations

Prior to taking into account the specific matters set out at **6.1.12.1** to **6.1.12.12** above the court is bound by an introductory requirement set out in the 1995 Act, s. 16(1) and the 1996 Act, s. 20(1) to ensure that such provision as the court considers proper exists or will be made for both the spouse and any dependent family members, depending on the circumstances of the case. This is a general standard which affords a certain amount of discretion to the court in deciding whether to make ancillary relief orders.

In the case of *J.D. v D.D.* (unreported, 14 May 1997, High Ct, McGuinness J) McGuinness J examined the provisions of s. 16 of the 1995 Act, and stated that:

'Even given these guidelines however, the court still has a wide area of discretion, particularly in cases where there are considerable financial assets'.

An additional factor set out in s. 20 of the 1996 Act is that the court *'shall'* have regard to the terms of any separation agreement which has been entered into by the spouses and which is still in force (s. 20(3)). While the issue of the terms of an order for judicial separation are not specifically adverted to, these are usually taken into account by the court in deciding whether or not to make ancillary relief orders on divorce. In *M.G. v M.G.* (unreported, 25 July 2000, Circuit Ct) Buckley J considered the general and specific statutory criteria which the court must apply when considering an application for divorce. Section 20 of the 1996 Act obliges the court to consider every aspect of the parties' financial and family situation before granting the decree, while 'having regard' for the existing agreements entered into between them. Buckley J examined a similar statutory provision in the Canadian Divorce Act 1985 and also reviewed the jurisprudence of the Canadian Supreme Court for guidance. He noted that the Irish Supreme Court had urged the need for finality in future arrangements for the family while the divorce legislation does not permit the application of a 'clean break' regime. Canadian case law requires that there be a 'sufficient change' which must be defined in terms of the parties' overall financial situation. Significantly, the fact that a change was objectively foreseeable does not necessarily mean that it was contemplated by the parties.

Both sections direct that if the court is considering making an order in relation to a dependent family member, it must take into account certain matters set out in s. 4(a) to (g). The overall criterion of each section is that the court must not make an order unless it would be 'in the interests of justice to do so'.

6.2 Procedure and Jurisdiction in the Circuit Court and High Court

6.2.1 THE CIRCUIT COURT

6.2.1.1 Introduction

Both the Circuit Court and the High Court have jurisdiction concurrently with each other to hear and determine applications for divorce, decrees of judicial separation, applications for orders under the Family Law Act 1995 and applications for decrees of nullity.

At present the majority of such applications are made in the Circuit Court as opposed to the High Court. If the assets of the couple are extremely substantial or if there are complicated issues of law or facts involved then it is more likely that proceedings will be issued in the High Court.

The Circuit Court Rules (No. 1) 1997, SI 84/1997, contain the rules for making applications to the Circuit Family Court for divorce, judicial separation, relief after foreign divorce or separation outside the State, nullity, declarations of marital status, the determination of property issues between spouses pursuant to s. 36 of the 1995 Act and certain other applications.

It is to be noted that these Rules do not deal only with divorce applications but also with nearly all types of matrimonial applications in the Circuit Court apart from simple applications for maintenance under the 1976 Act or applications under the domestic violence legislation.

The Rules came into operation on 27 February 1997.

6.2.1.2 Hearing venue

Rule 3 states that any of the above-mentioned proceedings are to be brought 'in the County where any party to the proceedings ordinarily resides or carries on any profession, business or occupation'. It is therefore possible to choose, in certain circumstances, whether a hearing should take place in, for example, Dublin or Cork. The wife may reside in Cork and the husband may reside or work in Dublin. The applicant may choose the location of the hearing based on the respondent's residence or place of business. If one or other parties to the proceedings has a number of businesses in various parts of the country then it is open to either party to issue proceedings in one of those areas.

6.2.1.3 Family law civil bill

All of the proceedings referred to above are to be instituted by the issuing of a Family Law Civil Bill at the County Registrar's Office for the appropriate county (r. 4.A). The only exception to this is where an application is being made for relief after foreign divorce or separation *outside* the State and then the Family Law Civil Bill can only be issued after an ex parte application has been made, grounded upon the affidavit of the applicant or solicitor for the applicant. Such an ex parte application is provided for in the Family Law Act 1995, s. 23(3). The affidavit must exhibit a draft of the Family Law Civil Bill to be issued and must further set out fully the reasons why relief is being sought. It must also clearly set out the domicile and residence of both parties. There must be substantial grounds for issuing such a Civil Bill, which must be clearly proven before proceedings can commence (r. 4.B).

Section 27 of the 1995 Act, which deals with the jurisdiction of the court to make relief orders, must be complied with.

Every Family Law Civil Bill must set out in numbered paragraphs the relief being sought and the grounds relied upon in support of the application (r. 5).

ANCILLARY ORDERS, PROCEDURE AND DISCOVERY

The Family Law Civil Bill for a decree of divorce should include as much relevant detail as possible and at least the following information:

(1) The date and place of marriage of the parties.

(2) The length of time the parties have lived apart, including the date of commencement of such living apart and the addresses of both of the parties during that time (where known).

It is sometimes quite difficult to ascertain precise addresses for both parties where they have been living apart for many years but as much detail as possible should be inserted.

In the event of a claim being made that the applicant and the respondent have been living apart from each other (whilst still under the one roof) then all relevant information to ground such a claim must be included in the Civil Bill.

In such cases the Family Law Civil Bill should include information as to: how the house is being divided up and what the arrangements are for using kitchen and bathroom facilities; what services the couple provide for each other, e.g. cooking, cleaning, etc.; what financial arrangements have been made in relation to the alleged separation; how the husband and the wife avoid meeting each other in the house; details of holidays and sexual relations or lack of same; details of any previous matrimonial relief sought and/or obtained; and details of any previous separation agreements entered into between the parties. A copy of any previous court orders or deeds of separation should be attached to the Family Law Civil Bill.

It is arguable that even where a decree of divorce is to be granted by consent that the terms of a deed of separation (if any) should be actually incorporated into the decree and orders made pursuant to the relevant sections of the Divorce Act. As a general rule this is not happening in practice in the Circuit Court but is strongly recommended. If ancillary relief orders are not made then there could be enforcement problems at a later date.

(3) The names and ages and dates of birth of any dependent children of the marriage, i.e. children who are still undergoing a full-time course of education up to a maximum of 23 years.

(4) Details of the family home and other residences of the parties including any former family homes or residences. It is sometimes quite difficult to obtain such information. It is also necessary to include details of the manner of occupation/ownership of the said properties. It is helpful to set out in detail how the family home was disposed of or transferred or sold or purchased.

(5) Details of the title to any property referred to in the Civil Bill. For example, is it registered in the Land Registry or Registry of Deeds? It is essential to carry out searches in this connection prior to the issuing of the Civil Bill. Such searches will also show any mortgages or charges on the property of which all parties must be made aware prior to a hearing.

(6) The basis of jurisdiction under the Family Law (Divorce) Act 1996.

(7) The occupation of each party. It is also common practice to insert the ages of each party.

(8) The grounds relied upon for the relief sought, e.g. that the parties have been living apart for at least four of the last five years and that there is no hope of reconciliation or any other relevant grounds.

(9) Each section of the Acts under which relief is sought.

Once the Family Law Civil Bill claiming a decree of divorce has been prepared and signed by the applicant's solicitor, the original is filed at the appropriate Circuit Court Office along with the s. 6 or s. 7 certificate, an affidavit of means and an affidavit of welfare and the County Registrar enters the case and allocates a Record Number.

The proceedings are then served pursuant to the Rules.

The Family Law Civil Bill, which claims a decree of judicial separation, is much the same as the Divorce Civil Bill, but excludes, obviously, any reference to how long the parties have lived apart and also need not contain copies of any earlier court orders.

The Family Law Civil Bill grounding a claim for relief after foreign divorce or separation outside the State pursuant to s. 23 of the Family Law Act 1995 is also similar but should include full details of the divorce or separation of the parties, a certified copy of the decree absolute or final decree of divorce/separation, together (where appropriate) with an authenticated translation attached to the Civil Bill (r. 5(c)(i)).

Details should also be given of the financial, property and custodial arrangements operating ancillary to the decree, together with the present marital status and occupation of each party. Most of the other information referred to in the Rules relating to divorce applications should also be included in this Civil Bill.

The details to be included in a Family Law Civil Bill for a declaration of marital status are similar.

A Family Law Civil Bill for nullity shall, in all cases, include details of:

  (1)   the date and place of marriage of the parties;

  (2)   the domicile of the spouses on the date of the marriage and on the date of the issuing of the proceedings, or (if one spouse has died) the domicile of the said spouse at the date of death;

  (3)   whether or not the spouses had been ordinarily resident in the State for one year prior to the issuing of proceedings;

  (4)   the address and description of each party;

  (5)   the number of children of the marriage;

  (6)   the grounds upon which the decree is being sought;

  (7)   the reliefs sought; and

  (8)   the issues to be tried (r. 5.D).

The details which need to be included in a Family Law Civil Bill for the determination of property issues between the spouses pursuant to s. 36 of the Family Law Act 1995 and for relief pursuant to s. 18 of the Family Law (Divorce) Act 1996 or s. 15(a) or s. 25 of the Family Law Act 1995 (orders for provision for a spouse out of the estate of the other spouse) are clearly set out in r. 5(f) and (g) respectively.

6.2.1.4   Service of family law civil bill

Rule 8(a) deals with service of Family Law Civil Bills. This can be by way of registered post on the respondent or the Family Law Civil Bill may be served personally on the respondent by any person over the age of 18 years. It is important to note that the appropriate certificate pursuant to s. 5 of the 1989 Act or s. 6 of the 1996 Act should also be served along with the Civil Bill. If there is a claim for ancillary financial relief then an affidavit of means must also be served at the same time, along with an affidavit of welfare if there are any dependent children of the marriage.

If a claim is being made for a pension adjustment order then notice must be served on the trustees of the pension scheme by registered post at their registered office or other appropriate addresses and an affidavit of service of such notice sworn and filed. A draft notice to trustees is attached to the Rules.

It is important therefore to investigate the pension situation in detail prior to issuing and serving proceedings and ensure that the names and addresses, etc., of all the trustees of any pension scheme are obtained so that they can be properly served.

It is also important to remember that when the hearing date is obtained a notice for trial must also be served on the trustees.

6.2.1.5 Appearance

Within ten days of the service upon the respondent of the Family Law Civil Bill, an appearance must be entered in court and a copy sent to the applicant's solicitors either by the respondent personally or by his or her solicitor (r. 9).

6.2.1.6 Defence

Rule 10(a) states that within a further ten days a defence and a s. 6 or s. 7 certificate (where appropriate) together with an affidavit of means if necessary and an affidavit of welfare if appropriate shall be served by the respondent.

It is unrealistic to expect, in many cases, such pleadings to be completed within such a short period of time.

Apart from the necessity to spend time in collecting information and preparing statements and documents, the respondent may need some time to come to terms with the fact that his or her spouse has issued proceedings in the first place.

Even if a defence is not filed, the respondent must file and serve an affidavit of means (if appropriate) and an affidavit of welfare (if there are any dependent children) within 20 days of service of the Family Law Civil Bill upon him or her (r. 10.C).

If this is not done within the time specified above then the court may enlarge or abridge such time upon such terms as to costs or otherwise as it sees fit (r. 36).

6.2.1.7 Motions for judgment (rule 11)

If there is a default on the part of the respondent in entering an appearance or filing a defence then the applicant may issue a notice of motion for judgment in default thereof.

The notice of motion must be served not less than 14 days before the hearing and the notice of motion shall not be returnable to a date less than 14 clear days from the date of service of the notice (r. 11.C).

Before the issuing of any such notice of motion the applicant or the applicant's solicitor must write to the respondent or the respondent's solicitor giving him or her a further 14-day period within which to either enter an appearance or defence, and also furnish a letter of consent to the late filing of same for a further period of 14 days. This letter must be produced at the time of issuing of the notice of motion and the 14-day period must have expired.

Rule 11.D states that if the appropriate appearance or defence is delivered to the applicant within seven days after the service of such notice of motion, and a copy of same is lodged in court not less than six days before the return date of the motion, then the motion for judgment will not be put into the Judge's list but will be struck out. Rule 11.D however states that 'the respondent *shall* pay to the applicant the appropriate sum for his/her costs of the said motion for judgment'.

In certain special cases, where there is a degree of urgency, the court or the County Registrar may abridge the time for service of such notices.

This could occur in situations where one or other of the parties to a divorce application is extremely ill and it is important to obtain a hearing date as quickly as possible.

If the court deals with the hearing of an application for judgment under r. 11, subject to the provisions of r. 11.D, it may make such order as to costs as it thinks fit.

6.2.1.8 Fast track divorce

Rule 11.H provides a simple and speedy procedure where both parties are agreed in respect of all the reliefs being sought. The Family Law Civil Bill (together with the affidavit of means and affidavit of welfare (where appropriate) are issued and served. The respondent can file a form of 'consent defence' and a notice can then be served by the applicant by way of notice of motion for judgment by consent.

This method is used to obtain speedy divorce decrees. It also lessens the stress on the parties concerned and minimises legal costs.

Many people simply require a decree of divorce without any ancillary relief. The provisions of this rule can also be availed of when there have been settlement discussions which have resulted in consent ancillary relief orders being agreed. These can subsequently be ruled on by the court at the same time as the granting of a decree of divorce with great speed if this procedure is availed of.

6.2.1.9 Notice of trial

Rules 12, 13 and 14 deal with this issue.

In Dublin a notice to fix a date for trial is issued and served and on that date the court will fix the hearing date in due course.

Outside Dublin, a notice for trial shall be served and listed for the sittings next ensuing after the expiration of the time mentioned in the notice. The same will operate to set down the action or matter for hearing at those sittings.

In certain circumstances the respondent may serve the notice for trial if the applicant fails to do so.

Rule 17(a) provides for the service of affidavits of representation by any notice parties, including in particular the trustees of a pension scheme. Such an affidavit should be filed by any such person who wishes to make representations to the court and should set out the basis on which such representations are being made and what the representations actually are.

6.2.1.10 Affidavit of means (rule 18)

In each case 'where financial relief under the Acts is sought' the parties must file an affidavit of means.

It is important to note that the rules state that this affidavit need only be filed where financial relief is being claimed. It follows therefore that if no financial relief is being sought then an affidavit of means is not necessary.

In Dublin it is certainly the practice that where there are no ancillary financial orders requested that such affidavits are not required by the Family Law office. However, outside Dublin, it appears that such affidavits are required in certain areas even where no claim for ancillary financial relief is being made.

What is a claim for financial relief? It seems clear from the practice of the Circuit Court in Dublin that an application for an order pursuant to s. 18(10) of the 1996 Act (an order blocking an application for provision out of the estate of a deceased spouse) is not a claim for financial relief and therefore does not lead to the necessity to swear an affidavit of means.

An application for a pension adjustment order is an application for financial relief and an affidavit of means will have to be filed. Such applications may need to be made in a large number of cases where no other relief is being sought.

The affidavit of means contains five schedules.

The first schedule must contain details of the assets of the party. It is important to list all assets whatsoever including those in which the applicant or respondent may have only an equitable interest. If acting for the applicant and wishing to bring a claim against other assets which are registered in the sole name of the respondent then these should be listed in this schedule also.

The second schedule must contain details of the income of both parties. This must cover income from any source whatsoever. It is helpful to state what the income is on a gross and a net basis. One should also set out all deductions made from the gross income on a regular basis, e.g., pension deductions, tax, PRSI, holiday fund, etc.

The third schedule should contain details of all debts and liabilities and details of the institutions that are owed monies.

The fourth schedule should contain a detailed list of the outgoings of the applicant and the respondent on either a weekly, monthly or annual basis. It is wise to have a very detailed schedule prepared with sub-headings and to furnish same to the applicant or respondent so that they can complete these themselves.

The fifth schedule should contain as much detail as possible relating to any pension schemes which exist. It is useful to attach a copy of the latest 'statement of benefits' received.

6.2.1.11 Affidavit of welfare

In any cases where there are dependent children involved (regardless of whether or not any financial relief is being claimed) an affidavit of welfare must be sworn and filed.

There are a large number of questions which both the applicant and the respondent need to answer. It is not necessary to prepare the affidavit of welfare in usual affidavit form but it is sufficient to simply reprint all of the questions and insert the appropriate answers in each section.

The affidavit of welfare must give details of the children born to the applicant and the respondent or adopted by them and details of other children of the family or to which *either* of the parties stand *in loco parentis*. Details must be furnished as to the address at which the children reside, the number of rooms in the house, whether it is owned or rented, educational arrangements for the children, details of their day-to-day care, etc.

The court has an obligation under the Act and the Constitution to ensure that the welfare of the children is properly catered for and the swearing of an affidavit of welfare concentrates the minds of both parties on this need.

6.2.1.12 Counterclaims

Any counterclaim is included in the defence and the same rules apply as if the counterclaim was actually the endorsement of claim in an original Family Law Civil Bill.

6.2.1.13 Interim applications

All interim applications are made by way of notice of motion and affidavit (r. 24(a)).

The only exception is a motion for discovery where no affidavit is needed in the Circuit Court.

Before issuing a notice of motion for discovery it is necessary under r. 24(b) to seek the necessary information in writing and to seek voluntary discovery at least 14 days prior to the issuing of the motion for discovery.

If on a date fixed for a full hearing of any application it is necessary for whatever reason to adjourn the proceedings, then the court may make such interim or interlocutory orders for relief as it shall feel are necessary. There is no necessity to issue a notice of motion in such circumstances (r. 25).

Rule 29 provides for ex parte orders exempting a marriage from the notice requirements of s. 32 of the Family Law Act 1995. It does seem somewhat absurd for s. 32 of this Act to state that a couple intending to marry must give not less than three months notice prior to the marriage ceremony to the Registrar in writing and yet permit such persons to obtain an exemption from such requirement on relatively flimsy grounds. Such applications for exemptions are made informally to the court and there is no need for lawyers to be involved. The reasons given by parties applying for such an exemption include ignorance of the law, age or illness of one or other of the parties and the fact that all the wedding arrangements have been made and it is too late to change them.

Rules 30, 31, 32 and 33 provide for applications pursuant to s. 8 of the Family Home Protection Act 1976 for a declaration that arrears of mortgage repayments which would normally give rise to proceedings for repossession of a family home shall be of no effect for the purpose of such proceedings once the arrears have been discharged.

6.2.1.14 Costs

The court may make any orders it sees fit as regards costs and it can order that these be taxed or in fact measure the costs itself (rr. 35 and 36).

6.2.2 THE HIGH COURT

6.2.2.1 Introduction

The Rules of the Superior Courts (No. 3) 1997, SI 343/1997, which came into operation on 1 September 1997, contain the rules for making applications to the Family Law High Court for a decree of divorce, a decree of judicial separation, any preliminary or ancillary applications relating to the granting of a decree of judicial separation or divorce and a wide range of other family law proceedings.

6.2.2.2 Family law summons

Rule 2 provides that all family law proceedings (other than an application to the court pursuant to s. 6(a)(iii) of the Guardianship of Infants Act 1964 (as inserted by s. 12 of the Status of Children Act 1987) shall be commenced by a Special Summons which shall be a Family Law Summons.

6.2.2.3 Special endorsement of claim

Rule 3 provides that the endorsement of claim shall be entitled 'special endorsement of claim' and shall state specifically, with all necessary particulars, the relief sought and each section of the Act or Acts under which the relief is sought, and the ground upon which it is sought. The Special Summons is given a return date before the Master of the High Court. The Master's role is to ensure that both parties have filed affidavits, affidavits of means and, if necessary, affidavits of welfare and have complied with any discovery orders made. Once the Master is satisfied, he can put the case into the Judges' List to fix dates, which usually takes place on a Friday in the High Court in Dublin.

On occasions when the respondent fails to file a replying affidavit or an affidavit of means the Master may remit the case to the Judges' List and direct that the respondent not be permitted to file a replying affidavit incorporating a counterclaim in certain circumstances. However, at the end of the day the High Court usually ignores such a recommendation, and permits all necessary pleadings to be filed prior to the hearing of the action.

6.2.2.4 Affidavit verifying proceedings

Rule 4 provides that, in any proceedings pursuant to rule 1(1), an affidavit verifying such proceedings or in reply thereto shall contain the following where applicable:

In the case of an application for a decree of divorce:

(1) the date and place of the marriage of the parties;

(2) the length of time the parties have lived apart and the addresses of both of the parties during that time;

(3) full particulars of any children of the applicant or respondent, stating whether each or any of them is or are a dependent child of the family and, if so, what provision has been made for each and any such dependent child of the applicant or respondent as the case may be;

(4) whether any possibility of a reconciliation between the applicant and respondent exists and, if so, on what basis the same might take place;

(5) details of any reliefs sought and/or obtained and details of any previous separation agreement entered into between the parties (where appropriate a certified copy of any relevant court order and/or deed of separation/separation agreement should be exhibited with the affidavit);

(6) where each party is domiciled at the date of the application commencing the proceedings or where each party has been ordinarily resident for the year preceding the date of application;

(7) details of the family home, occupation and ownership thereof;

(8) where reference is made in the summons to any immovable property, whether it is registered or unregistered land, and a description of the lands/premises so referred to. The importance of this information is that the Court Registrar, once an order affecting such land or property is made, must register same in the Land Registry or Registry of Deeds as the case may be.

The grounding affidavit, which is sworn by the applicant, and the replying affidavit, which is sworn by the respondent, are usually extremely detailed and set out a history of the marriage, the reasons for the breakdown, information relating to the acquisition of various assets and any other relevant financial information. The Special Summons generally sets out the reliefs which are sought by the applicant and the grounding affidavit contains the grounds for the claiming of such reliefs.

6.2.2.5 Certificate to be exhibited

Rule 5 provides that any affidavit filed under rule 4 shall where appropriate also exhibit the certificate required under s. 6 or, as the case may be, s. 7 of the 1996 Act, which shall be in Form 3 or Form 4 set out in the Schedule to the Rules.

6.2.2.6 Affidavit of means

Rule 6 deals with the affidavit of means.

Without prejudice to the right of any party to seek particulars of any matter from the other party to any proceedings or to the right of such party to make application to the court for an order for discovery, and without prejudice to the jurisdiction of the court under s. 17(25) of the 1996 Act (in relation to pension adjustment orders), in any case where financial relief under either of the Acts is sought each party shall file and serve an affidavit of means in the proceedings. It is clear that an affidavit of means does not need to be filed in the High Court unless some form of financial relief is being sought by the applicant or respondent.

A blocking order pursuant to the provisions of s. 18(10) of the Family Law (Divorce) Act 1996 is not a claim for financial relief. Thus, if the applicant is not seeking financial relief, and the respondent is not looking for it either, affidavits of means need not be exchanged. The affidavit of means shall be in Form 5 in the schedule to the Rules. It shall be served with the grounding affidavit, and the affidavit of means of the respondent shall be served with the replying affidavit unless otherwise ordered by the Master.

Subsequent to the service of the affidavit of means either party may request the other party to vouch all or any of the items referred to therein within 21 days of the request. In the event of a party failing to comply properly with the provision in relation to the filing and serving of an affidavit of means, or failing to fully vouch same, the court may, on application by notice of motion, grant an order for discovery and/or make any such order as the court deems appropriate including an order that such parties shall not be entitled to pursue or defend as appropriate such claim for ancillary relief under the Act save as permitted by the court and upon such terms as the court may determine as appropriate, or the court may adjourn the proceedings for a specified period of time to enable compliance with any such previous request or order of the court.

It is almost unheard of for the court to refuse to allow a party to pursue or defend a particular claim for ancillary relief because he or she has failed to make proper discovery or disclosure of financial matters. The court can and indeed does, however, take into account on occasion such a failure when deciding on the extent of particular ancillary relief orders which must be made.

6.2.2.7   Affidavit of welfare

Rule 7 provides that in any case in which there is or are a dependent child or children of the spouses or either of them an affidavit of welfare shall be filed on behalf of the applicant in Form 6 in the Schedule to the Rules. Where the respondent agrees with the facts averred to in the affidavit of welfare, he or she may file and serve an affidavit of welfare in the alternative form provided in Form 6 in the Schedule. This is a simple form wherein the respondent merely confirms his or her agreement to the contents of the applicant's affidavit of welfare. Where the respondent disagrees with all or any of the affidavit of welfare served and filed by the applicant a separate affidavit of welfare in Form 6 shall be sworn, filed and served by the respondent within 21 days from the date of service of the applicant's affidavit of welfare.

6.2.2.8   Interim and interlocutory relief

Rule 9 deals with interim and interlocutory relief. Preliminary orders under ss. 11, 12, 17(25), 37, 38(7) or 42 of the 1996 Act, or for any other interlocutory relief shall be by notice of motion to be served on the other party 14 clear days before the return date. The notice of motion shall be grounded upon the affidavit of the applicant concerned.

An application may be made ex parte to the court in any case in which interim relief of an urgent and immediate nature is required by the applicant. Any interim or interlocutory application shall be heard on affidavit unless the court otherwise directs. There is a repetition here of the provision in the Circuit Court Rules that where any oral evidence is heard by the court in the course of an ex parte application, a note of that evidence shall be prepared by the applicant or the applicant's solicitor and approved by the court and shall be served upon the respondent forthwith together with a copy of the order made, if any, unless otherwise directed by the court. In practice this rarely happens.

6.2.2.9 Applications relating to pension adjustment orders

Rule 10 deals with applications relating to pension adjustment orders. It provides that an applicant who seeks an order under Part III of the 1996 Act affecting any pension shall give notice to the trustees thereof in Form 7 set out in the Schedule to the Rules informing them of the application and of their right to make representations in relation thereto. It is essential that the appropriate notice to trustees is served. If it is not and an order is made by a court then such an order may very well not be binding on the trustees of a pension scheme. The notice in Form 7 provides that any representations to be made to the court under s. 17(18) of the 1996 Act may be made by way of affidavit of representation to be filed and served on all parties within 28 days of the service of the notice. There is no time limit within which the notice must be served on the trustees, but, presumably the Master will not send the case forward into the Judges' List until this has been done.

6.2.2.10 Notice of motion for directions

Rule 11 provides that an applicant or respondent may at any stage bring a motion for directions to the court in any of the following cases:

(a) where there are any dependent children who are *sui juris* and whose welfare or position is or is likely to be affected by the determination of the proceedings or of any issue in the proceedings;

(b) where an order is sought concerning the sale of any property in respect of which any other party has or may have an interest;

(c) where an order at any time is sought which will affect the rules of a pension scheme or require non-compliance therewith;

(d) where an application is brought seeking provision out of the estate of a deceased person, or in any other case in which it is appropriate.

This notice of motion shall be grounded upon the affidavit of the applicant and shall identify the parties whose interests are or are likely to be affected by the determination of the proceedings or any issue in the proceedings and who ought to be put on notice and given an opportunity to be heard.

6.2.2.11 Court's power to make appropriate order or directions

The court may upon such motion or of its own motion make such order or give such direction pursuant to the 1996 Act, s. 40 as appears appropriate, and may, where any order affecting the rules of the pension scheme is sought, direct that further notice be given to the trustees of such pension scheme in accordance with Form 7 set out in the Schedule to the Rules.

Section 40 refers to notices of proceedings being given by the person bringing the proceedings to the other spouse concerned or, as the case may be, the spouses concerned, and any other person specified by the court. A notice party who wishes to make representations must do so by affidavit which is to be filed and served on all parties within 28 days of service of the notice of application for relief.

6.2.2.12 Evidence at hearing

Rule 13 provides that the hearing of any interim or interlocutory application is to be on affidavit, subject to the rights of the parties to seek to cross-examine the opposing party on their affidavit. Notice to cross-examine may be served. The full hearing is to be on oral evidence. Where relief is sought under s. 17 of the 1996 Act evidence of the actuarial value of the benefit under the scheme shall be by affidavit filed on behalf of the applicant or respondent as the case may be.

It shall be sworn and served on all parties to the proceedings and filed at least 28 days in advance of the hearing and be subject to the right to serve notice of cross-examination. Where one of the parties has adduced evidence of the actuarial value of the benefit by such affidavit and the other party intends to dispute it he or she shall do so by affidavit which shall be filed at least 14 days in advance of the hearing, and be subject to the right to serve notice of cross-examination.

6.2.2.13 Adjournment where relief sought has not been specifically claimed

Rule 14 provides that where any relief is sought which has not been specifically claimed the court may adjourn the proceedings to allow the pleadings to be amended.

6.2.2.14 Transfer of action

Rule 15 provides that where any action is pending in the High Court which might have been commenced in the Circuit Court any party to the action may apply to the High Court for it to be remitted or transferred to the District or Circuit Court and if the High Court should 'in the exercise of its discretion consider such an order to be in the interests of justice' it shall remit or transfer such action to the Circuit or the District Court as the case may be. An application to remit may be made at any time after an appearance has been entered.

Case law

The case of *M.W. v D.W.* (unreported, 25 November 1999, Supreme Ct, Denham J, Barrington J and Barron J) deals with an application to remit a case from the High Court to the Circuit Court.

This case concerned an appeal from an order of the High Court made in April 1999 refusing to remit the action to the Circuit Court.

The applicant/wife was a home-maker who had issued proceedings seeking a decree of judicial separation and ancillary reliefs. The respondent/husband was the sole financial provider for the family.

Proceedings were issued by the wife in the High Court in Dublin although the parties resided in Cork. The husband said that he had a quintuple heart bypass in 1984 and had further serious heart trouble in 1997 and that he would find it most stressful to travel backwards and forwards to Dublin. All the witnesses who might be called resided in Cork, the respondent's accountants were based in Cork, the family home was in Cork and the solicitors of both parties were situated in Cork.

The husband further argued that he would be retiring in September 1999 and that his earning capacity would be totally diminished and the additional costs incurred in a High Court action would further dissipate the family assets at a time when the husband's employment was at an end.

The husband also pointed out that the wife had issued Circuit Court proceedings in 1997 in Cork which had eventually been settled.

The wife argued that the respondent's solicitors (who were the second firm acting on behalf of the husband) had served a notice of change of solicitors, a replying affidavit, a defence and counterclaim and that there had been a huge delay in making the application for remission. She further went on to argue that the husband had been slow and misleading in making discovery. She also pointed out that her husband at present was a man of considerable wealth and that he had just returned from a golfing holiday in South Africa and would shortly be travelling to Royal Ascot for the races. She therefore cast some doubt on his inability to travel.

Judgment

In the course of her judgment Denham J stated that 'the test to be applied is that an order to remit should be made in the interests of justice'. She further went on to say that delay was not a bar to seeking to remit an action in view of rule 15(2) which states that an application to remit may be made at any time after an appearance has been entered.

She went on to say that 'in this case the delay in seeking the order to remit was not such as to weigh against the respondent. However the issue of delay in general in the case was an important factor in considering the interests of justice'.

Denham J went on to consider various matters in reaching her decision namely:

(1)   the size of the assets both in this jurisdiction and suspected to be abroad;

(2)   the waiting list in Cork Circuit Court. The case would come on for hearing far quicker in the Family Law High Court in Dublin than in the Circuit Court in Cork;

(3)   if the case was heard in the Circuit Court in Cork and there was an appeal to the High Court it would be some years before the appeal was dealt with;

(4)   the lack of co-operation of the husband in making discovery.

In upholding the decision of the High Court and refusing to remit the case to the Circuit Court Denham J stated that:

'This is a dysfunctional family, of parents and children living under one roof pending the court decision on the action. In light of the circumstances time is an important aspect of this case. Also important is access to the court on interim and interlocutory applications to process the case. The probability is that proceedings in Cork would take longer and while the financial affairs on the surface appear not too complex the intricacy arises in the applicant's suspicion as to other assets and the intention to try and prove their existence. The court has a discretion. The discretion should be exercised to remit if that be in the interests of justice. In the circumstances of this case the refusal to exercise the discretion to remit was just. Further delay should be avoided. The case should be decided as soon as it is reasonably possible. Such procedure would be for the benefit of all the family'.

Finally, Denham J made reference to the costs to be incurred in lengthy litigation. She said 'if monies are spent on lengthy litigation it would be to the detriment of both parties and the children'. The issue of the costs involved could well be a factor relevant to a judge in determining the division of property between the parties or the issue of costs.

6.2.2.15   Hearing, transfer and consolidation

Rule 16 provides that the provisions of Ord. 49 rr. 1, 2, 3 and 6 (hearing, transfer and consolidation) shall apply to any proceedings commenced under r. 2 of the Rules.

6.2.2.16   Counterclaim

Rule 17 provides that a respondent may counterclaim by way of replying affidavit setting out clearly the relief claimed on the grounds upon which it is claimed in like manner as if he or she were the applicant.

6.2.2.17   Application for variation

Rule 19 provides that an application by either spouse or on behalf of a dependent member pursuant to s. 22 of the 1996 Act (e.g. for variation of an earlier order) may be made by notice of motion supported by a verifying affidavit which sets out fully 'when and in what respect circumstances have changed or what new evidence exists' as a result of which the court shall vary or discharge or otherwise modify in any respect an order to which the section applies.

6.2.2.18   Transactions intended to prevent or reduce relief

Rule 20 provides that an application under s. 37 of the 1996 Act (powers of the court in relation to transactions intended to prevent or reduce relief) may be made to the court by notice of motion in the proceedings supported by an affidavit verifying the facts alleged in relation to the disposition complained of and shall specify the relief claimed and the way in which the disposition is said to be intended to defeat the relief claimed or to affect it in any way.

6.2.2.19   Ancillary relief

Rule 22 provides that subsequent to the grant of a decree of divorce any party who seeks any further ancillary relief under Part III of the Act of 1996 shall do so by way of notice of motion in the proceedings grounded on an affidavit of the moving party.

6.2.3   CONCLUSION

It is sometimes difficult for practitioners to make decisions as to whether or not proceedings should be instituted in the Circuit Court or the High Court in a particular case. A solicitor advising a client must decide which court would be more beneficial for his or her client.

One of the major factors to be considered in reaching a decision as to whether to institute proceedings in the Circuit or the High Court is the extent of the assets. If there are very substantial assets available to one or both parties, or if there is a large family business involved in the case, then it is almost certainly more appropriate for proceedings to be issued in the High Court.

If a particular case involves complex financial issues or requires orders which may have far-reaching effects, then the High Court is probably the more appropriate forum.

In a growing number of cases a husband and a wife may be shareholders in a private limited company which runs a family business. In cases such as this it is not uncommon for proceedings under the Companies Acts to be issued along with family law proceedings. In such cases it is considered sensible for all proceedings to be dealt with in the same court and, since proceedings under the Companies Acts, in general terms, are issued in the High Court, then all proceedings will take place in that court.

There is no doubt, if one considers the level of awards made in the Circuit Court and the High Court, that lump sum orders, property adjustment orders and periodical payment orders are usually substantially higher or more wide-ranging when made in the High Court as opposed to the Circuit Court.

6.3   Discovery

6.3.1   INTRODUCTION

The process of discovery is of fundamental importance in both Circuit Court and High Court family law proceedings. It is a pre-hearing procedure which is intended to make available to both applicant and respondent all documents which exist (largely of a financial nature) and which may be relevant to the particular case or to the particular reliefs being sought.

In practice, an affidavit of discovery is sworn by both parties and the affidavit lists all documents which are in the possession of the deponent or within his or her power of procurement.

Such documents include copy bank statements, copy insurance policies, copy building society account books, copy credit union books, copy accounts of a business, etc. In addition, videos, computer discs and tapes may come within the terms of an order for discovery. In most cases such documents date from approximately three years prior to the issuing of proceedings.

One of the main purposes of discovery is to ensure that all relevant information and documents, whether beneficial or detrimental to the party's case are produced in advance of the hearing.

Particularly in 'big money' cases the process of discovery is essential in ensuring that the court is made fully aware of all assets, incomes, valuations and other financial matters before reaching a conclusion in relation to ancillary reliefs.

It is important however that the process is not abused. For instance, there is little point in pursuing the issue of discovery to a large degree if only one spouse is in employment and makes regular PAYE payments.

Discovery is of course relevant where one or both spouses have a number of different assets or monies offshore.

Until recently, in the Superior Courts it was not even necessary to file an affidavit setting out the reasons why one wanted an order for discovery but now the rules have changed quite substantially.

6.3.2 RULES OF THE SUPERIOR COURTS (NO. 2) (DISCOVERY) 1999

The Rules of the Superior Courts (No. 2) (Discovery) 1999, SI 233/1999, came into operation on 3 August 1999 and their main aim is to reduce the amount of unnecessary discovery applications in the High Court.

The Rules specify that every notice of motion should now specify the precise categories of documents in respect of which discovery is sought and shall be grounded upon the affidavit of the party seeking an order for discovery which shall:

(a) verify that the discovery of documents sought is necessary for disposing fairly of the cause or matter or for saving costs; and

(b) furnish the reasons why each category of documents is required to be discovered.

Rule 4 states that an order for discovery shall not be made unless:

(a) the applicant for discovery shall have previously applied by letter in writing requesting that discovery be made voluntarily, specifying the precise category of documents in respect of which discovery is sought and furnishing the reasons why each category of documents is required to be discovered;

(b) a reasonable period of time for such discovery is allowed; and

(c) a party or person requested has failed, refused or neglected to make such discovery or has ignored such requests.

The court, in certain unusual cases where the matter is urgent or the parties have consented, may make an order for discovery as appears proper without the necessity for such a prior application in writing.

6.3.3 CIRCUIT COURT RULES (NO. 1) 1997

The Circuit Court Rules (No. 1) 1997, SI 84/1997, provide in all cases where there is a claim for financial relief for the swearing and serving of an affidavit of means. Often this will be sufficient for the proper running of a case and there will be no need to pursue discovery.

Once an affidavit of means has been sworn and served either party may request the other party to vouch any or all items referred to therein (r. 18(a)).

In a substantial number of cases, however, particularly if one or other of the spouses is self-employed or runs a private business, it may be necessary to pursue the issue of discovery.

It is clearly preferable for both parties to agree to make voluntary discovery. Rule 24(b) states that:

> *prior to any interlocutory application for discovery or for information pursuant to s. 12(25) of the 1995 Act or s. 17(25) of the 1996 Act being made, the information being sought shall be requested in writing voluntarily at least 14 days prior to the issuing of the motion for the relief concerned . . .*

It is not possible therefore to bring a motion for discovery in the Circuit Court unless one has first requested voluntary discovery.

The making of full and proper discovery may often lead to a speedier settlement of all issues in a case and also a substantial reduction in legal costs.

In the High Court the application for an order for discovery may be made by way of notice of motion either to the Master of the High Court or, if the matter has already been put into the list to fix dates or listed for hearing, then to a judge of the High Court. In practice, however, the Master of the High Court endeavours to ensure that all discovery issues are dealt with before he transfers a matrimonial case to the Judges' List to fix dates.

Order 29 of the Circuit Court Rules provides that application is made to the court by way of notice of motion. There is still no grounding affidavit required in the Circuit Court although in practice, largely as a result of the new Superior Court Rules, the courts are beginning to insist upon clear reasons being given as to why discovery in relation to particular issues or areas is required.

6.3.4 COPYING OF DOCUMENTS

Once the affidavits of discovery have been filed and exchanged, both parties and their legal advisers are entitled to inspect the discovery documents of the other side. If the documents are not voluminous copies are usually furnished along with the affidavit. There is, however, no obligation on a practitioner acting for a particular party to carry out such copying. A practitioner may simply indicate to the other side that they may inspect the documents if they wish and take copies for themselves. Certainly such inspection often takes place where the number of documents to be copied is extremely large.

It is important to note that the term 'document' used in the context of discovery does not only refer to documents in the conventional sense but also includes photographs, tape recordings and computer discs.

If a spouse is dissatisfied with the affidavit of discovery sworn by the other spouse he or she may seek an order for further and better discovery. Such an order would not be made merely based on the belief that documents have been omitted. There must be some clear evidence or reason for believing that the affidavit is incomplete. The process cannot simply be used as a 'fishing expedition'.

6.3.5 CASE LAW

In the course of his judgment in the case of *M.W. v D.W.* (unreported, 25 November 1999, Supreme Ct), Barron J made a number of useful comments on the issue of discovery and stated that:

> 'In general where the issues are financial there are two basic questions:
>
> (a) what assets do the parties own?
>
> (b) what provisions should be made for the parties and their children (if any)?

Discovery of documents is not the most efficient way of dealing with the first issue, while the second issue cannot be resolved until the court is satisfied that all relevant financial details have been disclosed.

Too often in matrimonial cases where there are such issues there are lengthy inter-locutory proceedings whereby each party seeks discovery of documents from the other. In the course of such applications there are as a general rule allegations that assets are being hidden by one or other party. This results in applications for further and better discovery. Too often the financial situation of the parties is never totally clarified. In matrimonial proceedings time is really of the essence and after months if not years of wrangling in this fashion the party, still dissatisfied as to the information supplied, is nevertheless anxious to get on with the matter and too often the hearing is held before there has been total clarification of the appropriate assets.'

Barron J went on to discuss the new Superior Court Rules in relation to discovery and also pointed out that in many cases 'too great a leniency is given to persons in default' in making discovery. He did not feel that there was any adequate sanction for parties who deliberately delayed in making discovery or concealed documentation. He went on to say that 'in any event it is not documents which the other party really wants, it is facts. These are much more easily obtainable by cross-examination'.

In *F.R. v F.J.* [1996] 1 FLR 12 the applicant wife believed (wrongly as it transpired) that the husband had a substantial number of hidden assets and cash. In giving her judgment McGuinness J criticised the way in which the discovery process was pursued and refused to grant an order for costs in favour of the wife when she otherwise would have done so.

In *O'L v O'L* [1996] 2 Fam LJ 66 it was the applicant's wife who failed to make proper discovery. The case lasted a number of days in the Circuit Court and judgment was eventually reserved by McGuinness J. In the intervening period the applicant husband continued to enquire into the wife's finances as, despite many earlier demands, it was clear to him that she had failed to make full discovery. A number of matters came to light which showed that the wife had substantial additional monies in various accounts which had not been disclosed. When these were put to her at a later date she simply stated that she had forgotten about them.

McGuinness J stated in her judgment that she had intended to direct that the husband should pay a contribution towards the wife's costs but since the wife had failed to make proper discovery she would not do so.

6.3.6 'THE MILLIONAIRE'S DEFENCE'

The intention in pleading the 'Millionaire's Defence' is to minimise the amount of paperwork involved in a matrimonial case where the assets are extremely large. In such cases the respondent against whom discovery is sought claims that it would be oppressive in terms of costs and time for the areas of dispute between the parties to be enlarged by detailed financial investigations, valuations, reports etc. See *B v B* [1992] FLR 180.

This situation can occur in cases where the assets are extremely valuable. The 'Millionaire's Defence' has been availed of in the English courts on a number of occasions but it is felt now that the assets should certainly exceed £15m at today's values before this can be done.

The use of this defence in the Irish courts has been extremely rare to date but there is no doubt that it will become more relevant in the future.

If discovery were to take place in the normal way in such cases, the amount of paperwork involved would be undigestable and uncontrollable. A large number of documents which may have to be furnished will inevitably turn out to be entirely irrelevant to the proceedings. The case could not be properly dealt with by the lawyers involved or by the court and the costs which would be incurred could well be enormous and unnecessary.

In the case of *Van G v Van G* [1995] 1 FLR 328 the assets were valued at a figure in excess of £10m. The court, at the request of the respondent husband, accepted a summary of assets together with their values without the necessity for producing supporting documentation. The court also requested an estimate of the income of the husband prepared by his accountants and then proceeded to deal with the case.

6.3.7 ORDERS FOR WASTED COSTS

The English courts have the power to make orders for wasted costs. If the court feels that lawyers acting on behalf of the applicant or respondent have pursued discovery to an unreasonable or unnecessary degree the court may make an award of costs against the relevant solicitors.

In the case of *C v C* [1994] 3 FLJ 85 there was a very large amount of discovery which was pursued by various lawyers over a lengthy period. The amount of the award eventually granted by the court was a lump sum of £20,000. The legal costs incurred (largely as a result of the lengthy unnecessary discovery processes) were in the region of £130,000.

A subsequent hearing took place (which lasted for approximately 14 days) in order to decide who should be responsible for the large costs incurred in the main case. The court made orders against a number of firms of solicitors involved at one stage or another in the particular case as it held that they had improperly pursued discovery in certain instances.

It is not possible for the Irish courts to make such orders at this stage, although they may be given this power in the future.

6.3.8 CONCLUSION

The obtaining of orders for discovery and the examination of the documents produced as a result of such orders is taking up an increasing amount of time for practitioners involved in matrimonial cases. As the economy continues to expand and as individuals' financial affairs become more and more complex, it is essential that practitioners make all necessary enquiries into the other spouse's assets and income before attempting to finalise a matrimonial case, either by way of settlement or court hearing.

If such a process is not undergone fully and efficiently then it may leave the practitioner open to a claim for negligence in the future.

However, it is vitally important that a balance is maintained between the need for full disclosure and the unnecessary pursuit of a large number of irrelevant documents which disclose very little.

6.4 Court Forms

6.4.1 AFFIDAVIT OF MEANS

Record No

AN CHUIRT TEACHLAIGH CHUARDA

(THE CIRCUIT FAMILY COURT)

DUBLIN CIRCUIT   COUNTY OF THE CITY OF DUBLIN

IN THE MATTER OF THE JUDICIAL SEPARATION AND FAMILY LAW REFORM ACT 1989 AND IN THE MATTER OF THE FAMILY LAW ACT 1995 AND IN THE MATTER OF THE FAMILY LAW (DIVORCE) ACT 1996

BETWEEN/

JOAN MURPHY

APPLICANT

and

JIM MURPHY

RESPONDENT

AFFIDAVIT OF MEANS OF JOAN MURPHY

I, JOAN MURPHY of 5 Bloxham Green, in the City of Dublin, aged eighteen years and upwards MAKE OATH and say as follows:–

1. I say that I am the Applicant in the above entitled proceedings and I make this Affidavit from facts within my own knowledge save where otherwise appears and whereso appearing I believe the same to be true.

2. I say that I have set out in the First Schedule hereto all the assets to which I am legally or beneficially entitled and the manner in which such property is held.

3. I say that I have set out in the Second Schedule hereto all income which I receive and the source(s) of such income.

4. I say that I have set out in the Third Schedule hereto all my debts and/or liabilities and the persons to whom such debts and liabilities are due.

5. I say that my weekly outgoings amount to the sum of £   and I say that the details of such outgoings have been set out in the Fourth Schedule hereto.

6. I say that to the best of my knowledge information and belief all Pension information known to me relevant to the within proceedings is set out in the Fifth Schedule hereto (Where information has been obtained from the Trustees of the Pension Scheme concerned under the Pensions Act 1990 such information should be exhibited and where such information has not been obtained, the Deponent should depose to the reason(s) why such information has not been obtained).

FIRST SCHEDULE

(Here set out in numbered paragraphs all assets whether held in the Applicant/Respondent's sole name or jointly with another whether held legally or beneficially, the manner in which the assets are held, whether they are subject to a Mortgage or other Charge or lien and such further and other details as are appropriate).

SECOND SCHEDULE

[Here set out in numbered paragraphs all income from whatever source(s)].

THIRD SCHEDULE

[Here set out in numbered paragraphs all debts and/or liabilities and the Pensions/Institutions to which such debts and/or liabilities are due].

FOURTH SCHEDULE

WEEKLY INCOME

WEEKLY EXPENDITURE

MORTGAGE/RENT	:	£
HEATING	:	£
ELECTRICITY	:	£
TELEPHONE	:	£
GROCERIES	:	£
HOUSE INSURANCE	:	£
HOUSE CONTENTS INSURANCE	:	£
TV/VIDEO HIRE	:	£
TV LICENCE	:	£
CHILDREN'S CLOTHES	:	£
SCHOOL EXPENSES	:	£
MAINTENANCE PAYMENTS	:	£
REPAYMENT OF LOANS	:	£

PERSONAL EXPENSES

LIFE INSURANCE	:	£
PENSION CONTRIBUTIONS	:	£
REGULAR SAVINGS	:	£
TRAVEL EXPENSES	:	£
SUBSCRIPTIONS TO CLUBS ETC.	:	£
CLOTHING	:	£
DENTAL EXPENSES	:	£
DOCTORS EXPENSES	:	£
VHI	:	£

CAR EXPENSES

TAX	:	£
INSURANCE	:	£
SERVICE REPAIRS	:	£
PETROL ETC.	:	£
LEISURE/HOLIDAYS/ ENTERTAINMENT	:	£
CINEMA/SPORT ETC.	:	£
MAJOR EVENTS/BIRTHDAYS ETC.	:	£
TOTAL		£_____

FIFTH SCHEDULE

[Here full details of nature of Pension Scheme, benefits payable thereunder, normal Pensionable age and period of reckonable service should be listed to the best of the Deponent's knowledge, information and belief.]

SWORN by the said JOAN MURPHY

on the   day of   2000

at

in the City of Dublin before me a Commissioner for Oaths/Practising Solicitor and I know the Deponent.

. . . .
Commissioner for Oaths/Practising Solicitor

This Affidavit is filed on behalf of the Applicant by John Smith solicitors of Law School, Blackhall Place, Dublin 7 this   day of   2000.

Record No

AN CHUIRT TEACHLAIGH CHUARDA

(THE CIRCUIT FAMILY COURT)

DUBLIN CIRCUIT   COUNTY OF THE CITY OF DUBLIN

IN THE MATTER OF THE JUDICIAL SEPARATION AND FAMILY LAW REFORM ACT 1989 AND IN THE MATTER OF THE FAMILY LAW ACT 1995 AND IN THE MATTER OF THE FAMILY LAW (DIVORCE) ACT 1996

BETWEEN

JOAN MURPHY

APPLICANT

and

JIM MURPHY

RESPONDENT

AFFIDAVIT OF MEANS OF JOAN MURPHY

John Smith
Solicitors
Law School
Blackhall Place
Dublin 7.

6.4.2 AFFIDAVIT OF WELFARE

Record No

AN CHUIRT TEACHLAIGH CHUARDA

(THE CIRCUIT FAMILY COURT)

DUBLIN CIRCUIT   COUNTY OF THE CITY OF DUBLIN

IN THE MATTER OF THE JUDICIAL SEPARATION AND FAMILY LAW REFORM ACT
1989 AND IN THE MATTER OF THE FAMILY LAW ACT 1995 AND IN THE MATTER
OF THE FAMILY LAW (DIVORCE) ACT 1996

BETWEEN

JOAN MURPHY

APPLICANT

and

JIM MURPHY

RESPONDENT

AFFIDAVIT OF WELFARE OF JOAN MURPHY

I, JOAN MURPHY of 5 Bloxham Green, in the City of Dublin, aged eighteen years and
upwards MAKE OATH and say as follows:–

1.   I say that I am the Applicant in the above entitled proceedings and I make this
      Affidavit from facts within my own knowledge save where otherwise appears and
      where so appearing I believe the same to be true.

2.   I say and believe that the facts set out in the Schedule hereto are true.

      [In circumstances in which the Respondent does not dispute the facts as deposed to
      by the Applicant in his/her Affidavit of Welfare, the following averment shall be
      included, replacing Paragraph 2 hereof, and in such circumstances, the Schedule
      shall not be completed by the Respondent:

3.   I say that I am fully in agreement with the facts as averred to by the Applicant in
      his/her Affidavit of Welfare sworn herein on the day of
      20   and I say and believe that the facts set out in the Schedule thereto are
      true]

SCHEDULE
PART I – DETAILS OF THE CHILDREN

1. Details of children born to the Applicant and the Respondent or adopted by both the Applicant and the Respondent

    Forenames   *Surname*   *Date of Birth*

2. Details of other children of the family or to which the parties or either of them are in loco parentis

    Forenames   *Surname*   *Date of Birth*   *Relationship to Applicant/Respondent*

PART II – ARRANGEMENTS FOR THE CHILDREN OF THE FAMILY

3. Home Details

    (a) The address or addresses at which the children now live.

    (b) Give details of the number of living rooms, bedrooms, etc. at the addresses in (a) above.

    (c) Is the house rented or owned and, if so, name the tenant(s) or owner(s)?

    (d) Is the rent or mortgage being regularly paid and, if so, by whom?

(e) Give the names of all other persons living with the children either on a full-time or part-time basis and state their relationship to the children, if any.

(f) Will there be any change in these arrangements and, if so, give details.

PART III – EDUCATION AND TRAINING DETAILS

(a) Give the names of the school, college or place of training attended by each child.

(b) Do the children have any special educational needs? If so, please specify.

(c) Is the school, college or place of training fee-paying? If so, give details of how much the fees are per term/year. Are fees being regularly paid and, if so, by whom?

(d) Will there be any change in these circumstances? If so, give details.

PART IV – CHILDCARE DETAILS

(a)   Which parent looks after the children from day to day? If responsibility is shared, please give details.

(b)   Give details of work commitments of both parents.

(c)   Does someone look after the children when the parent is not there? If yes, give details.

(d)   Who looks after the children during school holidays?

(e)   Will there be any change in these arrangements? If yes, give details.

PART V – MAINTENANCE

(a)   Does the Applicant/Respondent pay towards the upkeep of the children? If yes, give details. Please specify any other source of maintenance.

(b)   Is the maintenance referred to at (a) above paid under Court Order? If yes, give details.

(c)   Has maintenance for the children been agreed? If yes, give details.

(d)   If not, will you be applying for a maintenance order from the Court?

PART VI – DETAILS OF CONTRACT WITH THE CHILDREN

(a)   Do the children see the Applicant/Respondent? Please give details.

(b)   Do the children stay overnight and/or have holiday visits with the Applicant/Respondent? Please give details.

(c)   Will there be any change to these arrangements? Please give details.

PART VII – DETAILS OF HEALTH

(a) Are the children generally in good health? Please give details of any serious disability or chronic illness suffered by any of the children.

(b) Do the children or any of them have any special health needs? Please give details of the care needed and how it is to be provided.

(c) Are the Applicant or Respondent generally in good health? If not, please give details.

PART VIII – DETAILS OF CARE AND OTHER COURT PROCEEDINGS

(a) Are the children or any of them in the care of a health board or under the supervision of a social worker or probation officer? If so, please specify.

(b) Are there or have there been any proceedings in any Court involving the children or any of them? If so, please specify. (All relevant Court Orders relating to the children or any of them should be annexed hereto)

Sworn by the said JOAN MURPHY
this   day of   2000

at

in the County of the City of Dublin before me a Commissioner for Oaths/Practising Solicitor
and I know the Deponent.

Signed

_____

COMMISSIONER FOR OATHS/
PRACTISING SOLICITOR.

Record No

AN CHUIRT TEACHLAIGH CHUARDA

(THE CIRCUIT FAMILY COURT)

DUBLIN CIRCUIT   COUNTY OF THE CITY OF DUBLIN

IN THE MATTER OF THE JUDICIAL SEPARATION AND FAMILY LAW REFORM ACT 1989 AND IN THE MATTER OF THE FAMILY LAW ACT 1995 AND IN THE MATTER OF THE FAMILY LAW (DIVORCE) ACT 1996

BETWEEN

JOAN MURPHY

APPLICANT

and

JIM MURPHY

RESPONDENT

AFFIDAVIT OF WELFARE OF JOAN MURPHY

John Smith
Solicitors
Law School
Blackhall Place
Dublin 7.

6.4.3   SECTION 5 CERTIFICATE

FORM NO 7

AN CHUIRT TEAGHLAIGH CHUARDA
(THE CIRCUIT FAMILY COURT)

DUBLIN CIRCUIT   COUNTY OF THE CITY OF DUBLIN

*IN THE MATTER OF THE JUDICIAL SEPARATION
AND FAMILY LAW REFORM ACT 1989 AND
IN THE MATTER OF THE FAMILY LAW ACT 1995*

BETWEEN   APPLICANT

AND

RESPONDENT

CERTIFICATE PURSUANT TO SECTION 5 OF THE JUDICIAL SEPARATION AND FAMILY
LAW REFORM ACT, 1989

_ _

I John Smith, the Solicitor acting for the above Applicant do hereby ceritfy as follows:

1.   I have discussed with the Applicant the possibility of reconciliation with the Respondent and I have given the Applicant the names and addresses of persons qualified to help effect a reconciliation between spouses who have become estranged.

2.   I have discussed with the Applicant the possibility of engaging in mediation to help effect a separation on an agreed basis with the Respondent and I have given the Applicant the names and addresses of persons and organisations qualified to provide a mediation service.

3.   I have discussed with the Applicant the possibility of effecting a separation by the negotiation and conclusion of a Separation Deed or written Separation Agreement with the Respondent.

Dated this   day of   2001.

SIGNED . . . .

John Smith,
Solicitor,
John Smith
Solicitors
Law School
Blackhall Place
Dublin 7.

104

6.4.4 SECTION 6 CERTIFICATE

AN CHUIRT TEAGHLAIGH CHUARDA
(THE CIRCUIT FAMILY COURT)

DUBLIN CIRCUIT   COUNTY OF THE CITY OF DUBLIN

IN THE MATTER OF THE JUDICIAL SEPARATION
AND FAMILY LAW REFORM ACT 1989 AND
IN THE MATTER OF THE FAMILY LAW ACT 1995

BETWEEN   APPLICANT
                                AND
                                                            RESPONDENT

CERTIFICATE PURSUANT TO SECTION 6 OF THE JUDICIAL SEPARATION AND FAMILY
LAW REFORM ACT, 1989
_____

I John Smith, the Solicitor acting for the above Applicant do hereby ceritfy as follows:

1.   I have discussed with the Respondent the possibility of reconciliation with the
     Applicant and I have given the Respondent the names and addresses of persons
     qualified to help effect a reconciliation between spouses who have become
     estranged.

2.   I have discussed with the Respondent the possibility of engaging in mediation to
     help effect a separation on an agreed basis with the Applicant and I have given the
     Respondent the names and addresses of persons and organisations qualified to
     provide a mediation service.

3.   I have discussed with the Respondent the possibility of effecting a separation by the
     negotiation and conclusion of a Separation Deed or written Separation Agreement
     with the Applicant.

Dated this   day of   2001.

SIGNED . . . .

John Smith,
Solicitor,
John Smith
Solicitors
Law School
Blackhall Place
Dublin 7.

6.4.5 FAMILY LAW CIVIL BILL

AN CHUIRT TEAGHLAIGH CHUARDA
(THE CIRCUIT FAMILY COURT)

DUBLIN CIRCUIT   COUNTY OF THE CITY OF DUBLIN

IN THE MATTER OF THE FAMILY LAW (DIVORCE) ACT 1996

BETWEEN

APPLICANT

AND

RESPONDENT

FAMILY LAW CIVIL BILL

YOU ARE HEREBY REQUIRED within ten days after the service of this Civil Bill upon you, to enter, or cause to be entered, with the County Registrar, at his/her Offices at Riverbank Courthouse, Merchant's Quay in the City of Dublin an Appearance to answer the claim of

in the County of City of Dublin the Applicant herein, as indorsed hereon.

AND TAKE NOTICE THAT, unless you do enter an Appearance, you will be held to have admitted the said claim and the Applicant may proceed therein and judgment may be given against you in your absence without further notice.

AND FURTHER TAKE NOTICE THAT, if you intend to defend the proceedings on any grounds, you must not only enter an Appearance as aforesaid, but also within ten days after the Appearance deliver a statement in writing showing the nature and grounds of your Defence.

The Appearance and Defence may be entered by posting same to the said Office and by giving copies to the Applicant and his/her Solicitor by post.

Dated the   day of   20 .

To:

INDORSEMENT OF CLAIM

1.   The Applicant and the Respondent herein were lawfully married to one another on the   .

2.   The Applicant and the Respondent herein are and were at the date of the said ceremony of marriage domiciled in Ireland.

3.   There are no children of the marriage between the Applicant and the Respondent herein.

4.   The Applicant and the Respondent herein have lived separate and apart from one another since in or about the   . Since that date the Applicant herein who is a   and is   years of age has resided at

     in the County of the City of Dublin. Since that date the Respondent herein who is a   and is   years of age has resided at   .

5.   The Applicant and the Respondent herein executed a Deed of Separation dated the   a copy of which is annexed to the within proceedings.

6.   The family home of the Applicant and the Respondent herein within the meaning of the Family Home Protection Act 1976 (hereinafter referred to as 'the family home') is situate at   in the County of the City of Dublin, and is held in the sole name of the Applicant herein. The Rateable Valuation of the said property does not exceed £   . Pursuant to the terms of the Deed of Separation dated the   it was agreed, *inter alia*, that the Respondent herein transfer her legal and beneficial interest in the family home to the Applicant herein and the Applicant herein assigned to the Respondent his legal and beneficial interest in other property therein referred to.

7.   The Applicant herein seeks a Decree of Divorce on the grounds that the Applicant and the Respondent herein have lived separate and apart from one another for a period of four years prior to the institution of these proceedings, there is no reasonable prospect of reconciliation between the Applicant and the Respondent herein and proper provision exists for the Applicant and the Respondent herein.

THE APPLICANT'S CLAIM IS FOR:–

(1)   A Decree of Divorce pursuant to the provisions of Section 5 of the Family Law (Divorce) Act 1996;

(2)   An Order and a Cross Order pursuant to the provisions of Section 18(10) of the Family Law (Divorce) Act 1996, that neither the Applicant nor the Respondent herein shall on the death of the other be entitled to apply for provision out of the Estate of the other herein pursuant to the provisions of the said Section;

(3)   Such further and other Order as to this Honourable Court shall seem proper;

(4)   An Order providing for and granting the Applicant the costs of these proceedings.

ANCILLARY ORDERS, PROCEDURE AND DISCOVERY

AND FURTHER TAKE NOTICE that, in any cases where financial relief is sought by either party you must file with the Defence herein or in any event within 20 days after the service of this Civil Bill upon you at the aforementioned Circuit Court Office an Affidavit of Means and where appropriate, an Affidavit of Welfare in the Manner prescribed by the Rules of this Court and serve a copy of same as provided by the Rules of this Court on the Applicant or his/her Solicitor at the address provided below.

Dated the   day of   20

The Address for service of proceedings upon the Applicant is as follows:–

John Smith
Solicitors
Law School
Blackhall Place
Dublin 7.

SIGNED . . . .

John Smith
Solicitors for the Applicant
Law School
Blackhall Place
Dublin 7.

To/

The County Registrar
Circuit Court Family Law Office
Riverbank Courthouse
Merchants Quay
Dublin 8.

and to/

TAKE NOTICE that it is in your interest to have legal advice in regard to these proceedings. If you cannot afford a private solicitor you may be entitled to legal aid provided by the State at a minimum cost to you. Details of this legal aid service are available at the following address:–

Legal Aid Board
St Stephen's Green House
Dublin 2

Telephone No (01) 6615811

where you can obtain the addresses and telephone numbers of the Legal Aid Centres in your area.

AN CHUIRT TEAGHLAIGH CHUARDA
(THE CIRCUIT FAMILY COURT)

DUBLIN CIRCUIT   COUNTY OF THE CITY OF DUBLIN

IN THE MATTER OF THE FAMILY LAW (DIVORCE) ACT 1996

BETWEEN   APPLICANT

AND

RESPONDENT

FAMILY LAW CIVIL BILL

John Smith
Solicitors
Law School
Blackhall Place
Dublin 7.

CHAPTER 7

PENSIONS ON SEPARATION AND DIVORCE

7.1 Financial Compensation Orders

7.1.1 INTRODUCTION

The Family Law Act 1995, s. 11 ('the 1995 Act') and the Family Law (Divorce) Act 1996, s. 16 ('the 1996 Act') govern financial compensation orders. The purpose of these sections is to give the court power by means of life insurance policies to provide, in a different way, for the financial security of a spouse or a dependent member of a family, or to compensate the spouse or the dependant for the forfeiture of the opportunity or possibility of acquiring a benefit, by reason of the decree of judicial separation (or divorce). It is proposed to discuss the legislative provisions in detail.

7.1.1.1 1995 Act, s. 11(1); 1996 Act, s. 16

Subject to the provisions of this section, on granting a decree of judicial separation or at any time thereafter, the court, on application to it in that behalf by either of the spouses concerned or by a person on behalf of a dependent spouse of the family, may, during the lifetime of the other spouse or, as the case may be, the spouse concerned, if it considers . . .

The order can only be made in the context of the granting of a decree of judicial separation (or divorce).

The order can be made on granting the decree or at any time thereafter during the lifetime of the other spouse. The application cannot be made if either spouse has died.

Either of the spouses may make the application (either applicant or respondent).

The application can also be made by a person on behalf of a dependent member of the family. This includes either spouse.

Under the 1995 Act, s. 11(2)(b) (1996 Act, s. 16) the order will cease to have effect on the remarriage or death of the applicant insofar as it relates to the applicant.

Under the 1995 Act, s. 11(2)(c) (1996 Act, s. 16) the court shall not make an order under this section if the spouse who is applying for the order has remarried.

7.1.1.2 1995 Act, s. 11(1)(a); 1996 Act, s. 16

The court must consider either:

(a) that the financial security of the spouse making the application ('the applicant') or the dependent member of the family ('the member') can be provided for either wholly or in part by so doing, or . . .

'Financial security' is not defined. The courts may therefore give it the widest possible meaning. A case in point might be where the respondent has been ordered to make periodical payments, but is unable to do so because, for example, of illness, in circumstances where the court cannot make a secured periodical payments order.

Even if this situation did not pertain at the time the decree of judicial separation (or divorce) was granted, clients should be advised of the possibility of this order being made 'at any time thereafter'.

7.1.1.3   1995 Act, s. 11(1)(b); 1996 Act, s. 16

Alternatively, the court can make a financial compensation order if it considers:

> *(b) that the forfeiture, by reason of the decree of judicial separation, by the applicant or the dependant, as the case may be, of the opportunity or possibility of acquiring a benefit (for example, a benefit under a pension scheme) can be compensated for wholly or in part by so doing.*

The forfeiture of the opportunity or possibility of acquiring the benefit must be solely 'by reason of the decree of judicial separation' (or divorce). The forfeiture can be either by the applicant or the dependant.

'Benefit' is not defined. Therefore the court may interpret it as widely or as narrowly as it wishes. This sub-paragraph seems intended to apply to benefits such as those under a pension scheme. For example, suppose that a pension scheme provides that a widow's pension, or a death gratuity, is only payable on the death of the spouse who is a member of the pension scheme to the other spouse if he or she is 'residing with' or 'cohabiting with' the spouse who is the member of the pension scheme at the date of his or her death. Clearly if a decree of judicial separation has been granted the surviving spouse would not be so residing or cohabiting. Therefore the court, on being satisfied by actuarial evidence of the value of the benefit being forfeited, could make a financial compensation order.

The granting of a decree of judicial separation (or divorce) will, of course, stop each spouse from making an application under the 1995 Act, s. 12(2) (1996 Act, s. 17(2)) for a pension adjustment order in relation to any retirement benefits accruing after the date of the decree of judicial separation (or divorce). Thus the court might use the 1995 Act, s. 11 (1996 Act, s. 16) to compensate a spouse for this loss. It might not, of course, be necessary for the court to make an order under the 1995 Act, s. 11 (1996 Act, s. 16) if the court could make an order under the 1995 Act, s. 12(3) (1996 Act, s. 17(3)) in relation to a contingent benefit such as a death in service payment.

It might also be possible to use the 1995 Act, s. 11 (1996 Act, s. 16) in a case where one spouse had placed his or her property in the joint names of himself or herself and a new partner, so as to defeat the inheritance rights of his or her spouse.

In either of the above circumstances the court may:

> *make a financial compensation order, that is to say, an order requiring either or both of the spouses to do one or more of the following:*

> *(i) to effect such a policy of life insurance for the benefit of the applicant or the member as may be specified in the order.*

This is the first type of financial compensation order.

It may not be possible for the respondent to take out a life insurance policy if he or she is, for example, terminally ill. Equally, it may be unrealistic for a court to make an order if the respondent does not have money to pay the premiums.

A situation might exist where the applicant could pay the premiums, although the policy is on the respondent's life.

The court may have to take taxation complications into account. Life policies and pension schemes operate under different tax codes. For example, a policy providing life cover

112

associated with a pension arrangement, effected under the Income Tax Act 1967, s. 235A, would qualify for tax relief on premiums. An ordinary life policy would not qualify for such relief. Tax relief may be important in certain circumstances, and should be brought to the attention of the court.

The court may order 'either or both of the spouses' to effect the policy, which may, therefore, be a joint policy.

The court may also make an order requiring either or both of the spouses:

> *(ii) to assign the whole or a specified part of the interest of either or both of the spouses in a policy of life insurance effected by either or both of the spouses to the applicant or to such person as may be specified in the order for the benefit of the member.*

This sub-paragraph refers to an existing policy.

It is not restricted to policies on the life or lives of either or both of the spouses.

The spouse might, for example, have effected a policy on the life of his or her parent or parents or his or her business partner or partners.

A policy effected by both spouses might, for example, be assigned to a person for the benefit of a dependent member of the family, in certain circumstances.

The court also has the power to require either or both of the spouses:

> *(iii) to make or to continue to make to the person by whom a policy of life insurance is or was issued the payments which either or both of the spouses is or are required to make under the terms of the policy.*

Thus, having made an order under (i) and (ii), the court may compel the respondent to pay the premiums, or the applicant, or both applicant and respondent may be ordered to pay the premiums.

7.1.1.4   1995 Act, s. 11(2)(a); 1996 Act, s. 16

These sections provide that:

> *The court may make a financial compensation order in addition to or in substitution in whole or in part for orders under ss. 8 to 10 and 12 [1996 Act, ss. 13 to 15 and 17] and in deciding whether or not to make such an order it shall have regard to whether adequate and reasonable financial provision exists or can be made for the spouse concerned or the dependent member of the family concerned by orders under those sections.*

Before it makes a financial compensation order the court must have regard to whether adequate and reasonable financial provision exists or can be made by way of periodical payments orders, lump sum orders, miscellaneous ancillary orders or pension adjustment orders.

The court is, however, not prohibited from making financial compensation orders in addition to the other orders just mentioned.

Practitioners must, however, present to the court all possibilities in relation to orders under the 1995 Act, ss. 8 to 10 and 12 (1996 Act, ss. 13 to 15 and 17) so that the court 'shall have regard' to these in the context of an application for a financial compensation order.

7.1.1.5   1995 Act, s. 11(2)(d); 1996 Act, s. 16

This refers to an order under the 1995 Act, s. 18(2) (1996 Act, s. 22(2)), which empowers a court:

> *. . . on application to it in that behalf by either of the spouses concerned or in the case of the death of either of the spouses, by any person who, in the opinion of the court, has a sufficient interest in the matter, or by a person on behalf of a dependent member of the family concerned, if it considers it*

proper to do so having regard to any change in the circumstances of the case and to any new evidence, by order vary or discharge an order to which this section applies, suspend any provision of such an order or any provision of such an order temporarily, revive the operation of such an order or provision so suspended, further vary an order previously varied under this section or further suspend or revive the operation of an order or provision previously suspended or revived under this section; and, without prejudice to the generality of the foregoing, an order under this section may require the divesting of any property vested in a person under or by virtue of an order to which this section applies.

The 1995 Act, s. 18 (1996 Act, s. 22) applies, inter alia, to financial compensation orders.

The 1995 Act, s. 11(2)(d) (1996 Act, s. 16(2)(d)) provides that an order under the 1995 Act, s. 18 (1996 Act, s. 22) in relation to orders under the 1995 Act, s. 11(1)(b)(i) or (ii) (1996 Act, s. 16(1)(b)(i) or (ii)) may:

make such provision (if any) as the court considers appropriate in relation to the disposal of

(i) an amount representing any accumulated value of the insurance policy effected pursuant to the order under the said paragraph (i), or

(ii) the interest or the part of the interest to which the order under the said paragraph (ii) relates.

This empowers the court to dispose of the insurance policy effected, or assigned, in an appropriate case where a financial compensation order has been varied.

A court can make a variation order if it considers it proper to do so having regard to any change in the circumstances of the case and to any new evidence.

A court could, for example, order that a life policy effected under a financial compensation order be surrendered and the proceeds divided between the spouses, or applied for the benefit of the children or similarly disposed of.

Note that a variation application can be made by either of the spouses concerned, by any other person who in the opinion of the court has a sufficient interest in the matter, or by a person on behalf of a dependent member of the family concerned.

7.2 Preservation of Pension Entitlements after Judicial Separation

7.2.1 1995 ACT, S. 13

Section 13 of the 1995 Act provides that on granting a decree of judicial separation or at any time thereafter the court may, in relation to a pension scheme, on the application of either of the spouses concerned, make during the lifetime of the spouse who is the member of the pension scheme, an order directing the trustees of the scheme not to regard the separation of the spouses resulting from the decree as a ground for disqualifying the other spouse for the receipt of a benefit under the scheme, a condition for the receipt of which is that the spouses should be residing together at the time the benefit becomes payable. Notice of the application shall be given by the spouses concerned to the trustees of the pension scheme, and the court shall have regard to their representations and to the representations of any other person specified by the court. Any costs incurred by the trustees shall be borne by either of the spouses or by both of them in such proportion and manner as the court determines. The court may make an order under s. 13 of the 1995 Act in addition to or in substitution for orders under ss. 8 to 11 of the 1995 Act, and in deciding whether or not to make such an order the court shall have regard to whether adequate and reasonable financial provision exists or can be made for the spouses concerned by orders under ss. 8 to 11 of the 1995 Act.

This section appears to refer specifically to pension schemes which contain a condition that the spouses should be living together at the time the relevant benefit becomes payable. Presumably, although it is not specifically mentioned in s. 13 of the 1995 Act, the court can make an order under s. 13 of the 1995 Act in addition to an order under s. 12 of the 1995 Act.

7.2.2 1995 ACT, S. 14

This section gives the court the power:

> *on granting a decree of judicial separation or at any time thereafter . . . on application to it on that behalf by either of the spouses concerned . . .* [to] *make an order extinguishing a share that either of the spouses would otherwise be entitled to in the estate of the other spouse as a legal right or on intestacy under the Act of 1965* [in certain circumstances].

One of the circumstances is that if the court is satisfied that:

> *adequate and reasonable financial provision exists or can be made under section . . . 11 . . . for the spouse whose succession rights are in question . . .*

In seeking to persuade a court to extinguish inheritance rights, a practitioner could present the court with the possibility of making a financial compensation order. To do so successfully the value of the inheritance rights would have to be assessed, or at least approximated. An order under the 1995 Act, s. 14 can only be made on the application of either of the spouses concerned, whereas an application for a financial compensation order can also be made by a person on behalf of a dependent member of the family.

7.2.3 CONCLUSION

Practitioners should make arrangements to be able to seek, at short notice, the advice of an appropriately qualified expert, such as an actuary, to assist them in making a presentation to the court for financial compensation orders.

It should be made possible, by rules of court, for an actuary's evidence to be presented in affidavit form.

7.3 Orders for Provision for Spouse Out of Estate of Other Spouse

The Family Law Act 1995, s. 15A (as inserted by the 1996 Act, s. 52) and the Family Law (Divorce) Act 1996, s. 18 govern orders for provision for a spouse out of the estate of the other spouse.

This section provides that where, following the grant of a decree of divorce, or following the grant of a decree of judicial separation, the court makes an order under the 1995 Act, s. 14 in relation to the spouse concerned (extinguishment of inheritance rights), and if one of the spouses dies, the court, on application to it in that behalf by the other spouse ('the applicant') not more than six months after representation is first granted under the Succession Act 1965 in respect of the estate of the deceased's spouse, may by order make such provision for the applicant out of the estate of the deceased spouse as it considers appropriate having regard to the rights of any other person having an interest in the matter if it is satisfied that proper provision in the circumstances was not made for the applicant during the lifetime of the deceased spouse under the 1995 Act, ss. 8, 9, 10(1)(a), 11 or 12 (or the 1996 Act, ss. 13, 14, 15, 16 or 17) for any reason (other than such conduct of that spouse which in the opinion of the court it would in all the circumstances of the case be unjust to disregard).

The court shall not make an order under this section if the applicant has remarried since the granting of the decree.

In considering whether to make an order the court shall have regard to all the circumstances including any lump sum order or property adjustment order made in favour of the applicant, and any devise or bequest made by the deceased spouse to the applicant.

The provision made for the applicant concerned under this section, together with any lump sum order or property adjustment order (valued at the date of the order) shall not exceed in total the share of the applicant in the estate of the deceased spouse to which the applicant was entitled or would have been entitled if there had not been an order under the 1995 Act, s. 14 or a decree of divorce. It is noteworthy that the 1995 Act, s. 15A only comes into operation where the court has made an order under s. 14 extinguishing inheritance rights. Thus, in the context only of a judicial separation, if inheritance rights have been waived otherwise than pursuant to the 1995 Act, s. 14 (and, of course, there must be a query over whether a person can waive their rights on a death intestate), the 1995 Act, s. 15A cannot come into operation. Section 15A of the 1995 Act is dependent on the 1995 Act, s. 14. However, the 1996 Act, s. 18, is not so dependent, and comes into operation where a decree of divorce has been granted. Presumably it overrides a renunciation under the Succession Act 1965, s. 113.

Notice of the application has to be given by the applicant to the spouse (if any) of the deceased spouse, and the court shall have regard to any representations made by the spouse of the deceased spouse and any other persons the court may direct.

The personal representative of the deceased shall make a reasonable attempt to ensure that notice of the death of the deceased spouse is brought to the attention of the other spouse, and where an application is made by the other spouse, the personal representative shall not, without the leave of the court, distribute the estate.

Where the personal representative has given notice of the death of the deceased to the other spouse concerned, and that spouse intends to apply to the court for an order under this section, or that spouse has applied for such an order and the application is pending, or an order has been made under this section in favour of that spouse, that spouse shall, not later than one month after the receipt of the notice, notify the personal representative of such intention, application or order as the case may be, and if he or she does not do so the personal representative may distribute the estate.

The 1995 Act, s. 15A(8) (1996 Act, s. 18(8)) provides that the personal representative shall not be liable to the spouse for the assets or any part thereof so distributed unless, at the time of such distribution, he or she had notice of the intention, application or order aforesaid.

A personal representative may be in a difficult position where he or she has not been able to find the surviving spouse and has to decide what is a 'reasonable attempt' to ensure that notice of the death is brought to the attention of the surviving spouse. The personal representative is certainly protected where notice of death is actually given to the surviving spouse (although the personal representative must be sure to be able to prove 'the receipt of the notice') but a personal representative would be in an invidious position if he or she knew of the existence or the possible existence of a surviving spouse, but could not serve notice on them. What is 'a reasonable attempt'?

On granting a decree, or at any time thereafter, the court, on application to it by either of the spouses concerned, may, during the lifetime of the other spouse, or as the case may be, the spouse concerned, if it considers it just to do so, make an order that either or both of the spouses shall not, on the death of either of them, be entitled to apply for orders under these sections.

7.4   Pension Adjustment Orders

7.4.1   GENERAL

Section 12 of the Family Law Act 1995 and s. 17 of the Family Law (Divorce) Act 1996 govern pension adjustment orders.

The benefits payable pursuant to a pension scheme are determined by the terms of the pension scheme and cannot be shared or interfered with by agreement between the member and the trustees of the pension scheme. In other words, the trustees who administer the pension scheme are bound by the terms thereof, irrespective of what the individual member wants. The individual member cannot change the terms of the pension scheme. Thus, for example, if a pension scheme provides that a pension is to be paid to the member's spouse when the member dies, there is nothing the member can do to deprive his or her spouse of that pension. It is therefore clear that separating spouses cannot, by means of a deed of separation, deprive one another of benefits under a pension scheme, or divide those benefits between them. A term in a deed of separation which purports to do either of these simply will not work.

If a member of a pension scheme wishes to have his or her views taken into account by the trustees of the scheme in the exercise of their discretion as to, for example, who should be regarded as a dependant on the death of the spouse who is a member of the scheme, the member can furnish the trustees with what has been loosely called a 'wishes letter' in which the member expresses his or her preferences to the trustees. If, however, the trustees have a discretion as to who to pay the benefit to, on the death of the member, they cannot allow their discretion to be fettered in any way.

Thus if the parties to a failed marriage resolve all of their differences by agreement they cannot have a retirement benefit or a contingent benefit to which either is entitled earmarked or split without an order of the court pursuant to the provisions of the 1995 Act, s. 12 (1996 Act, s. 17). These provisions are designed to give greater powers to the court to deal with the consequences of the breakdown of a marriage. An important new power given to the court is that of making a pension adjustment order pursuant to the 1995 Act, s. 12 (1996 Act, s. 17). This order is simply a further method whereby the court can ensure that adequate and proper provision is made for the spouses and dependent children of a marriage. Whether a pension order should be made, and its extent, must be viewed in the light of whether such proper provision can be made by the granting of other ancillary orders.

The 1995 Act, s. 12 (1996 Act, s. 17) brings into Irish law for the first time a procedure whereby a court may divide the benefits pursuant to a pension scheme between spouses. However it must be made absolutely clear that the 1995 Act, s. 12 (1996 Act, s. 17) can only be used as an ancillary order after the granting of a decree of judicial separation under the 1989 Act, s. 2, or a decree of divorce. Thus, where separating spouses intend to divide pension benefits they must not execute a deed of separation, because if they do so they will deprive the court of jurisdiction to make an order under the 1989 Act, s. 2, thus depriving the court of jurisdiction to make an ancillary order under the 1995 Act, s. 12. The recommended procedure is, therefore, for the separating spouses mutually to agree the terms upon which they are separating and then, if not already issued, proceedings should be issued under the 1989 Act whereupon a court settlement can be executed and an application made to the court to have the court settlement received and made enforceable and the relevant ancillary orders made by the court by consent.

As will be seen, the trustees of the pension scheme will have to be put on notice of the court application, and their costs paid by the spouses in such proportion as the court decides. The costs of the trustees will be minimised if their agreement is obtained in advance, and they do not have to be represented at the hearing. The recommended procedure is, therefore, for the form of the pension adjustment order to be agreed between the parties and the trustees of the pension scheme prior to the application being made to the court for the consent pension adjustment order.

It should also be noted that if spouses who have entered into a deed of separation subsequently become members of pension schemes (which they were not members of before the deed of separation), then under present legislation they cannot exclude each other from acquiring rights under the new pension scheme (because either could seek pension adjustment orders in divorce proceedings).

Section 12 of the 1995 Act (1996 Act, s. 17) applies to 'pension schemes'. In order to make a pension adjustment order the court will firstly require full details of the pension scheme and the trustees thereof. Practitioners will be familiar with the provisions of the Pensions Act 1990, s. 54, which requires trustees of occupational pension schemes to provide certain financial and other information about the scheme to, inter alia, members and their spouses.

The trustees of the scheme have a duty to furnish the following information to the members of the scheme and their spouses:

(1) the constitution of the scheme;

(2) the administration and finances of the scheme;

(3) the rights and obligations that arise or may arise under the scheme; and

(4) such other matters as may be prescribed by the Minister.

A weakness in s. 54, in the context of family law proceedings, is that it does not place the trustees under a duty to furnish details of the length of reckonable service of the member, or the value of his or her benefits.

Practitioners representing members' spouses will be able to use this section to obtain much information. The 1995 Act, s. 12(24) (1996 Act, s. 17(24)) provides that the Pensions Act 1990, s. 54, and any regulations made thereunder shall apply to a pension scheme if proceedings for a decree of judicial separation to which a member spouse is a party have been instituted, and shall continue to apply notwithstanding the grant of a decree of judicial separation. A practitioner's first step should therefore be to invoke the provisions of the Pensions Act 1990, s. 54, and obtain as much information as possible from the trustees.

7.4.2   DIFFERENT TYPES OF PENSION SCHEME

Pension schemes can be broken down into two categories:

(1) occupational pension schemes; and

(2) self-employed arrangements.

Occupational pension schemes are set up by employers to provide pension arrangements for their employees. They can in turn be broken down into two types:

(a) defined contribution schemes; and

(b) defined benefit schemes.

The distinction between these schemes is crucial to a proper understanding of the 1995 Act, s. 12 (1996 Act, s. 17), since the different types of scheme are treated in a different manner by that section.

The definition of 'pension scheme' (1995 Act, s. 2, 1996 Act, s. 2) not only refers to occupational pension schemes within the meaning of the Pensions Act 1990 which would include private occupational schemes and the Civil Service and semi-state schemes, but the 1995 and 1996 Acts also apply to:

any other scheme or arrangement (including a personal pension plan and a scheme or arrange-ment established by or pursuant to Statute or Instrument made under Statute other than under the

Social Welfare Acts) that provides or is intended to provide either or both of the following, that is to say

(i) Benefits for a person who is a member of the scheme or arrangement ('the member') upon retirement at normal pensionable age or upon earlier or later retirement or upon leaving or upon the ceasing of the relevant employment, or,

(ii) Benefits for the widow, widower or dependants of the member or for any other persons, on the death of the member.

Details of these latter schemes will have to be obtained by voluntary or compulsory discovery because s. 54 of the 1990 Act will not apply to them unless proceedings have been instituted under the 1995 Act, s. 12(24) (1996 Act, s. 17(24)). The Rules of the Circuit Court and of the Superior Courts provide that, where financial relief is being sought, pension details must be furnished in the affidavits of means. If at all possible pension details should be obtained prior to the issuing of proceedings so that the trustees of the relevant pension scheme can be given notice of the proceedings within the time limited by the Rules of Court after the institution of proceedings.

7.4.2.1   Defined contribution scheme

A defined contribution scheme is one where the employer, or both the employer and the employee, pay a defined percentage of the employee's salary into the scheme, to be invested by the trustees. The amount in the employee's pension account is then used at the date of retirement to purchase a pension for the employee, and the amount of the pension is clearly linked to the amount which is available to purchase it.

Self-employed arrangements are similar to defined contribution schemes except that the contributions to the scheme are made by the self-employed person only.

7.4.2.2   Defined benefit scheme

A defined benefit scheme is one in which a specific level of pension is promised to be paid by the employer to the employee at retirement, usually by reference to the salary at or near retirement and to the amount of service completed. The level of benefit is defined in advance and the employer, and in most cases the employee, must make sufficient contributions to ensure that the promised benefit can be paid at retirement. A defined benefit scheme usually operates on the basis that a person would get a particular fraction, usually 1/60th, of final pensionable salary for each year of reckonable service. For instance, a person who has worked 40 years would get 40/60ths (two-thirds) of his or her final pensionable salary. An example of a defined benefit scheme is the type of pension scheme operated in the Civil Service.

What benefits can be affected?

All benefits payable under a pension scheme can be the subject of pension adjustment orders. For the purposes of the Act, benefits are broken down into two categories:

(1)   retirement benefits; and

(2)   contingent benefits.

The Acts (1995 Act, s. 12, 1996 Act, s. 17) define 'contingent benefit' as:

a benefit payable under a scheme . . . to or for one or more of the following, that is to say the widow or the widower and any dependants of the member spouse concerned and the personal representative of the member spouse, if the member spouse dies while in relevant employment and before attaining any normal pensionable age provided for under the rules of the scheme.

Contingent benefits are often referred to as 'death in service' benefits.

'Relevant employment' means any employment or any period of self-employment to which a scheme applies.

7.4.2.3 Retirement benefit

Section 12 of the 1995 Act and s. 17 of the 1996 Act define 'retirement benefit' as 'all benefits (other than contingent benefits) payable under the scheme'. A retirement benefit would therefore cover the pension paid to a person who retires, or a pension payable to the widow or widower and any dependent member of the family on the death of the member after retirement. A pension payable to a spouse or dependant on the death of the member while in reckonable service is a 'contingent benefit'.

The importance of the distinction between 'retirement benefit' and 'contingent benefit' is that they are treated differently under the provisions of the 1995 Act, s. 12 (1996 Act, s. 17).

7.4.3 PENSION ADJUSTMENT

There are two basic concepts which are central to the operation of the 1995 Act, s. 12 (1996 Act, s. 17), namely 'ear-marking' and 'pension splitting'. Ear-marking means that a percentage of the whole or the part of a benefit should be paid directly to the other spouse or to another person for the benefit of a dependent member of the family. Ear-marking in respect of a 'retirement benefit' is provided for in the 1995 Act, s. 12(2) (1996 Act, s. 17(2)) and ear-marking in respect of a 'contingent benefit' is provided for under the 1995 Act, s. 12(3) (1996 Act, s. 17(3)). Orders made under the 1995 Act, s. 12(2) and (3) (1996 Act, s. 17(2) and (3)) are ear-marking orders and are called, in the Act, pension adjustment orders.

Pension splitting is a means whereby effect can be given to a pension adjustment order in respect of a 'retirement benefit' made under the 1995 Act, s. 12(2) (1996 Act, s. 17(2)). It has no relevance and no application to a pension adjustment order made in respect of a contingent benefit under s. 12(3) (1996 Act, s. 17(3)). Pension splitting means that a percentage of a 'retirement benefit' which has been ear-marked for the other spouse is valued and is used to provide a separate pension for the other spouse, either within the same pension scheme, or in another pension scheme, or by way of a bond. Pension splitting can come about in a number of ways, one of which is on foot of an application under the 1995 Act, s. 12(5) (1996 Act, s. 17(5)) by a spouse in respect of whom a pension adjustment order under the 1995 Act, s. 12(2) (1996 Act, s. 17(2)) has already been made.

7.4.3.1 1995 Act, s. 12(2); 1996 Act, s. 17(2)

Section 12(2) of the 1995 Act (1996 Act, s. 17(2)) provides that where a decree of judicial separation or divorce has been granted the court may, in relation to a retirement benefit under a pension scheme of which one of the spouses concerned is a member, on application being made at the time of the making of the decree or at any time thereafter during the lifetime of the member, by either of the spouses or by a person on behalf of a dependent member of the family, make an order providing for the payment of a benefit consisting of the whole, or a part, of that part of the retirement benefit that is payable under the scheme and has accrued at the time of the making of the decree.

The court may order the payment to be made either to the other spouse or to his or her personal representative, or to a person for the benefit of a dependent member of the family, but not to both.

A decree of judicial separation or divorce must have been granted.

The application may be made by either of the spouses (including the member) or by a person on behalf of a dependent member of the family.

The order may apply to the whole, or part, of the retirement benefit.

The payment can be made either to the other spouse or to his or her legal personal representative, or to a person on behalf of a dependent member of the family but not to both.

Pursuant to the 1995 Act, s. 12(23)(a) (1996 Act, s. 17(23)(a)) the court cannot make an order if the applicant spouse has remarried.

7.5 A Period and a Percentage

A pension adjustment order in respect of a retirement benefit can only be made in respect of the amount of the retirement benefit that has accrued up to the date of the decree of judicial separation or divorce. The order will specify two things:

(1) a period; and

(2) a percentage.

The period will be a period of reckonable service of the member prior to the granting of a decree of judicial separation or divorce.

The percentage will be a percentage of the amount of benefit accrued during the specified period of reckonable service which should be paid on foot of the order.

Reckonable service means service in relevant employment during membership of any scheme.

To take a practical example:

> If a member has been in the pension scheme for 20 years at the time of the grant of the decree of judicial separation the court could specify any period of time up to 20 years and any percentage of the retirement benefit accrued during that period. If, on this example, the court specified ten years and 50 per cent, then the person in whose favour the order is made would be entitled to receive 50 per cent of the retirement benefit which had accrued during the ten-year period, which, in a defined benefit scheme, would probably be 10/60ths, and the entitlement under the order would therefore be 5/60ths of the retirement benefit payable to the member. The part of the retirement benefit which is ear-marked for payment is called the 'designated benefit'.

The case of *J.C.N. v R.T.N.* (unreported, 15 January 1999, High Ct, McGuinness J) deals inter alia with the subject of pensions.

In that case the applicant wife sought a decree of divorce together with a number of ancillary orders including an order under s. 17(2) of the 1996 Act. The wife was 78 and the husband 74. The husband was retired and in receipt of a pension put in place by the Construction Industry Federation. The wife had no separate income. They were married in 1955 and they had two children born in 1956 and 1957. They entered into a deed of separation in 1975, in accordance with which the family home was sold and the proceeds divided. In addition, the wife received a lump sum of £30,000 together with some shares and a car. This was expressed as, and intended to be, a once-off final settlement.

The wife purchased a house for herself, but by 1980 she had exhausted the capital sum. The husband bought a house for himself also and in 1978 remarried in the Catholic Church. There had been no annulment of the original marriage. This second purported marriage had no legal validity.

In 1980, when the capital sum was exhausted, the wife brought maintenance proceedings and a consent order was made for £100.00 per week. Over the years further maintenance applications were made and in January 1999 the weekly maintenance was £211.08 per week. Neither of the children were dependent at the date of the judgment. The judge felt that the value of the wife's house was nearer to £225,000 than to the wife's estimate of £150,000.

The husband became registered as a member of the pension scheme in 1975, approximately the same time as he separated from the wife. All pension contributions were paid by his company, and the pension payable at his retirement at age 65 was to be two-thirds of his average salary over the three years immediately preceding retirement. No widow's pension was provided. In 1991 he paid a lump sum of £23,000 to enhance his existing pension benefits, just before he retired. The effect of this was that his personal pension was increased to £12,662.00 gross per year and a widow's pension became payable to his wife amounting to £8,442.00 per year, or £703.50 per month, in the event of his death in retirement.

The husband was enabled to do this by rule 10 of the scheme which provided that the scheme member could, subject to the consent of the trustees and the employer, arrange to provide a pension for a 'dependant' to commence after his death. This is what he did in 1991. At the date of the judgment the husband's pension had reached its maximum of £12,662.00 per year and would not increase further.

In addition to his pension the husband over the years had accumulated a considerable amount of capital. The present capital fund amounted to £170,000.00 from which the husband received deposit interest income of £5,440.00 per year. It was also possible that he might receive additional payments from the sale of land and stock, but the judge did not accept that this would make an appreciable difference to his annual income. His accountant projected that the husband would have an after-tax income of £15,846.00. His annual maintenance payments to his wife amounted to £10,400.00. The husband complained that his home was in very bad repair and valued it at £240,000, which the judge accepted. The judge also accepted that the husband was paying the maintenance partly out of capital. However, the judge made no change in the maintenance order but gave liberty to apply to either party once the taxation position became clear after the divorce decree was made. The court refused to make a lump sum order. The judge then went on:

> 'There remains the question of the wife's position should her husband pre-decease her. There is no doubt that this would leave her in a very precarious situation since the maintenance payments would cease on her husband's death and she has, by the separation deed, waived her rights under the Succession Act 1965.

> 'I appreciate that the husband built up the pension fund with a view to a pension being paid to his present partner. Nevertheless I must bear in mind not only the provisions of s. 5 of the 1996 Act but also the criteria set out in s. 20 of the Act. In particular in this case, I feel I must have regard to s. 20(2)(d) which refers to "the age of each of the spouses, the duration of their marriage and the length of time during which the spouses lived with one another". Mrs "N" is a lady of 78 years of age. She married the respondent 43 years ago and lived with him for some 20 years. It is clear that she is not able and will not be able to earn a living for herself. While this situation is far from satisfactory for any of the parties, I consider that some provision must be made for her out of the husband's pension fund. I will therefore order by way of pension adjustment order that, if the respondent pre-deceases the applicant, the trustees of the pension fund are to pay one-half of the annual pension, being a sum of £4,221.00 per annum, to Mrs "N", the applicant, the remaining half to be paid to [the second wife]. Should Mrs "N" pre-decease [the husband] the payment of the entire annual pension should revert to [the second wife].'

7.6   Contingent Benefit Under a Pension Scheme

In addition, the 1995 Act, s. 12(3) and the 1996 Act, s. 17(3) provide that where a decree of judicial separation or divorce has been granted the court may, in relation to a contingent benefit under a pension scheme of which one of the spouses concerned is a member, on application being made not more than one year after the making of the decree by either of the spouses or by a person on behalf of a dependent member of the family concerned, make an order providing for the payment, upon the death of the member spouse, of either the whole or a part of that part of any contingent benefit that is payable under the pension scheme in favour of the other spouse or in favour of a person for the benefit of a dependent member of the family, or both.

The order can be made both in favour of the other spouse and a person for the benefit of the dependent member of the family, or both.

It is assumed that a spouse can be a person in whose favour an order can be made for the benefit of the dependent member.

The order cannot be made in favour of a spouse who has remarried (1995 Act, s. 12(23)(a), 1996 Act, s. 17 (23)(a)).

An application for a pension adjustment order in respect of a contingent benefit may not be made after one year after the making of the decree.

An order under the 1995 Act, s. 12(3) (1996 Act, s. 17(3)) cannot be varied. It is not mentioned in s. 18(1) of the 1995 Act (1996 Act, s. 22(1)).

The question also arises as to whether more than one order can be made simultaneously against the same scheme under the 1995 Act, s. 12(2) (1996 Act, s. 17(2)). For example, can an order be made both against the respondent's personal pension, and against his widow's or dependant's pension arising on his death in retirement? In view of the wide definition of 'retirement benefit' it is felt by many practitioners that it is possible. Therefore, for example, an applicant might seek an order only against the widow's pension retirement benefit, and not against the member's retirement benefit. The question then arises whether these orders can be made against both the member's retirement benefit and the widow's pension retirement benefit. Expert opinion is divided as to whether this can be done. There would appear to be no reason why this cannot be done. However some practitioners feel that the period and the percentage must be the same, while others disagree. Judicial interpretation is necessary.

7.7   Nature and Effect of Pension Adjustment Order in Respect of Contingent Benefit

The order in respect of a contingent benefit will provide for a percentage of the benefit to be paid either to the other spouse or to another person for the benefit of a dependent member of the family or to both of them. If the payment is to be to both of them then the proportion which is to be paid to each must be specified by the court. A contingent benefit does not accrue with each year of service and the benefit is usually the same no matter how many years of service have been completed by the member. Therefore the court does not have to concern itself with how much benefit has accrued at the date of the decree of judicial separation, as it must do when it is dealing with a retirement benefit.

While an order under the 1995 Act, s. 12(3) (1996 Act, s. 17(3)) (relating to contingent benefits) shall cease to have effect on the death or remarriage of the spouse in whose favour it was made insofar as it relates to that spouse, a pension adjustment order under sub-s. (2) (in relation to retirement benefits) would appear to continue in force notwithstanding the remarriage of the dependent spouse, although, presumably, an application could be made by the respondent spouse under the 1995 Act, s. 18(2)(1996 Act, s. 22(2)) to have the pension adjustment order under sub-s. (2) varied or discharged, unless the court made an order under the 1995 Act, s. 12(26) (1996 Act, s. 17(26)) restricting or excluding the application of s. 18 of the 1996 Act. The 1995 Act, s. 12(26) (1996 Act, s. 17(26)) provides that an order under s. 12 may restrict or exclude the application of the 1995 Act, s. 18 (1996 Act, s. 22). Section 18 applies, inter alia, to orders under the 1995 Act, ss. 11, 12(2) and 13 (s. 22 applies inter alia to orders under the 1996 Act, ss. 16 and 17(2)).

7.8 Nominal Pension Adjustment Orders

The question sometimes arises as to how to ensure that neither spouse has any interest in the pension scheme of the other. This cannot be achieved by a waiver or disclaimer, but only by a form of pension adjustment order. For example, if the wife wants the husband to have no interest in her pension scheme, then they can agree to a nominal pension adjustment order being made. It appears that it is not possible to make a 'nil' pension adjustment order. A nominal pension adjustment order under the 1995 Act, s. 12(2) (1996 Act, s. 17(2)) would be, for example, for a period of one day, at the beginning of the period of reckonable service, and a percentage of .01 per cent. A nominal order under the 1995 Act, s. 12(3) (1996 Act, s. 17(3)) would be, for example, .01 per cent.

7.9 Variation of Pension Adjustment Order

Under the 1995 Act, s. 18(2) (1996 Act, s. 22(2)), the court may vary a pension adjustment order made under the 1995 Act, s. 12(2) i.e. retirement benefits (1996 Act, s. 17(2)), but there is no provision for a variation of an order made under the 1995 Act, s. 12(3) i.e. contingent benefits (1996 Act, s. 17(3)). However, under the 1995 Act, s. 12(26) (1996 Act, s. 17(26)) the court may restrict to a specified extent, or exclude, the application of the 1995 Act, s. 18 (1996 Act, s. 22) in regard to an order. Therefore a practitioner who is involved in a case where a pension adjustment order is granted pursuant to the 1995 Act, s. 12(2) (1996 Act, s. 17(2)) must give consideration as to whether the court should be asked to make an order restricting or excluding the provisions of the 1995 Act, s. 18 (1996 Act, s. 22), as in default of such restriction or exclusion the variation powers set out in the 1995 Act, s. 18(2) (1996 Act, s. 22(2)) continue to apply.

7.10 Pension Splitting

7.10.1 GENERALLY

Where the court makes an order in relation to a retirement benefit, payment of the part of the retirement benefit designated for the applicant would of course commence immediately if the designated retirement benefit had already commenced being paid to the member spouse; in other words in a situation where the member spouse had already retired.

Where payment of the designated benefit to the member spouse has not commenced, the applicant spouse has two options. He or she may either simply leave the part of the retirement benefit designated for him or her within the pension scheme, and the payment of the part of the member's pension which is designated to the dependent spouse will then be paid to him or her when the member's pension falls due. One could say, in this instance, that a portion of the pension has been ear-marked for the dependent spouse.

Alternatively the dependent spouse is entitled to have an amount of money from the scheme concerned (called a 'transfer amount') equal to the value of the designated benefit applied in accordance with the 1995 Act, s. 12(5) (1996 Act, s. 17(5)).

The 1995 Act, s. 12(5) (1996 Act, s. 17(5)) provides that where the court has made an order under 1995 Act, s. 12(2) (1996 Act, s. 17(2)) and payment of the designated benefit concerned has not commenced the trustees shall, when application is made to them by the dependent spouse, apply, in accordance with relevant guidelines, the transfer amount either:

(a) if the trustees and the spouse so agree, in providing a benefit for the dependent spouse under the same scheme that is of the same actuarial value as the transfer amount concerned; or

(b) at the determination of the dependent spouse, to a different occupational pension scheme, for example a scheme of which the dependent spouse is already a member, or, in making a payment into what is called 'an approved arrangement' which means an arrangement whereby the trustees effect policies or contracts of insurance that are approved of by the Revenue Commissioners. Where a transfer amount is applied under the 1995 Act, s. 12(5) (1996 Act, s. 17(5)) one could say that this is a form of 'pension splitting' where the benefit designated in favour of the dependent spouse has been split away from the retirement benefit of the member of the pension scheme.

Only a spouse can apply, and the application cannot be made by another person in whose favour a pension adjustment order has been made for the benefit of a dependent member of the family.

7.10.2 WHEN AN APPLICATION FOR PENSION SPLITTING CAN BE MADE

A spouse who has obtained a pension adjustment order in respect of a retirement benefit can apply to the trustees for pension splitting at any time from the date of such order until the date of the commencement of the payment of the designated benefit, that is, his or her part of the retirement benefit. The spouse making the application must furnish to the trustees such information as they may reasonably require (1995 Act, s. 12(5), 1996 Act, s. 17(5)).

7.10.2.1 Obligations of the trustees on receipt of such an application

The trustees must value the percentage of the retirement benefit which has been ear-marked under the order for payment to the applicant spouse. This is likely to be straightforward in the case of a defined contribution scheme where the value of the member's contributions up to a particular date is readily ascertainable. However the valuation is likely to be much more difficult in the case of a defined benefit scheme where the value of the percentage ear-marked for the applicant spouse is linked to the salary which the member will be receiving at or about the date of retirement. Such valuation is to be made having regard to relevant guidelines issued under the Pensions (Amendment) Act 1996, see SI 64/1997. Once the value has been ascertained this figure is what is called the 'transfer amount' (1995 Act, s. 12(4), (5), 1996 Act, s. 17(4), (5)).

Once the transfer amount has been ascertained, the trustees have two options. First, if they and the applicant spouse both agree, the trustees can hold the transfer amount within the scheme to provide a separate benefit for the spouse of an amount actuarially linked to the amount transferred. Secondly, the trustees can pay the transfer amount to another pension scheme, provided that the trustees of the receiving scheme are willing to accept it, or they may make a payment to such other approved arrangement as may be determined by the spouse. This arrangement could be by way of a buy-out bond provided by a life assurance company (1995 Act, s. 12(5), 1996 Act, s. 17(5)).

7.10.2.2 Pension splitting other than on application by a spouse

There are a number of circumstances which can bring about a form of pension splitting other than on foot of an application by a spouse who has obtained a pension adjustment order.

(a) The exercise of discretion by the trustees

When a court makes an order under the 1995 Act, s. 12(2) (1996 Act, s. 17(2)) in respect of a defined contribution scheme, and an application has not been brought by the other spouse for pension splitting, the trustees have a discretion to split the pension and to transfer the relevant transfer amount into another pension fund, where the trustees of that fund are willing to accept such a transfer, or they may pay such amount to another approved arrangement. The trustees choose the scheme or the assurance company which is to receive the transfer amount. The transfer is to be in accordance with the guidelines issued under the Pensions (Amendment) Act 1996, and these guidelines include provisions to prevent such a transfer into a pension scheme where higher fees or management charges are applicable.

Remember that trustees do not enjoy any discretion to exercise such a transfer in regard to a designated benefit payable under a pension adjustment order in respect of a defined benefit scheme (1995 Act, s. 12(6), 1996 Act, s. 17(6)).

(b) Death of a member spouse before the ear-marked benefit commences to be paid

When a pension adjustment order has been made in respect of a retirement benefit under the 1995 Act, s. 12(2) or the 1996 Act, s. 17(2) and the member dies before the payment of the designated benefit has commenced, the trustees of the scheme must for the purposes of giving effect to the order, within three months of the date of death, transfer to the person in whose favour the order is made an amount equivalent to the transfer amount (1995 Act, s. 12(7), 1996 Act, s. 17(7)). However in such a case the amount of contingent benefit payable in respect of the member under the rules of the scheme shall be reduced by the amount of the transfer amount (1995 Act, s. 12(16)(b), 1996 Act, s. 17(16)(b)). This reduction would not appear to be applicable to a contingent benefit which is payable pursuant to a pension adjustment order made under the 1995 Act, s. 12(3) or the 1996 Act, s. 17(3), as opposed to one made pursuant to the rules of the scheme.

(c) The cessation of membership of the scheme otherwise than on death

If the member ceases to be a member of the scheme, otherwise than on death, the trustees have a discretion to give effect to a pension adjustment order in a number of different ways. They can value the designated benefit and convert it into a transfer amount which they retain in the scheme to pay a separate benefit which is actuarially linked to the extent of the transfer amount. Alternatively they can make a payment of the transfer amount to another pension scheme, where the trustees of that scheme are willing to accept such amount, or they can make a payment into another approved arrangement, for example to a life assurance office by way of a buy-out bond. The option as to which course of action to take is at the discretion of the trustees (1995 Act, s. 12(8), 1996 Act, s. 17(8)).

(d) The recipient spouse dies before the commencement of the payment of the ear-marked benefit

Where a pension adjustment order has been made pursuant to the 1995 Act, s. 12(2) or the 1996 Act, s. 17(2) and the recipient spouse dies prior to the commencement of the designated benefit, the trustees are obliged to pay an amount equivalent to the transfer amount to the personal representative of the deceased spouse within three months of the date of death (1995 Act, s. 12(9)). However it should be noted that a pension adjustment order made under the 1995 Act, s. 12(3) (1996 Act, s. 17(3)) in respect of a contingent benefit ceases to have effect on the death or remarriage of the person in whose favour it was made, insofar as it relates to that person (1995 Act, s. 12(19), 1996 Act, s. 17(19)).

(e) The recipient spouse dies after commencement of payment of designated benefit

Where a spouse who has obtained a pension adjustment order under the 1995 Act, s. 12(2) (1996 Act, s. 17(2)) dies after the commencement of the payment of the designated benefit the trustees must within three months of the date of death pay to his or her personal representative an amount equal to the actuarial value, calculated in accordance with the relevant guidelines, of that part of the designated benefit which, but for the death of the recipient spouse, would have been payable to that spouse during the lifetime of the member spouse (1995 Act, s. 12(10), 1996 Act, s. 17(10)).

(f) The dependent member dies before the commencement of the payment of a designated benefit

Where a court makes a pension adjustment order in favour of a person for the benefit of the dependent member of the family pursuant to the 1995 Act, s. 12(2) (1996 Act, s. 17(2)) and the dependent member dies before the commencement of the payment of the designated benefit, the order ceases to have any effect in regard to the deceased dependant (1995 Act, s. 12(11), 1996 Act, s. 17(11)).

7.11 Information in Relation to Value of Retirement or Contingent Benefits

In deciding whether to make a pension adjustment order, and its nature and extent, the court will require information in regard to the value of the particular retirement or contingent benefit. In some cases it may be possible to obtain such information by simply writing to the trustees of the scheme under s. 54 of the Pensions Act 1990. However, if the necessary information is not obtained in this way, the 1995 Act, s. 12(25) (1996 Act, s. 17(25)) permits a court, of its own motion, or if so requested by either of the spouses or any other person concerned, to direct the trustees to provide certain information within a specified period. That information is the value and amount, determined in accordance with the relevant guidelines, of the retirement benefit that is payable under the scheme, and which has accrued at the time of the making of the order, and the amount of the contingent benefit that is payable under the scheme.

The 1995 Act, s. 12(25) (1996 Act, s. 17(25)) is useful in that it provides that the court may, of its own motion, or if requested by either of the spouses or any other person concerned, direct the trustees to provide the following:

(a) a calculation of the value and the amount of the retirement or contingent benefit concerned that is payable under the scheme and has accrued at the time of making of the order; and

(b) a calculation of the amount of the contingent benefit concerned that is payable under the scheme.

Although trustees should presumably give this information without the necessity of a formal order under the 1995 Act, s. 12(25) (1996 Act, s. 17(25)) it would appear from the Act that even if trustees unreasonably delayed in furnishing the information they would still be entitled to their costs under the provisions of the 1995 Act, s. 12(22) (1996 Act, s. 17(22)).

7.12   Notification to Trustees

There is an obligation to give notice to the trustees when certain applications are being brought under the 1995 Act, s. 12 (1996 Act, s. 17). This notice must be given when applications for orders are being brought under either the 1995 Act, s. 12(2) or (3) (1996 Act, s. 17(2) or (3)). Further notice must be given if a variation order is sought in respect of a pension adjustment order made in respect of a retirement benefit under the 1995 Act, s. 12(2) (1996 Act, s. 17(3)). In cases where it is obligatory to give notice to the trustees the court in deciding whether to make the order concerned, and in determining the provisions of the order, shall have regard to any representations that are made by the person to whom notice has been given.

Not every pension scheme will have trustees; for example, the Civil Service and semi-state schemes. However, because of the wide definition of the word 'trustees' in s. 12 of the 1995 Act in relation to a pension scheme which is not established under a trust, 'trustees' means the persons who administer the scheme.

7.13   Trustees' Costs

Any costs incurred by the trustees of a scheme by reason of:

(a)   receiving notification of an application; or

(b)   making representations in respect of an application; or

(c)   complying with the terms of a pension adjustment order; or

(d)   complying with the terms of a direction made for the purposes of a pension adjustment order; or

(e)   providing information as to the value of a benefit,

must be borne by the member or the other person concerned or both of them in such proportion as may be determined by the court, and in the absence of any such determination the costs shall be borne by them equally. Therefore it is important to obtain a determination as to who should bear the costs of the trustees, as in default of such determination the costs are born equally.

7.14   Other Costs

The trustees may decide to appear if the order sought is likely to involve additional costs for the scheme, so that the trustees can ensure that the spouses understand that there are additional costs and that they will have to bear these. Trustees may also wish to appear if they feel that a pension adjustment order is unnecessary because, for example, the value of the pension benefit is small and the cost of administering the order would not be justified. The 1995 Act, s. 12(22) provides that any costs incurred by trustees under s. 12(18) or in complying with a pension adjustment order or a direction under s. 12(20) or s. 12(25) shall be borne either by the member spouse or by the applicant or by both of them in such proportion as the court may determine. An order under s. 12(20) is basically an order giving the trustees such directions as the court thinks appropriate for the purposes of the pension adjustment order including directions which would involve non-compliance with the rules of the scheme concerned. The equivalent provisions are contained in the 1996 Act, s. 17.

7.15   Interaction with Other Family Assets

Will a court always, or usually, make a pension adjustment order? A court in deciding whether to make an order pursuant to s. 12 of the 1995 Act (1996 Act, s. 17), and in determining the provisions of the order, shall endeavour to ensure that such provision is made for each spouse concerned and for any dependent member of the family concerned as is adequate and reasonable having regard to all the circumstances (1995 Act, s. 16(1), 1996 Act, s. 20(1)).

Practitioners should note the substantial importance of s. 12(23)(b) of the 1995 Act (1996 Act, s. 17(23)(b)) which provides that the court may make a pension adjustment order in addition to or in substitution in whole or in part for orders under ss. 8, 9, 10 or 11 of the Family Law Act 1995 (1996 Act, ss. 13, 14, 15 and 16), and, in deciding whether or not to make the pension adjustment order, the court must have regard to the question of whether adequate and reasonable financial provision exists or can be made for the spouse concerned or the dependent member of the family concerned by orders under ss. 8, 9, 10 or 11 of the 1995 Act (1996 Act, ss. 13, 14, 15 or 16).

Section 8 of the 1995 Act (1996 Act, s. 13) refers to periodical payments orders, secured periodical payments orders, and lump sum orders.

Section 9 of the 1995 Act (1996 Act, s. 14) refers to property adjustment orders.

Section 10 of the 1995 Act (1996 Act, s. 15) refers to miscellaneous ancillary orders such as exclusion orders, orders directing the sale of the family home, orders under s. 36 of the 1995 Act (which replaced the Married Women's Status Act 1957, s. 12), and orders under the Family Home Protection Act 1976, the Family Law Act 1981, the Partition Acts 1868–1876 and the Guardianship of Infants Act 1964.

Thus, the court must first look at the possibility of making adequate and reasonable financial provision for the spouse concerned or the dependent members of the family by orders under ss. 8, 9, 10, or 11 of the 1995 Act (1996 Act, ss. 13, 14, 15 and 16) and only if such provision cannot be made, should the court embark on the consideration of making a pension adjustment order. As the making of a pension adjustment order can potentially be very complicated and costly, practitioners should, if possible, try to agree on the division of the family assets in such a way that a pension adjustment arrangement will not be necessary.

Practitioners must, therefore, carefully assess all of the family assets to see if adequate provision can be made under the 1995 Act, ss. 8 to 11 (1996 Act, ss. 13 to 16) before asking the court to make a pension adjustment order, because it is believed that a pension adjustment order could be a great deal more complicated than orders under, for example, ss. 8 to 11 (1996 Act, ss. 13 to 16).

When practitioners have obtained the necessary information about the pension scheme in question they will have to consider taking expert advice on the type of pension adjustment order to seek. This will depend on such things as the age of the spouses, the length of reckonable service, the length of the marriage and the length of time the spouses lived together, and of course the age of any dependent members of the family. Judges could not be expected to make pension adjustment orders without expert evidence, particularly in the light of the provisions of the 1995 Act, s. 12(2) (1996 Act, s. 17(2)) which state that the pension adjustment order under that section must specify the period of reckonable service of the member spouse prior to the granting of the decree and the percentage of the retirement benefit accrued during that period to be paid to the applicant or the dependent family member.

7.16 Notice to Trustees

Practitioners will have to be aware that it is provided under the 1995 Act, s. 12(18) that when an application is made under s. 12(2) or (3) or under s. 18(2) for the variation or discharge of an order under s. 12(2) the applicant must give notice of the application to the trustees of the scheme concerned and the court must have regard to any representation made by the trustees. The equivalent provisions are contained in the 1996 Act, s. 17(18). The pension scheme trust deed may provide an address for service of notices on the trustees, but, if there is no such provision, notice will have to be served on the trustees at their addresses as set out in the deed. The trustees may decide to appear at the hearing of the application and make representations. This will of course add to the costs of the proceedings. Practitioners should therefore, if at all possible, make contact well in advance of the hearing date with the trustees to ascertain any concerns the trustees might have and to allay these concerns. Obviously, the simplest approach would be for the spouses to agree the format of the pension adjustment order and get the trustees' agreement also. This would minimise costs. However, as we do not live in an ideal world, there will be cases where spouses will not agree or the concerns of the trustees will not be allayed and they will have to appear in the proceedings.

7.17 Expert Assistance

Practitioners would also have to obtain expert advice as to whether the applicant should leave the benefit designated by the pension adjustment order within the scheme, or apply under the 1995 Act, s. 12(5) (1996 Act, s. 17(5)) to have the designated benefit split from the member's benefit. If it is decided that it will be to the applicant's benefit to have the designated benefit split from the member's benefit then a formal application under the 1995 Act, s. 12(5) (1996 Act, s. 17(5)) may be made to the trustees at the time of the making of the order or at any time thereafter to have the split arranged in accordance with this sub-section.

7.18 Directions

A court may give such directions as it considers appropriate for the purposes of a pension adjustment order, including directions, compliance with which causes non-compliance with the rules of the scheme concerned, or the Pensions Acts 1990–1996. In such circumstances the trustee of a scheme shall not be liable in any court or other tribunal for any loss or damage caused by non-compliance with the rules of the scheme or the Pensions Acts, if such non-compliance was caused by his or her compliance with the direction.

7.19 Service of Order on Trustees

The 1995 Act, s. 12(21) (1996 Act, s. 17(21)) provides that the Registrar or clerk of the court concerned shall cause a copy of the pension adjustment order to be served on the trustees of the pension scheme concerned.

7.20   Conclusion

It will be clear from the above that practitioners should carefully consider the provisions of each pension scheme concerned and of the 1995 Act, s. 12 (1996 Act, s.17) before seeking a pension adjustment order as ancillary relief to an application for a decree of judicial separation or divorce. Although this new concept in Irish law contains complicated aspects with which practitioners have not been accustomed to cope until now, it is believed that the pension adjustment order will be a valuable asset for dependent spouses, particularly with the arrival of divorce.

7.21   Checklist

(With acknowledgement to Gerard Durcan S.C.)

1. Ascertain the extent of the assets and in particular whether either of the parties is a member of a pension scheme. If so, consider whether adequate and suitable provision for either of the spouses or for any dependent member of the family may require the making of a pension adjustment order.

2. If a pension adjustment order may be an appropriate option, then obtain a copy of the deed of trust and of the rules governing the pension scheme, and a copy of any explanatory booklet in regard to the scheme, if one is available. If necessary, invoke the provisions of s. 54 of the Pensions Act 1990 to obtain such information.

3. Obtain from the trustees, if necessary with the consent of the other side, details of the value of any retirement benefit which has accrued under the scheme and also of the amount of any contingent benefit that is payable.

4. Consider whether it is appropriate in the light of such information to seek a pension adjustment order either in respect of a 'retirement benefit' or a 'contingent benefit' or both. If necessary obtain the advice of a pension expert at this stage. Note that even if appearing for a respondent it may be appropriate to seek a pension adjustment order, together with an order under the 1995 Act, s. 12(26) (1996 Act, s. 17(26)) restricting or excluding the application of the provisions of the 1995 Act, s. 18 (1996 Act, s. 22).

5. Include a claim for a pension adjustment order or orders as appropriate in the endorsement of claim. Be careful to ensure that the pleadings accurately indicate exactly what claim is being made.

6. Consider whether it is necessary to bring an application pursuant to the 1995 Act, s. 12(25) (1996 Act, s. 17(25)) to obtain information from the trustees with regard to the value of any retirement benefit or the amount payable under the scheme by way of contingent benefit, and, if appropriate, bring an application pursuant to the 1995 Act, s. 12(25) (1996 Act, s. 17(25)) by way of notice of motion.

7. Remember that the person seeking a pension adjustment order will have to pay the costs of the trustees in such proportions as may be directed by the court or, if no direction is made, equally. Therefore, bringing an unnecessary application for a pension adjustment order can result in running up unneeded costs.

8. Ensure that the court has before it proof of the information which it will require to decide whether a pension adjustment order is to be made. Such information will include the period of reckonable service of the member spouse, the amount and value of retirement benefit which has accrued up to the date of the decree of judicial separation and the amount of any contingent benefit payable under the terms of the scheme.

9. Arrangements should be made to call a pension expert to give evidence to enable the court to decide whether a pension adjustment order should be made and if so what would be the effect of an order in particular terms.

10. Ensure that the court, if it decides to make a pension adjustment order under sub-s. (2), makes it in the appropriate format, that is, specifying the period of reckonable service of the member spouse prior to the granting of the decree to be taken into account, and the percentage of the retirement benefit accrued during that period to be paid. Also make sure that the court directs to whom the payment should be made, whether the other spouse, and in the case of death, his or her personal representatives, or such person as may be specified in the order for the benefit of a dependent member of the family.

11. Consideration should be given as to whether it is an appropriate case to seek to restrict or exclude the application of the 1995 Act, s. 18 (1996 Act, s. 22) in relation to the terms of the order. Remember that under the 1995 Act, s. 18(2) (1996 Act, s. 22(2)(a)) a variation order can be made in respect of a pension adjustment order made in respect of a 'retirement benefit' under sub-s. (2), unless the operation of that section is restricted or excluded under the 1995 Act, s. 12(26) (1996 Act, s. 17(26)).

12. Consideration should be given as to whether it is necessary to seek any directions for the purposes of the pension adjustment order including directions, compliance with which occasions non-compliance with the rules of the scheme concerned or the Pensions Act 1990. If appropriate such directions should be sought.

13. If a spouse obtains a pension adjustment order in respect of a 'retirement benefit' under sub-s. (2) of each Act consideration should be given as to whether the spouse should apply to the trustees to have the pension split pursuant to sub-s. (5) of each Act and if so what would be the optimum time to make such an application. This will involve consideration of whether it would be better to wait until near the date of retirement to have the pension split, in particular in the case of a defined benefit scheme.

14. If a decree of judicial separation has been obtained and no pension adjustment order in respect of a 'contingent benefit' has been obtained pursuant to sub-s. (3) then it would be important to consider whether such an application should be brought by either spouse since any such application must be brought within a year of the date of the decree of judicial separation.

15. In a case where a pension adjustment order is made in respect of a 'retirement benefit' pursuant to sub-s. (2) of each Act explain to the client that in the absence of an application under sub-s. (5) of each Act for pension splitting the trustees have a discretion as to what they may do for the purpose of giving effect to the order and explain what options are available to the trustees under sub-s. (6) of each Act.

16. Indicate to the client that the 1995 Act, s. 12 and the 1996 Act, s. 17 make provisions for contingencies which may occur, such as the death of the member of the scheme, the member leaving the scheme, the death of the person to whom the designated benefit is payable prior to the commencement of such designated benefit, the death of the person to whom such designated benefit is payable after the commencement of such designated benefit and the death of a dependent member of the family to whose benefit a pension adjustment order has been made.

17. Consideration should also be given as to whether it is necessary to seek an order under s. 13 of the 1995 Act directing the trustees not to regard the separation of the spouses resulting from the decree of judicial separation as a ground for disqualifying the other spouse from the receipt of a benefit under the scheme, a condition for the receipt of which is that the spouses should be residing together at the time the benefit becomes payable.

7.22 Cases

(With acknowledgement to Ciara Matthews, Solicitor)

7.22.1 CASE NOTE 1

Re *B v B*

Circuit Court order dated 2 July 1999.

Before Murphy J.

Facts

The husband sought a decree of divorce. The husband and wife had married on 30 March 1964 and had five children, none of whom were dependent at the date of the institution of the proceedings. One child suffered from Asperger's syndrome (a mild form of autism) and the wife claimed in her defence and counterclaim that he was dependent.

The parties separated in or around 1985 and entered into a deed of separation on 20 October 1989 wherein the following was agreed:

1. The family home was transferred to the wife.

2. A sum of £3,000 was paid by the husband in respect of the expenses arising on the transfer of the property and the remainder paid to the wife to enable her to decorate the exterior of the family home.

3. The husband redeemed the mortgage on the family home.

4. Both parties renounced their rights pursuant to the Succession Act 1965 with the proviso as follows:

    'Provided however that the husband shall ensure that the monthly pension entitlement payable in the event of his death shall be paid to the wife with any lump sum so payable specifically excluded from this Agreement'.

5. The husband agreed to pay to the wife a sum of £750 per month for her maintenance, to be increased in accordance with the Consumer Price Index.

6. The parties elected for joint assessment in relation to income tax.

7. The husband continued to pay VHI Plan level B for the wife and all the children, to cease upon each child ceasing to be a dependant.

8. The husband also agreed to discharge all reasonable accommodation costs, fees, books, tuition, etc., in relation to third level education save in respect of one of the children.

9. The wife retained all of the contents of the family home save for certain personal items, books, records and two paintings which the husband was to retain.

10. The husband agreed to pay the stamp duty payable on the execution of the deed of separation.

After the parties separated, the wife sold the family home and purchased smaller accommodation in which she was residing as of the date of the proceedings. The husband had purchased accommodation jointly with his new partner, worth approximately £150,000.

The husband was employed as a company secretary in a large corporation with earnings of approximately £80,000 gross per annum (inclusive of bonus). His other assets were savings and investments of approximately £32,000 and shares worth approximately £124,000 together with further share options in a company. He had liabilities of approximately £7,000.

The husband's pension allowed for retirement at 60 or 65 years of age. The current transfer value of the pension, as at the institution of the proceedings, amounted to approximately £360,000 and there were retirement, as well as contingent, benefits payable.

The wife in her defence acknowledged that she enjoyed a reasonably adequate lifestyle. She sought by way of counterclaim, periodical payment orders (pursuant to s. 13 of the 1996 Act) for both herself and one of the children who she claimed was dependent. She also sought lump sums for herself and that child and transfers of property for her own benefit and that of the 'dependent' child. She sought an order pursuant to s. 16 for a financial compensation order and orders pursuant to s. 17(2) and (3).

The wife had savings of approximately £10,500, together with a property worth approximately £150,000. She also acknowledged that she was owed a sum of £15,000 by her children in respect of a loan given to them. She acknowledged receiving maintenance from the applicant in the sum of approximately £930 per month (being the sum agreed in the separation agreement as index-linked) together with a small income from a craft business operated by her of approximately £80 per month. Her only debts amounted to £1,000 approximately.

The disparity between her income and her stated outgoings was approximately £30.25 per week. The husband commenced pensionable service in 1968 and had completed 31 years of service up to the date of the proceedings. If he were to remain in service until aged 65 he would have 38 years reckonable service. The benefits payable at normal retirement age (65) were:

1. Pension of £46,516 per annum (or £37,794 per annum if he retired at age 60) or a lump sum of £104,662 and a reduced pension of £36,255 per annum.

2. If the husband died after retirement a pension of £23,258 per annum would be payable to the surviving spouse.

3. On death in service there would be a lump sum payable of £220,341 to the husband's dependants and a pension of £23,258 per annum to the surviving spouse for the remainder of the spouse's lifetime or, if no spouse, a pension for the dependants.

4. 'Dependants' was defined in the scheme as:

   (a) a member's spouse;

   (b) a member's child aged under 18 or in full-time education or mentally or physically handicapped; or

   (c) any person who, immediately prior to the member's death, was wholly or partly dependent on the member for the provision of the ordinary necessaries of life.

5. The definition of 'spouses' in the rules of the scheme was 'a person with whom the husband was married before aged 60 and before retiring'.

A pensions expert was retained on behalf of the husband, who liaised with the trustees of the pension scheme. The wife also engaged a pensions adviser.

The husband was willing to secure the wife's maintenance on his death either in service or in retirement by way of a pension adjustment order. However, when the parties could not agree the percentages of the various pension adjustment orders to be made the matter fell to the court to be determined.

Orders

Having considered the evidence, the court made the following orders:

1. Decree of divorce.

2. Increase of maintenance to £15,000 gross per annum.

3. The husband to pay the wife's VHI.

4. The court had heard evidence from the pensions experts of the husband and the wife. The husband's pension expert noted that if the reckonable period to be specified by the court in granting an order under s. 17(2) was to be from commencement of the scheme in March 1968 to the date of the order (June 1999) a percentage of 33 per cent of the accrued retirement benefit would preserve the current maintenance payable to the wife. The husband had also given evidence that he was agreeable to the wife obtaining 33 per cent of the contingent lump sum and 70 per cent of the contingent spouse's pension payable on his death before retirement.

   However, if the husband were to die after retiring, the pension to the wife, under the rules of the scheme, would be halved. He suggested that the wife could, following the order being made by the court, ask the trustees to grant her a pension in her own right (which he calculated would be approximately the same actual value of the benefit which she would otherwise obtain) amalgamating the three benefits which she would receive into one (with no contingencies). (The pension expert was an actuary also, which was important.)

   What this would mean was that the accrued retirement benefit, the contingent lump sum benefit and the contingent spouse's pension would all be valued by the trustees and one pension, payable for the wife's life only (and not linked in any way to the husband's life) would be effected thus guaranteeing her income in the future even after the husband's death.

What is important here is the provisions contained in s. 12(5) of the 1995 Act and s. 17(5) of the 1996 Act:

> *if the* trustees and the spouse *so agree, the trustees can apply (in accordance with the relevant guidelines) the transfer amount (calculated in accordance with those guidelines) either in providing a benefit for or in respect of the spouse under the scheme that is of the same actuarial value of the transfer amount concerned or make a payment to such other occupational scheme as may be determined by the spouse. Had the trustees been in court to advise the court that, should the wife apply to have the transfer amount calculated and transferred to a pension in her own right within the same scheme [in this case it was a very favourable scheme] they would allow her to do so and would exercise their discretion accordingly.*

The ultimate orders made by the court were as follows:

4a. In relation to the contingent lump sum payable on the death before retirement of the husband, 33 per cent of same to the wife (s. 17(3)).

4b. In respect of the contingent spouse's pension payable on the death before retirement of the husband, 70 per cent of same (s. 17(3)) (Note that no reckonable period is specified in this order.)

4c. In respect of the accrued retirement benefits payable to the husband:

   38 per cent of same and the reckonable period was from the commencement of the member in the scheme (March 1968) to the date of the order (June 1999) (s. 17(2)).

To overcome the decrease in the wife's income should the husband predecease her post-retirement (and thereafter her income be halved) the court directed that the husband arrange that the wife would receive a sum of £20,000 in compensation (to be left in the most tax-efficient way for the husband). The court noted that the wife would be in receipt of a State pension. The court recommended to the wife that she approach the trustees of the husband's pension scheme and ask them to convert the pension benefits (the three of them) into a single life benefit. Finally the court directed that, should the wife predecease the husband, one-quarter of the lump sum to be paid to the wife's estate (pursuant to the benefits obtained under the pension scheme her pension would also pay a lump sum on her death) should revert to the husband.

This was a very complex situation which was dealt with on a very practical level by the judge.

Unfortunately, the case was appealed by the respondent wife to the High Court which then settled on the basis that the husband pay a contribution towards the wife's legal costs of £6,000 (compared to £3,000 ordered by the court).

7.22.2 CASE NOTE 2

Re *M v M*

30 July 1999.

Before Buckley J, Circuit Court.

Facts

The wife was the respondent in divorce proceedings instituted by her husband. The parties had married in June 1961 and had four children all of whom were dependent as at the date of the institution of the proceedings. The parties had entered into a deed of separation in 1984 in which it was agreed that:

1. The husband would pay to the wife the sum of £725 maintenance per month. Unusually, there was no provision made in the deed of separation for an increase in accordance with the Consumer Price Index.

2. The parties had elected for separate assessment for income tax purposes.

3. The husband agreed to transfer to the wife his interest in the family home in consideration of the wife surrendering her interest, as a joint tenant, in lands in County Wicklow and in consideration of her waiving her succession rights.

4. The wife agreed to take over the mortgage on the family home.

5. The husband agreed to continue to insure the property after it was transferred to the wife.

6. The husband agreed to continue to insure the wife and the children with VHI and pay any difference between hospital bills or doctors' fees in relation to the wife and the children exceeding the sum recoverable from the VHI.

7. The husband agreed to pay to the wife a sum of £750 to redecorate and refurbish the family home.

8. Both parties waived their inheritance rights pursuant to the Succession Act 1965.

9. The husband was to pay a portion of the wife's legal costs.

After the transfer of the family home to the wife it was subsequently sold by her in or around 1991 and she moved to the countryside and purchased alternative property. The wife was not in any employment either during the marriage or after the marriage and separation.

The husband (applicant) had his own business from which he was retired as of the date of the institution of proceedings although he continued to carry out some consultancy work. He resided in a property held in the joint names of himself and his partner, worth approximately £300,000. The husband had a child by that new relationship who was a dependant.

The husband sought a decree of divorce and an order pursuant to s. 18(10) of the 1996 Act.

The husband in his affidavit of means disclosed assets of a joint interest in his home worth approximately £300,000 with his new partner, an apartment in Spain, shares to the value of approximately £90,000, monies in a bank account in the sum of approximately £240,000 and other small savings of approximately £10,000. He disclosed a pension income of £59,000 approximately receivable from Equitable Life Assurance Society. He also was in receipt of approximately £30,000 gross in respect of his consultancy work. His outgoings amounted to approximately £4,000 per month.

The wife on the other hand had assets consisting only of her home, worth approximately £125,000, and no savings whatsoever. The wife's income was solely the maintenance received from the husband in the sum of £8,700 net per annum or £725 net per month. She had debts of approximately £2,000 and her outgoings amounted to £312 per week approximately. The wife had no pension. A notice to trustees was served on Equitable Life, the trustees of the husband's pension, by the wife. The wife sought a decree of divorce together with ancillary relief including periodical payment orders, lump sum orders, property adjustment orders, pension adjustment orders pursuant to s. 17(2) and (3), an order pursuant to s. 18(10) and an order pursuant to s. 19 providing for the sale of such property to give effect to the periodical payment orders and property adjustment orders sought. The wife also sought her costs.

The wife engaged the services of a pensions adviser. The husband had also engaged the services of a pensions adviser. However, the experts were of a different view as regards the interpretation of s. 17(2) which states:

> Where a decree of divorce has been granted the court, if it so thinks fit, may, in relation to *retirement* benefit *(not benefits)* under a scheme of which one of the spouses concerned is a member . . .

(The central issue is the definition of retirement benefit under s. 17(1) of the Act wherein a retirement benefit means 'all benefits (other than contingent benefits) payable under the scheme'.)

A further interesting point in this case was that the pension was an annuity contract with Equitable Life and came within the scope of s. 2(1) which defines a pension as 'A policy or contract of assurance approved by the Revenue Commissioners under Chapter 2 of Part 1 of the Finance Act 1992'. Under the definition, Equitable Life would also be considered the trustee or administrator of the scheme and the benefits payable to the husband and his spouse under the scheme fell to be considered retirement benefits. Under the policy, a gross annual annuity was paid of £61,359.91 and a spouse's pension of £53,274 on the member's death in retirement. As the husband had already retired the court did not have to specify the period of reckonable service when making the order pursuant to s. 17(2).

The objective of the wife's solicitors was to secure the wife's maintenance into the future (but they also wanted that sum of maintenance to be increased). An accountant was engaged to calculate the current level of maintenance being received by the wife in gross terms to determine the actual amount required by way of a pension adjustment order to secure the existing maintenance and also the projected maintenance which the wife hoped to receive.

The wife's pensions adviser requested that direct confirmation be sought from Equitable Life that they would be in a position to administer the pension adjustment order if one was served on them. However, Equitable Life stated that they could only answer that question upon actually seeing the court order that would be made.

The most significant issue in this case was that Equitable Life, the wife's pensions advisor and the Pensions Board all took the view that the court could *not* make an order which would purport to apply a different percentage to the husband's pension (being the member of the scheme) and the contingent widow's pension payable on the husband's death after retirement. This had been proposed by the husband, i.e. that his wife would not receive any of his pension (zero per cent of his pension would be treated as the designated benefit) but she would receive a percentage of the contingent widow's pension as would provide her with an income consistent with the maintenance that she would receive during his lifetime. The view of Equitable Life, the wife's pensions adviser and the Pensions Board is that a retirement benefit order must provide for the *same* percentage of each of the elements of the retirement benefit to be treated as a designated benefit for the non-member spouse. Clearly, it would be desirable to deal with each element of the retirement separately and some practitioners believe that this is possible as was seen in the previous case of *B v B*.

(The central issue is the definition of retirement benefit under s. 17(1) of the Act wherein a retirement benefit means 'all benefits (other than contingent benefits) payable under the scheme').

The practical difficulty in dealing with both retirement benefits together rather than separately was that in this instance (and this would be common in most pensions), the pension payable to the husband (being the member of the scheme) was greater than the pension which would be payable to the spouse of the husband (the wife). Therefore, if one percentage only is applied to both benefits two different figures are arrived at.

The court did not have to make a maintenance order given that the husband's pension was already being paid and therefore after the making of the pension adjustment order the income to the wife would derive directly from the pension (from Equitable Life).

The court noted that there had been no Consumer Price Index increasing provision in the deed of separation and that this was unusual. The court was advised by the wife's solicitors that the wife was not seeking to take into account all of the husband's assets, which were substantial, but merely to increase the periodical payment to be made by the husband to the wife and secure it by way of pension adjustment order.

Orders

Having considered the evidence, the court made the following orders:

1. A decree of divorce.

2. Mutual blocking orders pursuant to s. 18(10).

3. An order pursuant to s. 17(2) specifying the percentage to be 36 per cent of the retirement benefit payable to the husband under the policy.

4. The court awarded the wife her costs to be taxed in default of agreement.

As a consequence of the order the wife was to receive 36 per cent of the retirement benefit (£56,153, giving the wife a gross sum of £20,215 per annum), and, if the husband predeceased the wife, 36 per cent of the spouse's pension on death in retirement (£47,334 per annum giving the wife a gross sum of £17,040.24 per annum).

This was a very valuable annuity with provision for increases annually of 6 per cent for the first three years and 3 per cent per annum thereafter.

As with the previous case of *B v B* enquiries were made on behalf of the wife to Equitable Life to determine whether or not she could encash the retirement benefits granted in her favour (being 36 per cent of the husband's pension whilst he is alive and 36 per cent of the spouse's pension payable on the husband's death and a lump sum equal to the value of the designated benefits if the wife died first) and exchange them for an equivalent life pension payable to the wife for the remainder of her life. However this was not possible, given that the retirement benefit had already commenced being paid.

The wife received a compulsory purchase annuity which must be taxed under the PAYE system and PRSI must be deducted. Accordingly, the wife would receive payments net of income tax from Equitable Life and would not have to file any tax returns.

7.22.3 CASE NOTE 3

Re *D v D*

Circuit Court orders made on consent

Facts

The parties were married in June 1975 and had two children, one of whom was a dependant as of the date of the institution of the divorce proceedings. Both children were living with the wife.

The parties had separated in 1995 when the husband moved out of the family home and resided for one year in a second property owned by the parties, which was then sold with no profit. The husband, at the date of the institution of the proceedings, was residing with his sister. The wife had sold the family home and purchased alternative accommodation for herself and the children and paid to her husband the sum of £17,000 out of the proceeds of sale. The wife's new property had a mortgage of approximately £30,000. The wife was a self-employed person with a small income arising from her business, which was only getting off the ground. The husband worked for An Post.

The parties agreed that the husband would continue to pay to the wife £125 per week, being £50 for the wife and £75 for the dependent child for one year from the date of the settlement (to allow the wife to establish her business) and then reduce the maintenance payment to £75 only in respect of the dependent child.

The wife had no pension but the husband was a member of An Post superannuation scheme and An Post spouse's and children's contributory pension scheme.

Consent orders

The parties agreed a pension adjustment order pursuant to s. 17(2) directing the trustees of An Post to pay to the wife that part of the accrued retirement benefit deemed to have accrued from the date of their marriage up to 1993, being a period of 20 years, and that she be entitled to 50 per cent of the benefit accrued in that period. A non-variation order was made pursuant to s. 17(26) (that the provisions of s. 22 of the Act would not apply). Orders were also made pursuant to s. 18(10). The husband also agreed to make a will in which he would provide for payments of at least £8,000 for each of the children in the event of his death prior to them ceasing to be dependent. It was noted under the rules of the scheme that if the children were dependent they would be covered by the children's pension scheme with An Post also. The basis for the wife seeking a reckonable period of 20 years and percentage of 50 per cent was the length of the parties' marriage prior to it breaking down and she sought 50 per cent of same on the basis that she had looked after the children in the family home whilst her husband was employed and accruing benefits under the pension scheme.

7.22.4 CASE NOTE 4

Re *D v D*

Facts

The parties were married in August 1993 and had one child aged 12 at the date of negotiations to obtain a decree of divorce on a consent basis.

PENSIONS ON SEPARATION AND DIVORCE

The parties had separated in 1994 and concluded a deed of separation in September 1994 providing:

1. The husband was to pay to the wife a sum of £60 per week for the support of the dependent child, increasing it in accordance with the Consumer Price Index.

2. The husband also agreed to continue to ensure the wife and dependent child with the Garda Medical Aid Society and pay half of any excess in medical and dental costs not covered by the scheme.

3. The husband and the wife agreed to discharge all educational fees and expenses in respect of the child jointly.

4. The husband transferred the family home to the wife in consideration of a sum of approximately £25,000 and the wife also assumed responsibility for the existing mortgage.

5. The parties renounced their inheritance rights.

6. It was agreed that the husband would continue to discharge all payments necessary to maintain a life policy with Irish Life maintained through the Garda Representative Association. It was also agreed that should he predecease the wife at any time when the wife is a lawful spouse of the husband the wife shall be entitled to such widow's pension and/or life assurance payment as payable to the husband's widow and, if at the date of the husband's death, the wife is not the husband's lawful widow and the dependent child is under the age of 18 the life assurance payment should be paid to the wife to be held by her on trust for the child or, if she had attained the age of 18 but was still under the age of 23 and in full-time education, the life assurance payment would be paid directly to the dependent child.

What fell to be agreed in this case was securing the dependent child's maintenance after the parties divorced. On examining the life policy documentation it was clear that the benefit of same would be paid to the husband's estate for distribution under the terms of any will executed by him and therefore the clause in the deed of separation whereby the husband would leave the benefit of that policy to the wife or to the dependent child had been breached. On that basis details of the husband's pension benefits were sought so that whether or not to seek a pension adjustment order in favour of the dependent child could be ascertained. Because the husband was a member of An Gardaí Síochána, under the pension scheme he could retire at aged 50 on *full* pension. At that time the dependent child would be aged 17 years and could reasonably be a dependant for a further six years. It was therefore important that the maintenance for those six years be secured. Otherwise a situation could arise, in the event of the husband's death after retirement and whilst the child was still dependent, where all maintenance payments from the husband to the wife in respect of the dependent child would cease and any benefit that was payable under the life policy would be payable to the husband's estate and might not pass to the dependent child. Of course, the wife, on behalf of the dependent child, could institute a s. 17 application.

A pension adjustment order could be made in favour of the dependent daughter, payable to the wife. It will be noted that this order would cease upon the child ceasing to be a dependant. Consideration must also be given to seeking a financial compensation order pursuant to s. 16 of the 1996 Act, directing the husband to assign the benefit of the life policy, otherwise payable to his estate, to the wife for the benefit of the dependent child. From the husband's perspective, this order may be less favourable than a pension adjustment order as the financial compensation order would not cease upon the dependent child ceasing to be a dependant, in contrast to a s. 17(2) order.

This case is ongoing.

CHAPTER 8

RECOGNITION OF FOREIGN DIVORCE DECREES

8.1 Introduction

The recognition of foreign divorces was an important feature in Irish law until the introduction of domestic divorce in 1995. Before that date, couples whose marriage had broken down could not issue divorce proceedings in Ireland, as our courts had no jurisdiction to grant divorces. However, there was a jurisdiction that enabled foreign divorces to be recognised in this State. Spouses from marriages that were recognised as having been dissolved by a foreign decree were free to remarry under Irish law.

Although the introduction of divorce has eliminated the need for Irish couples to seek a divorce abroad, the law governing the recognition of such divorces is still important. This is because many couples who obtained foreign divorces before 1995 may have remarried, and so the validity of that second marriage in Irish law will depend on the validity of the previous foreign divorce. Additionally, many couples will continue to obtain foreign divorces for a variety of reasons, e.g., while they are working abroad, or they may have moved to Ireland for the first time and seek to have their marital status clarified.

Some importance attaches to the determination of these issues of status. For example, if a divorce is recognised as valid in one country, but not in another, a 'limping marriage' is said to arise in that the marriage limps from validity to invalidity as one considers its status from jurisdiction to jurisdiction. This is an undesirable situation, especially as mobility between countries increases.

The laws concerning the recognition of foreign divorces have changed on a number of occasions, and indeed they are still in a process of change. Because this area of family law has been developed from a common law base in a manner that can only be understood by reference to that base, the history of the development of the recognition jurisdiction should first be considered. While the Domicile and Recognition of Foreign Divorces Act 1986 governs the recognition of foreign divorces obtained after 2 October 1986, common law rules govern divorces obtained before that date. It must be noted that the law is in a state of some confusion concerning pre-1986 divorces.

8.2 Development of the Recognition Jurisdiction

The 1922 Constitution was silent as regards the law of divorce. At that time there was a recognised common law rule concerning the recognition of foreign divorces. The 1937 Constitution contained two provisions that dealt with divorce. The old Article 41.3.2 contained the ban that precluded Irish courts from granting divorces. Article 41.3.3

contained a statement that referred to foreign divorces, but its meaning was far from clear. It provided:

> *No person whose marriage has been dissolved under the civil law of any other State but is a subsisting valid marriage under the Law for the time being in force within the jurisdiction of the Government and Parliament established by this Constitution shall be capable of contracting a valid marriage within that jurisdiction during the lifetime of the other party to the marriage so dissolved.*

The first case to consider Article 41.2.3 was *Mayo-Perrott v Mayo-Perrott* [1958] IR 336. The principal question for the Supreme Court to decide was whether the Constitution banned the recognition of foreign divorces, or whether the common law rules were carried over into our law. As it turned out, the court split on the issue. Maguire CJ held that the provision barred the recognition of foreign divorce in Ireland. Kingsmill Moore J, on the other hand, held that the Constitution did not prevent the carrying over to our law of the recognition of foreign divorces as to do so would require an explicit statement to that effect. In the absence of such an explicit statement he felt it was open to the Irish courts to recognise foreign divorces on the common law basis.

Subsequent decisions adopted the approach of Kingsmill Moore J. This was first done by an English court in *Breen v Breen* [1964] P 144. The case of *Bank of Ireland v Caffin* [1971] IR 123 was the first time the question came up as a *ratio* issue. This case involved a dispute between the two widows of a Mr Caffin, deceased, as to which of them was his spouse for the purposes of the Succession Act 1965. His first marriage was solemnised, and later dissolved, in England while both he and his first wife were domiciled there. If that divorce was recognised, the second marriage was valid, and thus the second wife was his lawful spouse under Irish law. Kenny J in the High Court held that the common law rules for recognising a foreign divorce had been satisfied and thus the second marriage was valid. After this case there was no real doubt that Irish courts had the jurisdiction to recognise foreign divorces, though some judicial *dicta* tentatively suggested otherwise.

8.3   Basic Concepts

At common law, foreign divorces could be recognised if both spouses were domiciled in the jurisdiction of the court granting it at the date of the initiation of proceedings. Thus in *Gaffney v Gaffney* [1975] IR 103 the husband arranged a divorce in England from Ireland. He then brought his wife to Manchester where she petitioned for, and got, a divorce. Recognition was denied as neither spouse was domiciled in England at the relevant time. (There were other reasons why recognition may have been denied in this case which will be dealt with below at **8.7.2** and **8.7.4**).

This common law rule applied in Ireland until reformed by the 1986 Act. It still applies to foreign divorces obtained before that Act came into operation, though the common law rule itself has been developed by recent decisions and is now substantially different from this formulation.

The basic approach of Irish law to recognition is based on satisfying formal jurisdiction criteria, as opposed to substantive ones. In other words, Irish courts look to see whether the foreign court that granted the divorce was properly seised of the matter, thereby having jurisdiction to grant the divorce. Irish courts do not look to see whether the parties satisfied the substantive foreign law governing the grant of a divorce in the state (e.g., whether they lived apart for the required amount of time, etc.) Irish courts do not re-hear the divorce case when recognition is applied for. If the foreign court properly had jurisdiction over the couple according to Irish law, whether its internal rules for the grant of a divorce were satisfied are generally a matter for that court alone and are irrelevant for the most part as regards the recognition of the divorce (though there are a couple of exceptions, see below).

As a converse, if the foreign court did not properly have jurisdiction over the couple, that court did not have jurisdiction to grant the divorce and so the substantive law of that country was irrelevant. A divorce granted by a court with an insufficient jurisdiction over the couple could not be recognised under Irish law. Additionally, whether a foreign court has sufficient jurisdiction over a couple to divorce them will always be decided by Irish law. In fact, it is this rule that is at the root of the recognition of foreign divorces.

The traditional basis for deciding whether a foreign court had jurisdiction to grant a recognisable divorce was the law of domicile. If the couple were domiciled in the state where the divorce was granted at the time it was applied for, then that divorce would be recognised in this law. Domicile is thus sometimes called a connecting factor between individuals and a jurisdiction. While it is not the only such connecting factor, it has traditionally a special place in Irish law as regards these issues which may give rise to a conflict of laws. Recently, the notion of residence has gained an importance in this area, which shall be considered below. Whether a couple were domiciled in the relevant jurisdiction is always to be decided by reference to the Irish law of domicile.

8.4   The Law of Domicile

Domicile is a mixed question of law and fact. A person's domicile is not merely the place in which he or she resides. The place of domicile is a particular State or jurisdiction, not country. Thus, for example, each state of the USA is separate for the purposes of domicile. A domicile is a legal concept, though the fact of residence in a particular place is important. Being a legal concept, there are some peculiar elements to be considered when establishing a person's domicile. A practical guide to establishing domicile is to deal with the facts of a person's life in a chronological manner. The reason for this will be clear from the nature of the rules.

At birth, all persons are ascribed a domicile of origin. This is not determined by reference to the place of birth, but by reference to the domicile of one's parents at that time. A child born to married parents takes the domicile that his or her father has at the time of birth. A child born to unmarried parents takes the domicile of his or her mother at that time as the domicile of origin. The domicile of origin does not change through life, and it is never totally irrelevant because it may revive at any time if a person loses a domicile without gaining a new one: see *P.K. v T.K.* (unreported, 14 April 2000, High Ct, Murphy J).

During minority, a child takes a domicile of dependence. Again, this does not depend on the actual location of the child, but is rather dependent on the domicile of parents. Generally, a child born to married parents, or whose parents marry subsequent to birth, has a domicile dependent on its father. A child of unmarried parents is dependent on its mother. Thus, if the domicile of the relevant parent changes, so too does that of the child. (See generally, Power, 'The Domicile of Children: Towards a New Basis' [2000] 2 IJFL 21.)

Upon reaching adulthood, which occurs at 18 under Irish law, a person gets the capacity to acquire a domicile of choice. It is possible that domicile may immediately change to the place where the person has been residing for some time, possibly away from the relevant parent whose domicile ruled that of the child until adulthood. More usually, a domicile of choice is acquired when a person moves to a different jurisdiction. It is crucial to appreciate that more than a change of residence is required. There are two ingredients necessary to acquire a domicile of choice: residence in a particular place, coupled with an intention to reside there permanently or indefinitely (this latter is sometimes called the *animus manendi*). However, it has been said that the domicile of origin persists until it has been clearly shown to have been changed: see *Re Joyce* [1946] IR 277.

The residence factor is easy to comply with; no exacting standard or quality of residence is required *per se*. However, because of the requirement to show the intention to reside permanently or indefinitely, as a matter of proof some quality of residence must be established. There is no doubt that this second ingredient is difficult to establish. For example, if a person moved to France under a fixed five-year contract of employment and intended to return to Ireland when it expired, there would be little chance of establishing a domicile of origin in France during that time. The residence there could not be described as permanent or indefinite. For example, in *P.K. v T.K.* (unreported, 14 April 2000, High Ct, Murphy J), the fact that an American citizen was a student here for four years and acquired an Irish passport did not necessarily prove an Irish domicile.

Of course, it is possible to change one's intention and thereby gain a domicile of choice. In the first example above, if after three years in France the person decided not to return to Ireland but to remain in France indefinitely, then he or she would gain a French domicile of choice. On the other hand, if a person could establish that he or she intended to reside in a particular country permanently or indefinitely from the outset, a domicile of choice is established there from the time residence is taken up, which usually means the day of arrival (thus showing the, at least theoretical, minimal residence requirement).

Finally, if a person leaves a jurisdiction with a fixed determination not to return there, but with no particular place in mind to go, then any domicile of choice that might have been acquired in that place is lost. However, because in law no person can be without a domicile, the domicile of origin revives and remains that person's domicile until a new domicile of choice is acquired, if ever.

In order to prove that a domicile of choice has been acquired in a particular place an Irish court will require evidence of residence, and, more importantly, of intention. This is best shown by objective factors, rather than subjective declarations of intent, though these are relevant. In *Lambert v An tArd Chláraitheoir* [1995] 2 IR 372, Kinlen J said that an uncontradicted declaration of intention to acquire a domicile which was consistent with the party's actions could be regarded as evidence of an acquisition of domicile. On the other hand, where such declarations contradict the facts of a person's existence they will be of no effect: see *In re Sillar* [1956] IR 344.

Factors such as the ownership of land in a country, the network of roots established there, bank accounts, insurance policies, or pension plans based there are relevant to show that the person had made that place the centre of his or her existence. Other negative factors are also relevant, such as the absence of the above details in Ireland, and the absence of a settled intention to return here. If a person had returned to Ireland, the reasons for so doing will be important. If returning to Ireland was something unexpected or unforeseen, e.g. a business failure or illness, that is good evidence that until the enforced change the person intended to permanently reside abroad.

There is one matter that is now of historical evidence only, but which was the impetus for the changes introduced in the 1986 Act. Until that year, a wife had no independent domiciliary capacity and took the domicile of her husband as a domicile of dependence. Thus, if his domicile changed, so too did hers, even if her factual residence remained unchanged. In some ways this facilitated the recognition of foreign divorces before 1986 because, before then, both spouses had to be domiciled in the jurisdiction that granted the divorce. If the husband was domiciled there, then since his wife took his domicile, so too was she, and the divorce could be recognised, even if the wife remained in Ireland. But this could never happen the other way around, i.e. a wife could never move abroad without her husband and get a divorce that would be recognised here (though it might be perfectly valid in the place where it was granted). If he stayed here, so too, in Irish law, did her domicile. This inequality prompted the introduction of the Domicile and Recognition of Foreign Divorces Act 1986, which abolished the dependent domicile of a wife from 2 October 1986, and from that date on a wife was capable of gaining an independent domicile.

The rule of dependent domicile was also declared by the Supreme Court to breach the constitutional right of spousal equality in *W v W* [1993] 2 IR 476. It thus was not carried over into our law by Article 50 of the Constitution and is now wholly irrelevant in Irish law, even for pre-1986 foreign divorces.

8.5 Domicile and Recognition of Foreign Divorces Act 1986

The Domicile and Recognition of Foreign Divorces Act 1986 governs the recognition of foreign divorces that were applied for after 2 October 1986. In addition to abolishing the dependent domicile of a wife, it introduced new recognition rules, although these are based on the common law model. The central change was introduced by s. 5(1), which provides:

> *For the rule of law that a divorce is recognised if granted in a country where both spouses are domiciled, there is hereby substituted a rule that a divorce shall be recognised if granted in the country where either spouse is domiciled.*

Thus, if either spouse was domiciled in the jurisdiction granting the divorce at the date of the initiation of proceedings, the divorce is entitled to recognition in Ireland. This is true even where one spouse has never left Ireland.

In addition, the Act extends the recognition rules to allow for the recognition in Ireland of divorces that, while not granted in the place where either spouse is domiciled, are recognised in the place or places where both spouses are domiciled: see s. 5(4). (This extension applies only when neither spouse was domiciled in Ireland at the time of instituting proceedings.) For example, if, while a husband is domiciled in New York and his wife is domiciled in England, the husband applies for and obtains a divorce in Nevada which is entitled to recognition in both New York and England, the divorce will be recognised here.

There is one exception to the rule that each State or jurisdiction is treated separately for the purposes of recognition. This relates to the States which comprise the United Kingdom. Section 5(3) of the Act provides a special rule whereby a divorce granted in any of the following jurisdictions:

(a)   England and Wales;

(b)   Scotland;

(c)   Northern Ireland;

(d)   the Isle of Man; and

(e)   the Channel Islands

shall be recognised if either spouse is domiciled in any of those jurisdictions. Thus, if the husband remains domiciled in Ireland and his wife obtains a domicile of choice in England, and the wife applies for and gets a divorce in Scotland, that divorce is entitled to recognition in Ireland.

8.6 Pre-1986 Divorces

The rules introduced by the 1986 Act apply only to divorces applied for after 2 October 1986. For a time after the Act was passed the common law rules applied unchanged to the recognition of pre-1986 divorces (i.e. before 2 October 1986). Initially, this included the dependent domicile of the wife and the need for both spouses to be domiciled in the jurisdiction granting the divorce. However, there have since been substantial changes to the rules that apply to the recognition of pre-1986 divorces. These changes are important as many such divorces still come before the courts for a variety of reasons.

As noted above, the Supreme Court in *W v W* [1993] 2 IR 476 declared the rule of dependent domicile unconstitutional. That left a question about the common law divorce recognition rules which, unrealistically in the context of independent domiciles, expected both spouses to be domiciled in the foreign jurisdiction. The Supreme Court dealt with this by modifying the common law recognition rule to a position akin to that under the 1986 Act. The court said that a pre-1986 foreign divorce would be recognised once either of the parties was domiciled in the State granting the divorce. Blayney J said the court could modify the recognition rule because it was a judge-made rule, made in the light of a particular public policy. That policy had changed, as evidenced in the more lenient rules contained in the 1986 Act, and the court could modify the judge-made rules accordingly. The practical effect of *W v W* on the recognition of foreign divorces was to equalise the common law rules and those of the Act.

This uncomplicated picture has since changed again by a further decision, this time of the High Court in *G.McG. v D.W. (No. 1)* [1999] 2 ILRM 107 (see also the case note in (1999) 1 IJFL 26). In that case, McGuinness J recognised a divorce granted in England based on the ordinary residence of the petitioner in England. This represents a major change in the law away from the use of domicile as the basis on which to recognise foreign divorces. The notion of ordinary residence is free from the legal concepts that clutter the law of domicile, and focuses exclusively on the factual residence of a person.

The petitioner in *G.McG. v D.W.* satisfied the English jurisdictional requirement for obtaining a divorce there, which demanded that the petitioner be ordinarily resident in England for one year before the presentation of the petition. However, he was not domiciled there. By a coincidence, the English internal jurisdiction rule is the same as the jurisdiction requirement used here in respect of divorces under s. 39 of the Family Law (Divorce) Act 1996, in that to apply for a divorce in Ireland, one must be ordinarily resident in Ireland for one year before the application, or be domiciled here. McGuinness J felt that this demonstrated a clear public policy that the modern matrimonial jurisdiction of the State was not limited to a party's domicile. She also felt that the doctrine of the comity of the courts supported an extension of the rules as would the policy of the courts to avoid 'limping marriages'.

These reasons justified an extension of the common law rules to recognise a divorce granted on the basis of ordinary residence in England for one year. What is unclear is whether this was because:

(a)   residence in any jurisdiction for one year before the application will suffice to make the divorce recognisable here; or

(b)   whether one must merely satisfy whatever local jurisdiction rules are set by the place where the divorce is granted.

The first approach receives support from the references in the judgment to the Irish internal jurisdiction requirement; the second from the argument based on the comity of courts. This is a matter that has yet to be specifically ruled upon and clarified by the superior courts.

However, the first approach was preferred to the second by the Circuit Family Court in *B.B. v T.B.* (see (1999) 3 IJFL 20, Dublin Circuit, 16 March 1999). In that case, a divorce granted in Haiti in 1983 was not entitled to recognition here as neither of the parties was domiciled there, nor was either resident there to the same degree as required under Irish divorce law, i.e. one year. Although the divorce was recognised in Haiti and the petitioner satisfied local Haitian jurisdiction rules, it was held that because those rules were not as exacting as Irish rules, the divorce could not be recognised. This decision seems to put paid to any suggestion that, as regards couples domiciled in Ireland, Irish law will recognise pre-1986 'quickie' divorces, where the local jurisdiction rules are minimal, e.g. an overnight stay. This judgment also shows that despite any extension of the law, establishing domicile in the place where the divorce is granted entitles it to recognition here and that this remains the safest way of seeking recognition until the law is clarified.

While the *G.McG. v D.W.* judgment has been generally accepted as applying to pre-1986 divorces only, leaving post-1986 ones to be recognised exclusively under the 1986 Act, there was some debate as to whether the common law rules, as extended, could be used in relation to such post-1986 divorces. Another decision of the Circuit Family Court, *Blood Transfusion Services Board v H.L. and T.C.L.* (see (1999) 3 IJFL 19, Dublin Circuit, 1 February

146

1999), which concerned a 1991 English divorce, distinguished *G.McG. v D.W.* on the basis that the decision related only to a pre-1986 divorce. This could be seen as an indication that the courts see the decision as applying only to such divorces.

8.7   Bars to Relief

There are a number of considerations that may lead a court to deny recognition to a divorce decree that has been obtained abroad. While Irish courts reserve the right to refuse recognition, the fact that such refusals lead to limping marriages should be borne in mind. In addition, while public policy in Ireland may have been seen as anti-divorce in the past, the constitutional change to allow divorce here must be seen as a change in that public policy, which should lead to a greater willingness to recognise foreign divorces here.

8.7.1   NON-JUDICIAL DIVORCES

Traditionally, the only divorces that have been recognised are those granted by judicial authorities. Other more informal divorces, religious divorces or divorce by administrative measures were not originally recognised at common law. Examples include a *Gett* under Jewish Rabbinical law, which allows a husband to divorce his wife (but not the wife to divorce her husband) by letter. Under Moslem law a *Talaq* permits a husband to divorce his wife (but not the wife to divorce her husband) by verbally repudiating the marriage three times. Often, these divorces do not involve any judicial pronouncement.

There is English authority supporting the recognition of some such divorces, and a statutory provision there now clarifies the position. However, in the absence of any Irish authority, it must be doubted whether such divorces are valid here.

8.7.2   FRAUD

Fraud on the foreign jurisdiction can be used to deny recognition to an otherwise proper divorce. Although fraud is a wide concept, in the context of the recognition of foreign divorces it seems to be restricted in operation to the basis for the assumption of jurisdiction. In *Gaffney v Gaffney* [1975] IR 103 recognition was denied where a husband forced his wife to petition for an English divorce while she was based in Dublin. The English court granted the decree believing it had jurisdiction under its own rules, which it did not. The Supreme Court ruled that the decree was ineffective, and one of the grounds for doing so was the fraud of the husband.

8.7.3   DENIAL OF JUSTICE

This is a catch-all ground that recognises an inherent jurisdiction to deny recognition. For example, recognition may be refused if the petitioner took no reasonable steps to notify a respondent of the application for the foreign divorce, but there are other grounds also. A good example is the case of *L.B. v H.B.* (unreported, July 1980, High Ct), which involved collusion in obtaining the decree. That case involved a couple domiciled in France both of whom wished to divorce. In 1957 a divorce was obtained on the application of the husband. The decree was based on manufactured evidence of the wife's behaviour. If the French court had discovered this collusion no decree would have issued, though there was no basis in France to retract the decree once granted. Barrington J described the French proceedings as a charade and refused to recognise the decree.

8.7.4　DURESS

If one spouse forces the other into applying for the decree this will vitiate any subsequent decree, as would duress aimed at preventing a decree from being contested. This occurred in *Gaffney v Gaffney* [1975] IR 103, above, where an additional ground for refusing recognition was the fact that the husband had forced the wife to apply for the decree against her will. The scope of duress as a factor of non-recognition is not easy to establish as divorce, almost by definition, is a non-consensual process. Thus, the degree to which a court can refuse recognition on this ground must be limited.

8.7.5　ESTOPPEL

This concerns the issue of whether the conduct of a spouse may prevent him or her from denying the validity of a foreign decree. For example, if a spouse who petitioned for a decree later sought to deny its validity in order to make a claim, e.g. as a lawful spouse to the estate of the other, will the fact of being the petitioner doom the application?

The approach of the courts to this difficult issue, thus far, has been to deny the existence of any such estoppel as regards the validity of the decree. Divorce involves a question of status, and the courts have been of the view that such an issue is one of pure law; see e.g. *B.B. v T.B.*, and *Blood Transfusion Services Board v H.L. and T.C.L.* above. However, that is not to say that a spouse may be prevented from benefiting by such conduct financially and there has been no decision to specifically rule out estoppel from applying in such circumstances. Thus, while a person cannot be prevented from arguing against a decree for which he or she petitioned, he or she may arguably be denied the benefits if recognition is refused.

8.8　Consequences of Recognition

When a court recognises a foreign divorce decree the couple are seen by Irish law as being validly divorced. They are no longer spouses and are free to remarry validly under Irish law. The recognition itself brings no particular change to the couple, who will already regard themselves as divorced, but their status as such is secured.

8.9　Ancillary Reliefs

Until the passing of the Family Law Act 1995, there were some difficulties in securing proper ancillary relief following a foreign decree, most particularly as regards maintenance. The court that granted the decree may itself have made relevant orders, but there was no mechanism for applying for relief in Ireland. The couple were no longer spouses, and, for example, no application could be made under the Family Law (Maintenance of Spouses and Children) Act 1976.

Before the 1995 referendum permitted divorce in this country there was some doubt whether an Irish court could enforce foreign ancillary orders. In some cases it was held that to enforce such orders was contrary to the anti-divorce public policy of the time. However, there have been a number of decisions that rejected this argument and regarded the ancillary orders as independent and distinct remedies: see *Sachs v Standard Chartered Bank* [1987] ILRM 297.

In addition, mechanisms are now in place to facilitate the enforcement of maintenance orders between countries. The Maintenance Act 1994 brought the Rome Convention and the New York Convention into force in Ireland. The Rome Convention deals with enforcement between Ireland and other EU member states, while the New York Convention facilitates the enforcement of maintenance orders between Ireland and a wide range of other countries. A central authority has been established that assists applicants in the enforcement process.

Additionally Part III of the Family Law Act 1995 introduced a procedure whereby a person who was divorced abroad can apply in Ireland for certain reliefs. This applies only to divorces granted after 1 August 1996. Most orders available under the 1995 Act can be applied for, with the exception of preliminary orders. No relief will be granted to a divorcee who has remarried, and there are some special provisions to reflect the special nature of the circumstances in which relief is sought. Reliefs can also be applied for on behalf of dependent members of the family.

Before making an application for relief under Part III the applicant must get the leave of the court by way of an ex parte application. The court shall not grant such leave unless it considers that there is a substantial ground for so doing and a requirement specified in s. 27 is satisfied, whereby a relief order can be made if, but only if, at least one of the following requirements is satisfied:

(a) either of the spouses concerned was domiciled in the State on the date of the application for a relief order or was so domiciled on the date on which the divorce or judicial separation concerned took effect in the country or jurisdiction in which it was obtained; or

(b) either of the spouses was ordinarily resident in the State throughout the period of one year ending on either of the dates aforesaid; or

(c) on the date of the institution of the proceedings aforesaid either or both of the spouses had a beneficial interest in land situated in the State. (If this is the basis of jurisdiction, the range of orders that can be made is limited under s. 28.)

The court is not permitted to make a relief order unless satisfied that, in all the circumstances of the particular case, it is appropriate that such an order should be made by a court in the State and the court shall, in particular, have regard to the matters set out in s. 26, which include:

(i) the connection which the spouses concerned have with the State;

(ii) the connection which the spouses have with the country or jurisdiction other than the State in which the marriage concerned was dissolved or in which they were legally separated;

(iii) the connection which the spouses have with any country or jurisdiction other than the State;

(iv) any financial benefit which the spouse applying for the making of the order or a dependent member of the family has received, or is likely to receive, in consequence of the divorce or legal separation concerned or by virtue of any agreement or the operation of the law of a country or jurisdiction other than the State.

Under s. 24 where leave is granted to a person to make an application for a relief order, the court may, if appears that a spouse, or a dependent member of the family, concerned is in immediate need of financial assistance, make an order for maintenance pending relief. Section 25 allows a former spouse to apply for a share of a deceased former spouse's estate.

8.10 Practice and Procedure

An application under s. 29 of the Family Law Act 1995 is the most convenient method of seeking a declaration that a divorce is entitled to recognition within the State. This is specifically provided for in s. 29(4), in that a court can make a declaration that the validity of a divorce, annulment or legal separation obtained under the civil law of any other country or jurisdiction in respect of the marriage is entitled to recognition in the State.

Applications can be made to the High Court under ord. 70A of the Rules of the Superior Courts by way of a Family Law Summons and in the Circuit Family Court by way of a Family Law Civil Bill. There will often be a necessity to serve these proceedings out of the jurisdiction, as in many cases the respondent may not reside in Ireland. An application to court is necessary in order for this to be effected.

Orders under s. 29 are binding on the parties to the case. They are also binding on the State if the Attorney General is made a party to the action. The Attorney General can apply to be made a party, and the court shall join him or her if that occurs. There are some difficulties with this because the parties cannot force the Attorney General to become a party, and the meaning of an order binding the State is unclear: see *G.McG. v D.W. (No. 2)* (unreported, 31 March 2000, Supreme Ct). As a matter of practice it may be as well for applicants to forward a copy of the pleadings to the office of the Attorney General.

8.11 Conclusion

The recognition of foreign divorces raises important issues concerning the legal status of persons. This is all the more relevant as migration and emigration increase the number of people who seek to have such decrees recognised, not to mention historical factors that make the recognition important in Ireland. While the post-1986 rules are clear, those concerning pre-1986 divorces are in need of clarification.

It ought to be noted that the EU is proposing to introduce a new Convention to deal with the recognition of a range of family law decrees and orders. This is necessary, as such orders are not covered by the Brussels Convention, which regulates civil jurisdiction and the enforceability of civil judgments throughout the EU. If and when this new law enters into force the recognition of EU divorces will be made easier and quicker.

CHAPTER 9

TAX IMPLICATIONS OF MARRIAGE BREAKDOWN

9.1   Introduction

When dealing with marital breakdown, married couples have to confront many complex legal, financial and emotional issues in an effort to achieve a satisfactory resolution to their marriage breakdown. These issues include questions of maintenance, division of assets, custody of and access to children, succession rights, pension entitlements, occupation of the family home. Some of these issues may have tax implications.

A valid marriage ceremony recognised by Irish law attracts certain tax advantages not available to any other kind of relationship. To appreciate how marriage breakdown brings about certain changes from a tax point of view, it is necessary to have a basic understanding of the tax implications pertaining to the marital status. This chapter is divided into three sections:

    (a)   tax advantages of marriage: income and assets;

    (b)   maintenance; and

    (c)   transfer of assets.

The statutory references have been abbreviated for this chapter as follows:

Capital Acquisitions Tax Act 1976	—	CATA 1976
Family Law Act 1995	—	FLA 1995
Family Law (Divorce) Act 1996	—	FL(D)A 1996
Finance Act	—	FA
Health Contribution Regulations 1988	—	HC Regs 1988
Income and Capital Taxes Act 1988 (UK)	—	ICTA 1998
Social Welfare (Consolidation) Act 1993	—	SW (Con) A 1993
Stamp Duties Consolidation Act 1999	—	SDCA 1999
Taxes Consolidation Act 1997	—	TCA 1997

9.2   Tax Advantages of Marriage: Income and Assets

9.2.1   INCOME TAX

9.2.1.1   Statutory requirement

A marriage ceremony of itself does not give rise to any income tax advantage. To obtain any income tax benefits, a couple must be legally married and 'living together'.

Under the income tax rules a married couple are 'living together' unless either:

(a) they are separated under an order of a court of competent jurisdiction or by deed of separation, or

(b) they are in fact separated in such circumstances that the separation is likely to be permanent (TCA 1997, s. 1015(2)).

Accordingly, it is assumed that a married couple are living together unless there is a definite separation, either by court order or as a matter of fact.

The advantages obtained by a married couple living together include:

(i) entitlement to married allowance (double the single person's allowance) (TCA 1997, s. 461);

(ii) entitlement to double the single person's tax bands restricted in certain circumstances (TCA 1997 s. 15 (amended by FA 2000, s. 3));

(iii) entitlement to be assessed jointly, separately or as single people (TCA 1997, ss. 1015-1024).

9.2.1.2 Taxation options

Joint assessment

See TCA 1997, ss. 1018 and 1020 (as amended by FA 2000, s. 3). Joint assessment is not available for the tax year in which the marriage takes place and each spouse must be assessed as a single person. Joint assessment may apply for the second year of marriage either by actual election or deemed election. Either election may be withdrawn by either spouse before the end of the tax year. This must be done in writing.

When special provisions for married couples were introduced in the Finance Act 1980, it was enacted that the husband was assessable in respect of his own and his wife's total income and liable to pay any tax due on their joint incomes subject to certain exceptions (TCA 1997, s. 1017). A return of income would be submitted by the husband showing his own and his wife's income. He was granted the allowances and reliefs which a married couple were entitled to. Since 6 April 1994, a wife can also be the assessable spouse (TCA 1997, s. 1019(2)(a)).

Example:

Tax bill for 2000/2001 for a married couple living together and earning income as follows:

	£
Higher income spouse	40,000
Lower income spouse	8,000
Total and taxable income	48,000
28,000 at 22%	6,160
6,000 at 22%	1,320
14,000 at 44%	6,160
48,000	13,640
Less: Personal allowance (9,400 at 22%)	(2,068)
	11,572
Total tax due on joint assessment basis	11,572

In order to claim joint assessment, it is not necessary for both spouses to have income.

Therefore, joint assessment may be claimed if income arises to the husband only or wife only. However, if only one spouse earns income, the maximum amount of income taxable at the standard rate of tax is £28,000 rather than double the single person's standard tax rate band, i.e. £17,000 x 2 (FA 2000, s. 3).

Separate assessment

See TCA 1997, ss. 1023 and 1024 (as amended by FA 2000, s. 3). Separate assessment only applies where a married couple have elected for, or are deemed to have elected for, joint assessment and a special application for separate assessment is made. Under separate assessment, income tax is assessed, charged and recovered from each spouse as if they were not married. Where either a husband or wife elects for separate assessment, they can retain the tax savings, if any, of joint assessment and at the same time have their income tax assessments and returns of income dealt with separately. The personal allowances and reliefs available to both husband and wife are the same as in the case of joint assessment. In addition, the total tax payable cannot exceed the amount due if an election for separate assessment had not been made.

Any unused balances of allowances, reliefs and rate bands of one spouse are allocated against the income of the other spouse. The aggregate liability is exactly the same as under joint assessment.

Example:

Tax bill for 2000/2001 for a married couple living together and earning income as follows:

		£
Higher income spouse		40,000
Lower income spouse		8,000

	Higher income spouse's tax bill		Lower income spouse's tax bill	
	£		£	
Total and taxable income	40,000		8,000	
17,000 at 22%	3,740	8,000 at 22%	1,760	
*9,000 at 22%	1,980			
14,000 at 44%	6,160			
40,000	11,880		1,760	
Less: Personal allowance				
(4,700 at 22%)	(1,034)	(4,700 at 22%)	(1,034)	
	10,864		726	11,572

The aggregate liability is exactly the same as under joint assessment. The example shows that the unutilised 22 per cent tax rate band of the lower income spouse is transferred to the higher income spouse*.

Single assessment

See TCA 1997, ss. 1016 and 1018. Deliberate action must be taken by either party to a marriage if they wish to be taxed under the single assessment basis.

Since both spouses are effectively treated as single persons there is no provision whereby one spouse may transfer any balance of unused allowances or tax rate bands to the other spouse. The benefit of the unused allowances may therefore be lost and for this reason single assessment is generally less advantageous than joint assessment.

Example:

Tax bill for 2000/2001 for a married couple living together and earning income as follows:

	£
Higher income spouse	40,000
Lower income spouse	8,000

	Higher income spouse's tax bill		*Lower income spouse's tax bill*	
	£		£	
Total and taxable income	40,000		8,000	
17,000 at 22%	3,740	8,000 at 22%	1,760	
23,000 at 44%	10,120			
40,000	13,860		1,760	
Less: Personal allowance				
(4,700 at 22%)	(1,034)	(4,700 at 22%)	(1,034)	
	12,826		726	13,552

A comparison of the tax bills arising on the various assessment options shows:

Joint assessment	11,572
Separate assessment	11,572
Single assessment	13,552

By choosing single assessment, the married couple has an increased tax bill of £1,980.

Year of marriage relief

See TCA 1997, s. 1020. Married couples are taxed as single persons in the year of assessment, that is, the tax year in which the marriage takes place. If the total tax bill as single persons exceeds the amount which would have been paid if they were married and jointly assessed for the whole year, they are entitled, on making a joint claim, to an income tax refund. The refund is calculated as follows:

$$A \times \frac{B}{12} \quad Where$$

A = the additional tax payable as a result of being taxed as single persons rather than jointly assessed for the year in which the marriage takes place, and

B = the number of income tax months from the date of marriage to the end of the income tax year (parts of a month being treated as a month). An income tax month runs from the sixth day of the month to the fifth day of the following month.

Example:

Date of marriage 6 October 2000

	Higher income Spouse £	Lower income Spouse £	Total £
Tax payable			
– Single assessment basis	12,826	726	13,552
– Joint assessment basis			11,572
Excess			1,980
Time apportioned	£1,980 × $\frac{6}{12}$ =		990

The relief is allocated proportionately to the tax paid by each. In the above example, the higher income spouse would be allocated £937 of the relief (see *Note* below) and the lower income spouse would be granted the balance of £53.

A claim for relief must be made jointly and in writing after the end of the year of marriage.

Note: £990   × $\dfrac{£12,826}{£13,552}$ = £937

Non-resident spouses

If only one of the spouses is resident in Ireland for tax purposes, the Revenue takes the view that the couple are not entitled to elect for joint or separate assessment. This applies notwithstanding that the spouses are living together as defined in TCA 1997, s. 1015(2): *Fennessy v McConnelogue* [1995] ITR 133. However, if each spouse's income is fully chargeable in Irish tax then the Revenue will allow them to elect for joint or separate assessment. If the non-resident spouse has some income not chargeable to Irish tax then the Irish tax-resident spouse is taxed as a single person. The non-resident spouse will only be subject to Irish tax on Irish source income and will be entitled to a proportion of the personal allowance calculated by reference to Irish income over worldwide income (TCA 1997, s. 1032).

9.2.1.3   Children

Up to 1985/1986 inclusive, it was possible for a married couple to obtain a tax allowance for each child. However, this general relief was withdrawn from 6 April 1986. Since then, there are allowances available for particular categories of children. These can be summarised as follows:

(a) Incapacitated child allowance (TCA 1997, s. 465 (as substituted by FA 2000, s. 9))

An allowance for each incapacitated child of a taxpayer can be claimed or, subject to certain conditions, for any other incapacitated child for whom he or she has custody and maintains at his/her own expense.

In the case of an individual assessed jointly with his or her spouse, the allowance is given to the spouse on whom the joint assessment is made (TCA 1997, s. 1017).

In separate assessment cases, the allowance is divided equally between the spouses where the incapacitated child is their own child. For other children, such as informally adopted children, the incapacitated child allowance is given according as each spouse maintains the child (TCA 1997, s. 1024(2)).

The incapacitated child allowance (TCA 1997, s. 465(1) as substituted by FA 2000, s. 9(1)) is given for a tax year if, at any time during the year, the child is either:

(a) under the age of 18 years and permanently incapacitated by reason of mental or physical infirmity; or

(b) over the age of 18 years at the commencement of the year, and

    (i) is permanently incapacitated by mental or physical infirmity from maintaining himself or herself, and

    (ii) had become so permanently incapacitated before the age of 21 years or, if permanently incapacitated after the age of 21 years, had become incapacitated at a time when he or she was in receipt of full-time instruction at any university, college, school or other educational establishment.

A child under the age of 18 years only qualifies for the incapacitated child allowance if his or her mental or physical state is such that there would be a reasonable expectation that, if he or she were over the age of 18 years, he or she would be incapacitated from maintaining himself/herself (TCA 1997, s. 465(2)).

The reference in (b)(ii) above to a child being in receipt of full-time instruction at an educational establishment includes a case where the child was undergoing full-time training with an employer for any trade or profession in circumstances where the child was required to devote the whole of his or her time to the training for a period of not less than two years (TCA 1997, s. 465(5)). Consequently, a child who becomes permanently incapacitated when he or she is undergoing such training is a qualifying child although over 21 years. In any such case, the employer in question may be required to give the inspector information about the nature of the training that was involved. Furthermore, if the child becomes incapacitated after the age of 21 years while in full-time education, the Revenue Commissioners may consult with the Minister for Education and Science if there is any question as to entitlement to the relief.

'Child' includes a step-child, a child whose parents have not married and a child in respect of whom an adoption order under the Adoption Acts is in force (TCA 1997, ss. 5, 8). It also includes a child who is not a child of the taxpayer but who is in the custody of the taxpayer (TCA 1997, s. 465(4)).

The allowance is £1,600 granted at the standard rate of tax for each incapacitated child (TCA 1997, s. 465(2)). However, in the case of any incapacitated child over 18 years of age at the commencement of the tax year for which the claim is made, the amount of the allowance is reduced to the amount actually expended by the taxpayer in that year on maintenance for the child (if lower than £1,600) (TCA 1997, s. 465(3)(b)). In addition, if the incapacitated child's income for the tax year exceeds £2,100, the allowance is reduced £1 for each £1 by which the child's income exceeds £2,100 (TCA 1997, s. 465(6)). Therefore no allowance is available if the incapacitated child has income in his or her own right exceeding £3,700. In calculating the income of an incapacitated child, no account is taken of any income which the child may have as the holder of a scholarship, bursary or similar educational endowment.

If the allowance is claimed for two or more incapacitated children, the income test is applied separately for each child to reduce, if relevant, the allowance for the child in question.

If the incapacitated child allowance is claimed then the dependent relative allowance cannot be claimed (TCA 1997, s. 466).

(b) Allowance for widowed parent: TCA 1997, s. 463 (as amended by FA 2000, s. 7)

Widowed parents, either male or female, are entitled to an additional allowance, granted at the standard rate of tax, for each of the five tax years immediately following the tax year in which his or her spouse has died (but not for the year of death itself). The allowance for each of these tax years is as follows:

	£
First year after year of death	10,000
Second year after year of death	8,000
Third year after year of death	6,000
Fourth year after year of death	4,000
Fifth year after year of death	2,000

This relief applies to an individual whose spouse has died in 1988/1989 or any later tax year provided the following conditions are met (TCA 1997, s. 463(2)):

(a)   the individual has at least one 'qualifying' child residing with him or her for the whole or part of the year;

(b)   he or she has not remarried before the commencement of the year; and

(c)   the individual is not living together as man and wife with another person in the year.

The three conditions are applied separately for each of the five years so that if all the conditions are met in any one or more of the years, but not in the others or other, the allowance is given for the one or more years in which all the conditions are met.

A qualifying child is defined by reference to certain provisions in the TCA 1997, s. 462 (as amended by FA 1999, s. 5). This section deals with the single parent allowance and sets down certain conditions for a qualifying child who is applied for under s. 463 as follows:

(i)   the child must be, at the commencement of the tax year, under the age of 18 years or if over the age of 18 years be in full-time education (as defined) or be permanently incapacitated by reason of mental or physical infirmity from maintaining himself/herself and had become so permanently incapacitated before he/she had attained the age of 21 years or had become so permanently incapacitated after attaining the age of 21 years while in full-time education or training;

(ii)   the child can be a step-child, a child whose parents have not married or an adopted child. If the child is not the child of the widowed parent then he/she must have custody of the child; and

(iii)   the child must be maintained by the widowed parent.

A widowed parent can also claim the single parent allowance (see below).

(c) Single Parent Allowance: TCA 1997, s. 462 (as amended by FA 1999, s. 5 and FA 2000, s. 6)

A parent living alone can claim an additional allowance if the following conditions are met:

(a)   there must be no entitlement for that tax year either to the married person's allowance or to the widowed person's bereavement allowance;

(b)   the parent must not be a spouse living with his/her spouse in that tax year (i.e. where single assessment is in operation);

(c)   the parent is not a man living with a woman as man and wife (or vice versa) in that tax year; and

(d)   the parent proves that he or she has a 'qualifying' child residing with him/her for the whole or any part of that tax year.

This allowance is intended as an additional allowance for a single parent to assist in providing for the qualifying child or children living with him/her. The single parent may be an unmarried person, a deserted spouse, a separated spouse, a divorcee or a widowed person.

The Single Parent Allowance for 2000/2001 is as follows:

£

Widowed parent	
Tax year of bereavement	Nil
Following years	4,700*
Other single parent	4,700*

*Relief is only allowed by way of tax credit at the standard rate, i.e. 22 per cent for 2000/01.

Furthermore, the standard rate tax band for 2000/01 is increased by £3,150 so that the amount of income taxed at the standard rate of tax (22 per cent for 2000/01) is £20,150 rather than £17,000.

The allowance may be claimed if at least one 'qualifying' child resides with him or her for at least a part of the tax year. Only one allowance is given irrespective of the number of qualifying children living with the single parent in the relevant tax year.

A qualifying child is a child (TCA 1997, s. 462(1)(a) as amended by FA 1999, s. 5):

(a)   who is born in the tax year; or

(b)   who is under the age of 18 years at the commencement of the tax year; or

(c)   who, if over the age of 18 years at the beginning of the tax year, is:

(i)   in full-time education, or

(ii)   permanently incapacitated by mental or physical infirmity from maintaining himself or herself and who had become so incapacitated either before his or her 21st birthday, or, if after that birthday, while he or she was in full-time education or training, and

(iii)   who is a child of the individual, or if not a child of the individual, is in the custody of the individual and is maintained by the individual at the individual's own expense for the whole or part of the tax year concerned.

'Child' includes a step-child whose parents have not married and a child in respect of whom an adoption order under the Adoption Acts is in force (TCA 1997, ss. 6, 8).

The £4,700 allowance granted at the standard rate of tax cannot be given in respect of any qualifying child if that child's income for the relevant tax year exceeds £720. However, if there is more than one qualifying child, the allowance is given even if only one of those qualifying children has income not exceeding £720 for 2000/01. If the individual claiming the allowance has more than one qualifying child residing with him or her, and each of these children has income in excess of £720, then the child with the lower (or lowest) income is considered and the reduced allowance is calculated accordingly. The allowance is reduced £1 for each £1 by which the child's income exceeds £720.

A widowed parent may also be entitled at the same time to the allowance in TCA 1997, s. 463 (allowance for widowed parent).

(d) Income exemption limit (TCA 1997, ss. 187 and 188)

If an individual's total income does not exceed a specified amount, then the taxpayer's income tax bill is reduced to nil. The specified amount depends on the individual's age and whether he or she is single, widowed, or married. The specified amounts are:

		2000/01
Single/widowed	– under 65 years	4,100
	– over 65 years	7,500
Married couple	– under 65 years	8,200
	– over 65 years	15,000

In the case of taxpayers who have children living with them and who are in full-time education, the specified amount can be increased by £450 in respect of each of the first two children and £650 for each child in excess of two (TCA 1997, s. 187(2)).

Certain conditions regarding the child must be fulfilled. In general, these are similar to the requirements for Single Parent Allowance: TCA 1997, s. 46(1)(a), (4), (6) (as amended by FA 1999, s. 5):

(a) the child must, at the commencement of the tax year, be under the age of 18 years or if over the age of 18 years be in full-time education (as defined) or be permanently incapacitated by reason of mental or physical infirmity from maintaining himself and had become so permanently incapacitated before attaining the age of 21 years or had become permanently incapacitated after reaching 21 years while in full-time education or training;

(b) the child can be a step-child, a child whose parents have not married, or an adopted child. If the child is not the child of the parent then the parent must have custody of the child;

(c) the child must be maintained by the parent.

However, if there are two taxpayers claiming for the same child, there is only one increased allowance for each child. If a child is maintained by one individual only, then that individual is entitled to the increase. In the case of a child being maintained by more than one individual, each individual shall be entitled to claim a proportionate amount of the increase calculated by reference to that individual's share of the total maintenance expended on the child (TCA 1997, s. 187(3)).

(e) Home carers' allowances (TCA 1997, s. 466A (inserted by FA 2000, s. 12)).

This is a tax allowance of £3,000 granted at the standard rate of tax for families where one spouse works at home to care for children. In general, the allowance will be granted where a number of conditions are met:

(i) the taxpayer is married and assessed to tax under joint assessment rules (TCA 1997, s. 1018);

(ii) the child normally resides and is cared for by the taxpayer and his/her spouse (i.e. carer spouse); and

(iii) the carer spouse's income must not exceed £4,000. No account is taken of any carer's allowance from the Department of Social, Community and Family Affairs in calculating this income and, if the carer spouse's income exceeds £4,000, the allowance is reduced on a £3 per £1 basis, so that a reduced measure of relief will be available on income between £4,000 and £5,000.

The allowance is granted at the standard rate of income tax (22 per cent for 2000/01) and only one allowance will be granted irrespective of the number of qualifying persons being cared for.

If the income of the carer spouse exceeds the permitted limit, the allowance will be granted for that year if the taxpayer qualified for the allowance in the immediately preceding year.

This allowance and the increased standard rate tax band for certain two earner couples, i.e. £34,000 (FA 2000, s. 3) cannot be claimed simultaneously, but a taxpayer may opt for whichever is the more beneficial.

9.2.2 PAY RELATED SOCIAL INSURANCE (PRSI) AND HEALTH CONTRIBUTION LEVY (HCL)

Although PRSI and levies do not form part of the tax legislation, they are considered by the layperson to be another form of taxation, as in most cases, PRSI and the Health Contribution Levy are payable at the same time as income tax.

Marital status does not affect liability to PRSI and levies as this depends solely on the reckonable income of particular individuals. Therefore, a married couple is treated separately for determining a PRSI or Health Contribution Levy liability, if any.

In the case of self-employed individuals where joint assessment applies, the assessable spouse is liable from a collection point of view for any unpaid PRSI and HCL due by the non-assessable spouse subject to the right of the Revenue to seek payment from the non-assessable spouse if his/her liability remains unpaid (SW(Con)A 1993, s. 20(3) and HC Regs 1988, art. 3). Therefore, it follows that if either separate or single assessment applies, there is no question of one spouse being liable to discharge his/her spouse's unpaid PRSI or levies liability.

9.2.3 CAPITAL GAINS TAX

9.2.3.1 Statutory requirement

A marriage ceremony of itself does not give rise to any capital gains tax advantage. To obtain any capital gains tax benefits a couple must be legally married and 'living together' (TCA 1997, s. 5(2)).

Under the capital gains tax rules a married couple are 'living together' unless either:

(a) they are separated under an order of a court of competent jurisdiction or by deed of separation; or

(b) they are in fact separated in such circumstances that the separation is likely to be permanent (TCA 1997, s. 1015(2)).

Accordingly, it is assumed that a married couple are living together unless there is a definite separation, either by court order or as a matter of fact.

The advantages obtained by a married couple 'living together' include:

– entitlement to be assessed jointly or separately;

– each spouse is entitled to a £1,000 annual exemption;

– capital losses available to one spouse can be used by the other spouse; and

– entitlement to dispose of assets to each other without being subject to capital gains tax.

9.2.3.2 Taxation benefits

Choice of asssessment

Joint assessment (TCA 1997, s. 1028(1))

The tax due on gains arising to a married woman living with her husband in a tax year is normally assessed and charged on her husband. However, the capital gains tax payable by the husband cannot exceed the capital gains tax bill if they were separately assessed. The Revenue can request that she submit a return. The wife can also be assessed to her share of capital gains tax under TCA 1997, s. 1022 (as amended by FA 2000, s. 25) if her share of the capital gains tax remains unpaid. In addition, joint assessment can apply to gains arising in the year of marriage, i.e. from date of marriage to 5 April.

As for income tax a wife can be the assessable spouse since 6 April 1994 (TCA 1997, s. 931).

Separate assessment (TCA 1997, s. 1028(2))

An application for separate assessment can be made by either spouse giving notice in writing to the Inspector of Taxes within three months after the end of the relevant year of assessment. The application for a separate assessment is effective until it is withdrawn by the spouse who made the original application. This notice of withdrawal has no effect unless it is given within three months after the end of the tax year for which it is to take effect. Where such an election is made by either spouse, both are separately assessed for capital gains tax.

Annual exemption

Each taxpayer is entitled to realise an annual real gain after inflation of £1,000 before being subject to capital gains tax on any excess at the rate of 20 per cent, or in the case of certain assets 40 per cent (TCA 1997, ss. 28, 601; FA 1998, s. 65). The annual exemption is similar to an income tax personal allowance in that if it is not used in one tax year, it cannot be carried forward.

In the case of a husband and wife where both are chargeable to capital gains tax in a tax year (or would be so chargeable but for the annual exemption) and the gains of one spouse are less than £1,000, the unutilised portion of the annual exemption could be used by the other spouse, in addition to that individual's own annual exemption. This applied up to 5 April 1998.

Since 6 April 1998, spouses cannot transfer their unutilised annual exemption to each other (FA 1998, s. 75).

Losses

Losses realised by one spouse in a tax year and not absorbed by his/her gains can be set against the gains of the other spouse arising in that year. This applies not only to losses in the current year, but also to losses coming forward from previous years: TCA 1997, s. 1028(3).

This provision does not apply if either spouse gives notice to that effect within three months after the tax year to the Inspector of Taxes. Where such a notice is given, the losses are carried forward against subsequent gains of the spouse to whom the losses accrued.

Disposal of assets between spouses

If spouses are living together, disposals from one to the other are treated as being made at such a price as will give no gain or loss to the spouse making the disposal: TCA 1997, s. 1028(5), (6).

The above exemption supersedes the imposed 'arm's length' provisions normally applied between connected persons (TCA 1997, ss. 10, 549). The normal rule for acquisitions/ disposals between connected persons is that the assets are deemed to be acquired/disposed of at market value.

However, this exemption does not apply if the assets disposed of are trading stock of the spouse making the disposal, or if the assets form part of the trading stock of the spouse acquiring them.

On a subsequent disposal, the spouse acquiring the asset is treated as if that spouse had acquired the asset at the same date and cost as the disposing spouse had originally acquired it.

9.2.3.3 Children

There are no general capital gains tax exemptions available for parents who transfer assets to their children. If a parent transfers an asset by way of gift or otherwise to a child, then a capital gains tax liability may arise unless there is a specific exemption or relief. For example, a disposal of business assets by a parent may qualify for retirement relief if the conditions of TCA 1997, s. 599 are fulfilled.

A child is defined in TCA 1997, ss. 6 and 8 and includes:

(a) a step-child;

(b) a child adopted under the Adoption Acts; or

(c) a child whose parents have not married for disposals on or after 14 January 1988 only. Prior to 14 January 1988, a child born to parents who were not married to one another was a child only of its mother unless the parents married each other after the birth of the child or the child was adopted under the Adoption Acts.

9.2.4 CAPITAL ACQUISITIONS TAX

9.2.4.1 Spouses

All gifts and inheritances given by one spouse to another are exempt from capital acquisitions tax (CAT).

Inheritances have only been exempt since 30 January 1985 (FA 1985, s. 59). If at the date of the inheritance the spouse is a spouse of the donor, then inheritance is exempt from inheritance tax and does not have to be taken into account in calculating CAT on later gifts or inheritance from any source.

This exemption was subsequently extended to gifts with effect from 31 January 1990 where a gift is taken by an individual who at the date of the gift is the spouse of the donor (FA 1985, s. 127). Again, the gift is not taken into account in computing tax on later gifts or inheritances.

In the period from 30 January 1985 to 30 January 1990, the CAT exemption applied only to inheritances and did not extend to gifts unless the donor died within two years of the gift and the date of the gift was on or after 30 January 1985.

9.2.4.2 Children

As for other taxes, there is no exemption for the transfer of assets between parents and children. However, there is a generous lifetime allowance. It is possible for a child to receive a taxable benefit from either or both parents up to a total value of £300,000 (Year 2000 limit) without any CAT liability arising. This assumes that the child has not received any other benefit from his/her parents since 2 December 1988 (CATA 1976, Second Sch. (as amended by FA 2000, s. 145)).

A child is defined in CATA 1976, s. 2 (as amended by FA 1992, s. 223) and includes:

– a step-child;

– a child adopted under the Adoption Acts 1952 to 1991 or under a foreign adoption which is deemed to be a valid adoption within the meaning of the Adoption Act 1991. This definition is effective for gifts or inheritances taken on or after 30 May 1991.

The original section referred to the Adoption Acts 1952 to 1974. For gifts and inheritances taken on or after 26 July 1988 and before 31 May 1991, FA 1989, s. 80 extended the reference to the Adoption Acts 1952 to 1988.

An adopted child is treated as a child of his/her adoptive and not of his/her natural parents:

– in relation to gifts and inheritances taken on or after 14 January 1988, relationships are to be construed in accordance with the Status of Children Act 1987, s. 3 (TCA 1997, s. 8). This means that a child who is born to parents not married to each other is now treated as the child of both its parents for CAT purposes. Prior to that, such a child was treated as the child of its mother, unless the parents married each other after the birth or the child had been adopted under the Adoption Acts.

The lifetime exemption threshold, i.e. £300,000 (Year 2000 limit) applies only to benefits passing from a parent/parents to a child as defined by CATA 1976, s. 2. It would not apply to a child in relation to whom the disponer stands *in loco parentis*. Such a child would only qualify for the £30,000 or £15,000 exemption threshold unless he/she is a minor child of a deceased child. However, such a child can avail of the exemption for benefits received as 'maintenance, support or education' as outlined in CATA 1976, s. 58.

9.2.5   STAMP DUTY

9.2.5.1   Spouses

A married couple has always been entitled to reliefs from the normal rates of stamp duty for any property other than stocks and shares. Up to 17 July 1982, the rate of stamp duty on the transfer of assets between spouses was 1 per cent. Thereafter, the duty payable was restricted to 50 per cent of the duty that would otherwise be payable (FA 1982, Sch. 4).

The first full relief was only introduced in the Family Home Protection Act 1976, s. 14. This section relieved fully from stamp duty the charge arising where the family home (as defined) was transferred into the joint names of the two spouses where the home immediately prior to such a transaction was owned by either spouse or both spouses otherwise than as joint tenants.

This relief was further extended in the Finance Act 1990, s. 114 (as amended by FA 1992, s. 141, now SDCA 1999, s. 96) to include the transfer of all assets. The exemption now includes a direct transfer of an asset from one spouse to another or a transfer from one spouse into the joint names of both spouses. No adjudication is required.

The stamp duty exemption does not apply if the instrument transferring the property includes a transfer to a person other than the spouse, in a sub-sale situation or in transfers governed by the CREST legislation.

For example, if assets are transferred by way of trust to a spouse for life and on the death of the spouse to the children in equal shares, then the stamp duty exemption will not apply. However, if the property is transferred into a spouse's name first and that spouse creates a trust in favour of himself/herself for life and on his/her death to the children in equal shares, then the value of the property referable to the full interest followed by the creation of the life interest taken by the spouse is exempt from stamp duty. The value of the life interest for stamp duty purposes is calculated by reference to the Life Interest Tables set out in CATA 1976, Sch. 2. The remainder interest being transferred to the children, i.e. market value less life interest attributable to spouse, would attract a stamp duty rate equal to 50 per cent of the ad valorem rate.

9.2.5.2   Children

Under SDCA 1999, Sch. 1, any transfer of assets by parent(s) to a child is restricted to 50 per cent of the duty that would otherwise be payable unless the transfer relates to shares where the normal 1 per cent rate still applies.

'Children' are defined on a similar basis as for CAT purposes. The statutory references are: Adoption Act 1952, s. 27, FA 1972, ss. 44, 45 (amended by FA 1993, s. 214 and TCA 1997, s. 8).

9.2.6   PROBATE TAX

9.2.6.1   Spouses

When probate tax was first introduced (FA 1993, Ch. 1 Part VI) the transfer of assets, other than the dwellinghouse (as defined), by will or intestacy to a surviving spouse was not exempt from probate tax. However, this was rectified retrospectively in the Finance Act 1994.

If a spouse receives assets absolutely, no probate tax is payable. However, if assets are left to a spouse, e.g. by way of a trust for life, then the payment of probate tax is deferred until the spouse, i.e. life tenant, dies (FA 1993, s. 115).

If the surviving spouse gives up his/her limited interest for a cash sum, then no probate tax is due on part of the trust assets. This is calculated by reference to the proportion which the cash received bears to the value of the trust assets at the surrender date (FA 1993, s. 115A(1)).

If should also be noted that where the same property is held by one or more persons including the spouse, then only the probate tax relating to the share owned by the spouse is reduced to nil (FA 1993, s. 115A(1)(a)).

9.2.6.2 Children

There is only one probate tax exemption for assets passing by will or intestacy to a child (FA 1993, s. 112(d)). This relates to a dwellinghouse (as defined) which is taken by a child (para. **9.2.4.2**) who was, on the date of death of the parent, a dependent child (as defined) and whose normal place of residence was that dwellinghouse (FA 1993, s. 112(d)).

A dependent child is one who at the date of the parent's death is under 18 years of age or under the age of 21 years and in full-time education or if over 21 years was in full-time education continuously before reaching the age of 21 years (FA 1993, s. 109). To qualify for this exemption, the total income of the dependent child cannot exceed £4,892 (1999/2000). Total income is defined by reference to TCA 1997, s. 466(1). This equals the old age non-contributory pension and living alone allowance.

9.2.7 RESIDENTIAL PROPERTY TAX

This applied to houses and holiday homes but not to 'let' premises (FA 1983, Part VI). It only applied to residential property or properties occupied by individuals on 5 April each year. To be liable to residential property tax, two conditions had to be fulfilled:

(a) the market value of residential property as at the valuation date must exceed the market value exemption limit (for valuation date 5 April 1996, this was £101,000); and

(b) the total gross household income for the tax year ending on the valuation date must exceed the income exemption limits (for 5 April 1996, this was £30,100).

The rate of tax was 1.5 per cent on the value of the residential property exceeding the market value exemption limit. It was one of the few taxes where the existence or non-existence of a marriage did not confer any advantage or disadvantage.

Residential property tax was abolished for valuation date 5 April 1997 onwards.

9.3 Maintenance

9.3.1 INCOME TAX

9.3.1.1 Definition

Perhaps the most common monetary aspect of any legal separation or divorce is the maintenance aspect, i.e. where one spouse has to pay monies for the support of the other spouse and/or children. Essentially, maintenance means being provided either directly or indirectly with basic living essentials such as accommodation, food, clothes, etc. In order to obtain a tax deduction for maintenance payments, it is necessary for the maintenance provisions to comply with the requirements of TCA 1997, s. 1025. The most important requirement is that a benefit must accrue to a child or other party of the marriage. Payments other than direct monetary payments can qualify. Other requirements are the following:

Legally enforceable

The maintenance arrangements must be legally enforceable and made or done in consideration or in consequence of a separation or divorce referred to in TCA 1997, s. 1015. This separation may be factual or legal.

A maintenance arrangement is defined as 'an order of court, deed of separation, rule of court, trust, covenant or any other act which gives rise to a legally enforceable obligation'.

Post-7 June 1983

The provision applies only to legal obligations arising after 7 June 1983. It can apply where a pre-1983 maintenance arrangement is replaced by another post-7 June 1983 arrangement or, in fact, where both parties governed by a pre-1983 maintenance arrangement jointly elect for the 1983 provisions to apply.

Annual/periodical

To qualify as maintenance payments for the purposes of TCA 1997, s. 1025, the payments must be annual or periodic. Lump sum orders granted under FLA 1995, s. 8(1)(c), (2) and FL(D)A 1996, s. 13(1)(c), (2) do not qualify.

No deduction of tax

Maintenance payments are paid without deduction of standard rate income tax (22 per cent for 2000/2001). This is different from the pre-8 June 1983 position.

Spouse/children

The legislative provisions distinguish between maintenance payments made to the children and maintenance payments made to a spouse.

If a payment is directed to be made for the sole use and benefit of a child of the payer; and the amount, or the method of calculating the amount, of such payment is specified in the maintenance arrangement, then:

- the payments must be paid gross (i.e. without deduction of tax);

- the payer is not entitled to a deduction in computing total income for the payments;

- the payments do not rank as income of the child and are not taxable.

The Single Parent Allowance and/or Incapacitated Child Allowance may be claimed as the payments, whether direct or indirect, are a contribution towards the child's maintenance. Examples of indirect child maintenance payments could include payment of the child's school fees, holidays, courses, activities, sports, etc.

A child includes:

(a) a step-child (TCA 1997, s. 6);

(b) a child adopted under the Adoption Acts 1952 to 1991; or

(c) a child whose parents have not married (TCA 1997, s. 8).

All other maintenance payments are deemed to relate to the spouse where payments under a maintenance arrangement are made directly or indirectly by one spouse for the benefit of the other spouse:

- the payment must be made gross;

- the payer is entitled to a tax deduction for the maintenance payments;

- the payee spouse is taxable on the maintenance receipts.

Other jurisdictions

The provision is not confined to maintenance arrangements governed by Irish law only. It extends to maintenance arrangements made under any other jurisdiction also.

9.3.2 TAXATION OPTIONS

9.3.2.1 Single assessment

If a maintenance arrangement fulfils the conditions of TCA 1997, s. 1025, the separated couple are treated for tax purposes as single persons, each liable to tax in their own right.

A tax deduction can be obtained by the paying spouse for any maintenance payments made to the other spouse. The tax deduction is applied in computing total income. However, no tax deduction is available for maintenance payments for the benefit of the children of the marriage as defined above.

The maintenance payments are taxable in the hands of the recipient spouse as Case IV income but he or she is entitled to a Single Person's Allowance and single rate tax bands.

Example:

Couple separated, legally enforceable maintenance payable to lower income earning spouse of £6,000 annually. Income earned by each spouse in own right. Single assessment under TCA 1997 s. 1025, applies.

		£
Higher income spouse		40,000
Lower income spouse		8,000

	Payer spouse's tax bill £		Payee spouses's tax bill £	
Income	40,000		8,000	
Maintenance receipt	—		6,000	
	40,000		14,000	
Maintenance payment	(6,000)		—	
Taxable income	34,000		14,000	
17,000 at 22%	3,740	14,000 at 22%	3,080	
17,000 at 44%	7,480			
34,000	11,220		3,080	
Less: Personal allowance (4,700 at 22%)	(1,034)	(4,700 at 22%)	(1,034)	
	10,186		2,046	12,232
After-tax income	29,814		11,954	
Net disposable income	23,814	(1)	11,954	(2)

(1) £40,000 − (£6,000 + £10,186) = £23,814
(2) £14,000 − £2,046 = £11,954

9.3.2.2 Joint assessment

See TCA 1997, s. 1026. A married but separated couple can continue from a tax point of view as if they were not separated. To do this, there must be a maintenance arrangement as defined by s. 1025 in existence, both parties must be resident in Ireland during the tax year and there must be a joint election in writing for the provision to apply. It applies to separated and divorced couples. For divorced couples each ex-spouse must fulfil a further condition, i.e. neither spouse must have remarried.

At first sight, the provision is an election to joint assessment. The election for joint assessment is, in fact, a misnomer, as the legislation states that the separate assessment rules are to apply. Basically, this means that each spouse submits their own tax return, is entitled to his/her own personal allowances and tax rate bands but pays tax only on his/her own income. However, if either spouse has any unutilised personal allowances or tax rate bands, then these can be transferred to the other spouse. Since the decision to opt for TCA 1997, s. 1026 is a joint one, the usual time limits for separate assessment do not apply. The election may be made at any time during the year. In such a case the election cannot be 'deemed' to apply and must be specifically requested.

The main tax consequence of such an election is that there is no deduction for any maintenance payments paid and no liability attaching to the maintenance received (TCA 1997, s. 1026(2)).

Either party can withdraw from the election prior to the end of the tax year (TCA 1997, s. 1018(3)).

Example:

Married couple separated. Legally enforceable maintenance arrangement entered into, with higher income spouse agreeing to pay maintenance of £6,000 annually. Income earned by each spouse in own right. Both spouses elect for joint assessment under TCA 1997, s. 1026.

				£
Spouse				40,000
Spouse				8,000

	Payer spouse's tax bill £		Payee spouse's tax bill £	
Income	40,000		8,000	
Maintenance receipt	—		n/a	
	40,000		8,000	
Maintenance payment	n/a		—	
Taxable income	40,000		8,000	
17,000 at 22%	3,740	*8,000 at 22%	1,760	
*9,000 at 22%	1,980			
14,000 at 44%	6,160			
40,000	11,880		1,760	
Less: Personal allowance				
(4,700 at 22%)	(1,034)	(4,700 at 22%)	(1,034)	
	10,846		726	11,572
After-tax income	29,154		7,274	
Net disposable income	23,154	(1)	13,274	(2)

(1) £40,000 − (£10,846 + £6,000) = £23,154

(2) £8,000 − £726 + £6,000 = £13,274

* Balance of spouse's share of standard tax rate band, i.e. £17,000 − £8,000 = £9,000 is transferred to higher income spouse.

As a matter of practice, the Inspector of Taxes, if it is clear that only one spouse will have an income for a particular year, will apply the joint assessment rules for the year instead of separate assessment. This would mean that the income-earning spouse would be entitled to the Married Allowances and double rate tax bands up to a maximum of £28,000 with no additional amount taxable at the standard rate up to a maximum of £6,000. Only one Return of Income need be submitted.

Any decision to opt for joint assessment must take into account its impact on the entitlement to the Single Parent Allowance.

If the joint assessment election is not made, each spouse is entitled to a Single Person's Allowance (TCA 1997, s. 462). In addition, any child who is both resident with and maintained by a spouse will entitle the spouse to the Single Parent's Allowance. This need only be for part of the tax year. This could give two single person's allowances (£4,700 × 2) at the standard rate and an additional £3,150 X 2 of the additional standard rate tax band together with 2 × £4,700 Single Parent Allowance granted at the standard rate of tax. If a joint assessment election is made, only the Married Allowance, i.e. £9,400 granted at the standard rate, is available. The tax saving difference could amount to £3,454.

If a joint assessment election is made, it may be possible to claim the Homecarers' Allowance if one spouse is not working or if his/her income is less than £4,000 (see para. **9.2.1.3(e)**).

9.3.2.3 Variation of assessment

If the separated spouses agree, it is possible to change annually their decision between joint assessment and single assessment. Any decision to vary the previous year's treatment must, however, be notified to the Inspector of Taxes before the end of the tax year for which the new decision is to apply. A new decision for joint assessment must always be made by both spouses, but either spouse can revert back to assessment as single persons. However, generally speaking spouses do not tend to use this facility.

9.3.2.4 Non-resident spouses

If only the spouse paying the maintenance is resident in Ireland for tax purposes, it does not preclude him/her obtaining a tax deduction for such payments. The extent to which the non-resident recipient ex-spouse is liable to Irish tax will depend on whether or not there is a Double Taxation Agreement between Ireland and the country of tax residence. If there is no Double Taxation Agreement then the maintenance income is theoretically liable to Irish tax at the standard rate (22 per cent for 2000/01) upwards. There is no entitlement to personal allowances for a non-resident except in specific circumstances (TCA 1997, s. 1032). The Irish Revenue may have difficulty in taxing such maintenance receipts.

In the UK, maintenance arrangements entered into on or after 16 March 1988 are, in general, not taxable in the hands of the recipient spouse. Accordingly, it would appear that if the spouse paying the maintenance is resident in Ireland, and the recipient spouse is resident in the UK then the recipient spouse is not taxable on such maintenance (ICTA 1988, s. 347). This would not preclude the spouse paying the maintenance from obtaining his/her tax deduction for such maintenance payments in Ireland.

If only the spouse receiving the maintenance is tax resident here, then such income is taxable in Ireland and there is entitlement to full personal allowances and other reliefs. The non-resident paying spouse is not entitled to a tax deduction save to the extent that he/she has Irish source income.

9.3.2.5 Differences for separation, divorce and nullity

See TCA 1997, ss. 1025, 1026. In the case of legal separation, judicial separation, Irish or foreign divorce, it is possible for a payer spouse to obtain a tax deduction for maintenance paid to the payee spouse provided there is a maintenance arrangement in place as defined by TCA 1997, s. 1025. The payee spouse is taxable on such maintenance. Each spouse is subject to the single assessment rules.

In the case of a foreign divorce recognised in Ireland and only the ex-spouse paying the maintenance is resident in Ireland for tax purposes, it does not preclude him/her from obtaining a tax deduction for such payments. The extent to which the non-resident recipient ex-spouse is liable to Irish tax will depend on whether or not there is a Double Taxation Agreement between Ireland and the country of tax residence. If there is no Double Taxation Agreement then the maintenance income is subject to Irish tax at the standard rate (22 per cent for 1999/2000) upwards. There is no entitlement to personal allowances for a non-resident except in specified circumstances (TCA 1997, s. 1032). There may be practical difficulties in taxing this income.

If only the ex-spouse receiving the maintenance is tax resident here, then such income is taxable in Ireland and there is entitlement to full personal allowances and other reliefs. The non-resident paying ex-spouse is not entitled to a tax deduction save to the extent that he/she has Irish source income.

It is possible for a separated Irish tax resident couple to opt for joint assessment provided the spouses submit a joint election. In the case of a couple who have obtained an Irish divorce the joint assessment option is available to them provided both ex-spouses are tax resident in Ireland for the tax year and neither ex-spouse has remarried. If a couple have obtained a foreign divorce which is legally recognised here then they can elect for joint assessment if both are tax resident in Ireland and neither ex-spouse has remarried. Although the provisions of TCA 1997, ss. 1025 and 1026 extend to nullity situations, this is superfluous as the question of maintenance arrangements by order of the Circuit/High Court for the benefit of either party in the marriage will not arise. Therefore the joint assessment option under TCA 1997, s. 1026, will not be relevant. If there are children to the marriage, then the Circuit/High Court, if appropriate, will make maintenance provisions. However, as for separated or divorced couples, maintenance provisions for children are effectively treated as being made out of after-tax income.

In general, if either party to a marriage which is recognised here go through divorce proceedings which are not legally recognised under common law or the Domicile and Recognition of Foreign Divorces Act 1986, then the couple are treated as a separated couple and the consequences as outlined in para. **9.3.2** will apply. This assumes that a maintenance order has been made in the divorce decree or a separate legal document has been drawn up regarding this issue.

If a couple obtain a foreign divorce which is not legally recognised in Ireland and one of the parties to the marriage remarries, then this marriage is not recognised in Ireland. Therefore, it is not possible for the newly married couple to obtain any tax benefits. This is subject to one exception. From an income tax point of view, it is current Revenue practice to recognise such a marriage if a foreign marriage certificate is produced. However, if the second marriage is subsequently challenged, the Revenue will follow the legal position.

9.3.3   MORTGAGE INTEREST RELIEF

9.3.3.1   Single assessment

Any monies paid under a legally enforceable maintenance arrangement can qualify for a tax deduction in computing total income for the payer provided there is no joint assessment election under TCA 1997, s. 1026 (see **9.3.2**). These payments are then taxable in the hands of the payee.

If the payee uses the monies for expenditure which qualifies for tax relief, e.g. interest paid on a principal private residence, then the *payee* will get a tax deduction subject to the normal income tax rules.

169

Example:

Married couple living apart. Legally enforceable maintenance arrangement entered into with higher income spouse agreeing to pay £6,000 maintenance annually to lower income spouse for his/her maintenance. Lower income spouse to discharge mortgage repayments from maintenance and own funds. Higher income spouse lives in rented accommodation. Income earned by each spouse in own right. Single assessment under TCA 1997, s. 1025 applies.

	£
Higher income spouse	40,000
Lower income spouse	8,000
Mortgage interest payments (year 6 of mortgage)	1,100
Mortgage repayments (£35,000 for 15 years at APR of 5.50 per cent) say	4,800
Tax relief on mortgage interest for non-first time mortgage holder	1,100
Rent payments	4,200

	Payer spouse's tax bill £		*Payee spouse's tax bill* £	
Income	40,000		8,000	
Maintenance receipt			6,000	
	40,000		14,000	
Maintenance payment	(6,000)			
Taxable income	34,000		14,000	
17,000 at 22%	3,740	14,000 at 22%	3,080	
17,000 at 44%	7,480		—	
34,000	11,220		3,080	
Less: Personal allowance (4,700 at 22%)	(1,034)	4,700 at 22%	(1,034)	
Rent allowance (max) (750 at 22%)	(165)			
VHI (602 at 22%)			(132)	
Interest relief (1,100 at 22%)			(242)	
	10,021		1,672	11,693
After-tax income	29,979		12,328	
Net disposable income	19,779	(1)	7,528	(2)

   (1)   £40,000 (£10,021 + £6,000 + £4,200) = £19,779
   (2)   £8,000 + £6,000 (£1,672 + £4,800) = £7,528

Alternatively, the payer spouse may discharge directly payments due on mortgage for the principal private residence. It is possible for this spouse to obtain income tax relief for mortgage interest payments. If single assessment is opted for, the maximum interest relief available is for a single person only.

9.3.3.2   Joint assessment

If there are monies payable under a legally enforceable maintenance arrangement, it is possible for the couple to opt for joint assessment under TCA 1997, s. 1026. In this situation if either the payer or payee spouse pays the mortgage payments due on the principal private residence then the couple are entitled to the same mortgage interest relief as a married couple living together. As set out at **9.3.2**, the separate assessment rules are deemed to apply and accordingly each spouse is entitled to mortgage interest relief in the proportion that each has paid interest up to the relevant limit as set out in TCA 1997, s. 244. If one spouse pays all the mortgage interest then he/she is entitled to the tax relief on mortgage interest payments for himself/herself and his/her spouse subject to the overall limits set out in TCA 1997, s. 244.

Example:

Married couple living apart. Legally enforceable maintenance arrangement entered into with higher income spouse agreeing to pay £6,000 maintenance annually to lower income spouse for his/her maintenance. Higher income spouse to discharge mortgage repayments. Higher income spouse lives in rented accommodation. Income earned by each spouse.

Joint assessment under TCA 1997, s. 1026 applies.

	£
Higher income spouse	40,000
Lower income spouse	8,000
Mortgage interest payments (year 6 of mortgage)	2,200
Mortgage repayments (£70,000 for 15 years at APR of 5.50 per cent) say	9,600
Rent payments	4,200

	Payer spouse's tax bill £		Payee spouse's tax bill £	
Income	40,000		8,000	
Maintenance receipt			N/A	
	40,000		8,000	
Maintenance payment	N/A		—	
Taxable income	40,000		8,000	
17,000 at 22%	3,740	8,000 at 22%	1,920	
*9,000 at 22%	1,980			
14,000 at 44%	6,160		—	
40,000	11,880		1,760	
Less: Personal allowance (4,700 at 22%)	(1,034)	4,700 at 22%	(1,034)	
Rent allowance (max) (750 at 22%)	(165)		—	
Interest relief (2,200 at 22%)	(484)			
	10,197		726	10,923
After-tax income	29,803		7,274	
Net disposable income	10,003 (1)		13,274 (2)	

* Balance of spouse's share of standard rate band (i.e. £17,000 – £8,000) is transferred to higher income spouse.

(1) £40,000 – (£10,197 + £6,000 + £4,200 + £9,600) = £10,003
(2) £8,000 + £6,000 – (£726) = £13,274

9.3.3.3 General

It is also possible to have the mortgage, i.e. capital and interest payments, treated as maintenance payments by the payer spouse. To qualify as a maintenance payment it must be for the benefit of the other spouse.

For example, a mortgage on the family home is in joint names and the couple make a maintenance arrangement whereby the higher income spouse discharges the mortgage repayments on the family home and the lower income spouse continues to live in it with the children. As the home is in joint names, the higher income spouse is still obliged to pay his/her half of the mortgage. The higher income spouse's portion of the mortgage payment will qualify for interest relief but not as a payment for the other spouse's benefit and so not as maintenance.

The remainder may qualify for tax relief as maintenance. The lower income spouse would be taxable on these mortgage repayments made on his/her behalf but will qualify for interest relief on the interest element.

Furthermore, the higher income spouse can choose between interest relief and maintenance in relation to his spouse's share of the mortgage repayments. However, it must be done on a consistent basis. In general, it is more tax effective for the payer spouse to have the other spouse's share of mortgage repayments treated as maintenance.

Where interest is treated as legally enforceable maintenance, it is not subject to the interest tax relief restrictions. The entire mortgage repayment, both interest and capital, is allowable without restriction as a maintenance deduction. It is possible, as part of the maintenance arrangement, to make two distinct sets of payments, of which one can be regarded as interest qualifying for tax relief as interest and the other as maintenance.

9.3.3.4 Differences for separation, divorce and nullity

Under TCA 1997, s. 244 (as amended by FA 2000, s. 17) it is possible for a spouse to claim mortgage interest relief for mortgage payments made on a principal private residence occupied by his/her former or separated spouse with the quantum of tax relief available determined on whether single or joint assessment under ss. 1025 or 1026 of TCA 1997 is claimed.

If a nullity decree is obtained no tax relief for such mortgage repayments can be obtained.

9.3.4 VHI/BUPA RELIEF

9.3.4.1 Single assessment

If monies are paid under a legally enforceable maintenance arrangement then a tax deduction can be obtained by the payer spouse in computing total income if the assessment rules under TCA 1997, s. 1025 apply. These payments are then taxable in the hands of the payee spouse. If the payee spouse uses these monies to pay VHI/BUPA premiums then the payee spouse will get a tax deduction subject to the normal income tax rules. Tax relief for a year of assessment for VHI/BUPA premiums is granted at the standard rate of tax in respect of premiums paid in the preceding tax year (TCA 1997, s. 470).

9.3.4.2 Joint assessment

As for mortgage interest payments, if a joint assessment election is made under TCA 1997, s. 1026, then tax relief for VHI/BUPA premiums paid is firstly available to the spouse who paid the premiums and if such spouse has insufficient income to avail of the tax relief then the other spouse can claim the tax relief.

9.3.4.3 Differences for separation, divorce and nullity

If a couple are separated then if a spouse pays VHI/BUPA premiums for the benefit of himself/herself, his/her spouse and dependent children then he/she can claim tax relief under TCA 1997, s. 470. However, if the couple are divorced or obtain a nullity decree, then no tax relief is available to the payer spouse for VHI/BUPA premiums paid on behalf of the other ex-spouse or former spouse. This can be redressed by designating the VHI/BUPA payment as part of the maintenance arrangement and letting the payee spouse claim the tax relief.

9.3.5 INCOME EXEMPTION LIMIT

See TCA 1997, ss. 187, 188. When dealing with the tax implications of maintenance arrangements it is important to take cognisance of the various tax reliefs available including the exemption limit for income. Please refer to para. **9.2.1.3(d)** for the necessary conditions to claim the relief.

9.3.6 BUSINESS ASSETS

As part of a financial arrangement, it may be agreed or ordered by the court that assets owned jointly should be transferred to one spouse. In this situation, if a partnership existed between a husband and wife then upon the transfer of the partnership assets there is a cessation of trade for income tax purposes. This means that the cessation of trade rules will come into play for both spouses. In addition, a balancing allowance/charge may arise on the transfer of assets which qualified for capital allowances. In some circumstances it is possible to avoid the balancing allowances/charges, for example, by a joint election claim under TCA 1997, s. 289(5) for plant and machinery. The spouse acquiring the partnership assets will be subject to the commencement of trade rules for income tax. If the partnership carried on a farming trade and income averaging was claimed, the cessation of the partnership trade will give rise to a review of the income averaged for the two years prior to the last year of averaging. In addition, the spouse acquiring the partnership assets cannot claim income averaging until the fourth tax year of trading in his/her own name. These are some of the income tax issues other than capital gains tax issues which need to be considered if there is a transfer of business assets (see **9.2.3** for capital gains tax issues).

9.3.7 PENSION ADJUSTMENT ORDERS

9.3.7.1 Generally

Under FLA 1995, s. 12 and FL(D)A 1996, s. 17, the court has the power to adjust pension policy schemes as between spouses and dependent members of the family. The types of pension schemes included are occupational pension schemes, self-employed retirement annuity contracts, buy-out bonds and any other similar type schemes (FLA 1995, s. 2(1) and FL(D)A 1996, s. 2). Overseas pension schemes fall within the scope of the legislation but income continuance, permanent health insurance and other similar plans do not. Pensions and benefits provided under the Social Welfare Acts are also outside the scope of the legislation. Before making a pension adjustment order, the court must see if adequate provision can be made outside pension assets (FLA 1995, s. 12(23) and FL(D)A 1996, s. 17(23)). Either spouse can apply to the court for a pension adjustment order.

There are two types of orders which can be made by the court:

(a) Retirement benefits order

This refers to pensions, lump sums payable in addition to, or in substitution for all or part of a pension, periodic pension increases, benefits payable on death following retirement, and

173

preserved death benefits. These benefits could be payable at normal pension age, earlier or later retirement, or termination of reckonable service (FLA 1995, s. 12(2), FL(D)A 1996, s. 17(2)).

(b) Contingent benefits order

This refers solely to death in service benefits, i.e. benefits payable on the death of a member spouse while in relevant employment prior to the normal pension age (FLA 1995, s. 12(3), FL(D)A 1996, s. 17(3)).

9.3.7.2   Retirement benefits order

A retirement benefits order will require that part or all of a member spouse's accrued retirement benefit be payable to either the non-member spouse, or to a person for the benefit of a dependent member of the family. The amount that will be designated to a non-member spouse or dependent member of the family will depend on:

(1)   the period of pensionable service to be taken into account up to the date of granting of the judicial separation decree; and

(2)   the appropriate percentage of the retirement benefit accrued during the pensionable service period, which is to be paid to the person specified in the order (normally 50 per cent to date). It is called the Designated Benefit.

Such orders may be varied upon application unless the court otherwise orders (FLA 1995, ss. 12(26), 18(1), (2) and FL(D)A 1996, ss. 17(22), 22(1), (2)). It should be noted that unless the court makes some type of adjustment order, either a nominal one of no real import or of no real effect, then the blocking of the variation of the order cannot be achieved under FLA 1995, ss. 12(26), 18(1), (2) and FL(D)A 1996, ss. 17(26), 22(1) .

9.3.7.3   Member spouse

From a pension point of view, the amount designated to a non-member spouse is still part of the member spouse's retirement benefit for the purposes of determining the maximum benefits on retirement as is determined by TCA 1997, ss. 771–787 and Revenue Practice Notes (October 1996). The amount payable to the member spouse is reduced by the amount designated to the non-member spouse.

Pension payments are treated as income of the recipient and, depending on the scheme, are subject to PAYE deductions or deductions at the standard rate of tax (22 per cent for 2000/01).

With regard to the lump sum, the amount payable to the member spouse is the maximum amount allowed under TCA 1997, ss. 771–787 less any amount which could be receivable by the non-member spouse. Such lump sum payments can be received free of tax by the member spouse.

9.3.7.4   Non-member spouse

From a pension point of view, the retirement benefit designated to the non-member spouse by the court is not regarded as a benefit for the purposes of calculating the Revenue maximum benefits that may be provided under any other scheme for the non-member spouse. If the retirement benefit allocated to a non-member spouse is transferred into the member spouse's own scheme (treated as an independent benefit), any other occupational pension scheme, or under an approved insurance policy or contract, the independent benefit scheme must be approved by the Revenue.

As for the member spouse, any pension payments will be subject to PAYE deductions or deductions at the standard rate of tax (22 per cent for 2000/01).

At any time after the member spouse has retired, the non-member spouse may take his/her share of the retirement benefit partly as a lump sum and obtain a reduced pension. The maximum lump sum which a non-member spouse can obtain is based on the maximum lump sum receivable by the member spouse as at the date of transfer on the assumption that his/her employment had ceased then. Again, the lump sum can be obtained tax-free.

9.3.7.5   Contingent benefits order

This relates to any benefit payable on the death of a member spouse which is to be paid to the non-member spouse. It can relate to any lump sum and/or to a pension. Such orders must be applied for within one year of granting the decree of judicial separation or divorce decree. There is no power to vary an order in relation to a contingent benefit (FLA 1995, s. 18(1), FL(D)A 1996, s. 22(1)). Lump sum benefits are not subject to income tax or capital acquisitions tax in the hands of the non-member spouse. Pension payments would be subject to income tax.

9.3.7.6   Children

In general the type of pension adjustment orders that can be made for a non-member spouse can also be made for children. However, under the FLA 1995 and FL(D)A 1996, the definition of dependent member of a family is wider than the definition of children used for the purposes of the Taxes Consolidation Acts and Capital Acquisitions Tax Act 1976.

Any pension payments made to a dependent member of the family would be subject to PAYE deductions or deductions of income tax at the standard rate (22 per cent for 2000/01). Pension payments may have capital acquisitions tax implications, particularly those payable following the death of the member spouse. Lump sum payments would be received free of income tax but could be subject to capital acquisitions tax.

All pension payments cease when the person ceases to be a dependent member of the family as defined.

9.3.8   CHILD MAINTENANCE

9.3.8.1   Tax relief

Payment of maintenance to or for the benefit of a child does not have any income tax consequences. It is deemed to be paid out of after-tax income by the payer spouse. Correspondingly, the receipt of such maintenance by a child or by a spouse on behalf of the child does not give rise to an income tax liability in the hands of the recipient.

The maintenance orders that can be made by a court for a spouse can also be made for a dependent child. A dependent child is defined in both FLA 1995, s. 2(1) and FL(D)A 1996, s. 2(1) by reference to a dependent member of the family. A dependent member of the family means any child:

(a) of both spouses or adopted by both spouses under the Adoption Acts 1952 to 1991, or in relation to whom both spouses are *in loco parentis*; or

(b) of either spouse or adopted by either spouse under those Acts or in relation to whom either spouse is *in loco parentis*, where the other spouse, being aware that he or she is not the parent of the child, has treated the child as a member of the family.

The child must be under the age of 18 years or if aged 18 years or more:

–   must be receiving full-time education or instruction at any university, college, school or other educational establishment and must be under the age of 23 years; or

–   must have a mental or physical disability to such extent that it is not reasonably possible for the child to maintain himself or herself fully.

For judicial separation proceedings commenced prior to 1 August 1996, a dependent child was defined similarly but the upper age limit was 21 years where a child was in full-time education.

The upper age limit for a dependent child in full-time education for orders under s. 5 of the Family Law (Maintenance of Spouses and Children) Act 1976 as amended has been increased to 23 years with effect from 1 August 1996.

The definition of child has been extended in the Adoption Act 1998 to include 'simple' foreign adoptions.

9.3.8.2   Entitlement to single parent allowance

See TCA 1997, s. 462 (as amended by FA 2000, s. 6). When a married couple separate the children of the marriage may reside with either spouse for the full tax year. Alternatively, they may reside with both spouses at different times during the year. For example, the children may reside with the mother during the week and with the father at weekends or alternate weekends. In this situation, either or both spouses may be entitled to the Single Parent Allowance. For 2000/2001 this is £4,700 granted at the standard rate, i.e. 22 per cent with the normal standard rate tax band for a single person increased by £3,150 (FA 2000, ss. 3, 6).

For a parent to be entitled to this allowance, certain conditions must be fulfilled including:

–   the child must, during the tax year, be under the age of 18 years or, if over the age of 18 years, attending full-time education. Alternatively, the child must be permanently incapacitated by reason of mental or physical infirmity from main-taining himself and had become so permanently incapacitated before the age of 21 years or, if over the age of 21 years, was attending full-time education or training at the time of his permanent incapacity;

–   the child must be maintained at the parent's own expense for the whole or part of the tax year; and

–   the child must reside with the parent for the whole or part of the tax year. If the child is not a child of the parent then the parent must have custody of the child. Child includes a step-child, a child whose parents have not married and an adopted child adopted under the Adoption Acts.

–   If both spouses each maintain a child who resides with each parent for part of the tax year, it is possible for each parent to claim the full Single Parent Allowance. The Single Parent Allowance is not apportioned between the parents. Only one Single Parent Allowance is given to a taxpayer irrespective of the number of children (even if there is only one child) that may qualify. Maintenance for this purpose can be either voluntary, by court order or by legal agreement.

Example:

Married couple living apart. Children reside with one spouse during the week and with other spouse at weekends. No maintenance in respect of other spouse payable by either spouse. Each spouse maintains children when children are residing with them. Income earned by each spouse in own right.

			£
Higher income spouse			40,000
Lower income spouse			8,000

	Spouse's tax bill £		Spouse's tax bill £	
Total and taxable income	40,000		8,000	
20,150 at 22%	4,433	8,000 at 22%	1,760	
19,850 at 44%	8,734		—	
40,000	13,167		1,760	
Less: Personal allowance				
(4,700 at 22%)	(1,034)	(4,700 at 22%)	(1,034)	
Single Parent Allowance	(1,034)	(3,300 at 22%)	(726)	
(4,700 at 22%)	——	(1)	——	
	11,099		Nil	11,099
After-tax income	28,901		8,000	
Net disposable income	28,901	(2)	8,000	

(1) Single Parent Allowance limited to income taxable at the 22 per cent rate.
(2) £40,000 − £11,099 = £28,901

Three exclusions apply. These are:

(a) if a spouse is entitled to the Married Allowance, he/she cannot claim the Single Parent Allowance;

(b) if a separated spouse starts a household with a new partner then, in this case, he or she cannot claim Single Parent Allowance as the legislation precludes the relief being claimed where a man and woman are living together as husband and wife;

(c) if a child has income in his or her own right, then the Single Parent Allowance may be restricted. If the child's income exceeds £720 then the portion of the Single Parent Allowance granted at the standard rate is reduced £1 for each £1 by which the income exceeds £720. This is also done on a £1 for £1 basis. Scholarships, bursaries and other educational endowments are not taken into account as income for this purpose.

9.3.8.3   Entitlement to Incapacitated Child Allowance

Where a separated couple are assessed as single persons, the £1,600 Incapacitated Child Allowance granted at the standard rate of tax is apportioned based on the maintenance incurred by each spouse in maintaining the incapacitated child.

Where a couple are subject to joint assessment, then the allowance is divided equally between them unless the child is informally adopted where the allowance is apportioned based on monies expended on maintenance (TCA 1997, s. 1024(2)(ii), (iii)).

9.3.9 FACTUAL SEPARATION

9.3.9.1 Tax treatment: general

When a married couple decide to separate or live apart, one of the first tax consequences to arise is the change in their income tax status.

Both formal and informal separations are recognised for income tax purposes. It has been recognised by case law that not all couples living apart are necessarily separated. A separation may be due to business travel, illness, etc., of one of the spouses. There must be an intention by the parties to end the marriage. Therefore, couples living apart due to circumstances beyond their control are normally regarded for income tax purposes as living together. For example, in a 1947 High Court decision, it was held that the wife was 'living with' her husband where he, a Gardaí, was compelled to live at least 30 miles from her licensed premises: *D Ua Clothasaigh v Patrick McCartan* (1947) 2 ITC 237.

Examples of likely permanent separation could include one spouse leaving the marital home to live with a third party, living of separate lives but remaining under the same roof, etc.

This phrase 'living apart' has been recently considered in the UK. In *Holmes v Mitchell* [1991] STC 25, it was held that the Inland Revenue Commissioners were entitled to find that a couple who lived as separate households under the same roof were permanently separated for tax purposes. Following this case, the UK Revenue issued guidelines for similar cases. In particular, a UK inspector is instructed to ask questions along the following lines:

(1) How has the house been divided up and what are the arrangements for using kitchen and bathroom facilities?

(2) What services do they provide for each other, for example, meals, laundry, etc?

(3) What financial arrangements have been made in relation to the alleged separation?

(4) How do they manage to avoid each other?

It is likely that an Irish inspector would ask similar questions in order to reach a conclusion.

There have been no recent reported Irish tax cases on 'living together'. However, in January 2000, McCracken J, in *M.McA. v X. McA.* (unreported, 21 January 2000, High Ct), delivered a decision in the first reported contested divorce dealing with, inter alia, the concept of living apart while remaining in the same house. It was held that the issue of living apart means something more than physical separation and the mental attitude and intention of both spouses is of considerable relevance. Furthermore, marriage is not primarily concerned with where the parties live or whether they live under the same roof, and just as physically separated spouses can maintain a full matrimonial relationship, spouses who live under the same roof can be living apart from one another. In determining whether the parties were living apart the court must look to where the spouses reside and their mental attitude. This is a mixed test comprising both an objective and a subjective element. In this case where the spouses were not physically separated, the main test for determining 'living apart' was the mental attitude of both parties. McCracken J in reaching his decision did not raise such queries as considered in *Holmes v Mitchell* [1991] STC 25, above.

In a second High Court decision delivered by O'Sullivan J in June 1999 (*Moorehead v Tiilikainen*, unreported, 17 June 1999, High Ct), issued in the context of determining if a reconciliation of separated spouses had taken place, it was emphasised that both the mental attitude and physical togetherness of both spouses are necessary to determine if spouses are living together. O'Sullivan J also confirmed that, in this case, a three-month work absence did not mean that a couple are living apart.

9.3.9.2   Tax year of separation: separation likely to be permanent

In the year of separation, the couple are living together for part of the year and separated for the remainder. A question needs to be asked. Do the income tax rules for married couples or separated couples apply in the tax year of separation?

Joint assessment

An assessable spouse is entitled to the Married Allowance if the couple are taxed on the joint assessment basis (TCA 1997, s. 461(a)). There is no provision in the Taxes Consolidation Act for apportioning allowances on a time basis. If Married Allowance is due, it is due for the entire year.

The assessable spouse is liable to income tax for that tax year on his/her own income for the full year and on the spouse's income up to the date of separation.

The non-assessable spouse is taxed on his/her own income from the date of separation to the end of that tax year and is entitled to the Single Person's Allowance and single rate tax bands.

Example:

Date of factual separation: 5 July 2000

Tax bill for 2000/2001 for a couple earning income as follows:

		£
Assessable spouse		40,000
Non-assessable spouse – Up to 5 July 2000		2,000
– 6 July 2000–5 April 2001		6,000
		8,000

		Assessable spouse's tax bill £		Non-assessable spouse's tax bill £	
Total and taxable income	(s)	40,000		6,000	
	(w)	2,000			
		42,000		6,000	
28,000 at 22%		6,160	6,000 at 22%	1,320	
2,000 at 22%		440			
12,000 at 44%		5,280			
42,000		11,880		1,320	
Less: Personal allowance (9,400 at 22%)		(2,068)	(4,700 at 22%)	(1,034)	
		9,812		286	10,098
After-tax income (own only)		30,188		7,714	
Net disposable income		30,188	(1)	7,714	

(1)   £40,000 − £9,812 = £30,188

The married couple's tax bill of £10,098 in the tax year of separation is less than for a married couple living together, i.e. £11,572 (see para. **9.2.1.2**).

TAX IMPLICATIONS OF MARRIAGE BREAKDOWN

In this example, the wife's income has been apportioned on a time basis over the tax year. In practice, arbitrary apportionments cannot be made. Actual details of the wife's income from 6 April to the date of separation and from the date of separation to the following 5 April must be obtained.

Separate assessment

As for joint assessment, this remains in force for the tax year of separation. However, transfers of tax-free allowances and tax rate bands are permissible only up to the date of separation. In order to determine who is the assessable spouse, one has to consider TCA 1997, ss. 1017 and 1019. If the husband is the assessable spouse, then it is the wife who is taxed on her own income up to date of separation, with unused personal allowances and tax bands being transferred to the husband. The non-assessable spouse, i.e. the wife, would be subject to tax in her own right from date of separation to the following 5 April.

Example:

Date of separation: 5 July 2000

Tax bill for 2000/2001 for a couple earning income as follows:

	£	£
Assessable spouse		40,000
Non-assessable spouse – up to 5 July 2000		2,000
– 6 July 2000–5 April 2001		6,000
		8,000

(i) Assessable spouse (for full year)

	£	£
Total and taxable income		40,000
14,000 at 22%	3,080	
*14,000 at 22% (non-assessable spouse's unutilised share)	3,080	
12,000 at 44%	5,280	
40,000	11,440	
Less: Personal allowance		
(4,700 at 22%)	(1,034)	
(*2,700 at 22% non-assessable spouse's unutilised share)	(594)	
Tax bill	9,812	
After-tax income (own only)	30,188	
Net disposable income	30,188	(1)

    (1)   £40,000 − £9,812 = £30,188

(ii) Non-assessable spouse (pre-separation)

	£
Total and taxable income	2,000
*2,000 at 22% (note)	440
Less: Personal allowance	
*(2,000 at 22%)	(440)
Tax bill	Nil

Note:

Utilises part of £6,000 additional standard rate tax band granted to non-assessable working spouse.

*Excess personal allowances of £2,700 granted at the standard rate plus £14,000 of the standard tax rate band can be transferred to assessable spouse (see (i) above).

(iii) Non-assessable spouse (post-separation)

Total and taxable income	6,000
6,000 at 22%	1,320
Less: Personal allowance	
(4,700 at 22%)	(1,034)
Tax bill	286

The married couple's tax bill, i.e. £9,812 and £286 = £10,098 in the tax year of separation, is less than for a married couple living together, i.e. £11,572 (para. **9.2.1.2**).

Single assessment

Each spouse continues as before to submit his/her own tax return and pay their own respective tax bills. There is no change to their tax status in the year of separation.

9.3.9.3 **Subsequent tax years**

If the separation extends beyond the tax year of separation, the married couple are treated as two single people for income tax purposes. They are assessable on their own income, required to submit their own tax returns and make timely tax payments.

Example:

Date of separation: 5 July 2000

Tax bill for 2001/02 for a separated couple earning income as follows:

(2000/01 allowances and rates assumed to apply for 2001/02)

			£
Higher income spouse			40,000
Lower income spouse			8,000

No maintenance payable by either spouse

	Higher income spouse's tax bill £		Lower income spouse's tax bill £	
Total and taxable income	40,000		8,000	
17,000 at 22%	3,740	8,000 at 22%	1,760	
23,000 at 44%	10,120			
40,000	13,860		1,760	
Less: Personal allowance				
(4,700 at 22%)	(1,034)	(4,700 at 22%)	(1,034)	
	12,826		726	13,552
Net disposable income	27,174	(1)	7,274	(2)

181

(1) £40,000 − £12,826 = £27,174

(2) £8,000 − £726 = £7,274

The income tax bill for 2001/2002 shows a substantial increase over the 2000/2001 income tax bill for the tax year of separation or when they are living together:

	£
Living together	11,572
Tax year of separation (above)	10,098
Subsequent tax year (above)	13,552

9.3.9.4 Voluntary maintenance

Obviously, at this stage, the question of maintenance for a dependent spouse may need to be addressed. In a lot of cases, arrangements regarding maintenance may be informal for a period of time.

There is no tax deduction available for voluntary maintenance payments as the statutory provisions only allow a deduction in computing total income for maintenance payments made under a legally binding document. Correspondingly, the receipt of voluntary maintenance payments is not taxable. In this context, voluntary maintenance can be defined as maintenance payments made without agreement of the payee spouse. The Revenue also consider verbal maintenance agreements as voluntary due to the anticipated difficulties in enforcing an oral agreement.

Interaction of Married Allowance and voluntary maintenance

If a husband is wholly or mainly maintaining his wife, he is entitled to the Married Allowance (TCA 1997, s. 461(a)). As a rule of thumb, the Revenue grant the Married Allowance provided maintenance payments to his wife exceed income earned in her own right.

Up to 1995/96 inclusive, if a wife wholly or mainly maintained her husband, she was not entitled to the Married Allowance. For the tax year 1996/97 onwards, the Married Allowance is also given to a wife of the married couple not living together (FA 1996, Sch. 1).

It is understood that the Revenue will only grant the Married Allowance to the wife provided her own maintenance payments to her husband exceed income earned in his own right.

Since 1993/94, the Revenue have, as a matter of practice, been granting the Married Allowance to a wife in the same circumstances as for a husband.

Example:

Couple living apart and one spouse is mainly maintained by the other spouse. Voluntary maintenance of £6,000 annually is paid. Income earned by each spouse in own right.

	£
Payer spouse	40,000
Payee spouse	8,000

	Payer spouse's tax bill £		Payee spouse's tax bill £	
Income	40,000		8,000	
Maintenance receipt			n/a	
	40,000		8,000	
Less: Maintenance payment	n/a			
Total and taxable income	40,000		8,000	
17,000 at 22%	3,740	8,000 at 22%	1,760	
23,000 at 44%	10,120			
40,000	13,860	1,760		
Less: Personal allowance (9,400 at 22%)	(2,068)	(4,200 at 22%)	(1,034)	
	11,792		726	12,518
After-tax income	22,208		7,274	
Net disposable income	22,208	(1)	13,274	(2)

(1)   £40,000 − (£6,000 + £11,792) = £22,208
(2)   £8,000 − £726 + £6,000 = £13,274

Each spouse is taxed as a single person and the spouse paying the maintenance obtains the Married Allowance (TCA 1997, s. 461(a)). If the annual voluntary maintenance figure is less than the income earned by the payee spouse, the Revenue will not grant the Married Allowance to the payer spouse in practice. If the voluntary maintenance is split between spouse and children, then the children's maintenance is excluded in determining the level of maintenance payments for the purpose of determining entitlement to Married Allowance.

Impact on income tax reliefs: mortgage interest

When a couple separate, the tax reliefs available for mortgage interest relief may change.

If a couple separate and the higher income spouse continues to pay the mortgage repayments for the family home, then interest relief will be granted by the Revenue as if he/she were a single person. This will have effect for the second tax year of separation onwards (TCA 1997, s. 244). The reason for this is that the married couple's increased interest relief provisions only apply where the couple are jointly or separately assessed, i.e. assessed under TCA 1997, s. 1017.

It is also possible for a separated spouse to qualify for tax relief on interest payments both on his/her own residence and a separated spouse's residence. However, the single person's interest relief limit of £2,500 will still apply.

If a spouse claims tax relief for interest paid on a loan for his/her separated spouse's main residence, that interest will not be regarded as a maintenance payment. Therefore a spouse would not be entitled to Married Allowance unless further voluntary payments were made to wholly or mainly maintain his/her spouse and such payments exceed the income earned by the lower income spouse in his/her own right.

It should be noted that interest relief will not be available if the mortgage is in the name of, say, the lower income spouse and mortgage repayments are made by the higher income spouse who occupies the residence. This is due to the fact that the loan was not taken out by the spouse making the mortgage repayments.

9.3.9.5   Interim agreement

The process of resolving all matters pertaining to the separation may take some considerable period of time.

As no tax deduction is available for voluntary maintenance payments it is possible to draw up an interim agreement signed by both parties dealing with this issue pending resolution of other matters. Such an agreement would bring the maintenance payments within the scope of TCA 1997, s. 1025.

In some cases it may not always be possible for a separated couple to agree the amount of maintenance payable to one spouse. In other cases, one spouse, particularly the recipient spouse, may not agree to sign a document confirming the terms of the interim maintenance arrangement.

In such situations, it should be possible for one spouse to draw up a deed of covenant in favour of the other spouse to deal with the issue of interim maintenance. As long as the terms of the deed of covenant fulfil the conditions necessary under TCA 1997, s. 1025 the covenant would bring the maintenance payments out of the realm of voluntary payments and the paying spouse would be entitled to obtain a tax deduction for these payments. It is only necessary for one spouse to sign the document for the covenant to be legally effective. It is important to note that the covenant must be drawn up in consideration or in consequence of the separation and this must be set out in the covenant deed. The deed must be signed, sealed and delivered. The document must also be witnessed.

As the recipient spouse would be liable to income tax in respect of such covenanted maintenance monies, it is necessary that he/she is advised. This may then precipitate a court application on the part of the recipient. Proceedings for maintenance 'simpliciter' may be issued in the District Court under the Family Law (Maintenance of Spouses and Children) Act 1976, s. 5 (as amended).

The normal requirement to deduct income tax at the standard rate (22 per cent for 2000/01) on payment of the covenant monies does not apply (TCA 1997, ss. 792, 1025(3)).

A maintenance pending suit order granted under FLA 1995, s. 7 would also qualify as an interim agreement as would a similar order in FL(D)A 1996, s. 12.

9.3.10   COURT ORDERS

9.3.10.1   Lump sum maintenance order

Maintenance payments made on foot of a lump sum order granted under FLA 1995, s. 8(1)(c), (2) or FL(D)A 1996, s. 13(1)(a), (2) do not qualify as a tax deduction in the hands of the payer as they are not annual or periodic (TCA 1997, s. 1025).

9.3.10.2   Secured periodical payments order

A secured periodical payments order could represent maintenance, the payment of which is secured against a non-income producing asset such as land. Alternatively, as happens in the UK, a secured periodical payments order could require one spouse to transfer income-producing assets, such as shares, to trustees with the income to be used to pay maintenance to the other spouse. If the obligation to pay maintenance ceases, the trust ends and the assets revert to the settlor spouse. While the obligation to pay maintenance continues the recipient spouse must look to the trustees for the maintenance. The settlor spouse is under no personal obligation to pay the maintenance. On the face of it, a secured periodical payments order in favour of a spouse by way of trust is within the definition of maintenance arrangement as defined by TCA 1997, s. 1025. The income tax effect of the order is that the trust income distributed to the recipient spouse as maintenance is taxable as his/her income under Schedule D Case IV. Any surplus trust income not needed to pay maintenance is taxable as income of the settlor spouse. Even if the anti-avoidance provisions contained in TCA 1997, s. 791(2)-(4) applied to deem the income to be that of the settlor spouse, it is the writer's view that the provisions of TCA 1997, s. 1025 would come into play and the settlor spouse should be in a position to obtain a tax deduction for such maintenance paid to the recipient spouse.

If the secured periodical payments are ordered to be paid to a dependent child, it can be assumed following *Yates v Starkey* [1951] Ch 465, that the order creates a settlement for tax purposes particularly if the dependent child is under the age of 18 years. Consequently, the trust income will remain income of the parent and will not be income of the child. However, this merely reflects the general rule for child maintenance, which is that unless it can be included as part of the maintenance for a spouse, it is not the taxable income of the child and no tax relief is given to the payer spouse (TCA 1997, s. 1025). For a dependent child over the age of 18 years and under the age of 23 years, if still in full-time education, TCA 1997, s. 1025 would prevent the payer spouse obtaining a tax deduction.

In the event of a secured periodical payments order being made, the court should be made aware of the tax consequences of such an order. See also para. **9.2.3** for capital gains tax consequences. Secured periodical payments orders are not used frequently in Ireland. Attachment of earnings orders are more common.

9.3.11 PRSI AND HEALTH CONTRIBUTION LEVY (HCL)

When a couple separate the mere fact of separation does not give rise to any change in their respective PRSI and HCL liability.

Payment of voluntary maintenance does not give rise to a PRSI/HCL liability for the recipient spouse. The payer spouse cannot receive any refund of the HCL for income paid out as voluntary maintenance.

For the payer spouse PRSI refunds cannot be obtained for income paid out as voluntary maintenance.

The question of PRSI and HCL on maintenance payments and receipts only arises if a married couple choose to be assessed as two single persons under TCA 1997, s. 1025.

In the case of a spouse who is receiving maintenance payment from his/her spouse and is taxable as a single person in his/her own right, he/she will have a liability for the tax year 2000/2001 to pay PRSI for the self-employed at the rate of 5 per cent up to total income of £26,500. PRSI is not payable if gross income including maintenance is less than £2,500.

PRSI for the self-employed is not payable in respect of maintenance received if the recipient spouse pays PRSI as an employee. However, if the recipient spouse has a trade or professional income as a self-employed individual then PRSI will be payable on the maintenance receipt (SW (Con) A 1993, Sch. 1, Part III, para. 4).

In addition, health contributions at the rate of 2 per cent are also due. These are not payable for 2000/2001 if his/her gross income including maintenance is £14,560 or less. These percentages amount to 7 per cent and can represent a fairly hefty outflow from the recipient's maintenance income.

In addition, as the maintenance-paying spouse would, more than likely, have paid PRSI/HCL and levies on his/her own income, there is an element of double taxation. This is a further factor which should be borne in mind when considering whether or not to opt for single or joint assessment. This element of double taxation has been rectified for HCL for

1995/96 onwards in the Social Welfare Act 1995, s. 25. The maintenance paying spouse is entitled to a refund of HCL relating to income paid out as maintenance.

Example:

Couples separate. Legally enforceable maintenance payable to lower income-earning spouse of £6,000 annually. Infant children reside with and have to be supported by the lower income-earning spouse. Income earned by each spouse:

	£
Higher income spouse	40,000
Lower income spouse	8,000

	£	£
PRSI levies liability for 2000/2001		
(i) Higher income spouse (Class A1)		40,000
PRSI: Weekly salary	769.23	
Less: First £100 exemption	(100.00)	
	669.23	
PRSI at 4.5%	30.12	
This will be payable for 35 (34.45) weeks and amounts to		1,054
Levies		
Weekly salary	769.23	
Payable at rate of 2%	15.39	
Payable for 52 weeks	800.00	
Less: Refund due on income paid out as maintenance.		
£6,000 @ 2% (note)	(120.00)	680
Total		1,734

Note:
This refund can only be obtained after the end of the tax year, i.e. 5 April 2001. The application is made to the Collector General.

		£
(ii) Lower income spouse (Class A0)		8,000
PRSI: Weekly salary (note)	153.85	
Less: Exemption as weekly salary is less than £226	(226.00)	
	Nil	
PRSI at 4.5%	Nil	
Total PRSI for 2000/2001		Nil

Note:
No PRSI is payable on maintenance as PRSI is paid as an employee. This includes all PRSI classes except Class S1. If income was self-employed income, then the PRSI liability would be £648 (£8,000 + £6,000 − £1,040 @ 5 per cent)

Levies		
Weekly salary	153.85	
Weekly maintenance	120.00	
	273.88	
Levies at 2% are not due as income is less than		
£280 weekly or £14,560 yearly	Nil	
		Nil
Total		Nil

Where a married couple opt to be taxed under TCA 1997, s. 1026 then the maintenance payment and receipt is not recognised for income tax purposes and accordingly it is not recognised for PRSI or HCL purposes either.

In the case of a foreign divorce recognised in Ireland and only the ex-spouse paying maintenance is resident here, then a refund of levies but not of PRSI can be obtained. The extent to which the ex-recipient spouse would be liable to pay levies on this income will depend on whether such income is taxable here in Ireland. This will follow the income tax position. If the income liable to Irish tax is less than £14,560 (2000/2001 limit), then the question of levies does not arise. On the question of PRSI, no PRSI is payable provided he/she is not resident or ordinarily resident in Ireland and is not in receipt of Schedule D, Case I or II Irish source income, i.e. trade or professional income.

Where only the recipient ex-spouse is resident in Ireland then such maintenance payments are subject to levies only if reckonable income including maintenance exceed £14,560 (2000/2001 limit). With regard to PRSI, he/she will only be liable to pay PRSI on such maintenance payments if he/she has trading or professional income in Ireland.

9.4 Transfer of Assets

9.4.1 CAPITAL GAINS TAX

9.4.1.1 General

Both formal and informal separations are recognised for capital gains tax purposes.

See comments in **9.3.9** regarding a definition of 'living apart'.

From a capital gains tax point of view it is important to try to be definitive with regard to the date on when the separation is likely to be permanent. This is important for a number of reasons.

Joint/separate assessment

While a married couple are living together, the tax due on gains arising to a married woman living with her husband in a tax year are assessed and charged on her husband (TCA 1997, s. 1028(1)) unless the married couple have opted for the wife to be the assessable spouse. This will only apply up to the date that the separation is likely to be permanent. From that date, the non-assessable spouse, normally a wife, is assessed in her own name in relation to any gains arising after the date of likely permanent separation.

In the case of separate assessment, there is no change, i.e. each spouse is separately assessed in respect of their respective gains. If the claim for separate assessment is withdrawn for a particular tax year prior to 6 July after the end of the tax year, then the joint assessment rules, as outlined above, will apply for the tax year of separation.

Annual exemption

Up to 5 April 1998 inclusive, a spouse could transfer his/her unused annual exemption to his/her spouse. Unless a couple separated in circumstances likely to be permanent on 6 April, the benefit of TCA 1997, s. 1028(4) could be availed of, that is, a spouse's unutilised annual exemption could be used by the other spouse. If one spouse had a gain of less than £1,000, the excess would, under TCA 1997, s. 1028(4), be transferred to the other spouse. Unlike income tax, the total exemption available for the tax year of separation could not exceed £2,000. If one spouse had no gains, as a matter of practice, the other spouse could obtain the full £2,000 annual exemption even if a gain arose after the date of likely permanent separation. To this extent, the annual exemption was treated like a personal allowance. Once available on 6 April, it could not be withdrawn due to a change of circumstances during the tax year.

Since 6 April 1998, a spouse's annual exemption is not transferable to the other spouse. Therefore, the tax year of separation has no impact on the allocation of the annual exemption.

TAX IMPLICATIONS OF MARRIAGE BREAKDOWN

Losses

To the extent that losses crystallised by a spouse have not been used by his/her spouse, then any unused remaining losses as at the date of likely permanent separation can only be used by the spouse in whose favour they arose. That spouse can utilise those remaining losses against any gains arising after the date of likely permanent separation.

9.4.1.2 Transfer of assets: factual separation

From the date that the separation is likely to be permanent, any transfer of assets between spouses is not exempt from capital gains tax. This is different from income tax as the exemption only applies to the tax year or part of a tax year that the married couple are living together.

Voluntary transfer of assets

Although it is unusual for the transfer of assets to occur outside any legal arrangement relating to the separation, any such transfer could give rise to a capital gains tax liability unless an exemption or relief can be obtained. As the couple are still married, they are connected persons and market value will apply to the asset being transferred (TCA 1997, ss. 10, 549). Therefore the person acquiring the asset and the person making the disposal are treated as parties to a transaction otherwise than by way of a bargain made at arm's length.

Section 547 of TCA 1997 then provides that a person's disposal of an asset is deemed to be for a consideration equal to the market value of the asset where he disposes of an asset otherwise than by way of a bargain made at arm's length. Similarly a person's acquisition of such an asset is deemed to be for a consideration equal to its market value.

Example 1:

A married couple are separated, in circumstances likely to be permanent, since 6 July 1991. One of the assets owned by the couple is the former marital house, which the lower income spouse has occupied with the children since 6 July 1991. The family home was purchased in their joint names on 6 January 1986. It is now agreed that the higher income spouse will transfer voluntarily his/her share in the family home. The current value of the house is £300,000. The house cost £60,000 including expenses on 6 January 1986. The transfer date is 6 July 2000.

A capital gains liability for the transferring spouse arises as follows:

	£	£
Market value (50% share)		150,000
Less: Cost of 50% share	30,000	
Index factor at 1.497		
Indexed cost		(44,910)
Chargeable gain		105,090
Period of ownership 14 years + 6 months		
Principal private residence exemption applies to period of actual occupation plus last 12 months i.e. 6 years + 6 months (TCA 1997, s. 604)		
Exempt gain: 105,090 × $\frac{6.5}{14.5}$		(47,109)
Net chargeable gain		57,981
Less: Annual exemption		(1,000)
Taxable gain		56,981
Capital gains tax @ 20% payable on 1 November 2001		11,396

Example 2:

As part of the voluntary arrangement, the lower income spouse agrees to transfer to the higher income spouse 2,000 shares in an investment company owned equally by the married couple. The company was set up in May 1986 and the 2,000 £1 ordinary shares were issued at par. The shares are now valued at £15 each. A capital gains tax computation must be prepared for the lower income spouse.

		£	£
Market value at 6 July 2000			30,000
Less:	Cost in May 1986	2,000	
	Index factor at 1.432		
	Indexed cost		(2,864)
	Chargeable gain		27,136
Less:	Annual exemption		(1,000)
	Taxable gain		26,136
	Capital gains tax @ 20% payable on 1 November 2000		5,227

9.4.2 EXEMPT TRANSFER TO SPOUSE

The transfer of one or more assets will arise in marital breakdown cases. Up to 1 August 1996, the transfer of assets between spouses could give rise to capital gains tax liabilities. However, FLA 1995 introduced an exemption from capital gains tax on the transfer of assets from one spouse to another provided certain conditions were fulfilled. FL(D)A 1996 also provided for a similar exemption.

9.4.2.1 Separation

If a married couple formalise their separation by deed of separation or decree of judicial separation then any transfer of assets from one spouse to the other spouse effected on foot of a deed of separation or judicial separation court order will qualify for a capital gains tax exemption similar to that for married couples living together (TCA 1997, s. 1030).

9.4.2.2 Divorce

If assets are transferred from one ex-spouse to another as part of a divorce decree order then the transfer of assets from one ex-spouse to the other will not give rise to any capital gains tax liability in the hands of the transferring ex-spouse. The capital gains tax exemption for transfer of assets between spouses living together was extended to divorce: FL(D)A 1996, s. 35 (amended by TCA 1997, s. 1031).

9.4.2.3 Foreign divorce recognised in Ireland

Where a foreign divorce is granted which is recognised here and a relief order is granted then the transfer of assets arising from such a relief order qualifies for an exemption similar to the TCA 1997, s. 1028(5) relief: TCA 1997, s. 1030(2). This capital gains tax exemption does not apply to trading stock disposed of or acquired by either spouse. Foreign divorce court orders which provide for the transfer of assets from one ex-spouse to the other ex-spouse can qualify for the exemption under TCA 1997, s. 1030, provided the order is similar to relief orders dealt with in FLA 1995. This extension of the exemption is effective from 10 February 2000 (FA 2000, s. 76).

9.4.2.4 Foreign divorce not recognised in Ireland

In this situation, as the couple are legally married, a capital gains tax liability can arise if assets are transferred from one ex-spouse to another as part of a foreign divorce court order (see voluntary transfers at para. **9.4.1.2** above in the case of factual separations). However, if the disposal takes place on foot of a deed of separation, even if foreign, then no capital gains tax liability will arise.

If a couple obtain a foreign divorce, which is not legally recognised in Ireland and one of the parties to the marriage remarries, then this marriage is not recognised in Ireland. As a general rule, it is not possible for the newly married couple to obtain any tax benefits. This is subject to one exemption. From a capital gains tax point of view, it is current Revenue practice to recognise such a marriage if a foreign marriage certificate is produced. However, if the second marriage is subsequently challenged the Revenue will follow the legal position.

9.4.2.5 Nullity

After the decree of nullity, if there are any transfers of assets between the former spouses then these will not be exempt. It may happen that the transfer of assets between the spouses prior to the decree of nullity may not be exempt if they are not living together for tax purposes (TCA 1997, s. 1015).

9.4.3 CGT CLEARANCE APPLICATION

See TCA 1997, s. 980 (as amended by FA 1998, s. 74 and FA 2000, s. 70). For disposals prior to 1 August 1996, it would have been necessary to obtain a capital gains tax (CGT) Clearance Certificate if the sale proceeds or market value of the asset(s) transferred between spouses exceeded £100,000. This assumes that the spouses were not 'living together' under TCA 1997, s. 1015. This requirement applies to certain assets including:

- land in the State;

- goodwill of a trade carried on in the State; and

- shares in an unquoted company deriving their value or the greater part of their value directly or indirectly from land. It also applies to shares acquired as a result of a share for share transaction if the original shares derived their value from land.

If a sum of money exceeding £100,000 was paid for the transfer of the asset, the spouse purchasing the asset had to deduct 15 per cent from the monies and forward such sum to the Revenue unless a CGT Clearance Certificate was produced by the spouse transferring the asset.

If no sum of money passed and the assets were transferred in consideration of the separation, a CGT Clearance Certificate also had to be obtained. This requirement only applied to assets transferred after 17 July 1982. In such cases, the spouse who acquired the asset was obliged to advise the Revenue of the transfer within three months of its acquisition. This was only necessary if the spouse who transferred the asset failed to produce a CGT Clearance Certificate within two months of the transfer. Where the required information was not given to the Revenue Commissioners and the CGT payable was not discharged within 12 months of the due date, then the person who acquired the asset could be held responsible of the tax due. The tax could be assessed on him/her and collected from him/her. For such an assessment to be valid, it had to be made within two years of the original due date for the tax.

For disposals after 2 June 1995, if a CGT Clearance Certificate is not given to the acquiring spouse, then he/she has to, within seven days of acquisition of the asset, advise the Revenue Commissioners of the following particulars:

- the asset acquired;

- the consideration for acquiring the asset;

- the market value of that consideration, estimated to the best of that person's knowledge and belief and the name and address of the person making the disposal; and

- he/she must pay to the Collector General a sum equal to 15 per cent of the market value of the consideration so estimated.

This capital gains tax liability had to be paid within seven days of the person acquiring the asset and was payable without the making of an assessment. The tax paid could be recovered from the person disposing of the asset. This provision is effective from the date of the passing of the Finance Act 1995, i.e. 2 June 1995.

Although the transfer of assets between separated or divorced spouses is exempt (TCA 1997, ss. 1030-1031), it is still necessary to obtain a CGT Clearance Certificate if the original cost or acquisition value of the asset to the spouse transferring it exceeds £300,000 (£100,000 for disposals up to 26 March 1998 inclusive and £150,000 for disposals up to 1 April 2000 inclusive: TCA 1997, s. 980 (as amended by FA 1998, s. 74).

9.4.4 OTHER TYPES OF TRANSFERS

9.4.4.1 Trust for sale

Example: House placed into joint names of spouses on a trust for sale postponed until the youngest of the children is fully educated.

In the United Kingdom, this type of arrangement is known as a Mesher Order. It is based on a UK case called *Mesher v Mesher and Hall* [1981] All ER 126. In that case, the family home was jointly owned and there was a young child aged 9. It was ordered that the family home should be held in trust for the spouses in equal shares, but that the house should not be sold so long as the youngest child was under 17, or until further order. In the meantime, the wife had the right to live in the house rent-free provided she discharged all outgoings.

For capital gains tax, the key issue is whether a Mesher Order creates a settlement. The UK Revenue take the view (CGT Manual, volume 6, para. 65367) that a Mesher Order creates a settlement on the basis that the initial transfer of the family home to the spouses as trustees on trust for sale is a disposal of their interest in the home, irrespective of the fact that they may also be trustees and beneficiaries. The transfer is deemed to take place at the market value. However, because of the 'principal private residence' exemption, there will be no CGT liability for the spouse who has remained in the family home. There will be a liability for the non-occupying spouse if the Mesher Order is created more than one year after he/she permanently left the family home.

When the Mesher Order terminates on the child having reached the age specified in the order, the husband and wife in their capacity as trustees of the settlement are deemed to have disposed of the house and immediately reacquired it as bare trustees for themselves. However, for the duration of the Mesher Order a trust beneficiary, the wife, was entitled to occupy the house as her main residence under the terms of the order. Consequently, under TCA 1997, s. 604(10), the trustees should be entitled to claim a principal private residence exemption in respect of the gain arising during the period of the trust. However, a taxable gain may arise if there is a delay in selling the house after termination of the Mesher Order when the child reaches the specified age. The spouse who has departed will have a chargeable gain of the difference, after indexation, between that spouse's share of the sale proceeds and the market value of the house when the Mesher Order was terminated. Any such gain is likely to be small.

On the other hand, if the order does not create a settlement, a capital gains tax liability will not arise on the initial transfer of the house into joint ownership or as tenants-in-common even if the sole owner of the property prior to the transfer has not occupied it as his/her principal private residence for a period of time.

A variant of the order could require a husband who owned the house to put it into joint names of himself and his wife, and that they should thereafter own it in equal (or other) shares, with the sale being postponed. A further variant would be where the order expressly excluded the husband from occupation of the family home. In such cases it is the writer's view that a settlement is not created. It is also the writer's view that the wording in the Mesher Order can affect the tax consequences.

On the eventual sale of the property the non-occupying spouse will have a capital gains tax liability because he/she may not have occupied the house as his/her principal private residence for several years.

Mesher Orders are not common in Ireland.

9.4.4.2   Subject to a charge

Example: House transferred to one spouse, giving the other a charge on the property. The charge cannot be realised until a specific event. The charge may be of a fixed amount (i.e. £40,000) or for a share (i.e. 60 per cent).

From a tax point of view, the initial transfer will not give rise to a capital gains tax charge. On the sale of the house, no capital gains tax liability should arise if the house has been occupied as the principal private residence of the owner.

A problem may arise for the non-occupying spouse when the agreed portion of the sale proceeds is paid over. In the view of the writer, this CGT problem only arises if there is a variable deferred charge, e.g. the charge represents a share in the property. In essence, a variable deferred charge is a debt owed to the non-occupying spouse. A debt is an asset under TCA 1997, s. 532(1). The realisation of the deferred charge by the person in whose favour it has been granted will constitute a disposal. However, TCA 1997, s. 541 provides that no chargeable gain shall accrue to the original creditor, or his personal representatives, on the disposal of a debt, other than a debt on a security. It would appear that the variable deferred charge would not be a 'debt on a security' as considered by the House of Lords in *Aberdeen Construction Limited v IRC* [1978] STC 127, *W.T. Ramsey Limited v IRC* [1981] STC 174 and *Taylor Clarke International Limited v Lewis* [1997] STC 499. The House of Lords, while finding the meaning of the phrase obscure, held that it was not synonymous with a secured debt. Rather, it envisaged a debt which has characteristics attached to it which would enable it to be marketed (*per* Lord Wilberforce in *Ramsey* at 184).

A High Court decision of Morris J (*J.J. Mooney (Inspector of Taxes) v Noel Sweeney* [1997] 3 IR 424) approved Lord Wilberforce's approach in *Ramsay*. It appears that an argument could be made that a variable deferred charge is marketable and, accordingly, has the characteristics of a debt on a security. If so, then on receipt of the proceeds attributable to the subsequent sale of the property there would be a disposal for CGT purposes and a liability would arise. The right to the deferred sum has to be valued at the date of creation of the charge for CGT purposes.

Alternatively, if it is accepted that the variable deferred charge is not a 'debt on a security', one needs to consider the meaning of 'debt' in TCA 1997, s. 541, as outlined in the House of Lords decision *Marren v Ingles* [1980] STC 500. The issue considered by this case has not come before an Irish court to date. In *Marren v Ingles*, the taxpayer sold shares in the company for a fixed sum per share plus the right, in circumstances which might never occur, to receive a percentage of the value of the shares when they were resold by the purchaser. The taxpayer received additional payments when the shares were resold. The UK Revenue sought to charge capital gains tax on the additional monies received by the taxpayer. The House of Lords held that an asset was not a debt for the purposes of TCGA 1992, s. 251(1) (Irish equivalent TCA 1997, s. 541(1)) where it was a *possible* liability to pay an *unidentifiable* sum at an *unascertainable* date.

Unlike the debt considered in *Marren v Ingles*, a deferred charge on the family home is certain to mature at some future date, but both the timing and the amount receivable are uncertain. It seems possible, in the light of other dicta in the *Marren v Ingles* case, that Irish courts could regard these two factors as sufficient to preclude the deferred charge from taking advantage of the exemption for debts in TCA 1997, s. 541. Consequently, the non-occupying spouse could have a chargeable gain of the amount he/she receives on the realisation of the charge, less the indexed market value of the charge at its date of acquisition. However, the market value at its date of acquisition needs to be determined. It would appear that the relevant question is: at date of creation of the charge, what could this right to receive a stated percentage of the eventual sale proceeds of the house be worth on the open market?

To summarise, in the case of a deferred variable charge, there is a disposal of the house to the other spouse which qualifies for the exemption under TCA 1997, s. 1030. At the same time, the transferor spouse is acquiring a new asset, i.e. the right to receive deferred consideration. This right has to be valued at the date of acquisition. It is the writer's view that the value would equal the market value of the transferor spouse's interest in the house at the date of the transfer to the other spouse.

If the deferred charge is fixed, i.e. represented by a sum of money in favour of the non-occupying spouse, this deferred charge should constitute a debt within TCA 1997, s. 541. This assumes that he/she had disposed of his/her whole ownership of the house in return for the deferred charge. Consequently, any gain on the disposal of the house should be realised at the time of transfer to the occupying spouse, and there will be no capital gains tax charge when the deferred charge is ultimately realised. This interpretation is assisted by TCA 1997, s. 563(1) which enacts that the gain on the disposal of an asset is to be computed initially without regard to any postponement of the right to receive the consideration. In *Marson v Marriage* [1980] STC 177 it was held that the UK equivalent of this subsection, i.e. TCGA 1992, s. 48, presupposed a future consideration which was ascertainable in amount, and therefore had no application to a deferred consideration of uncertain amount. Conversely, it would appear that TCA 1997, s. 563(1), should apply to a fixed consideration.

9.4.4.3 Subject to a trust

Example: House placed in trust to spouse for life and thereafter to children.

In this situation, a settlement is being created. There would be a disposal from one spouse to the trustees and a capital gains tax charge may arise (TCA 1997, ss. 575, 577).

On the death of the life tenant no capital gains tax charge arises on the transfer of the family home by the trustees to the children (TCA 1997, s. 604(10)).

9.4.4.4 Sole occupancy to one spouse

Example: Sole occupancy given to one spouse for so long as the youngest child is under 18 years and thereafter to be sold with sale proceeds divided on an agreed basis.

If the family home is in the sole name of the non-occupying ex-spouse then, on the sale of the family home, a capital gains tax problem will arise for him/her as the house would not have been occupied as his/her principal private residence. Accordingly, a portion of the gain arising on the disposal of the property would be subject to capital gains tax. The taxable portion of the gain would be computed by reference to the period of non-occupation of residence (excluding the last 12 months of ownership) over the total period of ownership.

Similarly, even in the case of joint ownership, the non-occupying spouse could have a capital gains tax liability on the disposal of his/her half share in that property. On the other hand, it is unlikely that the occupying spouse would have a capital gains tax liability as the house would have been occupied by him/her as his/her principal private residence throughout the period of ownership.

For example, the court may order that 50 per cent of the net proceeds of sale are to be given to the occupying spouse in the case of a property owned by the non-occupying spouse. If the non-occupying spouse realises a gain on the disposal of the property and has to pay capital gains tax on part of the gain, then the 50 per cent share of the net sale proceeds payable to the occupying spouse is not reduced to take account of this fact.

9.4.4.5 Financial compensation orders

Under FLA 1995, s. 11 and FL(D)A 1996, s. 16 the court can make a financial compensation order requiring either or both spouses to:

(i)   effect a life assurance policy for the benefit of a spouse or dependent member of the family;

(ii) assign a life assurance policy to their spouse or dependent member of the family; or

(iii) make or continue life assurance policy premium payments as required under an assurance policy.

There are no tax implications arising from the making of such orders as outlined in (i) and (iii) above either on foot of payment of the life insurance premiums or payment of the life insurance policy proceeds. However, in the latter case, if the life insurance policy proceeds are paid to a dependent member of the family, then capital acquisitions tax may be an issue.

With regard to (ii) above, the assignment of a life insurance policy to a spouse or dependent member of the family will not give rise to any capital gains tax or capital acquisitions tax problems. However, the payment of the life insurance policy proceeds as a disposal by the spouse or dependent member of the family for capital gains tax purposes. Under TCA 1997, s. 593, if the person making the disposal is not the original beneficial owner and he/she acquired the rights or interests for a consideration in money or money's worth, then capital gains tax may be an issue. It may be necessary to consider this in particular situations. For example, if the assignment of the life insurance policy arises on foot of a court order then no capital gains tax charge will arise under TCA 1997, s. 593, as there has been no acquisition for a consideration in money or money's worth. However, if the assignment results under the terms of a settlement, then TCA 1997, s. 593 may need to be considered. The payment of the life insurance policy proceeds to a dependent member of the family will have capital acquisitions tax implications.

9.4.4.6 Secured periodical payments orders

Under FLA 1995, s. 8(1)(b) and FL(D)A 1996, s. 13(1)(b) the courts have power to award secured maintenance for a spouse and/or dependent member of the family. A secured periodical payments order could be defined as a maintenance order the payment of which is secured against a non-income producing asset such as land.

It could also, as in the UK, mean that one spouse is required to transfer income-producing assets, such as shares, to trustees with the trust income being used to pay maintenance to the other spouse. If the obligation to pay maintenance ceases, say on the death of a spouse, the trust ends and the assets revert to the settlor spouse. The latter type of secured periodical payments orders could cause capital gains tax difficulties. A transfer of income-producing assets into a trust appears to consist of the creation of a settlement which, while the trust continues, the transferor cannot claim to be absolutely entitled to as against the trustees. The transfer of the assets into trust therefore constitutes a chargeable disposal for capital gains tax purposes, notwithstanding the fact that the transferor may retain an interest in the trust capital. The transferor spouse and trustees are connected persons and the transfer is therefore deemed to be made for a consideration equal to the market value of the assets at the date of transfer.

The exemption available in TCA 1997, s. 1030 cannot be availed of, as the disposal is not to the other spouse.

If and when the obligation to pay maintenance ceases, the transferor spouse becomes absolutely entitled as against the trustees to a return of the assets. The trustees will therefore be deemed to have disposed of and reacquired the assets at their market value with a consequent potential chargeable gain, unless the reason for the reversion is the death of the spouse entitled to the maintenance. In the latter case, the transferor spouse will normally reacquire the assets at market value at the date of death (TCA 1997, s. 577). At present, secured periodical payments orders are not common. Attachment of earnings orders are used instead.

9.4.5 RPT CLEARANCE CERTIFICATE

For contracts signed on or after 1 April 1993, an RPT Clearance Certificate must be obtained in respect of any sale of a residential property if the sale proceeds exceed the market value exemption limit for the preceding 5 April (FA 1983, s. 110A).

If such a certificate is not obtained then a purchaser must deduct from the consideration a specified amount. This is based on the excess of the sale proceeds over the market value exemption limit of the preceding 5 April. This excess is subject to RPT at the rate of 7.5 per cent (maximum) and must be paid to the Revenue Commissioners. If the vendor has owned the property for less than five years then the rate is 1.5 per cent for each year of ownership.

The requirement to obtain an RPT Clearance Certificate will not arise in the case of a separated couple if there is no sale of residential property from one spouse to the other spouse or to a third party.

The Clearance Certificate procedures still apply notwithstanding the abolition of residential property tax. However, a Clearance Certificate is not required if a property was previously acquired after 5 April 1996. This applies to sales completed after 10 February 2000 (FA 2000, s. 118).

Charge on residential property

If a spouse transfers a residential property to the other spouse, then any RPT owing by the transferring spouse is charged on that property for a period of 12 years (FA 1983, s. 110A(9)). A charge is a liability or burden attaching to the property. If there is a subsequent sale or mortgage, the charge will not remain unless the sale proceeds or mortgage amount exceed the relevant market value exemption. Also, the tax or interest due will not remain as a charge against a bona fide purchaser or mortgagee for full consideration in money or money's worth without notice. On a subsequent sale, the transferee spouse can apply for a certificate of discharge (in duplicate) if a copy of the transfer deed is also forwarded. As a matter of practice, the Revenue will raise an assessment on the transferor spouse to collect the outstanding residential property tax.

9.4.6 CHILDREN

Court orders which result in assets being transferred to a dependent child or specified person on behalf of a dependent child can have capital gains tax implications. A dependent child is defined in FLA 1995, s. 2 and FL(D)A 1996, s. 2 as one who is:

- a child under 18 years;
- a child under 23 years in full-time education; or
- a child with a physical or mental disability.

For example, if an order was made for the assignment of a non-Irish assurance policy which was taken out after 20 May 1993, to a trustee on behalf of a dependent child, then CGT can arise for the transferor spouse (TCA 1997, s. 594). Also, if the court makes a property adjustment order by way of creation of a settlement for the benefit of the spouse for life and on his/her death to the children, the CGT will also be an issue (TCA 1998, ss. 574, 575).

9.4.7 CAPITAL ACQUISITIONS TAX (CAT)

See FA 1997, s. 142.

9.4.7.1 Separation

A deed of separation or decree of judicial separation does not have any impact on the capital acquisitions tax exemption on the transfer of assets between spouses as there is no change in their legal status.

9.4.7.2 Divorce

Property transfers between ex-spouses on foot of a court order governing an Irish divorce is exempt from capital acquisitions tax (FA 1997, s. 142).

9.4.7.3 Foreign divorce

Once a couple obtain a foreign divorce which is recognised here then the capital acquisitions tax exemption for gifts or inheritances passing between ex-spouses ceases. Accordingly, any transfer of assets between the spouses following the divorce decree could attract a capital acquisitions tax liability if the transferor ex-spouse is domiciled in Ireland or if the asset transferred is situated in Ireland. This applied up to 9 February 2000. A foreign divorce court order dealing with the transfer of property qualifies for an exemption provided it is similar to a relief order granted in Ireland under FLA 1995 (FA 2000, s. 132).

If a relief order is obtained, assets can be transferred from one ex-spouse to the other without any capital acquisitions tax consequences. If a relief order is obtained from an Irish court for the transfer of assets from the estate of a former deceased spouse, then the capital acquisitions tax exemption will apply to such a transfer (FA 1997, s. 142).

In general, if either party to a marriage which is recognised here go through divorce proceedings which are not legally recognised, then the couple are treated as a separated couple and the consequences as outlined above will apply on the transfer of assets as there is no change in their legal status as a married couple.

9.4.7.4 Children

Marriage breakdown only affects the legal status of spouses, and does not change the normal tax rules pertaining to the transfer of assets between parent and child/children.

9.4.8 STAMP DUTY

See SDCA 1999, s. 97 as amended by FA 2000, s. 31.

9.4.8.1 Separation

As for capital acquisitions tax (see **9.4.7.1**).

9.4.8.2 Divorce

As for capital acquisitions tax (see **9.4.7.2**).

9.4.8.3 Foreign divorce

As for capital acquisitions tax (see **9.4.7.3**).

9.4.8.4 Children

As for capital acquisitions tax (see **9.2.4.2** and **9.4.7.4**).

9.4.9 PROBATE TAX

See FA 1997, s. 143 as amended by FA 2000, s. 150.

9.4.9.1 Separation

As for capital acquisitions tax (see **9.4.7.1**).

9.4.9.2 Divorce

If an ex-spouse dies, the surviving ex-spouse provided he/she has not remarried can apply for provision out of the estate of the deceased ex-spouse (FL(D)A 1996, s. 18). No probate tax is payable on assets transferred to an ex-spouse following an order FL(D)A 1996, s. 18 (FA 1997, s. 143).

On the death of a spouse, the passing of assets whether by absolute or limited interest to the other spouse results in and abandonment/postponement of the tax. Obviously, if couples are divorced, no such relief is available. However, probate tax is abated to nil in the case of an absolute interest and postponed in the case of a limited interest in respect of assets given to a former spouse as a result of a relief order or foreign divorce court order (FA 1997, s. 143 as amended by FA 2000, s. 150).

9.4.9.3 Children

See **9.2.4.2** and **9.4.7.4**.

CHAPTER 10

DOMESTIC VIOLENCE

10.1   Introduction

The introduction of a separate civil remedy for 'domestic violence' in 1976 by the Family Law (Maintenance of Spouses and Children) Act 1976, s. 22 in many ways marked the introduction of personal/spousal law reform into the area of family law in Ireland. Prior to this spouses had to rely on the ordinary criminal law to protect them in the event of domestic violence. However, as such cases were heard in open court many people were reluctant to proceed with prosecutions. The 1976 Act introduced the remedy of a 'barring order' which excluded the violent spouse from the family home for a three-month period. The remedy was quite controversial when first introduced and there was much debate as to whether it was lawful to put a spouse out of the home even for reasons of domestic violence perpetrated against other family members. In 1981 the legislation was amended by the Family Law (Protection of Spouses and Children) Act 1981 enabling the making of barring orders for up to one year and the remedy of 'protection order' was also introduced. The latter remedy was introduced in order to protect the party seeking the barring order from the date of the institution of the barring proceedings until their final determination by the court. The domestic violence legislation has always been 'gender neutral' even though it is often used as the remedy of the 'battered wife'. Calls for the improvement and sophistication of the remedy came in the form of a *Report of Recommendations to Government of the Second Commission on the Status of Women* in January 1993. As the law stood, there were inconsistencies and anomalies in the legislation. The legislation covered only domestic disharmony between 'spouses'. Other people living in domestic relationships suffering domestic violence could not avail of the remedy. The benchmark Supreme Court decision of *O'B v O'B* [1984] IR 182 at 188 interpreted the legislative criteria of 'safety and welfare'. This case restricted the ambit of the 'safety' to cases of physical violence or threat of physical violence, and determined that the term 'welfare' could be interpreted widely but must always be referable to the conduct of the respondent spouse. Some 20 years after the introduction of the 'barring order' in 1976, the Domestic Violence Act 1996 was introduced.

10.2   Background

The Domestic Violence Act 1996 (the '1996 Act') came into operation on 27 March 1996. The preamble to the 1996 Act sets out the aims of the legislation, which are:

1.   to protect spouses and children and other dependent persons, and persons in other domestic relationships where their safety or welfare is at risk because of the conduct of the other person in the domestic relationship;

2.   to increase the powers of An Garda Síochána to arrest without warrant in certain circumstances; and

3.   to provide for the hearing at the same time of applications to court for other orders regarding custody and access, maintenance, conduct leading to the loss of the family home, restriction on the disposal of house chattels, and child care orders.

The first aim of the new legislation was to extend its cover from being an exclusively spousal remedy to a remedy available to those suffering from physical, sexual, emotional or mental abuse in a relationship which may or may not be based on marriage or cohabitation. The new legislation extends to cohabitants and family members. The safety and welfare of the victim must be at risk because of the other person in the domestic relationship. The term 'welfare' is now defined to specifically include:

the physical and psychological welfare of the person in question.

The legislation also increased the range of legal options available for the protection of a victim of domestic violence. It introduced a new remedy of 'safety order' and also made provision for the making of an 'interim barring order'. Commentators have queried the effect of this enlargement on the pre-existing position having regard to the *O'B v O'B* decision cited above, para. **10.1.1**. In that case the Supreme Court upheld the appeal of a husband against the making of a barring order in the High Court. The essential ground for the making of an order barring a spouse from the family home was, in the opinion of the Supreme Court, that the threat to the safety or welfare could be attributable to the conduct of the respondent spouse. The statutory inclusion of 'the physical and psychological welfare of the person in question' was a major departure.

The 1996 legislation also enlarged the remedy of a barring order by prohibiting the respondent, at the discretion of the court, from attending at or in the vicinity of, or watching or besetting the residence of the applicant or any dependent person. Watching and besetting is not expressly defined by the legislation but is negatively defined by the Non-Fatal Offences Against the Person Act 1997. (The 1997 Act, s. 9(2) provides that attending at or near the premises or place where a person resides, works or carries on business or happens to be, in order to obtain or communicate information, is not deemed a watching or besetting within the meaning of that legislation.)

The second task which the legislation set for itself was to increase the power of the police to arrest without warrant in certain circumstances. The remedy of barring order has been effective largely because of the power of arrest attached to it.

Finally, the legislation aimed to enable the court to make other determinations at the same time as the hearing of a domestic violence issue without the necessity of instituting separate sets of proceedings and consolidating them for a combined hearing.

10.3   Remedies Available

10.3.1   BARRING ORDER

This is an order directing the respondent, if residing at a place where the applicant or that dependent person resides, to leave such place, and prohibiting that respondent (whether resident or not) from entering such place until further order of the court or until such other time as the court shall specify. The order may also, if the court thinks fit, prohibit the respondent from:

(a)   using or threatening to use violence against the applicant or any dependent person;

(b)   molesting or putting in fear the applicant or any dependent person;

(c)   attending at or in the vicinity of, or watching or besetting a place where the applicant or any dependent person resides.

The court when considering the application for a barring order must be of the opinion that there are reasonable grounds to believe that the safety or welfare of the applicant or any dependent person requires the making of the order. It must consider the powers it has under the 1996 Act, s. 7 to make orders and to seek intervention by the Health Board under the Child Care Act 1991. It must also take into account any order or orders to be made under the Guardianship of Infants Act 1964, s. 11 (as amended by the Status of Children Act 1987) or the Child Care Act 1991 in respect of any dependent person.

If granted, the order may be made subject to such exceptions and conditions as the court may specify. A barring order if made by the District Court or by the Circuit Court on appeal from the District Court can last for up to three years or for such shorter period as the court may specify.

It must be noted that a dependent person under the 1996 Act is 'dependent' until 18, whereas under the Family Law Act 1995 and the Family Law (Divorce) Act 1996 dependency can exist for support purposes until the age of 23. The definition covers a natural or adopted child of either applicant or respondent or of both applicant and respondent. It also covers children to whom the applicant or respondent is *in loco parentis*. It also covers children of full age who have a physical or mental disability to such an extent that it is not reasonably possible for the child to live independently of the applicant.

Barring orders allow the victim of domestic violence to occupy a residence to the exclusion of the violent or abusive party. In a way, therefore, they can be thought of as 'occupation' orders. Given the Constitutional constraints imposed on the legislation, it can be seen that this category of order must be restricted, having regard to the Constitutional right to private property contained in Article 43 of the Constitution. An applicant who is not a 'spouse' seeking this type of remedy must, therefore, have an equal or greater interest in the property than the respondent.

Provision is made for the applicant in these non-spousal categories to state a belief that they have such an equal or greater interest in the property. Such belief is admissible in evidence by virtue of the 1996 Act, s. 3(4)(b). It has been suggested that this provision might have unforeseen repercussions, in that the issue of ownership might be treated as '*res judicata*' once the District Court order is made. The court is required to form an opinion regarding the legal or beneficial interest in the property as a preliminary issue where the applicant is a cohabitant or a parent of the respondent. Some District Judges have refused to make orders on the basis that they do not believe that the applicant has an equal or greater interest in the property even though the title deeds are in joint names. The District Family Court has jurisdiction under the Family Home Protection Act 1976 where the rateable valuation of the land does not exceed £20 by virtue of the Family Law Act 1995. It does not, however, have a remit in the determination of property disputes *per se*. Applications concerning the ownership of other property can be determined by the Circuit Family Court in accordance with the Family Law Act 1995, s. 36. Applications to determine the ownership of non-spousal property must also be made in the higher courts. An unsuccessful applicant or respondent may, of course, appeal the matter to the Circuit Court.

In effect therefore, there are only four categories of people who can seek a barring order:

(a) spouses and former spouses;

(b) cohabitants who have lived as husband and wife for six months in aggregate out of the previous nine months;

(c) a parent of an adult child who is not 'a dependent person' within the meaning of the Act; and

(d) a Health Board on behalf of an entitled 'aggrieved person' who may be an adult or a dependent person.

10.3.2 INTERIM BARRING ORDER

The District Court is now empowered to make an interim barring order either at the date of or in between the institution of the proceedings and their hearing. This means that the District Court can now give interlocutory relief in the nature of a barring order pending the determination of the barring proceedings. In exceptional cases such relief may be obtained ex parte. The criteria for the making of an interim barring order are: that there is an immediate risk of significant harm to the applicant or any dependent person if the order is not made immediately; and that the granting of a protection order would not be sufficient to protect the applicant or any dependent person.

Commentators have already pointed out that this new provision could fall into disrepute and render injustice unless a speedy return date is given for the hearing of the case. The District Court Rules, SI 93/1997, Form 59.7, Sch. C, provide for an 'Information' to be made by the applicant on oath and in writing prior to the granting of ex parte relief. In practice, the respondent or his or her solicitor must apply to the court for a copy of the 'Information' to see the nature of the evidence which led to the making of the order by the court. The 'Information' is normally a short and succinct document and may not contain all of the evidence given at the ex parte hearing. The Circuit Court Rules for ex parte applications, by comparison, provide that the applicant must apply for relief by affidavit or must prepare a note of the evidence tendered at the hearing and the respondent must be served with this: SI 84/1997, r. 26. The return hearing date for barring applications can be of significant duration in some District Family Court areas. This can lead to injustice where ex parte relief has been granted. However, SI 201/1998 provides that the return date for the hearing of the full application must be inserted into the body of the interim barring order.

The English cases of *Ansah v Ansah* [1977] Fam 138 and *Bates v Lord Hailsham* [1972] 1 WLR 1371 reinforced the basic principle that an order should not be made ex parte unless there is a real and immediate danger of serious injury or irreparable damage. See also *G v G (Ouster: Ex parte Application)* [1990] 1 FLR 395. The English Law Commission quoted with approval the judgment of Ormrod LJ in *Ansah v Ansah*:

> 'The power of the court to intervene immediately and without notice in proper cases is essential to the administration of justice. But this power must be used with great caution and only in circumstances in which it is really necessary to act immediately. Such circumstances do undoubtedly tend to occur more frequently in family disputes than in other types of litigation because the parties are often still in close contact with one another and particularly when a marriage is breaking up, in a state of high emotional tension; but even in such cases the court should only act ex parte in an emergency where the interests of justice or the protection of the applicant or a child clearly demands immediate intervention by the court. Such cases should be extremely rare, since any urgent application could be heard inter parte on two days' notice to the other side. . . . If an order is to be made ex parte, it must be strictly limited in time if the risk of causing serious injustice was to be avoided'

Service of the barring summons is by ordinary prepaid post in accordance with the District Court Rules. If a party is barred ex parte, however, personal service is more appropriate. In practice, personal service is usually ordered by the court in such an event. The return date for the hearing of the substantive barring case can, however, in some District Court areas, be several weeks away. To circumvent such difficulty in appropriate cases an application may be made under s. 13 of the 1996 Act to discharge the interim barring order. Such summons may be abridged down to two days' notice where the District Court Clerk is prepared to certify that the case is an urgent one pursuant to SI 93/1997, Ord. 59, r. 12.

10.3.3 PROTECTION ORDER

This is an order which stops short of putting the respondent out of the family home but orders the respondent not to use violence or threaten to use violence against, molest or put in fear the applicant or any dependent person. If the parties do not reside together, the respondent should not watch or beset the place where the applicant or dependent person resides.

The protection order does not have a life of its own but only lasts until the determination of the barring or safety order proceedings.

Protection orders are available to entitled persons who have commenced proceedings for either remedy. In practice the basis of the entitlement to the remedy must be set out in the

Information grounding the application for a protection order. It is essential therefore to ensure that the time frame is adequately addressed within the body of the Information in the case of 'cohabitants' seeking either remedy, and that the ownership of the property is addressed in the case of non-spousal applicants seeking a barring order.

10.3.4   SAFETY ORDER

This is a new remedy introduced by the 1996 Act which is in effect like a long-term 'protection order'. A safety order does not put the respondent out of the residence of the applicant but it prohibits the respondent from engaging in the following behaviour: using or threatening to use violence against, molesting or putting in fear the applicant or a dependent person; and if the respondent is residing at a place other than the place of the applicant or the dependent person, inhibiting the respondent from watching or besetting the place where the applicant/dependent person resides.

A safety order can not be granted in place of a barring order unless both remedies are sought. The court can make the order subject to exceptions and conditions, for example to facilitate access arrangements or the work of the respondent. The order may be made for up to five years. The safety order is a useful remedy in certain circumstances. For example, it can be useful if the respondent suffers from alcoholism and his or her behaviour becomes violent when under the influence of intoxicating liquor, where the applicant spouse wishes to support the respondent in treatment but also wishes to be protected in the event of the respondent becoming violent/abusive should he or she resume drinking in the course of the treatment programme. It can also be a useful remedy where spouses are factually separated and have not yet applied for a separation or divorce. In many such cases friction and tension can arise, particularly in relation to access.

Safety orders are available to five categories of applicants:

(a)   spouses;

(b)   cohabitants for six out of the previous 12 months;

(c)   parent of adult child;

(d)   persons of full age residing in mainly non-contractual relationships;

(e)   the Health Board on behalf of an entitled 'aggrieved person' who may be an adult or a dependent person.

10.4   Entitlement to Relief Under Domestic Violence Act 1996

The Act does not apply to all victims of domestic violence. It does not, for instance, help:

(a)   persons who are affected by a decree of nullity and fail to qualify as cohabitants;

(b)   cohabitants who do not satisfy the residence requirements or property entitlement requirements for a barring order;

(c)   adult siblings who want a barring order;

(d)   people who have a child in common but never 'cohabited'; and

(e)   a parent who wants to bar an adult child but the property is owned by the adult child.

The *Report of the Task Force on Violence against Women*, published in April 1997, recommended that the 1996 Act should be amended to cover situations where couples have a child in common but do not live together and also sought a change in the residence basis of entitlement to a barring order in the case of cohabitee applicants. The equivalent legislation in the UK introduced the concept of 'associated persons'. In this way the UK legislation covers a larger category of persons entitled to apply for either an occupation order or a non-molestation order: see the Family Law Act 1996, Part IV, s. 62(3). The UK legislation also discriminates between those who have 'matrimonial home rights' and those who have an entitlement to occupy a dwellinghouse by virtue of a beneficial estate or interest or contract or enactment conferring rights of occupation. Only the latter class may apply for 'occupation' orders in respect of a dwellinghouse, which is required to be the past, present or intended home of the parties. There is a *lacuna* in the UK legislation where the 'occupation' order is sought over a 'new' home. A non-molestation order is available, however, in such circumstances.

There are other remedies available to the victim of domestic violence. The Non-Fatal Offences Against the Person Act 1997 updated the Offences against the Person Act 1861. The 1997 Act deals with the crimes of assault, assault causing harm, assault causing serious harm, and threats to kill. It introduces new crimes of coercion and harassment which cover what is popularly known as 'stalking'. The Act also makes child abduction a crime. It also abolishes the common law rule in respect of immunity of teachers from criminal liability for punishing pupils. Domestic violence is also a crime and the victim is entitled to look to the criminal law for protection and redress. The remedy of civil injunction is still available in the higher courts.

10.5 Proofs to be Adduced

10.5.1 SPOUSES

The spouse has an entitlement to seek both a barring order (s. 3) and a safety order (s. 2). The first proof to be adduced is that the applicant and respondent are lawfully married. In certain District Court areas it is necessary to produce a marriage certificate. Where there are dependent persons seeking protection one must produce birth certificates of the children. This practice is not universal however. Unless the fact of the marriage is disputed, the oral evidence of the applicant generally seems to be sufficient in most District Court areas. In cases where there is a doubt over the entitlement to a barring order some practitioners issue both a barring and a safety application. This empowers the court to consider a safety order in default on the hearing of a barring application.

Proofs necessary to adduce a case of violence or behaviour causing a detrimental affect on the safety and welfare differ between District Court areas. Generally, in uncontested cases, the evidence of the applicant is sufficient to ground the application. Even in 'consent' cases the District Judge must hear sufficient evidence to enable him/her to exercise the judicial discretion required by ss. 2 and 3 of the Act. Where there is no appearance by the other side and proof of service is in order, the court must hear sufficient evidence to form an opinion that there are reasonable grounds for believing that the safety or welfare test is satisfied.

In contested hearings, substantial and detailed evidence is necessary from the applicant. In general the court does not want to go too far into the past. Evidence from a doctor, social worker or Garda is important. In cases based largely on psychological harm (safety and welfare) great care must be taken to show the nature of the behaviour of the respondent which is alleged to be the cause of the threat to the safety and welfare of the applicant or dependent person. It is essential to establish a causal link between the behaviour of the respondent and the harm to the applicant or dependent person. This may be established by both the evidence of the applicant and a social worker or Gardaí, or a medical witness. A medical report is admissible only by agreement with the solicitor for the respondent. Letters from the school concerning school attendance and performance may be proved in the like manner.

10.5.2 COHABITANTS

The second category of applicant entitled to seek relief is the cohabitant. There are two evidentiary hurdles to be jumped in these types of application. The first hurdle is the time frame requirement. As already stated, for the remedy of barring, the period of cohabitation 'as husband and wife' must be at least six months in aggregate during the period of nine months immediately prior to the application to bar and six months during the previous twelve months immediately prior to the application for a safety order. In practice, clients may be quite confused about the calculation of the cohabitation period. Many people are unclear about dates and this is something upon which one has to obtain very clear instructions before advising on the appropriate remedy. The expression 'as husband and wife' is not defined in the legislation. However, the social welfare legislation and attendant case law may be of some practical assistance in contested cases.

As the time frame is the 'gateway' to the relief for the cohabitant, problems of entitlement can arise where the cohabitation period is cut short because the cohabitant had to leave the place of cohabitation due to the behaviour of the respondent. The issue of 'constructive desertion' may arise. The case of *Counihan v Counihan* (unreported, July 1973, High Ct) was the first detailed judgment dealing with constructive desertion, stating that:

> 'an intention to disrupt the marriage or bring the co-habitation to an end must be shown in such a situation. However, the probable consequences of the conduct of a spouse can give rise to a presumption of such an intention, even if the spouse says he or she never wanted his or her spouse to leave'.

The concept was evolved in ease of the 'spouse' who had entered into the marriage contract for better or worse. See also *J.C. v J.H.C.* (unreported, August 1982, High Ct, Keane J). Section 3(12) of the 1996 Act has extended this concept of 'constructive desertion' to cohabitants who seek a barring order. The Family Law (Miscellaneous Provisions) Act 1997 inserted a further subsection into s. 3 of the Domestic Violence Act 1996 in this regard. This provides that where a cohabitant is in receipt of a barring order or an interim barring order and therefore does not have a cohabitation period of six out of the previous nine months by virtue of the said barring order, the requisite period of cohabitation is deemed to exist where the only reason for the shortfall lies in the fact that the respondent was not in occupation by virtue of the existence of the court order. This is relevant where a second barring application is being sought by a cohabitant. In practice, however, many District Judges will not grant a barring order during the currency or on the expiration of the existing barring order unless fresh evidence of further misconduct is adduced. This can sometimes be achieved by proof of breach of barring order. Where the cohabitant is merely seeking a 'safety order' it is necessary to establish a cohabitation period in which they lived 'as husband and wife' for at least six months in aggregate during the period of 12 months immediately prior to the application for the safety order. There is no equivalent of s. 3(12) in the Domestic Violence Act 1996, s. 2. There is no statutory extension, therefore, of the 'constructive desertion' provision where the applicant is a cohabitant seeking a safety order.

Proof of entitlement to apply for the remedy must be clearly set out in the 'Information' grounding a protection order. Useful indicators of the duration of cohabitation are the type of social welfare payment being received by the applicant or the tax status of the parties.

The second hurdle relates to the ownership of the property. One has to establish that the applicant has an equal or greater interest in the property from which the barring order is being sought. This factor must also be established in the body of the Information if interim relief is required. This can be dealt with by the expression of a belief in the Information. However, if there is to be an issue regarding the matter, more proof will be essential at the hearing stage. Other indicators are the rent book or letting agreement of the parties if they reside in rented accommodation. In the case of home owners, one must ascertain whether the property is in the joint names of the parties. One should ascertain when it was purchased and how it was financed. A joint tenancy by unequal contributions to purchase can pose practical problems. There is no proprietary requirement to be satisfied in the case of applications for safety orders.

10.5.3 RESPONDENT'S PARENT

The third category of applicant is the parent of the respondent who is not a dependant and has no interest, or a lesser interest in the property than the respondent has. In practice, most parents retain ownership of the family home. However, in some cases, property has been transferred to children with only a right of residence retained in favour of the parent. It is essential to check this out at the advice stage, as other proceedings in a different court might be more advisable. Where the application is for a 'safety order' there is no proprietary requirement to be satisfied.

10.5.4 OTHER APPLICANTS

The fourth category of applicant is entitled to seek a safety order only. This category appears to be quite broad and would cover those living in same sex relationships and siblings. The court has a wide discretion in relation to such an application and must consider: the length of time the parties resided together; the nature of duties performed by either applicant or respondent for the other or for any kindred person of the other; the absence of any profit or any significant profit made; and such other matters as the court considers appropriate in the circumstances.

There has not been a reported decision on this category of entitlement. It is unclear as to whether, for instance, it covers cohabitants who cannot satisfy the residence requirements of six out of the previous 12 months. It may be argued that it does not, given that the entitlement of cohabitants living 'as husband and wife' is already covered by the legislation. However, this would mean that applicants in a homosexual or lesbian relationship were treated more favourably than applicants in a heterosexual relationship. Can constructive desertion claims be used to extend the cohabitation period to be considered by the court under this category of application? There is a statutory extension of the doctrine of 'constructive desertion' to cohabitants living 'as husband and wife' under s. 3(12) of the Act, in the case of barring applications. There is no similar provision under s. 2 which deals with safety orders. Neither is the statutory extension of 'constructive desertion' provided for in the case of applicants of full age who reside with the respondent in a relationship the basis of which is not primarily contractual.

10.6   Applications by Health Boards

Section 6 of the 1996 Act empowers the Health Board to seek a remedy under the Act on behalf of an 'aggrieved person' which the person would him or herself be entitled to apply for. It would not be possible for a Health Board to obtain a barring order for someone who was not entitled to that relief under s. 3. For example, a Health Board could not obtain a barring order on behalf of a cohabitant who was not resident for six out of the previous nine months with the respondent. For the Health Board to have *locus standi* the following must apply:

(a)   they must be aware of an alleged incident or series of incidents which puts into doubt the safety or welfare of the victim (adult or dependent person called the 'aggrieved person');

(b)   they must have reasonable cause to believe that the aggrieved person has been subject to molestation, violence or threatened violence or otherwise put in fear of his or her safety or welfare;

(c) they must have a reasonable belief that, where appropriate in the circumstances, the aggrieved person would be deterred or prevented from pursuing the remedy for themselves or a dependent person out of fear of the respondent or molestation, violence or threatened violence;

(d) they must have ascertained, as far as reasonably practicable, the wishes of the aggrieved person, or, where the aggrieved person is a dependent person, the person *in loco parentis* to them and have considered those wishes.

This interesting and controversial provision provides that the consent of the victim or the adult carer of the victim is not a prerequisite, although they must be consulted. It is curious that the section does not require the Health Board to seek the views of the dependent person themselves, having regard to their age and understanding. Section 6(3) provides that the court, in determining whether and if so to what extent to make a safety order, barring order, interim barring order or protection order or whether to discharge any such order, shall have regard to any wishes expressed by the aggrieved person; the intimidated parent of a dependent aggrieved person; and, where the court considers it appropriate, the dependent person.

The United Nations Convention on the Rights of the Child 1989 requires State Parties to assure to the child who is capable of forming his or her own views, the right to express those views freely in all matters affecting the child. Those views should be given 'due weight' in accordance with the age and maturity of the child. For this purpose the Convention provides that the child should be provided with the opportunity to be heard in any judicial or administrative proceedings affecting the child either directly, or through a representative or an appropriate body, in a manner consistent with the procedural rules of national law. Section 6 can be viewed as allowing protective interventionism by the Health Board/court where the victim or the carer of the victim is disempowered from acting on their own behalf. This section has been used by Health Boards to obtain orders barring a spouse where the other spouse is accused of child sexual abuse. It has been used in this situation even where the other spouse opposes the intervention by the Health Board. The Health Board may under the Child Care Act 1991 remove the child who is the 'aggrieved person' and may prefer to do so unless assured that the other spouse will uphold the court order. In many cases, however, Health Boards prefer to remove the alleged perpetrator rather than the victim. There are many practical problems with this section, however useful it may seem at first reading.

Where the 'aggrieved person' is a dependent person then the Health Board does not have to establish that they are aware of an alleged incident or series of incidents which in their opinion puts into doubt the safety or welfare of the aggrieved minor. Nor do they have to establish that they have reasonable cause to believe that the aggrieved minor has been subjected to molestation, violence or threatened violence.

In such circumstances the Health Board need only adduce evidence that they are of the opinion that there are reasonable grounds for believing that such dependent person has been or is being assaulted, ill-treated, sexually abused or seriously neglected or such dependent person's health, development or welfare has been, is being or is likely to be avoidably impaired or seriously neglected.

If the order is made, the likelihood of harm to such dependent person will not arise or will be materially diminished.

Section 6(5) provides that the court may not make the order on behalf of a dependent person unless the Health Board can satisfy the court that the adult carer is willing and able to provide reasonable care for such dependent person.

10.7   Power of Court to Intervene and Order Section 7 Report

Section 7 of the 1996 Act empowers the court to consider an order under the Child Care Act 1991 where it considers such an order more appropriate in the circumstances of the case. This power extends to applications for relief under the 1996 Act, ss. 2, 3, 4 and 5, but not applications moved by a Health Board under s. 6. Therefore, where the court is hearing an application for a domestic violence remedy it may, having regard to the evidence before it and where there are dependent persons involved, take the view that the case warrants child protection intervention.

The court may then adjourn the proceedings and order an investigation by a Health Board into the circumstances of the dependent person. In addition the court can give directions under the Child Care Act 1991 as to the care and custody of the dependent person and make a supervision order under that legislation pending the outcome of the investigation by the Health Board.

The Health Board must consider whether it should:

(a)   apply for protection for the dependent person under the 1991 Act;

(b)   provide services or assistance for the dependent person's family;

(c)   take any other action in respect of the dependent person;

(d)   decline to take any action under the 1991 Act; and

(e)   inform the court of the reasons for inaction, or action taken or services given or intended to be given to the dependent person or their family.

Serious child protection concerns must present themselves in the course of the case before the section should be used. The solicitor must advise a client that the court may of its own motion request the Health Board to investigate a child care concern. While this power may be beneficial to the court in many cases, it can also have the effect of making clients feel more vulnerable should the respondent threaten to raise spurious child care concerns. Many parents feel vulnerable at the prospect of becoming exposed to the scrutiny of Health Board social workers and will need reassurance on this matter.

This section is quite different to an application by either party to the proceedings seeking a Social Report. Unfortunately, the District Court may not of its own motion seek a Social Report as the Guardianship of Infants Act 1964, s. 26 (as inserted by the Children Act 1997) has not been brought into force in the District Court. Where either litigant seeks such a Social Report they must bear the costs of the Report as ordered by the court. In cases where the parties are impecunious and not in receipt of civil legal aid, the court cannot seek a Social Report on the parties of its own motion.

The court may of course appoint a guardian *ad litem*/solicitor to act on behalf of the dependent person where the court is of the view that this is appropriate.

10.8   Protection of Household Chattels

Section 8 of the 1996 Act provides that spouses may not dispose of or remove household chattels between the institution of the domestic violence proceedings and the determination of them by the court. An application for permission to deal with household chattels in this period must be made to the court before which the proceedings have been instituted.

10.9   Contemporaneous Hearing of Related Proceedings

Section 9 of the 1996 Act enables the court to deal with issues of access, maintenance, restriction on conduct leading to the loss of the family home and the disposal of household chattels and orders under the Child Care Act 1991, without the need to issue another set of proceedings under the relevant legislation. In maintenance matters however, s. 23(4) of the Family Law (Maintenance of Spouses and Children) Act 1976, as inserted by the Family Law Act 1995, requires the mutual exchange of particulars of property and income. In effect, therefore, some District Courts will not deal with maintenance on an impromptu basis without statements of means being exchanged in advance. As a matter of practice therefore, a statement of means should be sought at the date of the institution of the barring proceedings or as soon as the solicitor is consulted in relation to such proceedings.

It is essential to remember that where there are issues of domestic violence, and violence to children (either physical or emotional) access should be viewed from the perspective of the child. Parental contact with children in cases where there has been domestic violence requires a significantly different approach. In each case the risk to the child must be assessed before access is agreed or ordered. The normal rule of thumb, that access is in the best interest of the child, does not automatically follow where there are issues of domestic violence. The primary question to be answered is whether the child needs to be protected. The nature of domestic violence ranges enormously. In some cases the parents may agree that access should take place but they may have concerns about boundaries and limitations, which should be built into any access order. Some parents may be better served by adjourning the proceedings to work out a 'parenting plan' through the auspices of the Family Mediation Centre. In other cases the help of a child 'expert' may be necessary before any decision can be taken. Similarly, there may be the need to engage a child expert where the relationship between the parent and the child has been damaged and requires restoration. In some instances the child may need to be independently represented either by a guardian *ad litem* (in the case of young children) or solicitor (in the case of an older child) where the child himself opposes access. Where access is agreed or ordered by the court and it transpires that the access is abusive of the child, application to court is needed to vary/discharge the order. Breach of access by the custodial parent may be the subject matter of proceedings by the parent who has an access order.

10.10   Taking Effect of Orders

Section 10(1) and (4) of the 1996 Act provide that any order made under the Act shall take effect on notification of its making being given to the respondent. Oral notification coupled with the production of a copy of the order shall, without prejudice to the sufficiency of any other form of notification, be taken as sufficient notification (s. 10(2)). The respondent who is present in court when the order is made is deemed to be notified of the making of an order (s. 10(3)). Notification is a very important issue, as the breach of an order has serious and far-reaching implications. The breach of an order made under the legislation is a criminal offence and the offender is liable on summary conviction to a fine not exceeding £1,500, or at the discretion of the court to imprisonment for a term not exceeding 12 months, or to both (s. 17). This statutory offence is without prejudice to the law as to contempt of court or any other liability, whether civil or criminal, that may be incurred by the respondent concerned. It is therefore vitally important to explain the serious consequences of breach of orders to respondent clients.

Section 11 provides that on the making, varying or discharge of an order under the 1996 Act, the court shall cause a copy of the order in question to be given or sent as soon as practicable to the applicant, the respondent, a Health Board in s. 6 cases, and the member in charge of the Garda Síochána in whose area the person for whose benefit the order was made resides.

Section 12 provides that an appeal of an order shall not operate as a stay on the order pending the appeal *unless* the court which made the barring order or the court to which the appeal is brought so determines.

10.11 Breach of Orders and Power of Arrest Under 1996 Act

Orders under the Act can be enforced by the Gardaí. This is what makes these orders more attractive than injunctions. The Gardaí may have powers of arrest under the Domestic Violence Act 1996, the Criminal Damage Act 1991, the Non-Fatal Offences against the Person Act 1997, the Dublin Police Act 1842 or the Criminal Law (Rape) Amendment Act 1990.

The Gardaí have a duty to investigate fully and promptly all incidents of domestic violence, including reports on these received from third parties. The Garda Síochána policy on domestic violence intervention has now been published and clearly states that all incidents of domestic violence must be recorded. The investigating member should provide the victim with a copy of the domestic violence information leaflet and make the victim aware of the relevant services in the area, such as: victim support groups; the Health Board; social workers; rape crisis centres; women's aid/refuges; local women's support groups; local GPs; Family Law courts; the Legal Aid Board; and any other agency which may be of assistance.

The 1996 Act provides for additional powers of arrest for the Gardaí where they have reasonable cause to believe that a person is being assaulted (occasioning actual bodily harm, malicious wounding or inflicting any grievous bodily harm) and the person is someone who could apply for a safety order or a barring order (s. 18(2)).

It is important for the client to receive clear advice from the solicitor outlining the enforcement mechanism in place for breach of the barring order once the case is over. Although the penalties for breach of the barring order will be clearly stated on the order it is essential to tell the client who is barred the consequences of breach of the order. There may be some confusion as to whether the barred client may call at the house to collect clothes, personal belongings, etc. The barred client may also believe that they can return to the house to collect the children for access, or if invited in by the spouse or children. These matters clearly need to be addressed orally once the case is over and the advice should be followed up in writing. If the client is to approach the residence for any reason then this needs to be specified in the order to avoid problems. If the order contains a watching and besetting clause then this must also be explained clearly to the client.

Research suggests that the victims of domestic violence may be in greater danger of serious violence after the legal system has intervened. It is equally important to tell the client who obtains a barring order how the 'breach of barring order' procedure works. They must also be told that the order is an order of court and that if they reconcile they must seek the discharge of the barring order by the court: it is not enough simply to invite the other party into the house for whatever reason. Notwithstanding the publication of the Garda Síochána policy on domestic violence intervention, the practice on the ground varies considerably. Section 18, which details the powers of arrest under the legislation, is not mandatory and where discretion is involved in any area it leads to differences in approach. In practice, it is wise to give the client adequate advice to enable him or her to secure the enforcement of the order obtained.

10.12 Instruction Sheet for Domestic Violence

CASE REFERENCE NO:

NAME OF CLIENT:

ADDRESS OF CLIENT:

TELEPHONE NO:

ADDRESS FOR CORRESPONDENCE:

MARITAL STATUS:

DATES OF COHABITATION:

ISSUES OF CONSTRUCTIVE DESERTION:

RESIDENCE/ FAMILY HOME DETAILS:

OWNERSHIP DETAILS:

CHILDREN:

OTHER DEPENDENT PERSONS:

HISTORY OF RELATIONSHIP:

PREVIOUS ORDERS:

HEALTH STATUS OF APPLICANT/RESPONDENT:

DETAILS OF GENERAL PRACTITIONER:

DETAILS OF PRIOR HOSPITAL ADMISSIONS

GARDA INTERVENTION DETAILS:

EXPLAIN NATURE OF DOMESTIC VIOLENCE REMEDIES:

BARRING ORDER/PROTECTION ORDER/INTERIM BARRING ORDER/SAFETY ORDER:

TAKE UP COPY OF INFORMATION WHERE ACTING FOR RESPONDENT:

HEALTH BOARD INTERVENTION:

ANCILLARY ORDERS:

MAINTENANCE:

ACCESS:

CUSTODY:

CHILD CARE ACT 1991:

ISSUES CONCERNING ACCESS TO CHILDREN:

EXPLAIN 'IN CAMERA RULE':

COURT DISTRICT/VENUE:

IS THE OTHER SIDE REPRESENTED?

ADVICE ON LEGAL AID:

STATEMENT OF MEANS REQUEST FOR HEARING:

CHAPTER 11

CHILD LAW

11.1 Private Law: Guardianship, Custody and Access

11.1.1 INTRODUCTION

Section 11 of the Guardianship of Infants 1964 Act (the '1964 Act') permits any person being a guardian of an infant to apply to the court for its direction on any question affecting the welfare of the infant. The court may give such directions as it sees proper regarding the issues of guardianship, custody and access and may order the father or mother to commence reasonable maintenance payments. Although an order can be sought under this section when the parties are residing together, it can have no effect so long as they reside together. Similarly, the order shall cease to have effect if the parties cohabit for a period of three months after the making of the order. An application regarding the custody of an infant and the right of access of his father or mother can be made to the court under s. 11 by the unmarried natural father of an infant by virtue of s. 11(4). Despite the terms of s. 6(1) which otherwise limit the rights of unmarried natural fathers under s. 11, references to the father or parent of the infant in s. 11 shall extend to the natural father of the infant. However, an application brought by the natural unmarried father can not include an application in relation to maintenance under s. 11(2)(b).

11.1.2 WELFARE

Welfare is defined by s. 2 of the 1964 Act as comprising the religious, moral, intellectual, physical and social welfare of an infant. Where proceedings are brought before the court, which relate, inter alia, to the custody, guardianship or upbringing of an infant, the court is obliged under s. 3 of the 1964 Act to regard the welfare of the infant as the first and paramount consideration. It is not the only relevant consideration, but it is apparently the most important. In the course of his judgment in *G v An Bord Uchtála* [1980] IR 32 at p. 76, Walsh J stated:

> 'The word "paramount" by itself is not by any means an indication of exclusivity: no doubt if the Oireachtas had intended the welfare of the child to be the sole consideration it would have said so. The use of the word "paramount" certainly indicates that the welfare of the child is to be the superior or most important consideration, in so far as it can be, having regard to the law of the provisions of the Constitution applicable to any given case.' (See also the dicta of McDermott LJ considering the corresponding English provision in *J v C* [1970] AC 668 and Henchy J in *MacD v MacD* (1979) 114 ILTR 66.)

The ostensible rule then (although this has been qualified by the constitutional preference for the marital family (see *K.C. and A.C. v An Bord Uchtála* [1986] 6 ILRM 65) is that where there is a conflict between the welfare of the child and other considerations (such as the rights of parents), the welfare of the child takes precedence over all other matters. This is sometimes known as the 'best interests test' although s. 3 refers specifically to the welfare of the child: see Walsh J in *G v An Bord Uchtála* at p. 76, who appears to suggest that the two terms may differ in meaning in certain contexts. This principle, that the best interests of the child must take preference in all matters concerning the child's welfare, is in line with Ireland's international obligations, in particular with article 3 of the UN Convention on the Rights of the Child 1989 (ratified by Ireland on 21 September 1992). For the purposes of clarity, the various constituent factors making up the concept of welfare shall be dealt with in turn.

11.1.2.1 Religious welfare

In determining the issue of the custody of a child in the past the court would most often make its decision in an attempt to ensure that the religious upbringing of the child was not affected by the award of custody.

Thus, for example, where one party was in a new relationship with a person of a different religion, awarding that parent custody would be seen as a threat to the religious welfare of the child. However, the court in *Cullen v Cullen* (unreported, 8 May 1970, Supreme Ct) was willing to accept the undertakings that the child would receive proper religious instruction. Therein, despite the mother's religious lapse, she told the court that she would see to it that her youngest child Jeffrey would be taught religion and would 'say his prayers'. (See *McD v McD* (1979) 114 ILTR 59 where the Supreme Court granted custody of a child being brought up as a Roman Catholic to his Protestant mother. The mother, furthermore, at the time was residing with a Protestant man. See also *Quinn's Supermarket v A.G.* [1972] IR 1; *McGrath and O. Ruairc v Maynooth College* [1979] ILRM 166 and *Campaign to Separate Church and State v Ireland* [1998] 3 IR 321, all of which seem to suggest a preference for buttressing the free practice of religion.)

Ultimately, however, the decision made by the court, although influenced to a certain extent by the religious welfare of the child, is made in the best interests of the general welfare of the child.

11.1.2.2 Moral welfare

It is no longer an invariable rule of law that a parent who is in an adulterous relationship should be deprived of custody in view of the danger this relationship poses to the child's moral welfare. In earlier cases the parent who committed adultery was often seen as a source of corruption and as a misguided example for the child. The Supreme Court in *J.J.W. v B.M.W.* (1971) 110 ILTR 49, a case where the respondent mother living in England had committed adultery, awarded custody of the three children of the union to their father on, inter alia, the grounds that their moral welfare was more likely to be protected away from the adulterous relationship. Finlay CJ stated:

> 'The fact is that the home which she has to offer to her children is one in which she continues an adulterous relationship with a man who has deserted his own wife and his own two children. A more unhealthy abode for the three children would be difficult to imagine.'

However, more recently it has been accepted that custody can no longer be awarded as a prize for good marital behaviour. Thus the committing of adultery by one parent does not automatically prevent forever his/her chance of obtaining sole custody of the children. Ultimately the court must examine the entire situation in light of the needs of each child and cannot immediately pass judgment on the parent who has acted in the 'immoral' manner. This more liberal attitude of the court was evidenced in the judgment of Walsh J in *E.K. v M.K.* (unreported, 31 July 1974, Supreme Ct) wherein he stated that:

> 'custody is awarded not as a mark of approbation or disapprobation of paternal conduct but solely as a judicial determination of where the welfare of the children lies.'

In *M.O'B. v P.O'B* (unreported, 5 January 1971, High Ct) Kenny J remarked in a similar vein that 'an award of custody is not reward for good behaviour'. This tendency has become more marked with the passage of time. In *S v S* [1992] ILRM 732, Finlay CJ in the Supreme Court stated that the conduct of the parents is relevant only insofar as it affects the welfare of the child, athough he did add that such conduct is relevant in considering the priorities of the parents in relation to the child. See also *P.C. v C.G* (unreported, 3 July 1983, High Ct, Ellis J).

Clearly although the moral welfare of the child remains a factor to be considered by the court when determining the issue of custody, the decision can only ultimately be made on the basis of the welfare of the child as a whole.

11.1.2.3 Intellectual welfare

The issue of intellectual welfare essentially relates to the intellectual and educational needs of a child. In considering this factor when deciding on the issue of custody the court must seek to ensure that the result of its decision is that the child is surrounded with intellectual stability and support.

11.1.2.4 Physical welfare

Physical welfare relates to the general physical health and well-being of the child. Traditionally, especially where younger children were concerned, the court applied the tender years principle (which is discussed in detail later) and deemed the mother most capable of looking after the physical well-being of the child. It was felt that mothers, all other things being equal, were best suited to the rearing of young children because of their nature and availability. More recent cases, however, have tended to dilute this inclination although the courts continue generally to regard the mother, all else being equal, as the more appropriate and competent care-giver. See dicta of McGuinness J in *D.F.O'S. v C.A.* (unreported, 20 April 1999, High Ct) and the discussion below at **11.1.2.7**.

11.1.2.5 Social welfare

The concept of social welfare was best described by Finlay P (as he then was) in the case of *J.C. v O.C.* (unreported, 10 July 1980, High Ct) as:

> 'their capacity to mix with and enter into and become part of the society in which they will be brought up'.

It is also interesting to note that Finlay P believed that keeping the children together 'is part of their social development as a family'.

The importance of the examination of these factors as a whole is highlighted by Walsh J in his judgment in *S v S* (1974) 110 ILTR 57 which was quoted favourably by McGuinness J in *C.C. v P.C.* [1994] 3 Fam LJ 85, who noted that it was stressed in a number of judgments that it is necessary for the court to take an overall view:

> 'All the ingredients which the Act stipulates are to be considered globally. This is not to be decided by the simple method of totting up the marks which may be awarded under each of the five headings. It is the totality of the picture presented which must be considered . . . the word ''welfare'' must be taken in its widest sense.' (See also *D.F.O'S. v C.A.* (unreported, 20 April 1999, High Ct, McGuinness J.)

It must be remembered, however, that although the welfare of the child is to be regarded as 'the first and paramount consideration' it is not the only factor to be considered by the court. In the Supreme Court judgment of *K.C. and A.C. v An Bord Uchtála* [1986] 6 ILRM 65, Finlay J stated:

> 'it does not seem to me that section 3 of the 1964 Act can be construed as meaning simply that the balance of the welfare as defined in section 2 of the 1964 Act must be the sole criteria for the determination by the court of the issue as to custody of the child'.

Nonetheless, ultimately the child's interests and welfare must be the primary concern of the court. O'Flaherty J in the course of his judgment in *Southern Health Board v C.H.* [1996] 2 ILRM 142, a case concerning the admissibility of a videoed interview where allegations had been made of abuse by the father, stated that:

'it is easy to comprehend that the child's welfare must always be of far graver concern to the court. We must, as judges, always harken to the constitutional command which mandates, as a prime consideration, the interests of the child in any legal proceedings'.

Later, O'Flaherty J states that:

'the first point to note about this case is that the judge is in essence required to *inquire* as to what is in the best interests of the child'.

The emphasis of the Supreme Court in this more recent case on 'the best interest of the child' contrasts with the approach of the Supreme Court in the slightly earlier case. Other than the issue of the welfare of the child as defined by s. 2 of the 1964 Act, the other relevant factors to be considered by the court when determining any issue relating to children are as follows:

11.1.2.6 Emotional welfare

Section 2 of the 1964 Act does not contain any reference to emotional welfare as an aspect to be considered when determining the issue of the welfare of the child. McGuinness J in *D.F.O'S. v C.A.* (unreported, 20 April 1999, High Ct) notes that to the list of factors contained in s. 2 which make up the definition of welfare, judges in the past have added the concept of 'emotional welfare'. McGuinness J in recognising emotional welfare as 'a most important aspect of welfare' suggested to the parents involved that in order to assist the emotional welfare of their children they should both attend individual counselling. Thus, it is suggested that this aspect of a child's welfare must now be considered by the court. Indeed, the emotional welfare of the child was recognised on a statutory basis in the Protections for Persons Reporting Child Abuse Act 1998, s. 1.

11.1.2.7 Tender years principle

As stated above, the courts have traditionally readily applied the tender years principle in determining the issue of the custody of younger children. O'Dalaigh CJ in his judgment in *B v B* [1975] IR 54 stated in reference to the young son of the parties that:

'in view of his tender age, there can be no doubt that the younger son should continue in the custody of his mother'.

However, the court does not apply this principle as a rule and in light of varying circumstances is willing to award the father the custody of young children, as in *J.J.W. v B.M.W.*, discussed above. In addition, in light of current attitudes and the changing roles of both fathers and mothers, decisions made now are less likely than before to adhere to the tender years principle. Fathers are increasingly more available as the principal carer in the family and are becoming more involved in the rearing of their families. This was made most evident by McGuinness J in her recent unreported decision of *D.F.O'S v C.A* wherein she discussed the merits of the tender years principle in light of current lifestyles and opinion.

'I do not entirely accept the old *tender years* principle: modern views and practices of parenting show the virtues of shared parenting and the older principles too often meant the automatic granting of custody to the mother virtually to the exclusion of the father.'

Thus in the instant case McGuinness J made an order of joint custody despite the fact that the child was merely four years old.

11.1.2.8   Parental caring capacity

In considering any application for guardianship, custody, access or even care proceedings the court must consider in each case the parental capacity of both parents. The court will be concerned to ensure that the custodial parent has the physical and mental resources to care for the child. Equally the court must be satisfied as to the physical and mental resources of any parent exercising access rights with the children. However this by no means will result in the 'weaker' spouse losing out on custody of the child.

Equally where the parent is incapable of fulfilling his/her role as parent they will not be granted custody of the child. This was evidenced in the case of *C.C. v P.C.* [1994] 3 Fam LJ 85. Here, the relationship between the boy and his father was such that in effect the child was living the role of the parent and the father was living the role of the child. In the words of McGuinness J the court feared there was a danger of the child becoming 'parentified, of protecting his father'.

11.1.2.9   Keeping siblings together

In general the courts prefer to keep siblings together, ideally in the family home. The courts favour continuity and stability for the children even where the behaviour of the custodial parent is in issue. O'Dalaigh CJ in the aforementioned *B v B* noted that:

> 'After the separation of the parents, there remain two lesser points of unity around which one would wish, if possible, to build: the first of these is the unity of the comradeship of the three children, and the second is the family home where these three children have grown up together.'

11.1.3   GUARDIANSHIP

Guardianship means the rights and duties of parents in respect of the upbringing of their children. It encompasses the duty to maintain and properly care for the child and refers to the decisions that must be made during the child's lifetime which relate to the general lifestyle and development of the child. Being a guardian requires a person to partake in the important decisions in a child's life, e.g. education, religion, general rearing etc.

11.1.3.1   Who can be a guardian?

The natural mother of a child is automatically a guardian of the child. Whether the father of a child is an automatic guardian depends upon his relationship with the mother. The married mother and father of a child are the most common guardians and they are so entitled by virtue of s. 6(1) of the 1964 Act. However for the father to have guardianship status the parties must be married at the time of the birth of the child. Alternatively he can acquire guardianship status if the parties marry after the birth of the child or become married at some time after the birth of the child. The natural father of the child who is not married to the mother of the child can apply to the court under the 1964 Act, s. 6A (as inserted by the Status of Children Act 1987, s. 12) to be appointed a guardian of the child. However the easiest way for the unmarried natural father to become a joint guardian of the child is by obtaining the mother's agreement and co-operation. Section 4 of the Children Act 1997 inserts a new s. 2(4) in the 1964 Act which enables a father to be appointed a guardian of the child with the mother's agreement provided they enter into a statutory declaration, declaring that they are the father and mother of the child, that they agree to the appointment of the father as a guardian of the child and they have entered into arrangements regarding the custody of and access to the child: see **12.7** below. Section 7 of the 1964 Act empowers a father (as defined under the Act) by will or deed, to appoint a person or persons to be the guardian or guardians of the child after his death. Equally under this section a mother can appoint such a testamentary guardian. A testamentary guardian acts jointly with the surviving parent of the child so long as the surviving parent remains alive unless the surviving parent objects to his/her so acting. A guardian can be appointed by the court under s. 7(4) on foot of an application by the testamentary guardian if the surviving spouse objects to the testamentary guardian or if the testamentary guardian considers the surviving spouse to be unfit to have custody of the child. The court is empowered to make an order that the testamentary guardian shall act as a joint guardian with the surviving spouse or equally can order that the testamentary guardian act as guardian of the child to the exclusion of the surviving spouse. In making the later order the court is also empowered by s. 7(6) to make the orders in relation to custody, access and maintenance as is appropriate in the circumstances. Where a child has no guardian an application can be made under s. 8(1) by one or more persons and the court can appoint the applicant(s) to be guardian(s) of the child. A guardian appointed to act jointly with a surviving spouse shall continue to act as a guardian after the death of the surviving parent. Section 8 equally allows a court to remove a guardian appointed by will or order of the court. In so doing, the court can appoint another guardian in place of the removed guardian.

11.1.3.2 Rights and powers of a guardian

Subject to any express terms of a deed, will or court order a guardian appointed under the 1964 Act shall be entitled to the custody of the child and shall be entitled to take proceedings for the restoration of his/her custody of the child against any person who wrongfully takes away or detains the child. Equally the guardian can act on behalf of the child for the recovery of damages for any injury to or trespass against the person of the child. The guardian shall also be entitled to the possession and control of all property of the child and shall manage all such property on behalf of and for the benefit of the child until the infant attains the age of 21 years or during any shorter period for which he has been appointed guardian and may take such appropriate proceedings in relation thereto as may be permitted.

11.1.3.3 Rights of natural fathers

Section 6(1) of the 1964 Act states simply that the father and mother of an infant shall be guardians of the infant jointly. However, this apparently wide definition is quickly limited by the definition of 'father' in s. 2 of the Act which excludes the natural unmarried father of a child. Several cases have come before the Supreme Court which have dealt with the right of a natural unmarried father to be appointed as guardian of a child. In *J.K. v V.W.* [1990] 2 IR 437, a case stated by Barron J from the High Court to the Supreme Court, it was held that s. 6A of the 1964 Act gave a natural father the right to apply to be appointed a guardian but did not give him the right to be a guardian; nor did it equate his position in law with the position of a father married to the mother of his child. Finlay CJ in the course of his judgment stated:

> 'The discretion vested in the Court on the making of such an application must be exercised regarding the welfare of the infant as the first and paramount consideration. The blood link between the infant and the father and the possibility for the infant to have the benefit of the guardianship by and the society of its father is one of the many factors which may be viewed by the court as relevant to its welfare'.

Another adoption case which came before the Supreme Court in 1996 by way of case stated was *W.O'R. v E.H. and An Bord Uchtála* [1996] 2 IR 248. Although most of the issues involved related directly to the matter of adoption one of the questions stated by the Circuit Court judge was in relation to the character and extent of the rights of interest or concern of a natural father: when do they arise in an application for guardianship and are such matters within the sole discretion of the trial judge? It was held by the Supreme Court that although the basic issue for the trial judge is the welfare of the children, consideration must be given to all relevant factors. The blood link between the natural father and the children will be one of the many factors for the judge to consider, and the weight it will be given will depend on the circumstances as a whole. Thus, in the absence of other factors beneficial to the children and in the presence of factors negative to the children's welfare, where the blood link is the only link between the father and the children it is of small weight and can not be the determining factor. But where the children are born as a result of a stable and established relationship and nurtured at the commencement of life by father and mother in a de facto family as opposed to a constitutional family, then the natural father on application to the court under s. 6(A) of the 1964 Act has extensive rights of interest and concern. However they are always subordinate to the paramount concern of the court which is the welfare of the child: see **13.11**.

11.1.4   CUSTODY

Custody is the right of a parent to exercise physical care and control in respect of the upbringing of their child on a day-to-day basis, *per* Denham J in *W.O'R. v E.H.* [1996] 2 IR 248. The married parents of a child are automatically joint guardians and custodians of their child. In the case of a child being born to an unmarried mother the mother is automatically the child's guardian and sole custodian. If the father of the child wishes to acquire custodial status, he can apply under s. 11(4) of the 1964 Act, even if he does not have guardianship rights at the time of making the application. Very often where one parent has left the home he/she is very reluctant to surrender any custodial rights. The fear exists that to do so would be to lose all control over their child's life. This belief arises from their inability to properly understand the concept of guardianship and the rights and duties that are retained by virtue of being a guardian. Joint custody is an option open to parents when the issues relating to the children are being determined. Section 9 of the Children Act 1997 amends s. 11 of the 1964 Act by inserting a section which makes it clear that in appropriate cases, custody of a child may be granted by the court to a father and mother jointly. However, the practicalities of life are such that most often children will reside with one parent whilst exercising access with the other parent. In the High Court case of *E.P. v C.P.* (unreported, 27 November 1998, High Ct) McGuinness J in awarding sole custody to the applicant wife and noting that joint custody is currently recommended, held that it cannot work satisfactorily for the children if there is a high level of conflict between the parents. She further noted that when couples cannot work together sensibly and happily in the interests of the children an order for joint custody is not suitable. Thus it appeared from this judgment that only where the spouses have an amicable relationship can joint custody be considered by the court. However, more recently, McGuinness J in *D.F.O'S. v C.A.* (unreported, 20 April 1999, High Ct) has in a situation of equal disharmony and conflict, made a decision to award joint custody to the unmarried parents of a child in the hope that

> 'if they accept the joint responsibility of caring for their daughter and promoting her welfare I hope it will encourage them to put their antagonisms behind them.'

In the course of her judgment McGuinness J at p. 25 noted that:

> 'As a general rule where there is deep hostility between the parents I am very reluctant to make an order granting joint custody, due to the probable inability of the parents to co-operate in caring for the child.'

Whilst admitting this to be her general position McGuinness J stated that in the instant case she feared that to award custody of the child to one parent could give rise to an increase in the present bitterness and resentment. Relying upon the evidence of an expert witness McGuinness J noted that although an acrimonious relationship existed between the parents they had both been able to maintain an excellent and individual relationship with the child. Thus, in the circumstances, it was held that joint custody was the most appropriate award to be made. Clearly the decision to be made by any court in relation to the issue of custody will depend entirely on the facts of each case. It can no longer be said that where a bitter relationship exists between the parents of a child an award of joint custody will not be made. It is apparent from this most recent decision of McGuinness J that where it is in the interests of all the parties involved, an order of joint custody can be made by the court.

11.1.5 ACCESS

The parent who does not obtain custody of a child but remains a guardian is entitled to apply for access to the child. The court will consider an application for access on the basis that the best interests of the child are of paramount importance. The right of access is ultimately thus a right of the child. If there is a conflict between what is in the best interest of the applicant parent and the child, the rights of the child will take precedence. It should be remembered that, as with a custody order, an access order is never a final order. It is always open to either parent to apply to the court to vary the access order if this is in the interests of the child. It is extremely unusual for a court to refuse a parent access with his child. The strong judicial tendency in favour of granting access is exemplified by *A.MacB. v A.G.MacB.* (unreported, 6 June 1984, High Ct). There, a father was granted access to his children despite strong evidence that the children were afraid of him. This was despite the additional fact that the father was alleged to have caused malicious damage to property. Barron J, nonetheless, considered at p. 13 of his judgment that it was 'essential that the children know that they have a father and . . . that their father is able to take the place of a father in their lives'. The court will often try to accommodate any case where access would be inappropriate by making an order of supervised access. In *O'D v O'D* [1994] 3 Fam LJ 81, for instance, the High Court granted supervised access to the father where there was a reasonable suspicion that he might have sexually abused his child.

The recent Children Act 1997 introduced on a statutory footing, the right of relatives to apply for access to a child. Section 9 of the 1997 Act which inserted (inter alia) s. 11B into the 1964 Act followed on from the High Court ruling in *D v D* [1993] 1 Fam LJ 34 wherein Carroll J stated that the right of the child to access extends beyond the right of access to his/her parents, to that of access to grandparents and the extended family of the child. In fact, in *Marckx v Belgium* (1979) 2 EHRR 330 the European Court of Human Rights held that 'family life' includes not only relations between parents and their children, but also extends to grandparents and grandchildren. The new s. 11B of the 1964 Act entitles any person who is a relative of a child or who has acted *in loco parentis* to a child to whom the original s. 11 does not apply, to apply to the court for an access order to the child on such terms and conditions as the court may order. The application, however, is not as straightforward as an application under the original s. 11 and the applicant under s. 11B must first apply to the court for leave to make the application. In deciding whether to grant leave for the making of the application, the court is obliged to have particular regard to the applicant's connection with the child, the risk of disruption to the child and the wishes of the child's guardians. It appears that a quasi hearing must occur before the main application can be made to the court.

The District Court (Custody and Guardianship of Children) Rules 1999 (SI 125/1999) have introduced new rules and forms for child custody and guardianship applications in the District Court. Order 58, r. 5(1) provides that for relatives or those *in loco parentis*, and who cannot apply under s. 11 (i.e. because they are not guardians of the child) to apply, the application for leave 'shall be preceded by the issue and service of a notice upon each guardian of the child'. The notice is set out in Form No. 58.15 of Schedule C. The substantive application for access is covered by Order 58, r. 5(3), which again requires service on all guardians of a notice set out in Form No. 58.19.

11.1.6 HEARSAY EVIDENCE

11.1.6.1 Generally

Section 23 of the Children Act 1997 permits the inclusion of hearsay evidence of any fact in all proceedings relating to the welfare of a child, public or private. The legislation also applies in cases relating to any person who has a mental disability to such an extent that independent living is not feasible. However, in all cases to which s. 23 relates, several conditions apply as listed below:

(a) The court must be satisfied that the child in question is either unable to give evidence by reason of age or that the giving of oral evidence (in person or by television link) would not be in the interests of the child's welfare (s. 23(1)).

(b) Evidence of a fact will only be admitted if direct oral evidence of such fact would also have been admissible (s. 23(1)).

(c) Such statement cannot be admitted if, in the opinion of the court, its inclusion would be to the detriment of the interests of justice, in particular if its inclusion would result in unfairness to any of the parties to the proceedings (s. 23(2)).

(d) Prior to hearsay evidence being admitted, all interested parties to the proceedings must be given notice of the proposal to submit such evidence. This should be accompanied by such particulars of, or relating to, the evidence as are considered reasonable and practicable in all the circumstances to allow the parties to deal with any matter arising from its being hearsay (s. 23(3)). This condition does not apply where the parties, by agreement, agree that it should not apply (s. 23(4)).

(e) Section 23 does not apply to proceedings started before the commencement of Part III of the 1997 Act, that is 1 January 1999.

11.1.6.2 Weight to be given to such evidence

When hearsay evidence is admitted by virtue of s. 23, the court must also turn its attention to the Children Act 1997, s. 24. This relates to the weight to be given to such evidence. The court is generally required to have regard to all circumstances from which any inference can be drawn as to its accuracy or otherwise, but in particular must consider the following:

(a) Was the original statement made at the time of or as soon as possible after the event to which it relates? Obviously the closer to the event, the greater the likelihood of accuracy.

(b) Does the evidence involve multiple hearsay (i.e. evidence of more than one statement made outside the confines of the court)?

(c) Does any person involved have any vested interest in concealing or misrepresenting the matter or matters? Take, for instance, the case of a person accused of abusing a child, informally questioning that child relating to the matter. It may be the case that the court would consider inadmissible evidence of the child's answers.

(d) To what extent, if any, was the original statement an edited account? To what extent, if any, was such statement made in collaboration with another for a particular purpose? Obviously an edited account will be of lesser weight, particularly where the person relating it has a vested interest in the case.

(e) Were the circumstances in which the evidence was gathered such as to suggest an attempt to prevent the proper consideration of its weight?

Section 25 of the Children Act 1997 allows evidence regarding the credibility of the child to be admitted, notwithstanding the fact that the child is not, strictly speaking, a witness.

Section 26 of the 1997 Act allows a copy of any document—which for these purposes includes a sound recording and a video-recording—to be admitted in evidence in proceedings where s. 23 allows hearsay evidence to be admitted. The document, by definition, need not be an original. Indeed, it is not necessary that the original document be still in existence. It is possible to produce a copy or facsimile thereof, and for these purposes it is not relevant how many removes there are between the copy and the original, i.e. the document may be a copy of a copy. The court may prescribe such means of authentication as to it appear proper.

Hearsay evidence may also be admitted in wardship proceedings. This was affirmed in *Eastern Health Board v M.K. and M.K.* (unreported, 29 January 1999, Supreme Ct) where the Supreme Court referred with approval to the changes in the Children Act 1997. It noted that, provided the court is satisfied that introduction of hearsay evidence is necessary and that its content is reliable, the court may admit it. The similarity to the provisions of the Act is obvious although the ability to give direct weight to such statements, by contrast with the 1997 Act, s. 24 remains uncertain.

11.2 Public Law: Child Care

The current legislation dealing with public law aspects is the Child Care Act 1991, which replaced the skeleton service that existed for children since the enactment of the Children Act 1908. The Child Care Act 1991 ('the 1991 Act') when introduced, represented an urgently required answer to the calls of many for reform in this area. Prior to its introduction Ireland lacked a definite infrastructure of child-care and family support services. The enactment of the 1991 Act formalised and updated the law for the protection of children whose welfare was under threat by virtue of their surroundings.

Those to be protected by the provisions of the 1991 Act are set out in the definition of 'child' contained in Part I thereof. 'Child' is defined by the Act as a person under the age of 18 years who has not married. Under the previous legislation there was a distinction made between a child who was under the age of 15 and a young person who was aged between 15 and 17.

11.2.1 WELFARE AND CARE

11.2.1.1 Introduction

Part II of the 1991 Act deals with the promotion of the welfare of children who are in need or in danger. Primarily, Part II sets out in detail the functions of the Health Board. It also deals with the area of voluntary care which allows a child to be taken into care by the Health Board with the consent of the child's parents and/or guardians. In addition to the general requirement that the welfare of all children in need be safeguarded, the Health Board has specific duties under the 1991 Act, s. 5 to ensure that the homeless child is adequately accommodated.

11.2.1.2 Importance of child's welfare

Section 24 of the 1991 Act provides that in any proceedings before the court in relation to the care and protection of a child that are brought under the 1991 Act, the court, having regard to the rights and duties of parents, whether under the Constitution or otherwise, is to regard the welfare of the child as the first and paramount consideration and, in so far as is practicable, give due consideration, having regard to his age and understanding, to the wishes of the child. It is not necessary for the child to be present at the hearing of the proceedings unless the court under s. 30 of the 1991 Act is satisfied that 'this is necessary for the proper disposal of the case'. However, where a child asks to be present, the court must under s. 30(2) grant his request unless it determines that to do so would 'not be in the child's interests' due to his age or 'the nature of the proceedings'.

11.2.1.3   Functions of the Health Board

Part II of the 1991 Act deals in part with the functions of the Health Board which are set out in s. 3 thereof. The basic function of the Health Board is to promote the welfare of children in its area who are not receiving adequate care and protection. In carrying out its duties the Health Board is required under s. 3(2)(a) to take such steps as it considers necessary to identify these children and in so doing to co-ordinate information from all relevant sources relating to them. The Health Board, although entitled to decide the level of involvement required, is obliged under s. 3 to take certain courses of action and does not retain any discretion in this regard. The obligations on the Health Board arising from this section are quite onerous as it appears that in promoting the welfare of children the Health Board must play an active and ongoing role in the lives of these children, rather than simply reacting to situations. When carrying out these functions the Health Board is obliged under s. 3(2)(b) to have regard to the rights and duties of parents as provided for by the Constitution and otherwise. The inclusion of this need for the Health Board to recognise the importance of parents' wishes may have saved this section from being declared unconstitutional as an otherwise unlawful interference with the rights of the family as protected by Articles 41 and 42 of the Constitution. However, despite the importance of the family as a whole, and the recognition of the role of parents, the welfare of the child must under s. 3(2)(b)(i) be regarded by the court as the first and paramount consideration. As in so many areas of family law, the welfare of the child is prioritised above all other matters. Furthermore, so far as is practicable, due consideration must be given to the wishes of the child having regard to his age and understanding. However, ultimately the court is required under s. 3(2)(c) to have regard to the principle 'that it is generally in the best interest of the child to be brought up in his own family'. Thus, in light of this principle a court must be satisfied of the need for Health Board intervention before it will consider granting any relief under this Act. Finally, a Health Board is assigned the duty under s. 3(3) of the 1991 Act to provide and maintain child care and family support services, including appropriate premises and such other provisions as are required or desirable, subject to any general directions given by the Minister under s. 69 of the Act. Therefore, where the Health Board considers intervention to be necessary, it should first consider whether a child not receiving adequate care and protection could receive such care by remaining with its family, with the provision of help from the Health Board by way of support services.

11.2.1.4   Voluntary care

It is the duty of the Health Board under s. 4 of the 1991 Act to take a child into care where it appears that the child, who is resident or is found in its area, requires care and protection which he is unlikely to receive unless he is taken into care. In such a case the Health Board is obliged to maintain the child for so long as his welfare requires it and to have regard to the wishes of a parent having custody of the child or a person acting *in loco parentis*. Section 4(2) prevents the Health Board from taking a child into care under this section without the consent of the parent(s). Thus this section envisages a situation where a parent accepts the existence of danger to the child and is willing to allow the participation and assistance of the Health Board, thereby preventing the necessity for proceedings to be instituted by the Health Board. Under this voluntary procedure where a parent wishes to resume care of the child the Health Board has no authority to maintain him in its care. In such circumstances, should the Health Board wish to continue its involvement, it must follow the procedures set out in Parts III, IV and VI of the 1991 Act. Where a Health Board has taken a child into its care under the voluntary care procedure it is obliged under s. 4(3) to maintain the child in its care so long as the board believes the welfare of the child requires it, up to the time the child reaches 18. In so doing the Health Board is required to have regard to the wishes of the custodial parent(s). Where the child in care is taken into care because he appeared lost or abandoned, the board in maintaining the child must endeavour to reunite him with his custodial parent where the board believes this to be in the child's best interests. If to reunite the child with his parents does not appear to be in the child's best interests or if one of the parents seeks the return of the child the Health Board may in appropriate cases institute care proceedings.

11.2.1.5 Homeless children

Section 5 of the 1991 Act deals with the needs of homeless children. Where a homeless child is discovered the Health Board is required to enquire into his circumstances and if it is discovered that there is no suitable accommodation available to him the board must take reasonable steps to make suitable accommodation available to him, unless the child is taken into care.

11.2.2 PROTECTION OF CHILDREN IN EMERGENCIES

11.2.2.1 Introduction

The protection of children in emergencies is governed by Part III of the 1991 Act. Part III grants both the Health Board and the Garda Síochána the powers necessary to carry out their functions in an emergency situation. A member of the Garda Síochána is empowered under s. 12 of the 1991 Act to remove a child to safety where there are reasonable grounds for believing that there is an immediate and serious risk to the health or welfare of the child and it would be insufficient for the protection of the child to await the making of an application for an emergency care order by the Health Board under s. 13. In exercising his rights under this section the member of the Garda Síochána may, accompanied by such other persons as may be necessary, without warrant, enter any house or other place using force if necessary. Where a child is removed in this manner he must be delivered up to the custody of the Health Board in the area as soon as is possible. The Health Board is obliged under s. 12(4) of the 1991 Act, where the child is not returned to the appropriate custodian/ guardian, to make an application for an emergency care order at the next sitting of the local District Court. In the event that the District Court in that district is not due to sit within three days of the date the child is delivered up, the application must be made at the sitting of a District Court to be held within the same three days as arranged under s. 13(4) of the 1991 Act as set out in more detail below.

11.2.2.2 Emergency care order

An emergency care order provides that the child shall be placed under the care of the Health Board for the area in which the child is for the time being, for a period of eight days or such shorter period as may be specified in the order. Section 13 allows for the making of an emergency care order by a justice of the District Court where he is of the opinion that there is reasonable cause to believe that:

(a) *there is an immediate and serious risk to the health or welfare of the child which necessitates his being placed in the care of a health board; or*

(b) *there is likely to be such a risk if the child is removed from the place where he is for the time being.*

These applications can be made on notice to the parents or person *in loco parentis,* or where the judge is satisfied that the urgency of the situation so requires the application can be made on an ex parte basis. The making of this order can be extended to allow for the issuing of a warrant for the purposes of delivering the child up to the custody of the Health Board. At report stage in the Dáil Debates a suggestion that this eight-day period be reduced to four days was agreed to be too short and almost inoperable in practice. Deputy Treacy (Dáil Debates Col. 2129, p. 304) stated that:

'A period of eight days strikes a reasonable balance between giving the Health Board time to prepare an application for a care order and ensuring that the parties are not deprived of the custody of their children for too long before having an opportunity to put their side to the court.'

Section 13(4) to (7) deals with procedural matters relating to the making of an emergency order under this section. Section 13(4) deals essentially with the issues of district and jurisdiction. It provides that an emergency order shall be made by the justice for the district in which the child resides or is for the time being, or where that district justice is not available, any district of the District Court. If the urgency of the matter so requires the application for an emergency order can be made ex parte and/or can be heard elsewhere than at a public sitting of the District Court. Of great importance is s. 13(5), which provides that an appeal from the making of an emergency order does not stay the operation of the order made. Section 13(6) states that it is unnecessary in an application or an order to name the child if such name is unknown. Section 13(7) empowers the district justice with the discretion to make orders as he thinks proper with regard to the withholding of the address of the place where the child is being kept, access issues and the medical or psychiatric examination, treatment or assessment of the child. There remains a presumption that the parents will be informed of the location of the child while allowing in appropriate circumstances for the justice of the District Court to make an order withholding such information. The Health Board is obliged under s. 14 to notify the parent or person *in loco parentis* of the child of the delivery or placement of the child in the care of the Health Board as soon as possible unless they are missing and cannot be found.

11.2.3 CARE PROCEEDINGS

11.2.3.1 Introduction

Part IV of the 1991 Act can be viewed as the main body of the Act which provides for the measures to be taken by the Health Board and the orders to be made by the court where a child is believed to have been or to currently be in danger. Where a Health Board is of the opinion that a child who resides or was found in its area is in need of care or protection which he is unlikely to receive unless an appropriate order is made by the court, it shall be the duty of the Health Board to make an application to the court for a care order or a supervision order, as it sees fit. The wording of this section makes it clear that the Health Board is compelled to take this course of action in the appropriate circumstances and retains no discretion in this regard.

11.2.3.2 Care order

The effect of a care order is to commit the child in need of care or protection to the care of the Health Board for so long as he remains a child or for a shorter period. Section 18 of the 1991 Act authorises the court on the application of the Health Board to make a care order where it is satisfied that:

(a) *the child has been or is being assaulted, ill-treated, neglected or sexually abused; or*

(b) *the child's health, development or welfare has been or is being avoidably impaired or neglected; or*

(c) *the child's health, development or welfare is likely to be avoidably impaired or neglected,*

and that the child requires care and protection which he is unlikely to receive unless the order is made.

The court is further entitled to extend that 'shorter' period upon its own motion or the application of another person, if it is satisfied that the grounds for the making of the order continue to exist.

Section 18(3) provides that where a care order is in force the Health Board has control over the child as if it were his parent. The Health Board is further obliged to do what is reasonable in all the circumstances to safeguard and promote the child's health, development or welfare. In particular the Health Board has authority to decide the type of care to be provided for the child under s. 36, which deals with the issues of accommodation and maintenance, to give consent to any necessary medical or psychiatric examination, treatment or assessment of the child, and to give consent to the issue of a passport to the child or of the provision of passport facilities to him to enable the child to travel abroad for a limited period. Any such consent given by the Health Board in this regard shall be deemed sufficient authority for the carrying out of whatever treatment or facility. Where a care order is made by the court, having regard to the means of the parties involved, it may further be ordered that the parent(s) of the child contribute to the Health Board a sum towards his maintenance. Finally, as an interim measure between the making of an application under s. 18 and its determination, the court may on its own motion or on the application of any person, make a supervision order (discussed below) which shall cease to have effect upon the determination of the application. Equally, under s. 18(5) where the court is satisfied on the facts that although it is not necessary or appropriate that a care order is made, it is desirable that the child be visited periodically in his home by or on behalf of the Health Board, the court may make a supervision order under s. 19 of the 1991 Act. Deputy Treacy at Report Stage in the Dáil Debates attempted to remove the discretion of the court in respect of the making of a supervision order in lieu of a care order. In light of similar recommendations by the Law Reform Commission, he proposed an amendment that the district judge would be placed under an obligation to satisfy himself that a supervision order made in place of a care order would adequately protect the child. However, this proposed amendment was not carried and the discretion of the court remains.

11.2.3.3 Interim care order

Section 17 makes provision for interim care orders which can be defined as an interim measure taken by the court to protect the child in the short term. An application for an interim care order must be made on notice to the parents or to the person *in loco parentis* except where the justice otherwise directs. Such an order can be made by a justice of the District Court where satisfied that an application for a care order has been or is about to be made and there is reasonable cause to believe that:

   (a)   the child has been or is being assaulted, ill-treated, neglected or sexually abused; or

   (b)   the child's health, development or welfare has been or is being avoidably impaired or neglected; or

   (c)   the child's health, development or welfare is likely to be avoidably impaired or neglected,

and that it is necessary for the protection of the child's health or welfare to be placed or maintained in the care of the Health Board pending the determination of the application for a care order. Section 17(2) provides that an interim care order requires the child to remain in the care of the Health Board for a period not exceeding eight days. However, if the parents or person *in loco parentis* consent, the interim care order can be granted for a period exceeding eight days. An extension of this period can be granted if the judge is satisfied that grounds for making the interim care order continue to exist with respect to the child. At this stage in the proceedings a justice of the District Court may also make such orders under s. 13(7) as he sees fit. Section 13(7) empowers the district justice with the discretion to make orders as he thinks proper with regard to the withholding of the address of the place where the child is being kept, access issues and the medical or psychiatric examination, treatment or assessment of the child.

11.2.3.4 Supervision order

The effect of a supervision order is to authorise the Health Board to visit the child at home on such periodic occasions as the Health Board may deem necessary in order to satisfy itself as to the welfare of the child involved and to give to his parents or person *in loco parentis* any necessary advice as to the care of the child. Section 19 of the 1991 Act provides that a court is empowered to make a supervision order where on application to it by the Health Board it is satisfied that there are reasonable grounds for believing that:

(a) *the child has been or is being assaulted, ill-treated, neglected or sexually abused; or*

(b) *the child's health, development or welfare has been or is being avoidably impaired or neglected; or*

(c) *the child's health, development or welfare is likely to be avoidably impaired or neglected,*

and it is desirable that the child be visited periodically by or on behalf of the health board.

In the Dáil Debates a supervision order was regarded as 'the first line of defence, simply to require that the child be monitored.' When compared to the gravity and resulting effect of a care order a supervision order was seen as a less intrusive order to be made in appropriate circumstances.

'It does not take the child out of his house setting; it does not impact on the child directly. Somebody from the Health Board will be keeping an eye on him and, obviously, there should not be very deep or profound grounds to require this to happen.'

Section 19(3) entitles any parent or person acting *in loco parentis* who is dissatisfied with the manner in which the Health Board is exercising its authority under this order, to apply to the court for such directions as it sees fit as to the manner in which the child is to be visited and the Health Board is obliged to comply with any such direction. Section 19(4) deals with the court's right on making a supervision order to give such directions as it sees fit as to the care of the child which may require the parents of the child or the person acting *in loco parentis* to cause him to attend for medical or psychiatric examination, treatment or assessment. Section 19(5) outlines the sanctions available to the court where a person fails to comply or facilitate with the operation of the terms of a supervision order or ancillary orders made under s. 19(4). Such a person shall be guilty of an offence and shall be liable on summary conviction to a fine not exceeding £500 and/or six months' imprisonment. The duration of a supervision order is dealt with by s. 19(6) which provides that a supervision order shall remain in force for the time specified by the court but for a maximum of 12 months. It shall cease to have effect should the child in respect of whom the order is made cease to be a child for the purposes of the 1991 Act. Although a supervision order can only be made for a maximum period of 12 months, the court is empowered under s. 19(7) to make a further supervision order on the application of the Health Board which would come into force upon the expiration of the original order.

These parts of the 1991 Act represent an admirable effort by the legislature to safeguard and protect the rights of children in need, by providing various remedies for the courts in the form of care orders, interim care orders and supervision orders, to be applied as the court sees fit. However, despite enabling the court to grant these powers to the Health Board, the rights of the parents are also included by the legislature and the courts are required to consider these at all times.

11.2.3.5 Guardian *ad litem*

Ireland, by entering into several international agreements aimed at increasing the role of the child in family proceedings, has committed itself to make family courts more child-friendly. The kernel of this reform lies in the Child Care Act 1991 and, in particular, in the introduction of the position of guardian *ad litem*.

The guardian *ad litem* is, effectively, an independent representative appointed by the court to represent the child's welfare, interests and wishes in proceedings under the Child Care Act 1991 and, in doing so, is to be independent of the parents and the Health Board. Section 26 of the 1991 Act allows the court to appoint a guardian *ad litem* in respect of a child involved in proceedings under Part IV (care and supervision orders), and Part VI (children in the care of Health Boards) of the Act. Section 25 allows the child to be added as a party to the proceedings, but where this does not occur, s. 26(1) allows a guardian *ad litem* to be appointed to act on the child's behalf. This is subject to the important caveat that the court be satisfied that such appointment is both necessary in the interests of the child and consistent with the requirements of justice. As with all proceedings under the Child Care Act 1991, s. 24 of the Act ranks the child's welfare as the first and paramount consideration in such cases although the court is also required to have due regard to the rights and duties of the parents. It further notes that in deciding to appoint a guardian *ad litem* the court should, in so far as practicable, have regard to the wishes of the child. The practicability of so doing will, as always, depend on the latter's age and understanding.

Beyond that, few other guidelines are laid down to aid the court in deciding whether it is appropriate to appoint a guardian *ad litem*. Section 26(4) stipulates that should the court see fit to add a child as a party to the proceedings under s. 25, any prior appointment of a guardian *ad litem* in respect of the same child shall be deemed to have ceased. In fact, it seems that s. 25 (allowing a child to be a party to a case) and s. 26 (allowing the appointment of a guardian *ad litem*) are mutually exclusive. This is so even where a child is added as a party not fully but only for certain purposes specified by the court.

The 1991 Act as it stands lays down no criteria governing the type of person who may be appointed as a guardian *ad litem*. It is, however, clear that the appointment of a guardian *ad litem* or lawyer has been made mutually exclusive by the Act. The 1991 Act is equally vague regarding the functions and role of the guardian *ad litem*. One point at least is necessarily implicit and that is that the guardian *ad litem* is to act independently of the parents and Health Board with a view to promoting the welfare and wishes of the child. Beyond that, the guardian *ad litem* is probably best advised to take direction from the presiding judge. He or she should first and foremost appraise the situation of the child. It is strongly suggested that for these purposes the guardian *ad litem* should be granted permission to have access to the child with a view to ascertaining his or her needs, wishes and concerns. Adequate access to records (such as health board and social workers' reports) should, arguably, also be afforded. Presumably the guardian *ad litem* has no role in interviewing the other parties to the case although it is suggested that the guardian *ad litem* should be permitted to make such enquiries to enable him or her to determine the best interests of the child.

11.3 Providing For Children In Care: Accommodation And Care

11.3.1 INTRODUCTION

Where a child has been placed in the care of a Health Board there are several options open to the Board in providing for his or her care. These are laid out in the Child Care Act 1991, s. 36. The Health Board may, subject to its control and its supervision, place the child in foster care. This would involve the placing of a child with a foster parent. A foster parent is defined (by s. 36(2)) as

> *a person other than a relative of the child who is taking care of the child on behalf of a Health Board in accordance with regulations made under section 39 of the Act.*

Alternatively, a child may be placed in residential care. This may take the form of a placement in a registered children's residential centre or in a residential home maintained by a Health Board. Each of these options is dealt with in more detail below.

The child may also, however, be placed in a school (presumably as a boarder) or other suitable place of residence as the Board sees fit. In appropriate cases the child, if eligible, may be placed for adoption, although this approach is likely to be used only in exceptional cases. It is worth noting at this juncture that a child of married parents may only be adopted in very extreme circumstances and in compliance with the exceptionally exacting requirements of the Adoption Act 1988 (see Chapter 13, at **13.14**). The adoption of a child born outside marriage is comparatively easier, although the Board would in these circumstances be required to obtain certain consents. In particular, consent would be required of the natural mother and/or guardian of the child and of any person who had care and control over the child at the relevant time. Provision is made for such consent to be dispensed with by a court but this can only be done where this is, in the opinion of the court, in the best interests of the child. A less drastic solution would be to place a child with a relative, an option explicitly contemplated by s. 36(1)(d). The listed options are not, however, exhaustive; s. 36(1)(d) allows for other suitable arrangements to be made as the Board thinks proper, making it clear that there is scope for creative solutions to child-care needs.

11.3.2 FOSTER CARE

11.3.2.1 Introduction

Foster care plays a central role in our child-care system. In 1998, 3,162 of the 3,984 children in the care of Health Boards were placed in foster care.

The placement of children in foster care is governed by the Child Care (Placement of Children in Foster Care) Regulations 1995 (SI 260/1995). In governing the issue of foster care, these regulations deal with the promotion of the welfare of the child, the pre-placement provisions, the monitoring of placements and the removal of children from placements where appropriate.

11.3.2.2 Foster parents

The definition of 'foster parent' under Part I of the regulations is 'a person other than a relative of a child who is taking care of the child on behalf of the health board' in accordance with s. 39 of the 1991 Act and these regulations.

11.3.2.3 Promotion of the welfare of the child

Part II of these regulations deals with the promotion of the welfare of the child. Although the Health Board is obliged to have regard to the rights and duties of parents it is required to consider the welfare of the child as its first and paramount consideration. In addition, in so far as is practicable, the Health Board must give due consideration to the wishes of the child, having regard to his age and understanding. Although neither the 1991 Act nor these regulations contain a definition of 'welfare', reference can and should be made to the definition contained in s. 2 of the Guardianship of Infants Act 1964 which refers to welfare as comprising the religious, moral, intellectual, physical and social welfare of the child (see **11.1.2**). The need to prioritise the welfare of the child underlies both the 1991 Act and the foster care regulations.

11.3.2.4 Panel of foster parents

Regulation 5(1) requires the Health Board to establish and maintain a panel of persons who are willing to act as foster parents. Regulation 27 provides that a Health Board is entitled to place a child with foster parents who are on a panel maintained by another Health Board. To be placed on a panel prospective foster parents must furnish the board with:

(i)   a written report from a registered medical practitioner on the state of their health;

(ii)   the names and addresses of two referees who are not related to them and whom the board may consult;

(iii) all necessary authorisations to allow the Health Board to establish from the Garda Síochána whether any convictions exist against them or their family; and

(iv) such other information as the board may reasonably require.

Furthermore, an assessment of the suitability of the prospective foster parents and their home must be carried out by an authorised person. A report in writing of this assessment must then be considered by a committee, established pursuant to reg. 5(3) of these regulations, as to the suitability of the applicants to act as foster parents on behalf of the Health Board. This committee is composed of persons with suitable expertise in matters affecting the welfare of children including persons with training or experience in relation to foster care. Finally in this regard the persons proposed as prospective foster parents must receive appropriate advice, guidance and training in relation to the foster care of children. Ultimately the applicants are entitled to be informed in writing under reg. 5(6) of these regulations as to the outcome of their application. (In addition, the Freedom of Information Act 1997, s. 18 allows the applicant to apply in writing to the head of the Health Board seeking reasons for the decision. In such a case (subject to certain exceptions) the latter will be obliged to furnish such reasons within four weeks of receiving the application.) These tests are clearly rigorous in order to ensure that a person accepted as a foster parent is entirely suitable to mind children.

11.3.2.5 Assessment of child

Regulation 6 governs the assessment of the circumstances of the child. Save for an emergency situation, the Health Board is obliged before placing a child with foster parents to carry out an assessment of the child's circumstances to include a medical examination of the child. However the medical examination is not compulsory where the board is satisfied, having regard to information and reports available in relation to the child, that such examination is unnecessary. Where an emergency situation arises and a child is placed immediately with foster parents, the board is obliged to carry out the assessment of the child's circumstances as soon as is practicable. Such assessment is necessary in order to ensure that both the Health Board and the foster parents are aware of the child's individual circumstances and needs, and can provide appropriately for him.

11.3.2.6 Choosing foster parents

When selecting persons from the aforementioned panel to foster a child in its care the Health Board under reg. 7 shall endeavour to ensure that those persons have the capacity to meet the needs of the child concerned. In relation to the religious upbringing of the child and the religion of the prospective foster parents, the Health Board in selecting the appropriate foster parents shall endeavour to respect the wishes of the child's guardians. However where it is not possible for the Health Board to comply with the wishes of the child's guardians, the board may make such arrangements for the care of the child as it considers reasonable and shall inform the guardians accordingly. Should a guardian be dissatisfied with the arrangements made the board must inform him of the right under s. 47 of the Child Care Act 1991 to make an application to the District Court for a direction. Again, the particular needs of the child will dictate to a certain extent the identity of the foster parents chosen. The religion of both the child and the foster parents will be of importance as the regulations seek to ensure that such beliefs are maintained and supported during the period of fostering.

11.3.2.7 Contract between health board and foster parents

Regulation 9 deals with the arrangements between the foster parents and the Health Board. Under this section the parties will be deemed to have entered into a contract and a copy of the contract (in the form set out in the First Schedule of the regulations) shall be given to the foster parents together with a copy of the foster care regulations. The formality of this contract ensures that the foster parents are made aware of the importance of their own role. Prior to placing a child with foster parents, in an attempt to ensure that the individual needs of the child are understood and that the foster parents are provided with a complete picture as to the particular facts pertaining to the child, the Health Board is obliged to furnish the foster parents with as much of the following information as is available to the board:

(i) name, sex and date of birth of the child;

(ii) religion;

(iii) reason for admission to care of the Health Board;

(iv) whether voluntary admission or pursuant to court order;

(v) particulars of previous placements (if any);

(vi) names and address(es) of child's parents;

(vii) names, ages and whereabouts of siblings (if any) of child;

(viii) arrangements for access;

(ix) particulars of any medical or nutritional requirements of child; and

(x) arrangements for child's attendance at school (where applicable).

Additional information may be made available to the foster parents as required.

11.3.2.8 Care and upbringing plan

Regulation 11 deals with the requirement that a Health Board, before placing a child in foster care, must prepare a care plan for the care and upbringing of the child. The care plan shall deal with:

(a) the aims and objectives of the placement;

(b) the support to be provided to the child, the foster parents and the parents of the child by the Health Board;

(c) the arrangements for access to the child by a parent or relative; and

(d) the arrangements for the review of the plan.

As with the assessment, where the child is placed with the foster parents in an emergency the care plan shall be prepared by the Health Board as soon as is practicable. In preparing the care plan the Health Board shall consult the foster parents and, where appropriate, the child and every person who in law is a guardian of the child. Finally, in this regard, the particulars of the care plan should be made known by the Health Board to the foster parents and, in so far as is practicable, to the child and every person who in law is a guardian of the child. By requiring a plan to be agreed and put in place before the child is placed in foster care, this ensures that the needs and requirements of the child are considered in advance by the Health Board, and whatever provisions are required are put in place. It also causes the Health Board to consider the issue of access between the child and his parents and to make appropriate arrangements to ensure that such access does take place, if appropriate.

11.3.2.9 Register

Under reg. 12 a Health Board is required to maintain a register which should contain particulars in relation to children placed in foster care by the Health Board. The register should include the name, sex and date of birth of each child, the names and address of his parents, the names and address of the child's foster parents, the date of the placement, and the date, where appropriate, of when the child ceases to be in placement. This in essence ensures that an official record exists in respect of each child who is under the care of the Health Board.

11.3.2.10 Case record

In addition to the aforementioned general register the Health Board must keep an up-to-date case record of every child placed in foster care. This case record contains the following documents:

(a) medical and social reports on the child, including background information on the child's family;

(b) a copy of any court order relating to the child or of any parental consent to the child's admission to the care of the board, as appropriate;

(c) the birth certificate of the child;

(d) a copy of the contract between the board and the foster parents;

(e) a copy of the care plan prepared under reg. 11;

(f) reports on the child's progress at school, where applicable;

(g) a note of any access visits between the child and his parent(s);

(h) a note of every review of the child's case pursuant to these regulations; and

(i) a note of every significant event affecting the child.

11.3.2.11 Financial and other support

A fostering allowance shall be payable under reg. 14(1) to foster parents in respect of any child placed with them, the amount to be specified by the Minister for Health from time to time. On 16 June 2000 Mary Hanafin TD, Minister of State at the Department of Health and Children, announced that foster care allowances were to be increased with immediate effect. The allowance for foster children under the age of 12 is now £71.55 per week and the allowance for children over the age of 12 is £85.75 per week. When addressing the annual conference of the Irish Foster Care Association on 11 November 2000 in Cavan, the Minister announced, in addition to the annual Christmas bonus paid to foster carers, a special extra bonus of £100 to be paid in Christmas 2000. In addition reg. 14(2) provides that a Health Board may provide further financial or other assistance as it considers necessary for the care of the child involved. Looking after and caring for a child will obviously give rise to expenses that the foster parents cannot be expected to pay. The provision of a fostering allowance is simply a practical arrangement which covers everyday expenses and should not be regarded as a form of remuneration for the service provided by the foster parents.

11.3.2.12 Duties of the foster parents

The duties of foster parents are set out in detail in reg. 16. Regulation 16(1) requires them to take all reasonable measures to promote the child's health, development and welfare. However, without prejudice to the generality of this requirement, reg. 16(2)(a)-(j) sets out that the foster parents shall in particular:

(a) *permit any person so authorised by the health board to see the child and visit the foster home from time to time as may be necessary in the interests of the child;*

(b) *co-operate with a person so authorised and furnish that person with such information as the person may reasonably require;*

(c) *ensure that any information relating to the child or the child's family or any other person given to them by the health board is treated confidentially;*

(d) *seek appropriate medical aid for the child if the child suffers from injury or illness;*

(e) *inform the health board as soon as practicable of any significant event affecting the child;*

(f)   inform the health board of any change in their circumstances which might affect their ability to care for the child;

(g)   co-operate with the health board in facilitating access to the child by a parent or other person who is allowed access;

(h)   give the health board at least 28 days notice of any intended change in their normal place of residence;

(i)   make good and proper arrangements for the care of the child in the case of absence by the child or both of the foster parents from the home; and

(j)   give the health board prior notice of any such absence the duration of which is likely to exceed 72 hours.

The guidelines which are provided for the foster parents in the form set out above are intended as a model for the management, care and control of the child. They also ensure that adequate communication and contact exists between the foster parents and the Health Board. These guidelines serve to protect the child's health and welfare by ensuring that the Health Board is kept abreast of all relevant developments.

11.3.2.13 Supervision by the health board of children placed in care

A child placed in foster care shall, under reg. 17(1), be visited by an authorised member of the Health Board as often as the board considers necessary, having regard to the terms of the plan for the care and upbringing of the child. Notwithstanding this general principle, the child shall be visited at intervals not exceeding three months during the first two-year period commencing on the date on which the child is placed with the foster parents, the first visit being within one month of that date, and thereafter at intervals not exceeding six months. Where following such a visit the board is of the opinion that a matter relating to the child's placement is not in compliance with the terms of these regulations, the Health Board must take appropriate action to ensure compliance. Finally, as set out under the provisions of the 'case record', a note of every visit to a child in care shall be entered in the case record relating to the child, with particulars of any action taken arising from the visit. By including minimum terms for the occurrence of visits by the Health Board it is hoped that no child in foster care will be allowed to go unsupervised by the Health Board for too long a period. However, this section of the regulations affords the Health Board a discretion to visit a child in foster care as often as the board considers necessary in the circumstances. The needs of each child and each situation will be set out in the case record, which will provide an indication of the anticipated requirements for visitation in each case.

11.3.2.14 Review of cases

Regulation 18(1) provides that a Health Board shall arrange for each case of a child in foster care and, in particular, the plan for the care and upbringing of the child to be reviewed by an authorised person as often as may be necessary in the particular case, but in any event, at intervals not exceeding six months for the first two-year period (with a review to take place within the first two months) and thereafter no less than once every year. Under reg. 18(4) where a Health Board initiates a review of the case of a child in foster care, the board shall inform the foster parents and in so far as is practicable, the child and every person who in law is a guardian of the child, and afford them an opportunity to be heard in person or otherwise to be consulted in relation to the review. In reviewing any case a Health Board is obliged to consider the following:

(i)   whether all reasonable measures are being taken to promote the welfare of the child;

(ii)   whether the care being provided for the child continues to be suited to the child's needs;

(iii)   whether the circumstances of the child's parents have changed;

(iv)   whether it would be in the child's best interests to be returned to the custody of his parents; and

(v)   where the child is due to leave the care of the health board, the child's need for aftercare within the meaning of s. 45 of the 1991 Act.

In considering the foregoing the Health Board is obliged to have regard to any views or information furnished by the child, the parents of the child, the foster parents and any other person consulted in relation to the review. In addition, reports relating to any visits made to the child during the period of foster care must be considered together with the latest available school report of the child where appropriate and any other relevant information. A note of every review and any subsequent action taken shall be contained in the case records and any decisions made shall be made known by the Health Board to the foster parents and, where applicable, to the child, every person who in law is a guardian of the child and any other person who the board considers ought to be informed. Regulation 19 permits any person having a bona fide interest in the matter to make a request in writing to the Health Board for a special review of the case of a child in foster care and the board is obliged to accede to that request unless it considers that such a review would be unnecessary. Such a decision to refuse a request must be transmitted in writing to the person who made the request. If the review is carried out the provisions of a review as set out above shall apply to a review under this regulation. Where a child is involved in frequent admissions to foster care, but the duration of the placements do not allow for a review in accordance with the time frames for reviews as set out above, the board shall carry out a review of such a case along the guidelines previously referred to.

When reviewing a case the progress of the parents of the child in foster care is of great importance to the Health Board. The Health Board is required to consider the parents' progress and whether returning the child to them would be in the child's best interests. The foster care currently being provided for the child must also be assessed and the Health Board must consider whether continuing in this care is in the best interests of the child. When read together with s. 3(2)(c) of the 1991 Act, which obliges the Health Board 'to have regard to the principle that it is generally in the best interests of the child to be brought up in its own family', where returning the child to his parents would be in the child's interests, this course of action should be taken by the Health Board.

11.3.2.15   Removal of children from placement

Removal at request of foster parents

Where the request for removal is made by the foster parents, the board must as soon as practicable arrange an alternative placement for the child. In so doing the board will request the foster parents to sign a statement in writing confirming that the removal is being effected at their request, this signed statement to be retained in the case record.

Termination of placement by the Health Board

Where the Health Board proposes to reunite the child and his parents or considers that the placement of the child with his foster parents no longer represents the most appropriate way of protecting the welfare of the child, the board must inform the foster parents of its intention to remove the child from their care. Where the foster parents object to this removal, they shall be afforded an opportunity to make representations to the Health Board. If the Health Board decides to proceed with the removal having heard their representations, the decision of the Health Board and the reasons therefor must be transmitted to the foster parents in writing. In furnishing the foster parents with its decision the board must also request that they deliver up the child to the board at such time and place as specified by the board. Where the foster parents neglect or refuse to deliver up the child the Health Board may apply to the District Court for an order under

s. 43(2) of the 1991 Act directing that the foster parents deliver up the child to the Health Boards such an order being made by the District Court judge where he believes it to be in the best interests of the child.

Counselling services

A Health Board shall in appropriate circumstances provide counselling services for foster parents where a child is removed from their custody in accordance with these regulations.

11.3.2.16 Miscellaneous provisions

Arrangements with voluntary bodies

It is open to the Health Board to make arrangements with competent and qualified voluntary bodies or other persons to assist in the performance of its functions under these regulations.

Inspection of Health Board practices

A person so authorised by the Minister for Health may inspect the practices and procedures of a Health Board in relation to the provision of foster care services and may examine such records as may exist, and interview those members of staff involved in the area of foster care. Thus the Health Board, although an inspection authority in itself, can also be the subject of supervision in order to ensure that it operates appropriately.

11.3.2.17 Current developments in foster care

Additional funding was announced in late 1999 to support existing foster parents and to create an additional 500 foster places. This development is very much needed in light of the expansion of the foster-care service in Ireland over the last 10 years. There are now nearly 3,500 children in foster care in Ireland. This increase in the number of children in foster care has resulted in an increased level of pressure on the services. Furthermore, many of the children in foster care have experienced more extensive trauma than before. The increased difficulties in our society are causing increased hardship and trauma for these children. Thus, the area of foster care must be monitored on an ongoing basis and supported in an appropriate and substantial manner.

11.3.3 RESIDENTIAL CARE

11.3.3.1 Introduction

If the Health Board chooses not to place the child in foster care it may place the child in residential care. This may be in a registered residential centre under Part VII of the 1991 Act or a residential home maintained by the Health Board, a school or other place of residence. The placement of children in residential care is governed by the Child Care (Placement of Children in Residential Care) Regulations 1995 which were introduced by SI 259/1995. These regulations are divided into six parts which apart from the preliminary and miscellaneous provisions deal with the promotion of the welfare of the child, the standards in residential care, the monitoring of placements and the issue of reviews.

11.3.3.2 Residential centre

Residential centre is defined in Part I of these regulations as 'any home or other institution whether operated by a health board, a voluntary body or other person which provides residential care for children in the care of a health board.' The definition goes on to further define what constitutes a residential centre by setting out what the definition does not include:

(a)   *an institution managed by or on behalf of a Minister of the Government;*

(b)   *an institution in which a majority of the children are being treated for acute illnesses;*

(c)   *an institution for the care and maintenance of physically or mentally handicapped children;*

(d)   *a mental institution within the meaning of the Mental Treatment Acts 1945–1966; and*

(e)   *an institution which is a 'certified school' within the meaning of Part IV of the Children Act 1908, functions in relation to which stand vested in the Minister for Education.*

11.3.3.3   Promotion of the welfare of the child

Part III of the regulations highlights the importance of the welfare of the child when the Health Board is making any decision relating to a child in its care. The Health Board is obliged to have regard to the welfare of the child as its first and paramount consideration when considering any matter relating to the placement of the child, the review of the case of a child in residential care or the removal of a child from residential care. In so doing the board must in so far as is practicable give due consideration to the wishes of the child as well as the rights and duties of the parents of the child.

11.3.3.4   Standards in residential centres

These regulations require that a Health Board must satisfy itself with the standards provided by each residential centre in respect of the following areas.

Care practices

A Health Board is required under reg. 5 to satisfy itself in respect of each residential centre that appropriate and suitable care practices and operational policies are in place having regard to the number of children residing in the centre and the nature of their needs.

Staffing

A Health Board under reg. 6 must satisfy itself as to the adequacy of the number, qualifications, experience and availability of the members of staff in each residential centre within its functional area (to include any residential centre outside its functional area in which the board has placed or proposes to place a child).

Accommodation

Regulation 7 requires a Health Board to be satisfied as to the adequacy and suitability of the accommodation provided by each relevant residential centre having regard to the number of children residing in the centre and the nature of their needs, and in particular that:

(a)   adequate and suitable furniture and bedding are provided;

(b)   a sufficient number of lavatories, wash-basins, baths and showers, supplied with hot and cold running water, and which ensure privacy as far as is practicable are provided;

(c)   adequate laundry facilities are provided;

(d)   the premises are adequately lit, heated and ventilated;

(e)   the premises are clean, appropriately decorated and maintained in good structural condition; and

(f)   adequate recreational facilities are provided.

Access arrangements

In respect of each relevant residential centre a Health Board is obliged under reg. 8 to satisfy itself that appropriate arrangements are in place to facilitate reasonable access and contact between the children residing in the centre and their parents, relatives and friends or any other person with a genuine interest in the children.

Health care and religion

There must be adequate arrangements in place to the satisfaction of the Health Board for access by children to general practitioner services and for their referral where necessary to medical, psychological, dental, ophthalmic or other specialist requirements. In relation to the children's religious beliefs the Health Board must be satisfied that in so far as is practicable, children placed in residential care are facilitated in the practice of their religion.

Food and cooking facilities

Children must be provided with food in quantities adequate for their needs which is properly prepared, wholesome and nutritious, which involves an element of choice and takes account of any special dietary requirements. For the purpose of this section and the centre's fulfilment of its obligations, the Health Board must be satisfied that:

(a)   suitable and sufficient catering equipment, crockery and cutlery are provided;

(b)   proper facilities for the refrigeration and storage of food exist; and

(c)   a high standard of hygiene is maintained in relation to the storage and preparation of food and the disposal of domestic refuse.

Fire precautions

Regulation 12 deals with the issue of fire precautions and the obligations that each residential centre must fulfil. However, these provisions are without prejudice to the detailed requirements of the provisions of the Fire Services Act 1981. Regulation 12(1) provides that evidence is required by a Health Board in respect of each residential centre from a chartered engineer or suitably qualified architect with experience in fire safety design and management confirming in writing that the relevant statutory requirements relating to fire safety and building control have been complied with. Furthermore the Health Board must be satisfied that adequate precautions have been taken against the risk of fire. This includes the provision of adequate means of escape in the event of fire, adequate arrangements in place for detecting, containing and extinguishing fires, the maintenance of fire fighting equipment and finally that all reasonable measures have been taken to ensure that the materials contained in bedding and the internal furnishings of the residential centre have adequate fire retardancy properties and have low levels of toxicity in the event of fire. In the event that structural alterations are carried out to the residential centre a Health Board may seek written confirmation of compliance in light of the changes. Finally, in relation to the issue of fire safety, a Health Board must satisfy itself that adequate arrangements are in place by means of fire drills and practices, to ensure that the staff and children in the centre are familiar with the relevant evacuation procedures to be followed in the event of a fire.

Safety precautions

Again these provisions are without prejudice to the requirements of another Act, in this case the Safety, Health and Welfare at Work Act 1989. Regulation 13 requires a Health Board to be satisfied as to the arrangements that exist to guard against the risk of injury occurring on the premises. Special mention is given to stairways, electrical and gas appliances and fittings, windows and doors, glazing and the storage of medicines, cleaning and other materials. Furthermore, a Health Board must be satisfied as to the adequacy of arrangements for the reporting and recording of accidents and injuries affecting children residing in the centre.

Insurance

A Health Board must be satisfied that each residential centre is adequately insured against accidents or injury to children placed in the care of the board.

Notification of significant events

Prompt procedures must be in place to the satisfaction of a Health Board for the notification by the centre to the Health Board of the occurrence of any significant event which affects any child who has been placed in the care of the board.

Records

Appropriate records must be maintained by each centre to the satisfaction of the Health Board and these records must be open to inspection by a person authorised by the Health Board.

Monitoring of standards

The Health Board must, in order to ensure that all elements of these regulations are maintained, provide that adequate arrangements are in place to allow for the entering and inspection of residential centres at all reasonable times by persons authorised by the Health Board. Where following such an inspection the Health Board is unhappy with the standard of any aspect of the requirements under these regulations, the board is obliged, if it intends to continue to have children maintained in that centre, to request the manager to take the necessary steps to ensure compliance with these regulations.

11.3.3.5 Monitoring of placements

Medical examination

When a child is placed in residential care the Health Board must arrange for the examination of that child by a registered medical practitioner unless the board is satisfied, in light of information and reports available on the child, that such examination is unnecessary. This requirement not only provides for the child's health to be checked, it also helps to ensure that the Health Board and the residential centre are aware of the particular needs of the child.

Register

A Health Board must keep a register in which particulars of each child placed in residential care shall be entered. An entry in respect of each child shall include the following particulars:

(a) the name, sex and date of birth of the child;

(b) the name and addresses of the parents of the child;

(c) the name and address of the residential centre in which the child has been placed;

(d) the date of placement in the centre; and

(e) the date on which the child ceases to reside in the centre.

As these particulars change, so too shall the contents of the register.

Case records

An up-to-date case record shall be compiled by the Health Board in respect of every child placed in residential care. The case record shall include such of the following documents as are available to the board:

(a) medical and social reports on the child, including background information on the child's family;

(b)   a copy of any court order relating to the child or of parental consent to the child's admission to the care of the board, as appropriate;

(c)   the birth certificate of the child;

(d)   reports on the child's progress at school;

(e)   a copy of the care plan for the child prepared by the Health Board under reg. 23 of these regulations;

(f)   a note of every visit to the child;

(g)   a note of every review of the child's case together with particulars of any action taken as a result; and

(h)   a note of every significant event affecting the child.

Care plan

Except in the case of an emergency a Health Board shall, before placing a child in residential care, prepare a plan for the care of the child. The plan shall deal, amongst other matters, with the aims and objectives of the placement, the support to be provided for the child, the residential centre involved and, where appropriate, the arrangements for access to the child by a parent, relative or other named person and the arrangements for the review of the plan. Where the emergency scenario arises the care plan will be prepared as soon as is practicable. Finally, in preparing the plan a Health Board is obliged to consult the manager of the centre and, in so far as is practicable, the child and every person who in law is a guardian of the child to whom particulars of the plan must be made known.

Supervision and visiting of children

A child placed in residential care shall be visited by a person so authorised by the Health Board as often as the board considers necessary, having regard to the care plan, but in any event, at intervals not exceeding three months during the first period of two years and thereafter at intervals not exceeding six months. Where, following such a visit, a Health Board is of the opinion that any matter relating to the child's placement is not in compliance with these regulations, the board shall take whatever appropriate action is required for compliance with these regulations. Regulation 24(5) requires that a note of every visit shall be entered into a child's case record together with the particulars of any action arising from the visit.

11.3.3.6   Reviews

Under reg. 25 a review must be arranged by the Health Board in respect of every child placed in a residential centre by the board. In addition the board must ensure the review of the plan for the care of the child by an authorised person. These reviews are to take place as often as may be necessary in each case, but at intervals not exceeding six months during the child's first two years in care and thereafter not less than once a year. Under reg. 25(4), on initiating a review the board is obliged, in so far as is practicable, to inform the parents of the child and every person who in law is a guardian of the child, and afford them the opportunity to be heard or consulted in respect of the review.

When reviewing the case of each child in residential care the board must consider the following:

(i)   whether all reasonable steps are being taken to promote the welfare of the child;

(ii)   whether the care being provided for the child continues to be suitable for the child's needs;

(iii)   whether the circumstances of the child's parents have changed;

(iv) whether it would be in the best interests of the child to be given into the custody of his parents; and

(v) the child's need for assistance and aftercare under s. 45 of the 1991 Act.

In considering the foregoing and determining the most appropriate course of action to be taken in the interests of the child, the board must have regard to the following:

(a) any views or information furnished by the child, the parents of the child, the manager and any other person whom the board has consulted in relation to the review;

(b) a report from the residential centre in which the child is residing;

(c) a report of any visits to the child in accordance with the aforementioned reg. 24(5) of the regulations;

(d) in the case of a child attending school, the latest available school report relating to the child; and

(e) any other information which in the opinion of the board is relevant to the case of the child.

To ensure that the most appropriate action in the circumstances is taken by the board all this information is gathered and considered. Whatever decision is made must be made known by the board to the manager of the residential centre, and, where practicable, to the child, any person who in law is a guardian of the child and any other person who the board considers ought to be informed. A note of every review and the action taken as a result (if any) must be entered in the case record.

Special review

Any person with a bona fide interest in the case of a child placed in residential care by a Health Board may make a request in writing to the board to carry out a review of the case and the board must accede to the request, having regard to the reports and information available, unless it considers that a review is unnecessary. Where the Health Board declines to accede to the request, it must inform the person who made the request of its decision in writing.

Frequent admissions to care

Where a child is placed in residential care by the Health Board on more than one occasion in a period of 12 consecutive months, the board shall carry out a review of the child's case under the terms of the aforementioned reg. 25.

Removal of a child from residential care

Where the Health Board which has placed a child in a residential centre decides to reunite the child with a parent or considers that the continued placement of the child in that centre is no longer in the best interests of the child, the board shall inform the manager of its intention to remove the child from the centre and the reason therefor. Should the manager object, the Health Board shall afford the manager an opportunity to make representations to the Health Board. If having considered these representations the board decides to proceed with the removal, it shall give notice in writing to the manager of its decision and the reason therefor and request the manager to deliver up the child on a specific date. Should the manager refuse to comply, the Health Board can apply to the District Court for a direction.

11.3.3.7 Miscellaneous provisions

Support services

A Health Board must make available such support services as it considers necessary to each residential centre wherein children are placed.

Voluntary bodies

A Health Board may make arrangements with competent and appropriately qualified voluntary bodies or other persons for assistance in the performance of its functions.

Inspections

Regulation 31 provides for the inspection of the practices and procedures operated by the Health Board in relation to the provision of residential care by a person authorised by the Health Board. In particular this regulation authorises a person so authorised to enter any residential centre maintained by the Health Board and to examine the state and management of the centre and the treatment of the children therein and further to examine the records of the centre and to interview the members of staff who are involved in residential care services.

11.3.3.8 Standards of residential care

The standards that must be maintained by residential centres are governed by the Child Care (Standards in Child Care Residential Centres) Regulations 1996, SI 397/1996. Part I of the regulations defines 'children's residential centre' as 'any home or other institution for the residential care of children in the care of health boards or other children who are not receiving adequate care and protection'. The 'register' within the context of these regulations means 'a register of children's residential centres established under s. 61 of the Child Care Act 1991, and in relation to a particular health board means the register established by the board'.

11.3.3.9 Application for registration

The schedule to these regulations sets out the form in which an application can be made for registration as a children's residential centre under Part VII of the Child Care Act 1991.

11.3.3.10 Standards in residential centres

Operational policies

The registered proprietor and person in charge of the residential centre must satisfy the relevant Health Board that appropriate and suitable care practices and operational policies are in place, having regard to the number and needs of the children residing in the centre.

Accommodation

The registered person in charge (as *per* reg. 7) has the responsibility of satisfying the Health Board that adequate and suitable accommodation is provided in each case in light of the needs of the children and the number of them. In particular there must be:

(a)   adequate and suitable furniture and bedding provided;

(b)   sufficient number of lavatories, wash basins, baths and showers, supplied with hot and cold water with appropriate privacy, as far as is practicable;

(c)   adequate laundering facilities;

(d)   adequately lit, heated and ventilated premises;

(e)   clean and appropriately decorated premises, maintained in good structural condition; and

(f)   adequate recreation facilities.

Access arrangements

The registered proprietor and person in charge of a centre must satisfy the Health Board that arrangements are in place to facilitate reasonable access to children by parents, relatives and friends or other persons with a bona fide interest in the children.

Health care and religion

Children being maintained in the centre must have access to general practitioner services and the facility must exist for their referral to medical, psychological, dental, ophthalmic and other specialist services as required. As regards religion, the registered proprietor and person in charge must satisfy the Health Board that appropriate arrangements are in place to enable children residing in the centre, in so far as is reasonably practicable, to practise their religion.

Food and cooking facilities

Regulation 12 requires each centre to have suitable and sufficient catering equipment, crockery and cutlery, proper refrigeration and storage facilities and a high standard of hygiene. Adequate provisions of food must be supplied which is properly prepared, wholesome and nutritious, involves an element of choice and takes account of any special dietary needs.

Fire precautions

Confirmation is required from a chartered engineer or suitably qualified architect relating to compliance with the relevant fire safety and building control requirements, including that:

(a)   adequate precautions have been taken by the centre against the risk of fire, including the provision of adequate means of escape in the event of fire;

(b)   adequate arrangements are in place for detecting, containing and extinguishing fires, and for the maintenance of fire-fighting equipment; and

(c)   all reasonable measures have been taken by the centre to ensure that the materials contained in the bedding and the internal furnishings of the centre have adequate fire retardancy properties and have low levels of toxicity.

Safety precautions

The registered proprietor and person in charge must satisfy the Health Board that adequate arrangements exist to guard against the risk of injury occurring on the premises, particularly with regard to stairways, appliances, windows and doors, storage of medicines, cleaning and other material.

Miscellaneous

Regulations 15–17 deal with the issues of insurance, notification of the Health Board of significant events and the requirement that appropriate records are kept in relation to the children being maintained in the centre. This last requirement, although vitally important, is not dealt with in any detail in these regulations.

11.3.3.11   Inspection of premises and enforcement of regulations

Regulation 18 requires the registered proprietor and members of staff of a residential centre to permit authorised persons to enter and inspect the premises and afford them the required facilities and information. These authorised persons are further permitted to examine and take up copies of all records save those relating to the medical records of the children in the centre. Access to those records will be limited to a medical practitioner. Finally, reg. 19 provides that these regulations shall be enforced and executed by each Health Board in respect of each children's residential centre in its own functional area.

11.3.3.12 Current developments in residential care

On 10 October 1999, the Social Services Inspectorate launched the report of the findings relating to inspection of residential centres run by the Health Boards. The report is based on the first 12 inspections that were carried out across the 10 Health Board areas. The inspections covered a range of residential centres, including several children's residential centres for children in the care of the Health Boards. Many of the staff at the centres were found to be committed and caring workers who had earned the respect of the children but the inspectors found that there were high levels of staff turnover in some centres that did little to ensure children in those centres were provided with the continuity of care they needed. Furthermore, it was found that too many staff were employed on temporary contracts and in some centres there were few staff with the relevant qualifications for child-care work. Care planning was found to be lacking in so far as inspectors found that there was insufficient attention given to care planning by social workers. It was noted by the Inspectorate that although in most cases a useful placement plan was drawn up by the residential staff to guide their work, it was not within the context of an overall care plan, when the placement commenced. Without more attention being given to care planning, inspectors voiced their concerns that children may remain in residential care longer than is necessary. On the whole the findings of the Inspectorate were regarded as encouraging, which reflects the progressive improvement of the services provided to children in residential care.

In relation to financial assistance, Mr Frank Fahy TD, Minister of State at the Department of Health and Children, in November 1999 announced a £28 million National Child Care Investment Strategy. The focus of the strategy was stated to be on supporting vulnerable children in the family and community, and setting and attempting to avoid where possible, the necessity of residential care. In addition, in response to the funding needs of Health Boards in respect of residential care, the Minister of State also announced an allocation of £1 million to the Department of Education and Science for the development of targeted educational responses in respect of certain children who are at risk. This initiative was stated to form part of a multi-agency approach to the needs of children released from (inter alia) residential care centres.

11.3.3.13 Foster care versus residential care

Whether a child who is in need of care and protection from the Health Board is placed in foster care or residential care will depend on the particular needs of the child as well as his individual circumstances.

Needs of child

The requirements of an individual child may determine the decision of the Health Board in relation to his suitability for foster care or residential care.

The religious beliefs of the child may also play a role in this decision process. Where the foster parents available to take the child practise a different religion from the child, a difficulty may arise in particular circumstances where the parents and/or guardians of the child hold strong views in this regard. In such a case a residential centre may be the only option available to the Health Board who are obliged to consider the issue of religious belief.

Needs of parents

Section 37 of the 1991 Act places an obligation on the Health Board to facilitate the parents and/or guardians of a child in care with reasonable access. This requirement is emphasised by the regulations governing both foster care and residential care as both require the Health Board to take account of the wishes of the child's parents and/or guardians.

11.3.4 ACCESS TO CHILDREN IN CARE

In all cases where a child is in the care, voluntary or otherwise, of a Health Board, it is possible to make provision for granting of reasonable access to the child's parents and other relatives. Section 37 of the 1991 Act obliges the Board, in such cases, to facilitate reasonable access to the child by his or her parents, by any person acting *in loco parentis* in respect of the child or by any other person who has a bona fide interest in the child. The last-mentioned person may include a grandparent or grown-up sibling. Such access as is permitted may include provision to allow the child to reside temporarily with such person. For instance, a child residing with foster parents may be permitted to spend the last weekend of every month with his natural father or to stay overnight, once a month, with his grandparents.

Some persons may be unhappy with the arrangements made. If so, it is open to that person, or indeed any person, to apply to the court for appropriate directions. In such a case the court may make an order, in such terms as it considers appropriate, regarding access to the child by that person. This order may, however, be varied or discharged on application by any person. It is also open to the court, on the application of the Health Board only, to preclude access by a named person. This may be done only where the court deems it necessary to do so in order to safeguard or promote the child's welfare. The order precluding access may, furthermore, be varied or discharged by the court on the application of any person. It may be possible, however, for the child himself to seek the direction of the court on this or any other matter relating to access, under the 1991 Act, s. 47.

It is noteworthy, incidentally, that the terms of s. 37 reflect a rather parent-centred attitude to access. The section speaks of access 'by' a parent 'to' a child whereas surely it is the reverse that should concern the court. Is it not more apt to speak of the *child's* right of access *to* its parents and other relatives? If the primary concern of the court is with the welfare of the child, should not this section be worded accordingly? The divergence is subtle, no doubt, but revealing.

Before leaving this topic, it is worth noting developments in the international legal arena. In *Eriksson v Sweden* (1989) 12 EHRR 200, the European Court of Human Rights held that the natural family relationship is not terminated by reason of the fact that a child is taken into care. The enjoyment by a child and a parent of each other's company, it said, is a fundamental element of family life. The curtailment or denial of access would thus be a prima facie violation of article 8 of the European Convention on Human Rights. It would, furthermore, be deemed a full violation thereof unless it could be shown in accordance with law, that such denial of access had an aim or aims that is or are legitimate under article 8(2) and was 'necessary in a democratic society'. Access, according to the Court, is an automatic right of the child in care, not to be denied unless there is clear evidence that it is contrary to the welfare of the child to permit access. This approach is also to be found in the 1989 UN Convention on the Rights of the Child, article 9(3) of which makes specific provision for:

> 'the right of the child who is separated from one or both parents to maintain public relations and direct contact with both parents on a regular basis unless it is contrary to the child's best interests.'

From this flow two prevailing principles to be observed when considering access arrangements:

(a) the appropriateness or otherwise of making access arrangements should be considered primarily by reference to the welfare of the child; and

(b) access to parents and other relatives should invariably be considered to be in the best interests of the child, unless the contrary is clearly demonstrated.

The Strasbourg Court in *Olsson v Sweden* (1988) 11 EHRR 259, noted that there was an obligation on national authorities to take appropriate practical measures to facilitate reunion with parents. The three Olsson children in that case were taken into foster care and placed with different foster parents a considerable distance from each other and from their parents. The geographical distance between the members of the family resulted in contact being cut off between them. The court found that this gave rise to a violation of article 8. More importantly, it attributed little weight to the administrative difficulties alluded to in the case, such as a lack of appropriate foster families. Unfortunately, the court did not provide instruction as to what is an acceptable distance by which children and parents can be separated.

11.3.5 TERMINATION OF CARE

11.3.5.1 Generally

There are certain situations where a child may be deemed no longer to be in the care of the Health Board:

(a) First and foremost, a child who has reached the age of 18 is no longer deemed to be a child for the purposes of the Act. Thus, the jurisdiction of the Health Board in respect of that child is ended. A child who marries is likewise deemed no longer to be the responsibility of the Board.

(b) Where a child has voluntarily been placed in the care of the Health Board (under the 1991 Act, s. 4), such care will be terminated by the decision of the parents to resume custody (s. 4(2)).

(c) Where under the 1991 Act, s. 18(8), a care order is discharged by the court.

(d) Where an emergency care order made under s. 13 or an interim care order created by means of s. 17 expires and is not renewed.

It goes without saying that where, on appeal or judicial review, a care order is reversed or quashed, the effect of such appeal shall be to terminate the Health Board's lawful custody of the child in respect of which the order has been made.

11.3.5.2 Removal from placement

Where a child has been placed in accordance with the 1991 Act, s. 36 he or she may be removed from such placement under the provisions of s. 43. This allows the Health Board to terminate any placement of a child, seemingly with little comeback for the persons having custody, for the time being, of the child. The removal of a child from custody has the effect of bringing to an end any contract between the Health Board and the aforementioned person(s) in respect of the child's care.

Should any person having custody, for the time being, of a child refuse to comply with the request, or alternatively ignore it, the Board may seek the direction of the court. The court may thus order such person to return the child to the custody of the Board. The judge, nonetheless has a discretion in this regard. He or she may refuse to grant the order if he or she considers that it is not in the best interests of the child to do so (s. 43(2)).

Where an order is, however, made, any person who fails to comply therewith may be guilty of contempt of court. If such person unlawfully retains custody of the child following the making of an order under s. 43(2), it is possible, furthermore, that such person may be found guilty of an offence under s. 43(3) of the Act. This is conditional on the person having been shown a copy of the order in question or having been required by the Health Board or a person acting on its behalf, to deliver up the child. The Health Board will be deemed however, to have satisfied this condition where the person in question was present at the court sitting at which the order was made. A person so convicted faces a maximum penalty of six months in jail or a fine of £500 (630 euros) or both at the discretion of the court.

11.3.5.3 Unlawful removal of a child from care

Where a child is unlawfully removed from the care of the board or of any person having lawful custody of the child, the 1991 Act, s. 46 allows the board to take steps to restore the child to the lawful custody of any person. This will include a situation where a child, having been in the lawful custody of a person for a temporary period, has been prevented from returning to a place of lawful custody at the end of that lawful period.

The Health Board is empowered by s. 46(2) to request the assistance of the Garda Síochana in searching for the child unlawfully detained with a view to his return to lawful custody. To this end the Gardaí may take all reasonable measures to secure such return. It is possible, furthermore, to obtain the order of the court regarding the child's return (s. 46(3)). This allows the judge to order that a named person produce and return a child to the custody of the Board. This may be done only where the judge is satisfied by information on oath that there are reasonable grounds for believing that the child can be produced by the person named in the application. An application under s. 46(3) may be made ex parte (s. 46(7)). In addition to the possibility of conviction for contempt of court, a failure or refusal to comply with such order will amount to an offence under s. 46(4). This, again, is conditional on the person having been shown a copy of the order in question or having been required by the Health Board or a person acting on its behalf, to comply with the requirement. The Health Board will be deemed, however, to have satisfied this condition where the person in question was present at the court sitting at which the order was made (s. 46(5)). A person so convicted faces a maximum penalty of six months in jail or a fine of £500 (630 euros) or both at the discretion of the court.

It is also possible for a warrant to be issued permitting a member of the Garda Síochana to enter a place in which, it is reasonably believed, the child is being detained (s. 46(6)). Such a place may include a house or any other place, including a building or part thereof, and any tent, caravan or other temporary or other movable structure. It is possible also to make an order in respect of a vessel, vehicle, aircraft or hovercraft. Upon the making of such an order a member of the Gardaí, accompanied by any person deemed necessary (including other Gardaí) may enter and search the place stated in the order, using such force as is necessary in the circumstances.

It is possible for an order under s. 46(3) or (6) to be made, should the urgency of the case so require, other than at a public sitting of the District Court (s. 46(8)). Such an order or warrant will usually be issued by a judge of the district in which the person or place specified in the information is to be found (s. 46(9)). Where this is not possible, however (where the judge is not 'immediately available'), an order may be made or warrant issued by any district judge.

11.3.6 APPLICATION FOR DIRECTIONS

Where a child is in the care of the Health Board, any person may apply to the court for directions as to any matter affecting the child's welfare. It is also possible for the court to issue such directions on its own initiative. The court should consider the prospect of such directions as it thinks proper, with reference always to the predominant requirement that the child's welfare be promoted. Such directions as are given may, however, be varied or discharged by the court, should it see fit.

11.3.7 AFTERCARE

Where a child reaches the age of 18 he or she is no longer technically deemed to be in care. Few parents, however, see fit to sever all links with their children on their reaching the age of majority. In a similar vein the Health Board (notwithstanding s. 2(1)) is empowered, should it see fit, to make continuing provision for persons formerly in its care. Section 45 allows the board to assist such persons until they have reached the age of 21, should it be satisfied that such assistance be needed. This may include:

(a)   making provision for visits to the child or other practical assistance;

(b)   arrangements to assist the completion of education by the former child and the provision of maintenance to assist him or her while completing this education. Such arrangements may be continued after the child has reached the age of 21 should it be necessary to facilitate the completion of that person's education;

(c)   placing the former child in a suitable trade, calling or business and paying such fees as are required to facilitate such placement (presumably this refers, *inter alia,* to a vocational apprenticeship); and

(d)   arranging appropriate accommodation (including hostel accommodation). This may involve (e) consulting and co-operating with local and voluntary housing authorities with a view to securing appropriate accommodation.

These provisions are facilitative only and not mandatory. The reality is that a Health Board, hard pressed and under-resourced, may choose to devote its scant resources to children in need rather than for providing aftercare to persons who are now no longer 'children' for the purposes of the Act.

11.3.8 VARIATION OR DISCHARGE OF CARE ORDERS AND SUPERVISION ORDERS

11.3.8.1 Introduction

Pursuant to s. 22 of the 1991 Act the court may on its own initiative or on the application of any person:

(a)   vary or discharge a care order or a supervision order; or

(b)   vary or discharge any condition or direction attaching to the order; or

(c)   in the case of a care order, discharge the care order and make a supervision order.

11.3.8.2 Invalid orders

Section 23 specifies the powers of the court in cases where a care order proves to be invalid. If a court makes such a declaration of invalidity in any proceedings for whatever reason, it may refuse to exercise any power to order the delivery or return of the child to a parent or any other person if it is of the opinion that to do so would not be in the best interests of the child. In such circumstances the court has the power to make a new care order or remit the matter to the relevant District Court so that it can consider whether to make a new care order. This section enables the status quo concerning the child's care to be maintained whilst a new care order is obtained. However this section should only be applied where the court is of the opinion that it is not in the best interests of the child to be returned. The terms of this section are very broad and enable the child who is considered to require care to be safeguarded against technical or fundamental matters which invalidate care orders and thereby facilitate the automatic return of the child to his parents or person acting *in loco parentis.*

11.3.9 PRACTICE AND PROCEDURE OF CHILD CARE PROCEEDINGS

11.3.9.1 Introduction

Part V of the 1991 Act sets out the jurisdiction and the powers and procedures of courts in relation to child care proceedings.

11.3.9.2 Jurisdiction

Section 28 of the 1991 Act provides that the District Court and the Circuit Court on appeal have jurisdiction to hear and determine proceedings brought under Parts III, IV or VI of the 1991 Act. The proceedings are to be heard otherwise than in public and are to be as informal as is practicable and consistent with the administration of justice in the circumstances. Section 31 sets out restrictions on the publication of matter likely to result in members of the public identifying a child who is or has been the subject of child care proceedings. Any breach of this is a summary offence, which carries a penalty of 12 months imprisonment or a fine of £1,000 or both. There is also the possibility of the person who is in breach of these restrictions being found in contempt of court.

11.3.9.3 Reports on children

Section 27 of the 1991 Act provides that the court in proceedings under Part IV or VI of the 1991 Act may procure a report from a nominated person on any question affecting the welfare of the child. In determining whether to obtain such a report the court is to have regard to the wishes of the parties before the court where these are ascertainable but the court is not bound by these wishes. The court may also order an assessment when making an interim care order or emergency care order. A copy of the report is to be made available to the representatives of each party to the proceedings or the party himself if he is not legally represented. The report may be received in evidence in the proceedings. The court if it thinks fit, or any party to the proceedings, may call the person making the report as a witness. The fees and expenses of a person preparing the report are to be paid by such party or parties to the proceedings as the court orders.

11.3.9.4 Family law proceedings

Section 20 of the 1991 Act links the Act with proceedings brought under the Guardianship of Infants Act 1964, the Judicial Separation and Family Law Reform Act 1989, the Family Law Act 1995 and the Family Law (Divorce) Act 1996. In the course of private family law proceedings a court may order a section 20 report where it believes that in order to adequately protect the children in a case a care order or supervision order may need to be made. In a private family law case the court can of its own motion or on the application of any person, adjourn the proceedings and direct the Health Board to undertake an investigation of the child's circumstances. The court may also give directions as to the care and custody of the child or make a supervision order pending the outcome.

11.3.10 CONCLUSION

In an attempt to make adequate and appropriate provision for children in need, the legislature has introduced numerous statutes and statutory instruments, some of which are detailed above. The foundations of child care law are now contained in the 1991 Act upon which all other legislative enactments are now based. The central role of the Health Board is evident from the contents of the 1991 Act. For example, the powers of the Health Board to take a child in need into care provide for both voluntary, contentious and emergency situations. Furthermore, the involvement of the Garda Síochána is included in the provisions of the 1991 Act, as their intervention, forceful or otherwise, may be required from time to time. This chapter has also set out in detail the issues of foster care and residential care for children in need. The detail contained in the relevant statutory instruments and the appropriate sections of the 1991 Act serve to reflect the extensive obligations imposed on those practising in this area. The concept of welfare arises for consideration with every issue and ultimately the welfare of the child is the basis for all actions taken and decisions made by the Health Board. The law relating to child care is required to be both detailed and extensive because of the many complications that can arise in every case. This is evident from the variety of references included in this brief section dealing with the legislature's approach to the issue of children at risk.

CHAPTER 12

THE NON-MARITAL FAMILY

12.1 Introduction

The term non-marital family includes not only two single people living together with their children, but also where one party has obtained an annulment from the Roman Catholic Church and has entered a ceremony of marriage in that church with their partner, or it can include a separated person living with another, or someone who has entered into a foreign divorce which is not recognised as valid within this jurisdiction.

12.2 The Constitution

Article 41 deals with the rights of the family. Many judgments of the Irish courts have held that the only family recognised and given protection by the Constitution is a family based on marriage, for example:

(a) *In re M (an infant)* [1946] IR 334;

(b) *In re Cullinane (an infant)* [1954] IR 270;

(c) *State (Nicolaou) v An Bord Uchtála* [1966] IR 567;

(d) *In re J (an infant)* [1966] IR 295;

(e) *McN v L* (unreported, 12 January 1970, High Ct, Kenny J);

(f) *G v An Bord Uchtála* [1980] IR 32;

(g) *W.O'R. v E.H.* [1996] 2 IR 248.

Article 41.1.2 pledges the State to guarantee to protect the family in its constitution and authority, as the necessary basis of social order.

Article 41.3.1 pledges the State to guard with special care the institution of marriage, on which the family is founded and protect it against attack.

Although parents who have not married do not benefit from the rights enunciated in Articles 41 and 42 of the Constitution it has been held that non-marital children have the same 'natural and imprescriptible rights' as marital children. These rights include the right to religious and moral, intellectual, physical and social education and the right to free primary education. They have also been said to include 'where possible, the right to the society and support of their parents': *W.O'R. v E.H. and An Bord Uchtála* [1996] 2 IR 248 at 267.

12.3 The Mother

Does the non-marital mother enjoy the same constitutional rights as a married mother? The Supreme Court has considered this question in detail in a number of cases. In *Re M (an Infant)* [1946] IR 334 Gavin Duffy P treated the non-marital child as having the same 'natural and imprescriptible rights' under Article 42 of the Constitution as the marital child. However, the learned President held that the constitutional guarantees for the family, outlined in Article 41, were not available to the mother of a non-marital child. The Supreme Court approved Gavin Duffy P's judgment in *State (Nicolaou) v An Bord Uchtála* [1966] IR 567.

Walsh J at p. 644 of the *Nicolaou* judgment stated:

'her natural right to the custody and care of her child and such other natural personal rights as she may have fall to be protected under Article 40.3 (personal rights clause) and are not affected by Article 41 or Article 42 of the Constitution'.

O'Higgins CJ in *G v An Bord Uchtála* indicated that the rights of the mother are neither inalienable nor imprescriptible, similar to the rights of the family under Article 41. Her rights can be alienated or transferred in whole or in part and either subject to conditions or absolutely. In addition they can be lost by the mother, if her conduct towards the child amounts to an abandonment or abdication of her rights and duties.

12.4 The Father

In Ireland, the Constitution provides the State with its fundamental laws and therefore its perspectives on the parent-child relationship naturally influence the formulation and interpretation of laws influencing this relationship. Articles 41 and 42 of the Constitution confer upon the 'married family' rights and duties which are described as inalienable and imprescriptible. These articles insist on preserving rights in married parents in circumstances where those rights have been constantly abused or, even more absurd, where the parents have no interest in the exercise of those rights. On the other hand these articles exclude the unmarried father from having any constitutional rights in relation to the child.

The leading case is *State (Nicolaou) v An Bord Uchtála* where it was stated that 'as far as Article 41 is concerned the guarantees therein are confined to families based upon marriage' [1966] IR at 576. The Supreme Court rejected the father's claim that he had been discriminated against under Article 40.1. Walsh J said:

'it has not been shown to the satisfaction of the court that the father of an illegitimate child has any natural rights as distinct from legal rights, to either the custody or society of that child, and the court has not been satisfied that any such right has ever been recognised as part of the natural law' (see **12.6** and **12.7**).

12.5 Legitimacy

Unless the parents of a child are married to one another either at the child's date of birth or at the time of conception the child is not regarded as legitimate. However, a child may be legitimated by the subsequent marriage of its parents: Legitimacy Act 1931, s. 1 (as amended by the Status of Children Act 1987, s. 7(1), (2)). The child is legitimated from the date of the parents' marriage. Prior to the coming into effect of the Status of Children Act, a child would not have been legitimated by the parents subsequent marriage if the parents could not have married at the child's date of birth or ten months prior to the birth.

There is no difference between the constitutional position of the legitimate child and the legitimated child. The natural father's consent is needed if an adoption order is to be made for a legitimated child.

12.6   Guardianship

Prior to the coming into effect of the Status of Children Act 1987, the natural mother and not the natural father was the guardian of the child born outside marriage. A guardian of a child has the right to be consulted on all matters affecting the upbringing of the child, e.g. the signing of passport forms, change of name, permission to marry, etc. The natural father may now apply to court to be appointed as joint guardian of the child with the mother: Status of Children Act 1987, s. 12. If there is no such application the mother remains the sole guardian: Status of Children Act 1987, s. 11. In cases where the mother consents to this appointment and the father is registered on the birth certificate there is a special informal procedure: Status of Children Act 1987, s. 9.

In the past, parties were deterred from seeking relief by way of a nullity decree when they realised that it rendered their children illegitimate and that the father would no longer be a guardian of the children. The Status of Children Act 1987, s. 9 now provides that if a nullity decree is obtained in respect of voidable and of certain void marriages the father remains as guardian of the children born during the marriage.

If a father is guardian of a child his consent will have to be obtained to an adoption order (Adoption Act 1952, s. 14). If a guardianship order is made it will have implications for the making of a care order. In all guardianship applications before the court the guiding principle is that of the Guardianship of Infants Act 1964, s. 3, i.e. the welfare of the child is the first and paramount consideration.

Application can be made under the Guardianship of Infants Act 1964, s. 8(4) to remove from office any guardian appointed by will, deed, or by court order. The fact that the guardianship order was made can be submitted in evidence in subsequent civil proceedings for the purposes of proving paternity (Status of Children Act 1987, s. 45).

If a couple approach a solicitor together for advice, they should be interviewed separately. They should be advised of the implications of guardianship orally and in writing.

12.7   Guardianship Rights of the Natural Father

Until recently the only method for a non-marital father to obtain guardianship rights was to make an application to court under the Guardianship of Infants Act 1964, s. 6A (as inserted by the Status of Children Act 1987). Such an application was fraught with uncertainties and was held in *J.K. v V.W.* [1990] 2 IR 437 to give natural fathers no more than a right to apply to be appointed guardian. The real bar to appointment was the opposition of the natural mother or the placement of the child for adoption. If the mother supported the application, success was almost assured. However, there was still the necessity, and cost, of going to court. Indeed, with over one-fifth of children being born outside marriage, had their fathers all brought such an application the courts would have come to a standstill.

Section 4 of the Children Act 1997 introduces a new s. 2 into the Guardianship of Infants Act 1964. Included is a new and simplified method of appointing a natural father as guardian of the child that does not involve a court appearance. Instead the parents make a statutory declaration in which they:

(a)   declare that they have not married each other;

250

(b)   declare that they are the father and mother of the child concerned;

(c)   agree to the appointment of the father as a guardian of the child; and

(d)   have entered into arrangements regarding the custody and, as the case may be, access to the child.

The form of the statutory declaration is set out in the Guardianship of Children (Statutory Declaration) Regulations 1998, SI 5/1998. The declaration does not have to recite the particular custody or access arrangements agreed; the fact of agreement will suffice. It should also be noted that there is no need for the couple to be living together to make the declaration, or for that matter to be separate. A separate statutory declaration should be made in respect of each child. Once the father has been appointed he can only be removed from office by the court.

The requirement of a statutory declaration attaches the necessary degree of formality to the process. This aspect of the procedure is designed to emphasise its importance as not only does the prescribed form remind parents that making the agreement will seriously affect their legal position, it also suggests that they both seek legal advice before the form is completed. The effect of the 1997 Act is to remove the need to attend court where the father and mother are in agreement on the question of guardianship.

There are practical difficulties with the operation of this section. For example, where does one 'file' the declaration? Furthermore, if the father is not registered on the birth certificate and presents the statutory declaration to the Registrar, it is likely that the Registrar will not accept the declaration and will require a court order. Significantly, by virtue of the Registration of Births Act 1996, s. 1(3), a surname must now be chosen on registration. Previously a surname could be chosen after registration. Indeed, the child could obtain a birth certificate in either name. The main difficulty of course arises when the father's wish and application to be appointed a joint guardian is contested by the natural mother. The position in relation to these applications has not been altered by the 1997 Act, s. 4.

12.8   Custody/Access

Custody is the day-to-day care and control of the child. Access is the right to see and to communicate with the child. While the natural mother's right to custody is now recognised as a constitutional right, the natural father has no such right. However, the natural father may under the Guardianship of Infants Act 1964, s. 11(4) (as amended by the Status of Children Act 1987) seek a custody, access and maintenance order.

This type of application was rare until the Courts Act 1981 transferred jurisdiction in relation to the Guardianship of Infants Act 1964 to the Circuit and District Courts from the High Court. The most frequent applications by natural fathers are for access. However, in circumstances where a child is not being looked after by the mother, the father may seek custody of the child. A s. 11 order is not enforceable if a couple reside together and it ceases to have effect if they continue to reside together for three months after the order is made. As with guardianship applications the welfare of the child is the first and paramount consideration of the court in hearing these applications (Guardianship of Infants Act 1964, s. 3).

12.9   Maintenance

An unmarried cohabitee has no legal right to seek maintenance from his/her cohabitee for themselves. Maintenance can be sought for the support of children pursuant to the Family

Law (Maintenance of Spouses and Children) Act 1976 as amended by the Status of Children Act 1987. Maintenance can also be obtained under the Guardianship of Infants Act 1964, s. 11(2)(b).

If a married woman is separated from her husband and is cohabiting then the husband can issue variation proceedings to have the maintenance attributable to her discharged on the basis of desertion. Under the 1976 Act, s. 5(2), as originally drafted, desertion was an absolute bar to maintenance and adultery was a discretionary bar. A change was introduced in the Judicial Separation and Family Law Reform Act 1989, s. 38 and desertion is now only a discretionary bar to relief while adultery was removed as a bar (see **5.6**).

12.10 Status of Children Act 1987

Part IV of the Status of Children Act 1987 deals with maintenance. A maintenance order cannot be made unless it is proved on the balance of probabilities that the respondent is the parent: Status of Children Act 1987, s. 15. Even though corroboration is not required, it is helpful to look at the guidelines set out in *Morrissey v Boyle* [1942] IR 514. Note that 'dependent child of a family' now includes a child whose parents are not married to each other, and a child where the spouse acts in *loco parentis* to a child, though he is aware that he is not the parent of the child: Status of Children Act 1987, s. 16.

Where there is a maintenance dispute between spouses, the court will take into account their financial responsibilities towards any dependent children (including children from outside their marriage) in accordance with the Status of Children Act 1987, s. 17. Section 18 makes similar provisions with regard to parents who are not married to each other, in setting out what is to be taken into account in assessing maintenance. This applies to a couple who had been married to each other, e.g. are lawfully divorced, but maintenance is still required for the children. An agreement made on maintenance between parents of children who are not married to each other can now be ruled in court, and become a maintenance order for the purposes of the Family Law (Maintenance of Spouses and Children) Act 1976, ss. 8 and 8A, provided the court is satisfied that the agreement is a fair and reasonable one which adequately protects the interests of the child.

Lump sum payments for incidental expenses of the birth or funeral of a child, whether born in a marriage or not, can be recovered, up to £750 maximum (Status of Children Act 1987, s. 21).

12.11 Succession

Since 14 June 1988, children born outside of marriage have the same succession rights as legitimate children. The Status of Children Act 1987 amended the Succession Act 1965 to provide that all relationships for the purpose of the Succession Act are to be regarded equally irrespective of the marital status of a person's parent. The 1987 Act overturns the decision in *Re the Goods of Walker: O'Brien v S and A.G.* [1985] ILRM 86 which held that a non-marital child could have no succession rights to its father's estate. On intestacy the child born outside marriage is entitled to a share in the parent's estate. By s. 31, a child born outside marriage can bring s. 117 proceedings challenging the will of a parent if they are disappointed in their inheritance, irrespective of whether the will was executed before or after 14 June 1988. Although the unmarried cohabitee has no succession rights to the estate of the other party, provision can be made in wills for cohabitees. However, a married spouse can claim his or her legal right share.

The children born to parents who are not married to each other are now in the same CAT thresholds as legitimate issue. They are now in class (a), i.e. with a threshold of £300,000 (see **9.2.5.2**). Even though a parent is dead a declaration of parentage can be sought under the Status of Children Act 1987. A finding of parentage in guardianship, maintenance or social welfare cases is admissible as evidence in subsequent proceedings (Status of Children Act 1987, s. 45).

It is essential for a single mother to make a will nominating persons to be guardians of her child, in the event of her death. Otherwise, the child will have no guardian, unless an order under the Guardianship of Infants Act 1964, s. 6A (as inserted by the Status of Children Act 1987) has been made.

12.12 Declarations of Parentage

The Status of Children Act 1987, ss. 33 to 36, provides for declarations of parentage. A person can seek an order in the Circuit Court that a certain person is his mother or father. This can be done even though the parent is dead. Section 35 of the Status of Children Act 1987 enables a person, other than an adopted person, to apply to the Circuit Court for a declaration that an individual named in the application is his father or mother as the case may be, or that both the individuals are his/her parents: see *I.O.T. v B.* (unreported, 3 April 1998, Supreme Ct). The court order is binding on all the parties and on any party claiming through a party to the proceedings. It is likely that such declarations will be of importance in probate cases. The Attorney General can be joined as a party, and if a declaration is made, it will be binding on the State. Note that under the Status of Children Act 1987, s. 35(8), the court can make a positive declaration of paternity. Evidence of paternity may consist of proof that the couple were living together at the time of conception, as in *G.N. v K.K.* (unreported, 30 January 1998, High Ct).

12.13 Blood Tests

The definition of blood test includes DNA profiling. The Status of Children Act 1987, s. 38 provides that in any civil proceedings, in which parentage is in question, the court can give a direction for the use of blood tests, and the case is then adjourned for the test to be done: see *J.P.D. v M.G.* [1991] ILRM 217. A blood sample will not be taken without the person's consent, though if he does not consent, under s. 42 of the Act, the court may draw inferences from the fact of failing to take any step required, after a direction has been given for blood testing to take place. The question of whether or not a respondent or applicant is likely to consent to the taking of blood samples should be ascertained at the earliest possible time so as to avoid bringing witnesses to court.

In cases of conflict or disagreement it is generally advisable to undergo the tests, as testing can now establish to an extremely high degree of probability that some person is or is not the father of a child. A client should be advised that there is a penalty for impersonation.

12.14 Presumption of Paternity

The Status of Children Act 1987, s. 46 abolishes the presumptions of legitimacy and illegitimacy. It replaces them with the presumptions of paternity and non-paternity. All of these presumptions are rebuttable by the normal standards of proof, i.e. on the balance of probabilities.

The presumption of paternity provides that a married woman's husband is the father of her children unless the contrary is proved. However, in certain circumstances the husband will be presumed not to be the father of the child. This is where a married woman is living apart from her husband under either a decree of *divorce a mensa et thoro* or a deed of separation for longer than ten months prior to the birth of the child (Status of Children Act 1987, s. 46(3)).

The effect of the old rule in *Russell v Russell* [1924] AC 487, HL, was to prevent parents from giving evidence which would result in their child being regarded as illegitimate. However, in *S v S* [1983] IR 68 it was held that this rule was inconsistent with the constitutional guarantees of fairness in procedures. This decision has been given statutory recognition by the Status of Children Act 1987, s. 47(1).

Under the Status of Children Act 1987, s. 45, a finding of parentage in guardianship, maintenance or certain social welfare proceedings can be submitted in evidence in subsequent civil proceedings for the purposes of proving that a person is the parent. The original proceedings can be either prior to or post 14 June 1988, which is the date of the commencement of the Status of Children Act 1987.

12.15 Registration of Births

In the past it has been difficult for a mother of a child born outside marriage to have the natural father registered on the birth certificate. The procedures are detailed in the Status of Children Act 1987, s. 49, which amends the Births and Deaths Registration Act (Ireland) 1880, s. 7. This provides that if the mother or father of a child born outside marriage wants the natural father's name put on the birth certificate, it can be inserted either at the request of one or both if they both sign a statutory declaration that he is the father or there is a court order in existence naming him as the father. This is a court order to which the Status of Children Act 1987, s. 45, relates. If a child is born to a married woman, where her husband is not the father, the birth can be registered to include the name of the natural father if in addition to the above procedures there is:

(a) a statutory declaration by the husband that he is not the father; or

(b) a statutory declaration by the mother indicating that she had been living apart from her husband for more than ten months prior to the birth under a decree of *divorce a mensa et thoro* or a deed of separation; or

(c) a court order naming the father.

If there is no father's name on a birth certificate, the birth can be registered to have the father's name inserted. The procedures are similar to those outlined above. The birth of a child must be registered within three months of the child's birth.

If a child is born before the mother and the father get married to each other the birth can be registered under the Legitimacy Act 1931. If the father's name is not to be on the birth certificate then the column for the father's name and occupation is left blank. Sometimes a married woman who is pregnant by another man will change her name by deed poll to allow the father and mother to have the same surnames on the birth certificate. If a husband's name has been put down as the father and the wife subsequently admits that he is not the father it is possible to have a registration changed on the basis that there is an error of fact or substance on the record.

Generally, the Registrar General's office at 8/11 Lombard Street, Dublin 2 are very helpful with any queries.

12.16 Deed Poll

Sometimes a cohabiting woman may want to change her surname to that of her boyfriend. She can do this by executing a deed poll which is enrolled in the High Court. The surname of a child born within marriage may not be changed without the husband's consent. However, if the husband does not consent one can write to the Registrar of the High Court explaining the position. The matter can then be brought before the President of the High Court for a decision. A married woman may revert to her maiden name without the necessity of a change by deed poll.

12.17 Protection Against Violence

The Domestic Violence Act 1996 extended the protection of barring and protection orders to cohabitees. The Domestic Violence Act 1996 came into force on 27 March 1996 and substantially extended the jurisdiction and powers of the District Court and the penalties available to deal with cases of domestic violence. The Act is discussed in Chapter 10.

12.18 Property Rights

A cohabitee is not protected by the Family Home Protection Act 1976. Further, the Family Law Act 1995, s. 36 and the Family Law (Divorce) Act 1996, s. 15(1)(b) do not apply to property disputes between unmarried couples unless the couple were engaged. Section 5 of the Family Law Act 1981 sets out the law applicable to the determination of disputes regarding property which arise between people whose agreement to marry was terminated. Section 44 of the Family Law (Divorce) Act 1996 clarifies an ambiguity in s. 36(8) of the Family Law Act 1995 by providing that the latter section shall apply to the parties to an engagement which has terminated, as if the parties to the agreement were married to each other, in relation to property in which either or both of them had a beneficial interest while the agreement was in force.

The determination of property disputes between a cohabiting couple remains outside the ambit of the family law courts. The only avenue left open to such a couple is to bring an application under the Partition Acts 1868–1876.

12.19 Cohabitation Agreements

Cohabiting by the voluntary act of living together as husband and wife to the exclusion of others but in circumstances where the parties are not married to one another is differentiated by the law from marital cohabitation in that there is no legal recognition of the relationship if it breaks down.

In Ireland, a cohabiting couple is not recognised as a 'family' even in circumstances where the parties have lived together for a number of years, or where they have children and effectively live as a family as recognised under the Constitution. The High Court decision of *Ennis v Butterly* [1997] 1 ILRM 28 is sigificant in that it gave the court an opportunity to consider the legal status of cohabitation agreements. It was noted that the position in England and Wales was succinctly stated by Millet J in *Windeler v Whitehall* [1990] 2 FLR 505 in the following terms:

'If this were California this would be a claim of palimony, but it is England and it is not. English law recognises neither the term nor the obligation to which it gives effect. In this country a husband has a legal obligation to support his wife even if they are living apart. A man has no legal obligation to support his mistress even if they are living together.'

Kelly J in *Ennis v Butterly* cited the foregoing decision with approval, noting that:

'the law in [Ireland] is no different and, if anything, would lean more strongly against [cohabitation contracts] having regard to the special position of marriage under the Constitution.'

Marriage and the family under the Constitution are afforded a particular place in society and are protected by the State in its laws. It is the policy of the State and the law to ensure that marriage and the family founded in the Constitution remain intact. In those circumstances, de facto families are outside the ambit of this constitutional protection. Indeed, as Kelly J stated in *Ennis v Butterly* at p. 42):

'To permit an express cohabitation contract . . . to be enforced would give it a similar status in law as a marriage contract. It did not have such a status prior to the coming into effect of the Constitution, rather such contracts were regarded as illegal and unenforceable as a matter of public policy. Far from enhancing the position at law of such contracts the Constitution requires marriage to be guarded with special care.'

In summary, the decision of the High Court in *Ennis v Butterly* is clear. Non-marital contracts are not recognised by Irish law as such contracts are contrary to public policy and are unenforceable. Finally, as Kelly J opines (at p. 39):

'This absence of intervention on the part of the legislature suggests to me that it accepts that it would be contrary to public policy, as enunciated in the Constitution, to confer legal rights on persons in non-marital unions akin to those who are married.'

CHAPTER 13

ADOPTION

13.1 Introduction

Before addressing the substantive law on adoption it is important to put adoption in context. Adoption was legalised in this jurisdiction by the enactment of the Adoption Act 1952. Since the enactment of the Adoption Act 1952, dramatic changes have occurred in the whole area of adoption, so much so that adoption as it was understood in the 1950s has more or less ceased to exist. This can largely be attributed to a lessening of the social stigma attached to the birth of a child outside marriage and to the improved social and financial services available to single parents. It should be borne in mind that the Unmarried Mother's Allowance first became available in 1973. Up until then it was very difficult, if not impossible, for an unmarried mother to retain custody of her own child, unless the mother herself came from a liberally-minded and financially comfortable family.

13.2 Legal Consequences of Adoption

Section 24 of the Adoption Act 1952 provides:

Upon an adoption order being made:

(a) The child shall be considered with regard to the rights and duties of parents and children in relation to each other as the child of the adopter or adopters born to him, her or them in lawful wedlock;

(b) The mother or guardian shall lose all parental rights and be freed from all parental duties with respect to the child.

Consequently when an adoption order is made the legal nexus between the natural parents and their child ceases completely.

If, for instance, a maintenance order has been in existence directing the father to pay the mother periodic maintenance in respect of a child, and the child is adopted, the said maintenance order ceases to have any effect. Similarly, an order granting the father access to his child would also lapse: see *W.O'R. v E.H.* [1996] 2 IR 248. Furthermore, the adopted child has no rights against its natural parents under the Succession Act 1965, the Status of Children Act 1987 or otherwise.

13.3 Role of Adoption Board

The Adoption Board ('An Bord Uchtála') consists of a chairman and eight ordinary members. It is the Board (and not a court) which makes adoption orders. The Board registers adoption societies and offers advice and guidelines to adoption societies and Health Boards, and through its social workers it monitors placements. Furthermore, pursuant to the Adoption Act 1991, the Adoption Board has the function of deciding whether or not to recognise foreign adoption orders and to make preliminary decisions in relation to the suitability and eligibility of persons who want to adopt children in other jurisdictions.

Up until 1979 there was some legal uncertainty in relation to the Constitutional position of the Adoption Board. Article 37.1 of the Constitution provides:

> *Nothing in this Constitution shall operate to invalidate the exercise of limited functions and powers of a judicial nature, in matters other than criminal matters, by any person or body of persons duly authorized by law to exercise such functions and powers, notwithstanding that such person or such body of persons is not a judge or a court appointed or established as such under this Constitution.*

In the course of a number of cases which came before the High Court and Supreme Court in the 1970s it was argued (though never decided by any court) that the Adoption Board was acting unconstitutionally because it was acting in a judicial capacity. Because of this legal uncertainty a referendum was held in 1979 and the Sixth Amendment of the Constitution Act was passed which inserts at Article 37.2 the following:

> *No adoption of a person taking effect or expressed to take effect at any time after the coming into operation of this Constitution under laws enacted by the Oireachtas and being an adoption pursuant to an order made or an authorisation given by any person or body of persons designated by those laws to exercise such functions and powers was or shall be invalid by reason only of the fact that such person or body of persons was not a judge or a court appointed or established as such under this Constitution.*

There are various different circumstances which may give rise to an adoption, including the following:

(a) adoption by a married couple of a child who has been placed with them by an adoption society;

(b) adoption by the natural mother and her spouse;

(c) adoption by the natural father and his spouse;

(d) adoption by foster parents;

(e) foreign adoptions.

13.4 Role of Adoption Societies

The role of a registered adoption society in the context of the adoption process is to act as an intermediary or 'go-between' between the natural parent or parents on the one hand and the prospective adopters on the other hand. It is the role of the adoption society to place the child for adoption with suitable prospective adopters, to monitor the placement and to provide back-up counselling and other social services for both the natural parent (or parents) and the prospective adopters.

13.5 Persons Capable of Adopting

Those capable of adopting are:

(a) a married couple living together;

(b) the natural mother;

(c) the natural father;

(d)   a relative of the child (pursuant to the definition given to 'a relative' in the 1952 Act, a relative was only traceable through the mother of the child; however, pursuant to the Adoption Act 1998, the definition of 'relative' has been widened so as to include relatives traceable through the father of the child);

(e)   a widow;

(f)   a widower (under the Adoption Act 1974, s. 5 there were certain restrictions placed on the adoption by widowers which did not apply to widows. This provision of the Act was held to be unconstitutional in *T.O'G. v Attorney General* [1985] 5 ILRM 61);

(g)   a married man or a married woman who is legally separated or who has been deserted;

(h)   a single person (pursuant to the Adoption Act 1991, s. 10).

The potential adopter must be of good moral character, must have sufficient means to maintain a child, must be of good health and must be a suitable person to act as a parent.

The potential adopter (or adopters) must be ordinarily resident in the State and have been so resident during the year ending at the date of the making of the adoption order (Adoption Act 1991, s. 10(6)).

13.6   Children Capable of Adoption

An adoption order may be made in respect of a child who is:

(a)   an orphan;

(b)   a non-marital child;

(c)   a legitimated child whose birth has not been re-registered under the Legitimacy Act 1931;

(d)   an abandoned child (where in High Court proceedings it has been established that the parents of the child have for physical or moral reasons failed in their duty towards the child).

Originally, pursuant to the Adoption Act 1952, 'a child' was any person under 21 years of age, but now, pursuant to the Adoption Act 1998, no-one over the age of 18 years can be adopted.

The nationality or citizenship of the child is irrelevant but the child must be resident in the State. Pursuant to the Adoption Act 1974, s. 8, a child cannot be adopted unless he has attained the age of six weeks.

Pursuant to the Adoption Act 1952, s. 10 (as amended), if a child is over 7 years of age at the date of the application for his adoption the Board is under a statutory obligation to give due consideration to his wishes, having regard to his age and understanding.

13.7   Who May 'Place' a Child for Adoption

The following may place a child for adoption:

(a)   a Health Board;

(b)   a registered adoption society;

(c)   a parent, provided the child is being placed with a relative.

Subject to certain exceptions and pursuant to the 1952 Act, s. 7A (as inserted by the Adoption Act 1998, s. 4) an adoption agency shall not place a child for adoption unless the child has attained the age of four weeks.

13.8 Religious Requirements

The Adoption Act 1952, s. 12(2), provided that the child had to be of the same religion as the adopters, which meant that a married couple who were each of a different religion were not capable of adopting. In *M v An Bord Uchtála* [1975] IR 81 this provision of the 1952 Act was held to be unconstitutional. The situation is now governed by the Adoption Act 1974, s. 4, which stipulates that a person whose consent is required for the adoption must be informed of the religion of the adoptive parents.

Since most adoption societies are run under the auspices of the Roman Catholic Church, it is very difficult in practice for non-Catholic couples or couples of mixed religions to adopt a child.

13.9 Placement of Child for Adoption

This is the process whereby a mother agrees to put forward her child for adoption and places the child with an adoption society or directly with a prospective adopter or adopters (in circumstances where the prospective adopter or adopters are related to the child). This process is often referred to as the first (or initial) consent. However this process is an *agreement* rather than a *consent*. Finlay P, as he then was, distinguished between the two in *S v Eastern Health Board* (unreported, February 1979, High Ct, Finlay P) when he pointed out that an agreement, unlike a consent, was only capable of being rescinded by mutual agreement. If an adoption society or Health Board is placing the child for adoption the mother will be requested to sign a formal agreement to place, which is known as Form 10. The natural father of the child is only required to agree to the placing of a child for adoption if the child is a legitimated child or if the father is the guardian of the child or if he has custody of the child. The mother's agreement (and the father's when it is required) must be free and in the full knowledge of the consequences of placing a child for adoption: see *G v An Bord Uchtála* [1980] IR 32.

13.10 Consents Required

An adoption order cannot be made unless the child's mother or guardian or any person having charge or control over the child consents to the making of the adoption order. The father's consent is required in the case of a legitimate child or in the case where the father is the guardian or custodian of the child.

A consent is not valid unless the child has attained six weeks of age and it cannot be given earlier than three months before the application for adoption: see *Re J* [1966] IR 295.

Under the 1952 Act, s. 15(2) (as amended) the Board is under a duty to satisfy itself that every person whose consent is necessary has given his or her consent and fully understands the nature and effect of the consent and of an adoption order. In the course of his judgment in *McL. v An Bord Uchtála and Attorney General* [1977] IR 287, O'Higgins CJ stated:

> 'Section 15(2) imposes a statutory obligation on the Board to be satisfied that not merely has the formality of a written consent been observed, but that it is a genuine and real

consent in the sense that its nature and effect are fully understood by the person consenting'.

In this case the mother had signed her 'final' consent some 11 months after her child had been placed with prospective adopters, and very shortly after signing her consent she married the father of her child. The court held that at the time she signed the consent the mother did not know that she was still entitled to revoke her consent before the adoption order was made. The court held that the adoption order was void for this reason and for the further reason that although she was entitled to be heard by the Adoption Board, she was not informed of the date when the application for adoption was listed for hearing. As a consequence of this case the Adoption Act 1976 was enacted, which rendered valid all consents given and orders made prior to its enactment insofar as they might have been invalid by reason of the defects existing in the case. The 1976 Act, s. 3(1)(a) provides that a person whose consent is necessary is to be informed of his or her right to withdraw it at any time prior to the making of the order and of his or her right to be heard on the application for the order. Section 3(2) of the 1976 Act provides that if a person does not wish to be heard by the Board or to be consulted again in relation to the order, the Board does not have to inform or consult him or her.

Section 39 of the 1952 Act places an onerous duty on adoption societies to explain the consequences and effect of adoption and the consents involved.

13.11 The Role of the Natural Father

13.11.1 INTRODUCTION

The role of the natural father under the Adoption Act 1952 (as originally enacted) was very limited. Pursuant to the Adoption Act 1952, s. 16(1), the father was not listed amongst the categories of persons who are entitled to be heard by the Adoption Board on an application for an adoption order. By virtue of being a person having charge of or control over a child, the father (not as a father *per se*) has a right under the 1952 Act to be heard by the Board, and indeed by virtue of being a person having charge or control over a child he is someone whose consent is required for the making of the adoption order.

The role of the natural father *per se* was given some limited statutory recognition in the Adoption Act 1964 pursuant to which the father's consent is required in relation to a child legitimated by the subsequent marriage of his or her parents whose birth has not been re-registered under the Legitimacy Act 1931. (Where such child's birth is re-registered, parental consent is not, of itself, sufficient for an adoption order to be made as the child is then regarded as a legitimate child born to married parents.)

The role of the natural father in the adoption process was improved significantly by the enactment of the Status of Children Act 1987. Pursuant to this Act the natural father can now apply to court to be appointed a guardian of his child and if such order is made then the father becomes a person whose consent is required for the making of an adoption order. The father in effect gets into a 'veto' situation because an adoption order cannot be made unless he so consents and his consent cannot be dispensed with unless he had in the first place agreed to the placement of the child for adoption.

13.11.2 CONSTITUTIONAL POSITION

The constitutional rights of the natural father were considered at great length in *State (Nicolaou) v An Bord Uchtála* [1966] IR 567. It was submitted on behalf of Nicolaou that the Adoption Act 1952 discriminated against him by according a status to the mother which was not accorded to the father contrary to Article 40.1 of the Constitution. This submission was unequivocally rejected by the Supreme Court and the court also held that the Act was not contrary to Article 40.3 as the father 'had no personal rights in relation to the child'; nor was it contrary to Articles 41 and 42 as these Articles related solely to a family and parenthood based on marriage.

The constitutional position of the natural father came up for debate again in the Supreme Court in *J.K. v V.W.* [1990] 2 IR 437 when the Supreme Court had an opportunity of revisiting the judgment in the *Nicolaou* case. However, the Supreme Court again quite categorically concluded that a natural father does not have a constitutional or natural right to the guardianship of his child. The Supreme Court held that the right of the natural father conferred by statute and not by the Constitution was merely a right to apply for guardianship. (In *J.K. v V.W.* [1990] 2 IR 437 the father obtained an order for custody and guardianship in the Circuit Court but ultimately he lost on the mother's appeal to the High Court after the case had been stated by that court to the Supreme Court.) Subsequent to the ultimate determination of this case by the High Court the natural father instituted a case in the European Court of Human Rights arguing that his rights under Articles 6 and 8 of the European Convention on Human Rights and Fundamental Freedoms had been violated. In its judgment in *Keegan v Ireland* (1994) 18 EHRR 342 the court stated:

'The fact that Irish law permitted the secret placement of the child for adoption without the applicant's knowledge or consent, leading to the bonding of the child with the proposed adopters and to the subsequent making of an adoption order, amounts to an interference with his right to respect for family life.'

The court also found that the father had no rights under Irish law to challenge the decision to place his child for adoption, either before the Adoption Board or before the courts, or any standing in the adoption procedure generally.

13.11.3 ADOPTION ACT 1998

Whilst the judgment of the European Court of Human Rights in *Keegan v Ireland* (1994) 18 EHRR 342 was not binding on Irish domestic law, new procedures were introduced by the Adoption Board into the adoption process quite soon afterwards to give the natural father an opportunity, where possible, to appear before the Board before any adoption order was made. Immediately after the European Court's judgment in *Keegan v Ireland* the Government set about introducing legislation to give statutory effect to the rationale of the European Court of Human Right's judgment and after some time the Adoption Act 1998 was enacted.

By virtue of the Adoption Act 1998 the natural father now has statutory rights during the course of the adoption process and pursuant to s. 5 of the Act he has a right to be heard by the Adoption Board prior to the making of any adoption order. More importantly however, adoption societies are obliged to make every reasonable effort to involve the natural father during the pre-placement stage. If the identity of the father is known to the adoption agency, the agency shall before placing the child for adoption take such steps as are reasonably practicable to consult the father for the purpose of:

(a) informing him of the proposed placement;

(b) explaining to him the legal implications of, and the procedures relating to, adoption; and

(c) ascertaining whether or not he objects to the proposed placement.

If the father indicates to the adoption agency that he has no objection to the placement, the adoption agency may at any time thereafter place the child for adoption. If the father objects to the proposed placement of the child for adoption, the agency must notify the father and the mother that it is deferring the placement for a period not being less than 21 days for the purpose of affording the father an opportunity to make an application under the Guardianship of Infants Act 1964, as amended by the Status of Children Act 1987. If the father issues such proceedings then the adoption agency shall not place the child for adoption until the proceedings are concluded. If the natural father does not indicate that he has any objections to the proposed placement or if, having done so, he does not issue the aforementioned proceedings the adoption agency may after a period of time place the child for adoption.

If an adoption agency is unable to consult the father it shall notify the Adoption Board to that effect and the Board may, where it is satisfied that the agency has taken such steps as are reasonably practicable to consult the father, authorise the agency to place the child for adoption.

Furthermore, if the Board is satisfied that, having regard to the nature of the relationship between the father and mother and the circumstances of the conception of the child, it would be inappropriate for the agency to contact the father in respect of the placement of the child, the Board may authorise the agency to place the child for adoption.

Furthermore, the Board has power to authorise the adoption agency to place a child for adoption in certain circumstances notwithstanding that the mother has refused to reveal the identity of the child's father.

13.11.4 LIMITATIONS ON RIGHTS OF NATURAL FATHER

Whilst the rights of the natural father have been improved significantly by virtue of the Status of Children Act 1987 and the Adoption Act 1998, the constitutional and statutory rights of the father are still very limited relative to the rights of the natural mother. The weight to be attached to the natural father's rights and the strength of his position in the adoption process will very much depend on the facts and circumstances of each case. The Adoption Board and the courts have enormous discretion. The essence of the rights given to the natural father pursuant to the Adoption Act 1998 is to give him a say and a fair hearing during each stage of the adoption process. The most important right of the natural father in the entire adoption process is the right to apply for guardianship and custody under the Guardianship of Infants Act 1964 and the Status of Children Act 1987 because, as already stated, by virtue of obtaining guardianship or custody the father becomes a person whose consent is required for the making of an adoption order, and no adoption order can then be made without his consent. Also, as stated earlier, his consent cannot be dispensed with unless he has already been a party to an agreement to place (which a natural father would not be a party to if he objected to an adoption in the first place). See *K.C. and A.C. v An Bord Uchtála* [1985] 5 ILRM 302, also known as *In re J.H.* [1985] IR 375. In this case, when the natural mother placed her child for adoption and signed Form 10 she was unmarried. Subsequent to giving her 'final' consent she revoked her consent and married the father of the child, thus making the child a legitimated child. The prospective adopters made an application, pursuant to the Adoption Act 1974, s. 3, to have the natural mother's and natural father's consents dispensed with, but this was dismissed, and Lynch J held that the natural father's consent was not capable of being dispensed with, given that he had not agreed to the placement of his child.

13.11.5 CASE LAW

Since the enactment of the Status of Children Act 1987 there have been many applications (usually to the District Court) by natural fathers to be appointed guardians of children in circumstances where the natural mother has either placed the child for adoption or intends to do so. This was the situation in *J.K. v V.W.* [1990] 2 IR 437 though neither the Supreme Court nor the High Court gave much guidance on how such a guardianship application should be determined in circumstances where an adoption is pending. This issue or question arose again for the Supreme Court in *W.O'R. v E.H.* (unreported, 23 July 1996, Supreme Ct). This was a consultative case stated by the Circuit Family Court in Cork to the Supreme Court. In this case the applicant father had been involved in a relationship with the respondent mother from 1981 until 1992, during which time two children were born to the parties, a daughter on 31 May 1982 and a son on 2 July 1991. Having lived together as a family for six years, the mother and father separated when their son was 11 months old and some 14 months later the natural mother married another man. Shortly after the natural mother married she and her husband applied to the Adoption Board for an adoption order in respect of her two children, and the natural father applied to the District Court for an order appointing him a guardian. The natural father's application was refused by the District Court and he appealed to the Circuit Family Court at which stage His Honour Judge Moran referred the matter to the Supreme Court. The natural father had been exercising access to his children and had obtained an access order from the District Court. The Adoption Board indicated that they would not make an adoption order in favour of the respondent and her husband until the said access order had been vacated (since the Adoption Act 1952, s. 24(b) provides that the mother or the guardian of a child, on an adoption order being made, shall lose all parental rights and be free from all parental duties with respect to the child).

The learned Circuit Court judge submitted for the determination of the Supreme Court the following questions:

(1) On hearing of an application by a natural father to be appointed guardian under the Guardianship of Infants Act 1964, s. 6A, is it proper for the court to take into account a specific pending application for adoption of the children of the natural parents by the natural mother's husband when deciding whether or not to appoint the natural father as a guardian to his children, in particular in circumstances where the natural father is not seeking to change the custodial status of the children?

(2) If the answer to (1) above is in the affirmative, is it proper for the court to take into account the natural father's intention to oppose the adoption application?

(3) If the answer to (1) above is in the affirmative, is it proper for the court to have regard to this specific adoption application pending?

(4) What are the character and extent of the rights of interest or concern of the natural father (referred to by the Supreme Court in the decision of *J.K. v V.W.* [1990] 2 IR 437) and when do same arise in the context of a guardianship application and are such matters within the sole discretion of the trial judge?

(5) Is the concept of de facto family ties as referred to in the European Court of Human Rights decision of *Keegan v Ireland* (1994) 18 EHRR 342 afforded recognition under the Constitution and what rights, if any, accrue to the applicant arising from same?

(6) Is a natural father's right to apply for guardianship and/or access or an order for access already made extinguished on the making of an adoption order?

(7) If the answer to (6) above is in the negative, does the Adoption Board have the right to direct that an access order already made be vacated before making an adoption order?

Five interesting judgments were delivered in the Supreme Court by Hamilton CJ, O'Flaherty J, Denham J, Barrington J and Murphy J.

In his judgment Hamilton CJ answered questions (1), (2), (3), and (6) in the affirmative and all four other judges concurred with him though their reasoning differed to some extent. All five judges gave their individual responses to questions (4) and (5), which could not be simply answered in the affirmative or in the negative and since question (6) was answered in the affirmative question 7 did not arise for determination.

It will be seen from the Supreme Court judgments in the above case that the natural mother's wish to have her child adopted and the natural father's opposition to such adoption must be taken into consideration by the court when determining that natural father's application. However, Hamilton CJ stated in his judgment that:

'The trial judge must however make his own decisions based on his own independent assessment of the whole case as presented to him and should not regard his decision as merely a means of predetermining the outcome of the adoption proceedings in favour of any party.'

Up until the decision of the Supreme Court in *W.O'R. v E.H.* [1996] 2 IR 248 there was uncertainty as to whether or not the Adoption Board could make an adoption order in circumstances where the natural father was exercising access to his child pursuant to a court order and the view of the Adoption Board, until the judgment in this case, was that an adoption order should not be made in such circumstances. Quite clearly the Supreme Court determined that any access order in favour of a natural father is extinguished by the making of an adoption order.

13.12 Dispensing with Consents

13.12.1 GENERALLY

Prior to 1974 the Board could only dispense with a mother's consent if:

(a)   she was incapable of giving her consent because of mental infirmity; or

(b)   because she could not be found.

The Adoption Act 1974, s. 3 provides as follows:

(1) In any case where a person has applied for an adoption order relating to a child and any person whose consent to the making of an adoption order relating to the child is necessary and who has agreed to the placing of the child for adoption either

(a) fails, neglects or refuses to give his consent; or

(b) withdraws a consent already given,

the applicant for the adoption order may apply to the High Court for an order under this section.

(2) The High Court, if it is satisfied that it is in the best interests of the child so to do, may make an order under this section:

(a) giving custody of the child to the applicant for such period as the court may determine, and

(b) authorising the Board to dispense with the consent of the other person referred to in sub-section (1) of this section to the making of an adoption order in favour of the applicant during the period aforesaid.

(We will see later on that in very restricted circumstances and pursuant to the Adoption Act 1988 an adoption order can be made where a child has been abandoned notwithstanding that the mother (or father) has not agreed to the placing of the child for adoption).

It will be seen from the above that before the court can make an order authorising the Adoption Board to dispense with the mother's consent (and father's consent if required) the court must be satisfied that a valid agreement to place exists.

13.12.1 CASE LAW

There is an abundance of case law dealing with what constitutes a valid agreement to place and also dealing with the inter-relationships between the adoption process and the constitutional rights of the natural mother.

It is quite clear from the Supreme Court judgment in *G v An Bord Uchtála* [1980] IR 32 and the judgments in all the subsequent cases that in order for there to be a valid agreement to place it is essential that the natural mother must be fully informed of her rights including the right to give or withhold consent at any time before the making of an adoption order. In the course of his judgment in *G v An Bord Uchtála*, Walsh J stated:

> 'I am satisfied that having regard to the natural rights of the mother, the proper construction of the provision in section 3 of the Act of 1974 is that the consent, if given, must be such as to amount to a fully informed, free and willing surrender or an abandonment of these rights. However, I am also of the opinion that such a surrender or abandonment may be established by her conduct when it is such as to warrant the clear and unambiguous inference that such was her fully informed, free and willing intention. In my view a consent motivated by fear, stress or anxiety or consent or conduct dictated by poverty or other deprivations does not constitute a valid consent.'

A strict interpretation and application of the judgment of Walsh J would make it almost impossible to establish to the satisfaction of the court that a valid agreement to place exists and McWilliam J in *McF v G* [1983] 2 ILRM 228 endeavoured to give a practical interpretation and application to the judgment of Walsh J when he stated:

> 'I am of opinion that these considerations must be considered from a practical point of view. The mere fact of having an illegitimate child causes stress and anxiety and, if there were plenty of money, arrangements could be made for care and accommodation without the necessity of involving the Adoption Board at an early stage. But in most cases there is stress and anxiety and there is not sufficient money and there is not adequate accommodation and if absolute rules as to fear, stress, anxiety or poverty were to be applied there could hardly be a case found in which one or other of them would not be present so that it could be argued a consent was not valid.'

In *S.H. v E.H.B.* (unreported, February 1979, High Ct, Finlay P) the agreement to place was mutually rescinded when the prospective adopters returned the child to the natural mother at her request. Subsequently the natural mother changed her mind and returned the child to the prospective adopters. At the time of returning the child to the prospective adopters she did not sign another agreement to place (which she had previously done). However, she did sign her final consent to the making of an adoption order. Some two weeks after giving her final consent the mother once again changed her mind and requested the return of her child. The prospective adopters refused to do so on this occasion and they subsequently instituted proceedings under s. 3 of the Act. Finlay P (as he then was) held that by signing the consent to the making of an adoption order the natural mother had also agreed to the placing of her child for adoption. He held therefore that there was a valid agreement to place and that the court should dispense with the natural mother's consent.

In *McC v An Bord Uchtála* [1982] 2 ILRM 159 the circumstances were similar. In this particular case McWilliam J found that the initial agreement to place was invalid. However, he held that by virtue of the mother signing the 'final' consent to adoption she had also validly agreed to the placing of her child for adoption so as to permit the court to make an order under s. 3 of the 1974 Act.

In *Re D.G. (an infant)* [1991] 1 IR 40, otherwise known as *O.G. v An Bord Uchtála* [1991] 1 ILRM 154, Finlay CJ in the course of his judgment stated:

> 'A mother agreeing to place a child for adoption could not be said to reach a fully informed decision so to agree, unless at the time she made the agreement she was aware that the right which she undoubtedly had to withdraw that consent or to refuse further

to consent to adoption, is subject to the possibility that, upon application by the prospective adopting parents, the court could conclude that it was in the best interests of the child to dispense with the mother's consent and if following upon such decision the Board decided it was appropriate to order the adoption of the child, she, the mother, could lose forever the custody of the child.'

It will be noted from these judgments that 'consent' and 'agreement' are used inter-changeably (perhaps mistakenly).

13.12.3 BEST INTERESTS OF THE CHILD

If the prospective adopters in their proceedings under the Adoption Act 1974, s. 3, get over the first hurdle of establishing that there was a valid agreement to place they must also then establish to the satisfaction of the court that it is in the best interests of the child to have the consent dispensed with. The status quo and the time factor are of crucial importance when determining the best interests of the child. If a child is placed with prospective adopters at four weeks old and if by the time the court hears a s. 3 application the child has been living with the prospective adopters for two or more years, then the prospective adopters would normally have no difficulty in establishing that it is in the best interests of the child to have the consent dispensed with.

Conversely, if the child has only been living with the prospective adopters for a few months or if the child has been living with various different sets of carers for different periods of time, then it would be difficult for the prospective adopters to win on the 'best interests' test assuming that the natural mother and her circumstances are capable of providing proper care for her child. There are many cases where it is quite clear what is in the best interests of the child, given the bonding which has occurred between the child and the prospective adopters and the unequal home circumstances and personalities of the prospective adopters on the one hand and the natural mother on the other. However, there are many cases where the 'best interests' test is far from clear and in such circumstances it is usual for the court to rely on the evidence of expert witnesses, particularly consultant child psychiatrists. Consultant child psychiatrists see their role in these cases as giving evidence on behalf of the child as to what his best interests are, irrespective of which side the psychiatrist has been retained by. It is important, however, to note that child psychiatry is no science and that child psychiatrists can differ from one another and be very much influenced by their own personal and professional views and attitudes. Choosing or agreeing on one psychiatrist rather than another can, in some cases, greatly influence or indeed determine the outcome of the case.

In *G. v An Bord Uchtála* [1980] IR 32 a majority of the Supreme Court determined that once the mother had validly agreed to the placement of her child for adoption, any constitutional rights she possessed as a mother cease to be a determining factor that should influence the court's decision in determining what is in the best interests of her child.

13.13 Practice and Procedure in Section 3 (Dispensing with Consent) Applications

All applications pursuant to the Adoption Act 1974, s. 3 must be heard, at first instance, by the High Court. Quite often an application pursuant to the Adoption Act 1974, s. 3 is brought in response to an application for custody by the natural mother (and/or father) which may have been instituted in the Circuit Family Court pursuant to the Guardianship of Infants Act 1964, and if this is the case the guardianship/custody proceedings would normally be remitted to the High Court to be heard at the same time as the adoption case.

13.13.1 WHEN ACTING FOR A NATURAL MOTHER

When a practitioner is consulted by a natural mother who has placed her child for adoption and who wants to regain custody of her child it is absolutely essential that he acts immediately because the longer the prospective adopters have de facto custody of the child the stronger their case becomes in relation to establishing that the best interests of the child is to stay with them. When consulted by a natural mother in these circumstances it is quite often the case that the natural mother would not know the identity of the prospective adopters; in such circumstances a letter should be sent to the adoption society requesting (or indeed demanding) the return of the child. A copy of this letter should also be sent to the Adoption Board. If the child is not returned immediately then it is essential that an application for custody be issued immediately. An application for custody can be issued at first instance in the District Court, the Circuit Court or the High Court. If issuing proceedings in the High Court such proceedings can be instituted pursuant to the Guardianship of Infants Act 1964 by way of special summons or alternatively by issuing habeas corpus proceedings. If it is expected that the prospective adopters will contest any application for custody and issue proceedings under the Adoption Act 1974, s. 3, then it is advisable that the natural mother's custody proceedings are issued in the High Court, so as to avoid delay. If the proceedings are issued in the District Court or the Circuit Court very long delays can be caused in having the case determined by a court. If, for instance, the custody proceedings are issued in the District Court or the Circuit Court the legal representatives for the prospective adopters might wait until nearer the hearing date of the said proceedings before applying for an adjournment on the grounds that they intend to issue proceedings in the High Court under the Adoption Act 1974, s. 3, and this could increase the delay in having the case heard by several months.

13.13.2 WHEN ACTING FOR PROSPECTIVE ADOPTERS

The reality of the situation is that the longer the prospective adopters have de facto custody of the child the stronger their case becomes in relation to the best interests test. Just because a natural mother is taking longer than expected to sign her 'final' consent is no reason for the prospective adopters to go rushing in to the High Court on foot of a s. 3 application. Prospective adopters should be advised to postpone issuing a s. 3 application until time has elapsed or until they are forced to do so in response to the natural mother's application for custody. An application pursuant to s. 3 of the Adoption Act 1974 on behalf of prospective adopters is instigated by way of special summons in the High Court grounded on an affidavit sworn by the prospective adopters. The High Court procedures ensure that anonymity is maintained in adoption cases and the parties are known by their initials and any identifiable information is either specifically excluded from the pleadings or simply tippexed therefrom. The prospective adopters are the applicants in any such proceedings and An Bord Uchtála are the respondents. Proceedings are served on the Chief State Solicitor as solicitors for An Bord Uchtála. The Adoption Board, in conjunction with the Chief State Solicitor's Office, arranges for the proceedings to be served on the natural mother and subsequently, by way of a notice of motion to the High Court, the natural mother is made a notice party to the proceedings. In circumstances where the natural mother herself has issued custody proceedings, arrangements are made to have the prospective adopters made a notice party to her proceedings. The natural mother's custody proceedings and the prospective adopters' adoption proceedings would be set down for hearing by the same judge on at least two separate days. So that anonymity can be maintained each party gives evidence in court on separate days without the other party being present (except for the other party's legal representatives).

13.13.3 WHEN ACTING FOR A NATURAL FATHER

As already mentioned, no adoption can occur if the natural father has been appointed a joint guardian of the child (unless he so consents). Consequently, where an adoption is being contemplated by the natural mother, it is of vital importance for the natural father to apply to court for guardianship, assuming that the natural mother does not agree to him being so appointed. However, it may not be appropriate for proceedings to be issued on behalf of the natural father pursuant to the Status of Children Act 1987 shortly after the child's birth, because to do so might encourage the natural mother to take up a defensive position and not allow the natural father to have any contact with the child which she might otherwise have allowed. In advance and in anticipation of a guardianship application by the natural father it is important that he should establish as much meaningful contact with the child as possible and to do so in a manner which avoids or minimises hostility. The natural father's application for guardianship will be determined in accordance with the criteria set out in the Guardianship of Infants Act 1964, s. 3, and in accordance with the judgment delivered by the Supreme Court in *W.O'R. v E.H.* [1996] 2 IR 248 already mentioned.

13.14 Adoption Act 1988

The Adoption Act 1988 permits the non-consensual adoption of a child, including but not limited to a marital child, in exceptional and very limited circumstances.

While an application must, initially, be made to the Health Board, it must be followed by an order of the High Court permitting such adoption. Section 2 of the Adoption Act 1988 only empowers the Health Board to make a conditional order in respect of a child. The second tier of the process, then, involves an application to the court by the Health Board in whose functional area the child is at the relevant time. In the absence of the permission of the High Court, or the Supreme Court on appeal, the adoption cannot proceed.

The court itself, however, may only grant such an adoption if it is satisfied of all of the following:

(a) The parents of the child, for physical or moral reasons, have failed in their duty towards the child for a period of not less than 12 months immediately preceding the making of the application. The failure must, according to the Supreme Court in the Article 26 references of the Adoption (No. 2) Bill 1987 (*In the matter of Article 26 and the Adoption (No. 2) Bill 1987* [1989] IR 656) be 'total' in character. Poverty alone, or other 'externally originating circumstances', will not suffice to amount to a failure for these purposes.

(b) Such failure must be likely to continue without interruption until the child has reached the age of 18. The use of the term 'without interruption' seems to underline the need to prove a total abdication of duty on the parents' part.

(c) Such failure must, furthermore, amount to abandonment on the part of the parents of all parental rights, whether of constitutional or other origin, in respect of the child. In *Western Health Board v An Bord Uchtála* (unreported, 10 November 1995, High Ct) the court refused to make an order in respect of a child of married parents. Lardner J held that there had been a failure on the part of the child's parents, which failure had lasted at least 12 months and was likely, furthermore, to continue until the child was 18 years old. He was not satisfied, however, that the evidence was such as to prove abandonment of parental rights on the parents' part. The Supreme Court agreed, noting that the failures envisaged by (a) and (b) above did not automatically amount to an abandonment of all parental rights. This largely mirrors the comments of the Supreme Court in the Article 26 reference of the

Adoption (No. 2) Bill 1987 at p. 664, where it observed that a failure to carry out parental duties did not automatically, and of itself, amount to an abandonment of rights under (c).

(d)   Finally, it is necessary to establish that because of such failure, it is appropriate that the State 'as guardian of the common good, should supply the place of the parents'.

Each and every one of the foregoing conditions, according to the Supreme Court in *Article 26 reference of the Adoption (No. 2) Bill 1987* at p. 664 is an 'absolutely essential proof'. 'Failure in any one of these proofs', it observed, 'absolutely prohibits the making of an authorised order, no matter how strong might be the evidence available of its desirability from the point of view of the interests of the child'. Even if each of these stipulations is satisfied, however, it will still be necessary to establish to the court's satisfaction that, all things considered, the adoption is in the best interests of the child.

The Adoption Act 1988 passed constitutional scrutiny precisely because it is so rigorous and exacting. It is this very factor that is its biggest drawback. The procedures required by the Act have proved themselves to be 'lengthy and cumbersome' (see the criticisms of Darling, [1994] 4 IJFL 2 at 4) and the requirements thereof often difficult to make out (see *Western Health Board v An Bord Uchtála*).

13.15   Adoption Act 1991

13.15.1   INTRODUCTION

The Adoption Act 1991, as amended by the Adoption Act 1998, was enacted primarily to cover the legal situation relating to Irish people adopting foreign babies from foreign countries, in particular Romania. It deals primarily with the law relating to the recognition of foreign adoptions. However, it also amends existing legislation to allow in certain circumstances the adoption of a child by a single person.

A 'foreign adoption' is comprehensively defined in the Adoption Act 1991, s. 1, and it will be noted from its definition that a foreign adoption must in essence conform with our concept of an adoption.

Section 10 of the Adoption Act 1998 substitutes a new paragraph (a) in the definition of 'foreign adoption' under the 1991 Act, s. 1. The effect of this amendment is that if a simple adoption can be converted into a full adoption in the foreign jurisdiction, the adoption may be recognised as a 'foreign adoption', capable of recognition, provided the consent to the 'full adoption' is obtained.

13.15.2   QUALIFYING ADOPTIONS

In order to qualify for recognition as a foreign adoption under the Adoption Acts 1991–1998, the following conditions must be satisfied:

The first requirement for recognition is that consent to the adoption of all persons necessary under the foreign law has been obtained or dispensed with. The consent to the adoption is therefore dealt with in accordance with the laws of the foreign jurisdiction and so the Act conveniently sidesteps the complications attaching to the issue under Irish domestic adoption law. The Irish court must accept the competence of the foreign jurisdiction to determine the consent requirement.

The second condition outlined in the definition requirement of a 'foreign adoption' is that the 'adoption' made in the foreign jurisdiction is essentially the same as a domestic adoption. Some jurisdictions have quite different concepts of adoption from that in Ireland.

For example, some jurisdictions recognise 'simple adoptions', which do not sever the legal links between the birth family and the child. It is instructive to note that paragraph (b) of the 1991 Act has been substituted by the 1998 Act, as follows:

> *the adoption has, for so long as it is in force, substantially the same legal effect as respects the guardianship of the child in the place where it was effected as an adoption effected by an adoption order.*

This new section is substantially different from the previous one. It is clear from the Parliamentary Debates that the purpose of this amendment was to facilitate the recognition of adoption orders made in jurisdictions like China, where adoptions may be terminated in certain defined circumstances.

The third policy consideration is that the foreign jurisdiction should undertake enquiries into the adopters, the child and the parents or guardians. At the very least, this policy requirement ensures that some rudimentary enquiries are made in both jurisdictions.

The fourth policy requirement is that the court or other authority or person by whom the adoption was effected in the foreign jurisdiction had given due consideration to the interests and welfare of the child, before making the adoption order. The original section 1 of the 1991 Act defined the welfare criterion as follows:

> *(d) the law of the place where the adoption was effected required the court or other authority or person by whom the adoption was effected, before doing so, to give due consideration to the interests and welfare of the child.*

In contrast the new s. 1(d), as substituted by the 1998 Act, s. 10(a)(iii), states:

> *the adoption was effected for the purpose of promoting the interests and welfare of the child, . . .*

The original sections appear to have been directed towards ensuring that the foreign jurisdiction went through some formal determination that the child was suitable for adoption abroad. The substituted section applies, without question, a less onerous standard. Such a standard could be achieved by asserting that the adoption was in fact carried out to promote the interests and welfare of the child, even if the foreign jurisdiction did not have a procedure in place in its laws to ensure that the welfare of the child was considered in advance of an adoption order being made.

The final policy consideration is that no money should have changed hands in relation to the adoption. Only foreign adoptions which satisfy the foregoing policy considerations have been recognised under the 1991 Act. The requirements set out by the legislation as a prerequisite to recognition have proved to be exacting in practice.

13.15.3 ADOPTERS ORDINARILY RESIDENT IN IRELAND

Section 5 of the Adoption Act 1991, as amended by the 1998 Act, s. 13, deals with the recognition of foreign adoptions where the adopters are ordinarily resident in Ireland. The following conditions must be complied with:

(a) the adopters must be eligible to adopt under the 1991 Act, s. 1, as amended by the 1998 Act, s. 10;

(b) the adopters must be ordinarily resident in Ireland on the date of adoption;

(c) where the adoption was effected before 1 April 1992, An Bord Uchtála must declare in writing that it is satisfied that the adopters are persons in whose favour an adoption order may be made under s. 1 as amended; and

(d) where the adoption took place on or after 1 April 1992, An Bord Uchtála must declare in writing before the date on which the adoption was made (i) that the adopters satisfy the provisions of s. 1 as amended, and (ii) that following an assessment by the relevant Health Board or registered adoption society, the adopters are suitable persons under the Adoption Act 1952, s. 13.

13.15.4 REGISTRATION

Pursuant to the Adoption Act 1991, s. 6, the Adoption Board is obliged to establish and maintain a register of foreign adoptions and a certified copy of an entry in the register is evidence that the adoption to which it relates is a foreign adoption deemed to have been effected by a valid adoption order.

CHAPTER 14

CHILD ABDUCTION

14.1   What is Child Abduction?

Child abduction, in simple terms, occurs when a child is removed from a person who has the legal right to custody of the child, referred to as 'the custodial parent', without that person's authority or consent. (The use of the term 'custodial parent' should not obscure the fact that a non-parent may also be awarded custody of a child in certain circumstances and a child may be wrongfully abducted from that person's care and custody also.) Such a situation of wrongful removal constitutes abduction within the meaning of the relevant international Conventions and in Irish law, and both international and domestic law have dedicated provisions aimed at securing the return of the child to the jurisdiction of his or her habitual residence and vindicating the custodial parent's rights.

An act of wrongful retention, where a child is lawfully removed from the jurisdiction of the child's habitual residence to another jurisdiction (e.g. for a holiday or access visit with the consent of the custodial parent) but is unlawfully retained in that jurisdiction and the abductor refuses to return the child to the custodial parent, will also attract sanctions under the relevant Conventions and in domestic law.

Similarly, where a child is taken out of the jurisdiction of the child's habitual residence without the authority or consent of a person who has non-custodial rights in respect of the child (e.g. a legal guardian or a person who has a right of access to the child), steps may also be taken to vindicate such rights under international and domestic law.

As with other crisis situations involving children, the wrongful removal or wrongful retention of children causes great emotional distress to all parties involved and requires swift responses on the part of the person whose rights have been denied and his or her legal advisors. The object of the applicable international and domestic legal regimes is the speedy restoration of the *status quo ante*. The guiding principle is that the courts of the jurisdiction in which the child is habitually resident is the proper forum for the vindication of the rights of the child and for the determination of the best interests of the child. Accordingly, the central aim of the international and domestic legislative framework is to ensure the return of the child to the jurisdiction of his or her habitual residence as quickly as possible and, if there are any disputes, for example, regarding custody of or access to the child, these should be litigated before, and determined by the courts of the jurisdiction of, the child's habitual residence and not by the courts of the jurisdiction into which the child has been abducted. Indeed, the Irish Supreme Court has indicated on a number of occasions, and most recently in the case of *T.M.M. v M.D.* (unreported, 8 December 1999, Supreme Ct, Denham J) that proceedings instituted under the Hague Convention on the Civil Aspects of International Child Abduction 'are intended to be summary and completed in a speedy fashion. This is the type of case which should be on a fast-track management process.'

14.2 International Responses to the Problem

The rise in the number of abductions of children across international frontiers prompted the adoption of the United Nations Convention on the Rights of Child, art. 11, which required member states to take measures to combat child abduction. Arising from this commitment, two further Conventions were drawn up to address the issue, the Hague Convention on the Civil Aspects of International Child Abduction ('the Hague Convention') and the European Convention on Recognition and Enforcement of Decisions Concerning Custody of Children and on Restoration of Custody of Children ('the Luxembourg Convention'), both of which were signed by the original Contracting States in 1980 and brought into force in Ireland on 1 October 1991 with the enactment of the Child Abduction and Enforcement of Court Orders Act 1991. At that time, both Conventions had been operating for almost 11 years. The Hague Convention had been signed by the original Contracting Party States on 25 October 1980 under the auspices of the Hague Conference on private international law. The Luxembourg Convention was initially signed on 20 May 1980 under the auspices of the Council of Europe and, indeed, in 1985 the Irish Law Reform Commission had recommended that Ireland should ratify and implement the Hague Convention and should consider ratifying the Luxembourg Convention: Law Reform Commission Report on the Hague Convention on the Civil Aspects of International Child Abduction and Some Related Matters (LRC 121985) (June 1985).

Prior to the incorporation of the principles of the Conventions into Irish law in 1991, abduction, wrongful removal and wrongful retention disputes which came before the Irish courts were dealt with in accordance with the well-established principle of comity of courts, i.e. the Irish courts recognised and enforced decisions and orders made by courts in jurisdictions with comparable legal systems. While, in general, the principle of comity resulted in the Irish courts recognising the validity of a foreign order, there have been situations in which the Irish courts have refused to return children to the jurisdiction of their habitual residence where to have done so would have resulted in a breach of rights guaranteed under the Irish Constitution. See the cases of: *Northampton County Council v A.B.F. and M.B.F.* [1982] ILRM 164; *Kent County Council v C.S.* [1984] 4 ILRM 472; and *Saunders v Mid-Western Health Board* [1989] ILRM 229. However, the introduction of the principles of the aforesaid Conventions into Irish law in 1991 resulted in a streamlined approach to all cases of abduction, wrongful removal and wrongful retention involving children who had been habitually resident or retained in or removed to the territory of Contracting States.

With regard to abduction of children or wrongful removal from or wrongful retention in a non-contracting State, the pre-existing comity principles apply, and with regard to children brought to or retained in this jurisdiction, it is to be anticipated that, although not bound thereby in such circumstances, the courts will be mindful of the Convention principles in determining such cases: *A.S. v E.H. and R.M.H.* (unreported, May 1996, High Court, Budd J).

14.2.1 THE HAGUE AND LUXEMBOURG CONVENTIONS: GENERAL

As set out above, both the Hague and the Luxembourg Conventions are concerned with securing the expeditious return of abducted children or children who have been wrongfully retained in or improperly removed to a jurisdiction back to the country in which they are (or had been prior to the wrongful removal or retention) habitually resident. This general policy of return is based upon the assumption that the courts of the Contracting States are all equally capable of fairly determining the issues between the parties and of protecting the welfare of children:

> 'The whole jurisdiction under the Convention is, by its nature and purpose, peremptory. Its underlying assumption is that the courts of all its signatory countries are equally capable of ensuring a fair hearing to the parties and a skilled and humane evaluation of

the issues of child welfare involved. Its underlying purpose is to ensure stability for children, by putting a brisk end to the efforts of parents to have their children's future where they want and when they want, by removing them from their country of residence to another jurisdiction chosen arbitrarily by the absconding parent.' (In *P v P (Minors) (Child Abduction)* [1992] 1 FLR 155, cited with approval by Keane J in *Wadda v Ireland*[1994] ILRM 126.)

The Hague Convention has a greater geographical application than the Luxembourg Convention and, at present, the Hague Convention covers 46 countries world-wide (Argentina, Australia, Austria, Bahamas, Belgium, Belize, Republic of Bosnia and Herzegovina, Burkina-Faso, Canada, Chile, Colombia, Costa Rica, Republic of Croatia, Republic of Cyprus, Czech Republic, Denmark, Ecuador, Finland, France, Georgia, Federal Republic of Germany, Greece, Honduras, Hong Kong Special Administrative Region of China, Republic of Hungary, Republic of Ireland, Iceland, Israel, Italy, Grand Duchy of Luxembourg, the former Yugoslav Republic of Macedonia, Republic of Mauritius, Mexico, Principality of Monaco, Moldova, Netherlands, New Zealand, Norway, Panama, Paraguay, Poland, Portugal, Romania, Republic of Slovenia, Spain, St. Kitts & Nevis, Sweden, Switzerland, United Kingdom, United States of America, Republic of Venezuela, Federal Republic of Yugoslavia, Republic of Zimbabwe). Belarus, Brazil, Fiji, Malta, Turkmenistan, Uruguay and Uzbekistan have acceded to the Hague Convention The Luxembourg Convention applies to 24 European countries (Austria, Belgium, Cyprus, Denmark, Finland, France, Germany, Greece, Ireland, Italy, Liechtenstein, Luxembourg, Netherlands, Norway, Poland, Portugal, Spain, Sweden, Switzerland and the United Kingdom).

Similarities between the Conventions include:

(a)   the welfare of the child is of paramount importance;

(b)   both emphasise expeditious processing of applications for return of children;

(c)   both apply to children under 16 years of age;

(d)   both establish Central Authorities to facilitate the operation of the Conventions;

(e)   both emphasise that a decision under the Conventions is not to be taken as a determination on the merits of the custody/access issue;

(f)   both emphasise that in determining whether the child should be returned, the judicial or administrative authority should not adjudicate on the merits of the custody/access issue;

(g)   both envisage that the views of the child should be considered where appropriate;

(h)   both provide 'defences' which may be pleaded by the abducting or retaining party.

The most significant substantive difference between the two Conventions is that, in order to activate the Luxembourg Convention, an applicant must be in a position to demonstrate that he or she has a court order (a *decision* relating to custody), whereas under the Hague Convention, the focus is on a breach of *rights* of custody and it is not necessary to have a formal court order 'confirming' the rights.

The Conventions will be considered in turn.

14.2.2   THE HAGUE CONVENTION

The Hague Convention on the Civil Aspects of International Child Abduction was signed by the original Contracting Party States on 25 October 1980 and has now been ratified by 46 countries world-wide. The central principle of the Convention is that, in cases of wrongful removal or wrongful retention of children in breach of rights of custody, Contracting States are required, in almost every case, to return a child to the jurisdiction of the child's habitual residence.

14.2.2.1 Principal features

Article 1 of the Convention provides that the objectives of the Convention are 'to secure the prompt return of children wrongfully removed to or retained in' a Contracting State and 'to ensure that rights of custody and of access under the law of one Contracting State are effectively respected in the other Contracting States.'

Article 2 commits the Contracting States to taking 'all appropriate measures to secure within their territories' the implementation of the said objectives of the Convention and, to this end, they 'shall use the most expeditious procedures available'.

The removal or retention of a child is stated to be wrongful for the purposes of the Convention (art. 3) where 'it is in breach of rights of custody attributed to a person, an institution or any other body, either jointly or alone, under the law of the State in which the child was habitually resident immediately before the removal or retention' and 'at the time of the removal or retention those rights were actually exercised, either jointly or alone, or would have been so exercised but for the removal or retention.'

In the first instance, therefore, a person, institution or body seeking the return of a child must establish that they enjoyed and actually exercised 'rights of custody' under the law of the State in which the child was habitually resident immediately prior to the removal or retention.

14.2.2.2 Rights of custody

Article 3 of the Convention declares that rights of custody 'may arise in particular by operation of law or by reason of a judicial or administrative decision, or by reason of an agreement having legal effect under the law of that State' and art. 5 defines 'rights of custody' as including rights relating to the care of the person of the child and, in particular, the right to determine the child's place of residence.

The fact that the legal code in another jurisdiction may utilise a different description of the concepts of custody and access is not material. For example, the terms used in the United Kingdom to describe what, in Irish law, are defined as 'custody' and 'access' are 'parental responsibility' and 'contact' respectively. In the decision of *W v W* [1993] 2 FLJ 47 at p. 67, Lardner J held that the right of parental responsibility (as defined in English law) includes the concept of custody.

The proper scope of the term 'rights of custody' received considerable attention in the High Court decision in *H.I. v M.G.* [1999] 2 ILRM 22 and later in the Supreme Court on appeal. The case concerned a child born in New York to an Egyptian father, the plaintiff, and an Irish mother, the defendant. Although the parties went through an Islamic marriage ceremony, the marriage was not recognised by New York law.

As a non-marital father, the plaintiff did not enjoy any automatic rights of custody, although the child's mother never disputed the matter of paternity and he acted as *de facto* joint custodian of his son for five and a half years. Following the removal by the defendant of her son to this jurisdiction, the child's father instituted proceedings pursuant to the Hague Convention. It was agreed by both parties that the issue of the presence or absence of rights of custody on the part of the child's father must be resolved as a preliminary matter. It was argued on behalf of the plaintiff that, as he was entitled to apply to the New York courts for rights to custody of or access to the child once the issue of paternity was formally confirmed, he had inchoate rights in respect of the child which had been breached by the defendant's action in removing the child to Ireland.

In the High Court, Laffoy J noted that the term 'rights of custody' must be construed in a manner which accords with the overall objective of the Convention, such objective being, in the view of the learned judge, to spare children already suffering the effects of the breakdown of their parents' relationship the further disruption suffered when they were taken arbitrarily from their settled environment and moved to another country in the search for a more sympathetic forum or a more convenient base. Thus, in her view, the term should, in most cases, be given the widest possible interpretation.

In this instance, the defendant acknowledged that the plaintiff was the father of the child and Laffoy J thus concluded that the inchoate rights of the plaintiff father to custody, which would almost certainly have crystallised into established rights in the event of the approval by a New York court of the mother's acknowledgement of custody, amounted to rights of custody within the meaning of art. 3 of the Convention.

The Supreme Court reversed the finding of the learned trial judge. Keane J, as he then was, delivering judgment for the majority, noted that the removal of a child in circumstances in which his or her dispossessed parent or other appropriate person or body, not yet having rights of custody, has instituted proceedings for the purpose of securing such rights, shall be wrongful within the meaning of the Convention. Likewise, in the absence of such proceedings, a removal may nonetheless be wrongful as a violation of custodial rights attributed to a *court* which has made an order prohibiting the removal of a child without the consent of the dispossessed party or without a further order of the court itself, since the court's right to determine the custody or to seek to prohibit the removal of the child necessarily involves a determination that, at least until the circumstances change, the child's residence should continue to be in the State in question.

The Supreme Court, however, rejected the assertion that the term 'rights of custody' embraced 'an undefined hinterland of inchoate rights of custody not attributed in any sense by the law of the requesting state to any party asserting them or to the court itself.' On the facts at issue, there were no proceedings in being in New York regarding the plaintiff father's right of custody and neither was there a New York court order prohibiting the defendant from removing the child to another jurisdiction without the consent of the plaintiff or without further order of the court. The plaintiff did not therefore enjoy anything amounting to a right of custody as defined and the Supreme Court ruled that he could not invoke the Hague Convention to secure the return of his child.

14.2.2.3 Habitual residence

The definition of the term 'habitual residence' for the purpose of determining the place of the child's habitual residence prior to his or her wrongful removal or retention has been given considerable judicial attention.

Ms Justice Laffoy in the decision of *Z.S.A. v S.T.* (unreported, August 1996, High Ct, Laffoy J) stated that the determination of the place of the child's habitual residence is a question of fact and is 'not to be treated as a term of art with some special meaning' but, rather, the words are to be given their 'ordinary meaning'. Thus, the matter is not governed, for example, by the same rigid rules of dependency as apply in the context of the law of domicile. (In this regard, see *In the matter of C.M.* [1999] 2 ILRM 103.)

In the case of *K.L. v L.C.* [1993] 2 Fam LJ 79, Blayney J, following the approach of the English courts, ruled that habitual residence is to be equated with ordinary residence.

In the English case of *Barnet London Borough Council v Shah* [1983] 2 AC 309, it was held that, to establish the place of habitual residence of a child, there has to be 'a settled purpose with a sufficient degree of continuity'.

Although it takes time to establish an habitual residence, it was held in the English case of *C v S* [1990] 3 WLR 492 that it takes no time at all to terminate it. If a person leaves a place with a settled intention not to return, the loss of the former habitual residence follows, but while the habitual residence may be lost immediately on departure, a person does not acquire a new habitual residence overnight. In the *C v S* case, less than six months' residence was considered sufficient to establish habitual residence.

The courts will examine the intention of the party seeking to prove that a new place of habitual residence has been established. In the decision of the English Court of Appeal in

Re F [1992] 1 FLR 548, the court approved of the finding of a lower court that a family had acquired a new place of habitual residence after only one month in a new country.

Where habitual residence has been established in a country, it was held in the case of *Oundijan* [1980] 1 FLR 19 that periods of absence, with an intention to return, will not change it.

14.2.2.4 Consent and acquiescence

A deprivation of the right to exercise custody shall not be 'wrongful' if an abducting parent may show evidence of consent to the removal or retention of a child on the part of the dispossessed parent or other relevant person or body, although continued detention without the consent or contrary to the wishes of such a parent may be deemed wrongful. See *N.K. v J.K.* [1994] 3 IR 483.

A consent must be an unconditional one. Thus, a consent conferred by a dispossessed father upon his estranged wife for the purposes of the removal of their children from England to Ireland in order to enable them to set up a new home and life there, when granted on the understanding and condition that he would follow them to their new home in order to effect a reconciliation, shall not suffice: see *M.D. v A.T.D.* (unreported, 6 March 1998, O'Sullivan J). On the facts, O'Sullivan J rejected the father's argument that his consent was a conditional one of the kind described above. Similarly, Morris J concluded in *D.C. v V.L.C.* (unreported, January 1995, High Ct, Morris J) that a statement by one spouse to the effect that the other spouse should leave and take their child with him, for example in the course of an argument, did not constitute a consent to leave the jurisdiction.

The presence of consent does not, however, determine matters. The Supreme Court noted in *B.B. v J.B.* (unreported, 28 July 1997, Supreme Ct) that a trial judge shall retain a discretion to return a child to a parent who has consented to the removal or the retention. The Supreme Court outlined a checklist of eight factors to which a judge exercising his or her discretion should have regard. Thus, a trial judge shall consider, *inter alia*:

(a) the habitual residence of the child at the time of the removal;

(b) the law relating to its custody and access in the place of habitual residence;

(c) the overall policy of the Convention and its objective to secure protection for rights of access;

(d) the need to ensure respect for rights of custody and of access under the law of Contracting States in the laws of other Contracting States;

(e) the circumstances of the child including information relating to the social background of the child;

(f) the nature of the consent in question and the circumstances in which it was given;

(g) any relevant litigation in the place of the child's habitual residence;

(h) any undertaking(s) given.

(The above factors do not represent an exhaustive list, and were considered by O'Sullivan J in *M.D. v A.T.D.* above.)

An 'abducting parent' may seek to resist an allegation of abduction by claiming that the custodial parent acquiesced in the removal or retention of the child. The difference, in this context, between 'consent' and 'acquiescence' is merely one of timing. Consent precedes the wrongful taking or retention, while acquiescence follows it. Acquiescence, like consent, may be active, arising from express words or conduct, or passive, arising by inference from silence or inactivity. It must be real in the sense that the dispossessed parent or institution must be informed of his, her or its general right of objection, but precise knowledge of legal rights and remedies, including the specific remedy under the Convention, is not necessary.

The test to be employed, in this regard, is an objective one and a court must determine whether a parent conducted himself or herself in a manner which is consistent with the seeking of a summary order for a child's return at a later date.

In *P v B* [1995] 1 ILRM 201 endorsing the test set out by Waite J in *W v W (Child Abduction: Acquiescence)* [1993] 3 FLR 211, Budd J in the High Court concluded that as the 'abducting parent' and members of her family had informed the father of the child that she and the child were merely returning to Ireland in order to enable her to recuperate, thereby giving rise to an inference that she would in due course return to the place of the child's habitual residence, a six-month lapse between the date of wrongful return and the date on which the request for return was received by the Irish authorities did not amount to a 'long-term acceptance of a state of affairs' and thus the plaintiff was not precluded from seeking relief pursuant to the Convention. The Supreme Court endorsed this approach on appeal. In *S v S* [1998] 2 IR 244, the Supreme Court likewise concluded that there was no such long-term acceptance by the plaintiff father as he had used the two months prior to the institution of proceedings to secure a reconciliation with his wife and thus to encourage her to return with the children to their place of habitual residence. See also the comments of Donaldson LJ in *Re A (Minors: Abduction: Acquiescence)* [1992] 2 FLR 11.

Therefore, where an applicant can demonstrate to the court that the child in question is under 16 years of age, was the subject of custody or access rights in favour of the applicant, that there has been a breach of those rights and that the child was habitually resident in a Contracting State before the breach thereof, art. 12 directs that, where a period of one year has not yet elapsed since the date of the wrongful removal or retention, the court 'shall order the return of the child forthwith'. Where the proceedings have been commenced after the expiration of a period of one year since the date of the wrongful removal or retention, art. 12 provides that the court 'shall also order the return of the child, unless it is demonstrated that the child is now settled in its new environment'.

14.2.2.5 Delay

In *S v S* [1998] 2 IR 244, the Supreme Court expressed its concern about the fact that some 18 months had expired between the date of the commencement of the High Court proceedings seeking the return of the children in question and the date on which the matter concluded in the Supreme Court. Denham J, noting that delay serves to defeat the purpose of the Convention, referred to the duty on parties and professionals to proceed with all due expedition in cases of this nature. The Supreme Court decision in *P v B (No. 2)* [1999] 2 ILRM 401 espouses the view that a significant culpable delay on the part of the dispossessed party and the inferences which may be raised from such a delay are matters to which a court should have regard when considering whether to return a child to its place of habitual residence. On the facts before it, the court concluded that a delay of over 20 months between the date of removal of the child from her place of habitual residence to this State and the institution of proceedings for return were not adequately explained by the child's dispossessed father. Furthermore, such delay had caused the child in question to spend a critical period of her development in this State and had enabled her to put down roots in her new community. The court concluded that the child was settled, from both a physical and psychological point of view, in her new environment. Reversing the conclusion of the trial judge, the Supreme Court refused to order the return of the child.

14.2.2.6 Relevant considerations

In the consideration of an application for the return of a child under the Convention, the provisions of the Convention quite clearly provide in art. 16 that the court 'shall not decide on the merits of the rights of custody until it has determined that the child is not to be returned' under the Convention or unless an application under the Convention has not been lodged within a reasonable time after receipt of the notice of the wrongful removal or retention.

Accordingly, the Supreme Court has unequivocally determined that, within Hague Convention proceedings, the Irish courts are not required to make enquiries pursuant to the Guardianship of Infants Act 1964, s. 3, regarding the welfare of the child: *P v B* [1994] 3 IR 507, *per* Denham J. Similarly, Lardner J, in the case of *W v W* [1993] 2 FLJ 47, stated that the courts do not have to decide what would be for the long-term benefit of the child.

Similarly, art. 19 provides that 'a decision under this Convention concerning the return of the child shall not be taken to be a determination of the merits of any custody issue.'

In considering an application pursuant to art. 13, the court 'shall take into account the information relating to the social background of the child provided by the Central Authority or other competent authority of the child's habitual residence.' Thus, for example, McGuinness J in *T.M.M. v M.D.* (unreported, 20 January 1999, High Ct) relied upon the negative assessments of the family environment contained in social work reports compiled by the relevant English authorities.

14.2.2.7   Defences

For a defendant in proceedings under the Hague Convention, recourse may be had to the 'defences' provided by the Hague Convention, arts. 13 and 20.

Article 13 provides that, notwithstanding the provisions of art. 12, the court is not bound to order the return of the child if the person, institution or other body, which opposes its return, establishes that:

(a)   the person, institution or other body having the care of the person of the child was not actually exercising the custody rights at the time of removal or retention, or had consented to or subsequently acquiesced in the removal or retention; or

(b)   there is a grave risk that his or her return would expose the child to physical or psychological harm or otherwise place the child in an intolerable situation.

Article 18 of the Hague Convention provides that the court of the requested State may return a child despite the fact that the case falls within the parameters of one of the exceptions set out in art. 13. Article 13 itself provides that the requested State 'is not bound' to order the return of the child if it is shown that the relevant circumstances exist. Thus, as Keane J noted in *B.B. v J.B.* (unreported, 28 July 1997, Supreme Ct) the jurisdiction to refuse to return, which art. 13 confers, is permissive, and the courts retain a discretion throughout. In this regard, reference should be made to the decision of the Supreme Court in the above case, where the court endorsed the trial judge's finding that the dispossessed parent had in fact consented to the removal of the child, yet overturned his order refusing to return as the learned trial judge had failed to exercise the discretion which arts. 13 and 18 conferred.

'Grave risk'

These provisions of art. 13(b) have often been invoked by abducting parents as a means of resisting an application for return. The attitude of the superior courts to this defence has varied and, over time, an increasingly restrictive interpretation has been placed on the phraseology of art. 13(b) of the Convention, particularly since the judgment in *C.K. v C.K.* [1994] 1 IR 250.

In the earlier case of *M.A. v P.R.* [1993] 2 Fam LJ 52, the High Court refused to order the return of a child to a father who had behaved in an extremely violent manner towards the family and whose behaviour had first forced his wife and children out of the family home and into a refuge prior to her departure with the children to this State. The High Court accepted that the defendant was forced to leave because she was stricken with fear and, furthermore, acknowledged that the violence inflicted by her husband was physically affecting the children and the defendant. The court accepted that there was a grave risk of further physical and psychological harm to the children if returned to their father.

A similar conclusion was reached by Costello J in *R.G. v B.G.* [1993] 2 Fam LJ 55, where the learned judge accepted the evidence of the mother of the children that her husband drank to excess and was violent while drunk. Perhaps the most lenient application of all may be found in *P.F. v M.F.* (unreported, 13 January 1993, Supreme Ct), wherein the Supreme Court invoked the final clause of art. 13(b) and refused to order the return of children to their father in Massachusetts on the grounds of his previous record of gross financial irresponsibility. Returning them to such an environment would, the court concluded, expose the children in question to an intolerable situation.

It is clearly arguable that, in the above cases, the Irish courts tended towards a consideration of the merits of the custody issues and, in effect, the courts began to tread into territories more properly the preserve of the courts of the State of the child's habitual residence in custody and related proceedings.

The decision in *C.K. v C.K.* [1994] 1 IR 250 clearly envisages, however, that the defence may be successfully invoked in limited circumstances. The court therein drew attention to the preamble of the Hague Convention which states that a child's interests are of paramount importance and that such interests are best served by the return of the child to the jurisdiction in which he or she was habitually resident in order to enable the courts of that jurisdiction to determine issues of custody and related matters. The court concluded that the defendant had not shown that the courts in Australia, being the jurisdiction to which it was proposed to return the children, would not adequately consider the children's welfare.

The decision of the Supreme Court in *S v S* [1998] 2 IR 244 is in a similar vein. While acknowledging that grave risk may take many forms and furthermore that there was a *prima facie* case of sexual abuse of one of the children by the father who sought to secure return, the court nonetheless refused to apply the art. 13(b) defence. The court concluded that there was no grave risk involved in returning the child in question to the *jurisdiction* of the courts of England and Wales, although it refused to order her return to her father pending full custody proceedings in the said courts. The evidence in the case did not sustain a finding that there would be a grave risk of psychological harm in returning the child to the family home, if the plaintiff father was absent.

In the more recent case of *T.M.M. v M.D.* (unreported, 20 January 1999, High Ct) the plaintiff mother sought to secure the return to England of her two children, aged 11 and 8 years. The children had been brought to this jurisdiction by their maternal grandparents and had been resident here for a period of one and a half years by the time the matter came on for hearing in the High Court before McGuinness J. The evidence before the learned judge indicated that the plaintiff had a ten-year history of alcoholism and had suffered from bouts of depression. Evidence of child neglect was borne out by a social welfare report compiled by the English authorities. McGuinness J and the Supreme Court on appeal concluded that there was a very real risk of physical and psychological harm to the two children and thus refused to order the return of the children. McGuinness J distinguished this case from *S v S* [1998] 2 IR 244 by adverting to the fact that, unlike the earlier case, there was no satisfactory carer for the children in England if returned there.

The decision in *M.D. v A.T.D.* (unreported, 6 March 1998, High Ct, O'Sullivan J) should also be noted at this juncture. In that case, the defendant relied, inter alia, upon the psychological harm which separation from his mother would cause to the child in question, in order to resist her husband's application to secure return. The defendant indicated that she would not return to England as she wished to stay in this State with her other, older, child (who was not the subject of an application under the Convention by the plaintiff). O'Sullivan J rejected her attempt to rely on this provision, stating that 'a court should be astute not to permit an abducting parent to set the Convention at naught by refusing to travel with a returning child.'

The child's wishes

A court may also refuse to return a child if it finds that the child objects to being returned and has attained an age and degree of maturity at which it is appropriate to take account of his views. Article 13(c) provides a separate and distinct ground for refusal to return on this basis and, thus, this defence may be invoked in the absence of allegations of grave risk of physical or psychological harm.

The Irish courts have, however, noted that whilst it is a separate ground, 'a decision not to return a child to the country of its habitual residence is a decision of the court and care should be taken [t]hat it is not, nor does it appear to be, the decision of the child.' (*Per* Denham J in *T.M.M. v M.D.* (unreported, 8 December 1999, Supreme Ct).)

Great care must be taken in the exercise of this judicial discretion, and the courts shall not rely upon a child's objections unless satisfied that they are raised for mature and cogent reasons: *per* Morris J in *D.C. v V.L.C.* (unreported, January 1995, High Ct, Morris J). The questions whether a child objects to being returned and furthermore whether he or she has attained an age and degree of maturity at which it is appropriate to take account of his view are questions of fact peculiarly within the province of the trial judge and the courts have resisted the call to adopt guidelines setting out the procedure to be employed by judges when ascertaining these facts: see *D.C. v V.L.C.* cited above.

Article 20 defence: fundamental principles

Article 20 supplements the art. 13 defences by providing that '[t]he return of the child under the provisions of article 12 may be refused if this would not be permitted by the fundamental principles of the requested State relating to the protection of human rights and fundamental freedoms.'

However, art. 18 provides that nothing in Chapter III of the Hague Convention shall limit the power of a judicial or administrative authority to order the return of the child at any time.

Conclusion

The present attitude of the courts, following the lead of the Supreme Court, for example, in such cases as *C.K. v C.K.* [1994] 1 IR 250, is to favour a very strict interpretation of the defences provided in the Hague Convention. The presumption underlying the Hague Convention (that the best interests of the child are served by the prompt return of the child to the jurisdiction of origin) is not easily surmountable, and any risks identified to the court by the defendant will often be regarded as best dealt with by the relevant authorities in the jurisdiction of origin.

Communications between the Central Authorities (note that in this regard it is envisaged that the Central Authorities will 'co-operate with each other and promote co-operation amongst the competent authorities in their respective State to secure the prompt return of children and to achieve the other objectives of the Convention': Hague Convention, art. 7) and the provision of undertakings to the court by one or both parties will often be regarded as adequate interim protection, pending a resolution of the custody or access issues before the courts in the jurisdiction of origin.

14.2.2.8   Undertakings

The High Court frequently seeks undertakings from the plaintiff parent as a prerequisite to an order for return. Undertakings may be drafted in negative terms, such as those which envisage that, if a child is returned to the place of habitual residence, his or her plaintiff parent shall not reside in the family home pending the resolution of custody or other relevant matters, an example thereof is found in *S v S* [1998] 2 IR 244, mentioned above, or may alternatively impose positive obligations such as a duty to make interim maintenance payments or to provide accommodation for the abducting parent pending the resolution of relevant court proceedings in the place of habitual residence. In that regard, see the judgment of O'Sullivan J in *P v B* [1994] 3 IR 507, also cited above.

In *P v B*, the Supreme Court agreed that the use of reasonable and enforceable under-takings, designed to ensure the welfare of the child during the transition from one jurisdiction to another, is entirely consistent with the 1991 Act and with the Hague Convention. Such undertakings, the court added, accord with the constitutional protection of the welfare of the child and they may also protect a parent in their role and in the exercise of their rights under the Constitution.

The courts have on occasion rejected the argument that a child should not be returned to the place of his or her habitual residence by reason of a grave risk that he or she would suffer physical or psychological harm at the hands of the plaintiff parent, and have instead insisted upon the acceptance and adoption of appropriate undertakings by that parent. Thus, as mentioned above, the Supreme Court in *S v S* concluded that the child in question should be returned to England but that the plaintiff parent, in respect of whom allegations of sexual abuse against the child were made, should not reside in the family home pending the resolution of proceedings before the English courts.

In *T.M.M. v M.D.* (unreported, 20 January 1999, High Ct), on the other hand, McGuinness J in the High Court distinguished the facts before her from those in the *S v S* case. The learned trial judge noted the mother's difficult history of alcoholism and also referred to the fact that the children's father had ceased to play any role in their upbringing and was thus clearly not a satisfactory alternative carer for the children. There was therefore no safe environment for the children in England. McGuinness J accepted that the English courts would enforce any undertakings imposed but concluded, nonetheless, that there was a very real risk of physical and psychological harm which could not be met by any form of undertaking. The approach of the learned trial judge was endorsed by the Supreme Court on appeal.

14.2.2.9 Disputes concerning rights of access

Rights of access are defined as including 'the right to take a child for a limited period of time to a place other than the child's habitual residence'. It is clear from the wording of the preamble and of art. 3 of the Hague Convention that the primary objective thereof is the protection and enforcement of custody rights. By contrast, the terms of the Convention do not warrant the return of children and their custodial parent to the jurisdiction in which they were formerly habitually resident merely to enable the non-custodial parent to exercise his or her rights of access. This holds equally true in those cases in which a court order granting access to the dispossessed parent is also deemed to prohibit the removal of the child without the consent of that parent or further order of the court, *per* Keane J in *W.P.P. v M.D.* (unreported, 14 December 1999, Supreme Ct). The enforcement of access rights is assigned by the Convention to the administrative channels of the Central Authorities designated by the Contracting State.

14.2.3 THE LUXEMBOURG CONVENTION

14.2.3.1 Principal features

The European Convention on Recognition and Enforcement of Decisions Concerning Custody of Children and on Restoration of Custody of Children, known as the Luxembourg Convention, is primarily concerned, as its long title suggests, with the recognition and enforcement of custody decisions made in any of the Contracting States and, accordingly, also has a role in the restoration of custody of children.

A decision relating to custody is, for the purposes of the Convention, 'a decision of an authority in so far as it relates to the care of the person of the child, including the right to decide on the place of his [or her] residence, or the right of access to him [or her]' (Luxembourg Convention, art. 1).

Improper removal is defined in art. 1 as meaning:

> *the removal of a child across an international frontier in breach of a decision relating to his [or her] custody which has been given in a Contracting State and which is enforceable in such a State; improper removal also includes:*
>
> *(a) the failure to return a child across an international frontier at the end of a period of the exercise of the right of access to this child or at the end of any other temporary stay in a territory other than that where custody is exercised;*
>
> *(b) a removal which is subsequently declared unlawful within the meaning of article 12.*

The Luxembourg Convention also establishes a Central Authority to carry out the functions provided for by the Convention and the Central Authorities are also required to co-operate with each other and promote co-operation in a manner akin to that required pursuant to the Hague Convention.

In order that the provisions of the Convention may be activated therefore, a *decision relating to custody* made by the relevant authority in a Contracting State must be in existence. Furthermore, like the Hague Convention, the child the subject of the decision must be under 16 years of age.

14.2.3.2 Recognition and enforcement

Where a person who has obtained such a decision wishes to have that decision recognised or enforced in another Contracting State, an application must be made to a Central Authority in accordance with the procedural requirements set out in the Luxembourg Convention, arts. 4, 13 and 14. Article 7 provides that '[a] decision relating to custody given in a Contracting State shall be recognised and, where it is enforceable in the State of origin, made enforceable in every other Contracting State.'

Articles 9 and 10 outline the circumstances in which an application for recognition and enforcement may be refused:

(a) Where procedural defects exist, e.g. if a decision in respect of custody or access was made in the absence of the defendant or his or her legal representative, if the defendant was not duly served with the initiating document in sufficient time to enable him or her to arrange his or her defence (unless service was not effected due to the defendant's concealment of his or her whereabouts): see art. 9(1). Note also that proceedings for recognition and enforcement may be adjourned on grounds set out in art. 10(2).

In the case of *S.D. v R.B.* [1996] 1 FLR 291 Costello P refused to endorse the decision of the English courts regarding the custody of two children brought to this jurisdiction by their mother. The High Court, however, found that notice of the proceedings before the English courts had not been properly served on the mother and that she had been made aware of the impending court hearing a mere two days before it took place. She was not therefore in a position to secure legal assistance and representation nor arrange her own travel to the proceedings. The learned judge noted that the child's father had been aware of the whereabouts of the mother and had nonetheless failed to inform her of these matters. This approach was endorsed in *P.M. v V.M.* (unreported, 4 November 1997, High Ct, Kinlen J; unreported, 20 February 1998, Supreme Ct), see also *S.D. v R.S.* [1996] 3 IR 524.

(b) If the effects of the decision are manifestly incompatible with the fundamental principles of the law relating to the family and children in this State: see art. 10(1)(a).

(c) Where, by reason of a change in circumstances (including the passage of time, not including a mere change in the residence of the child after an improper removal), the effects of the original decision are manifestly no longer in accordance with the welfare of the child: see art. 10(1)(b).

(d) Where, at the time when the proceedings were instituted in the State of origin, the child was an Irish national or was habitually resident here and no such connection existed with the State of origin: see art. 10(1)(c)(i).

(e) Where, at the time when the proceedings were instituted in the State of origin, the child was both an Irish national and a national of the State of origin and was habitually resident in Ireland: see art. 10(1)(c)(ii).

(f) Where the decision is incompatible with a decision given in Ireland, or a decision enforceable here having been given in a third State, pursuant to proceedings commenced before the submission of a request for recognition or enforcement, and if the refusal is in accordance with the welfare of the child: see art. 10(1)(d).

In accordance with the judicial stance taken in the context of the Hague Convention, the courts have taken a restrictive approach to the interpretation of the circumstances in which an application for the return of a child under the Convention will be refused. See, for example, *R.J. v M.R.* [1994] 1 IR 28 and *S.M. v A.J.B.* [1994] 3 IR 491. The applicable standard of proof according to these cases is one of 'high probability', 'something more than the probability appropriate for ordinary proof in civil actions'.

If, at the time of the removal, there is no custody order in force, the Luxembourg Convention, art. 12, provides that this Convention may apply to an order made after the removal if it also contains a declaration that the removal was wrongful.

14.2.3.3 Conclusion

Given the more limited 'defences' available to defendants and the narrower margin of discretion available to the courts in proceedings instituted under the Luxembourg Convention, it would appear to be in the interests of a person seeking the return of a child wrongfully or improperly removed or retained to institute proceedings under the Luxembourg Convention as opposed to the Hague Convention where possible to do so.

14.3 Interaction between Irish Law and International Law

As indicated above, the Child Abduction and Enforcement of Court Orders Act 1991 (the '1991 Act') brought both the Hague and Luxembourg Conventions into force in Irish law on 1 October 1991. The Conventions do not oust jurisdiction of the Irish court. Indeed, the 1991 Act, s. 11, provides that nothing in Part II of the Act (the Part dealing with the Hague Convention) 'shall prevent a person from applying in the first instance to the court, whether or not under the Hague Convention, in respect of the breach of rights of custody of, or breach of rights of access to, a child removed to the State'.

The court referred to in the 1991 Act is the High Court and, in addition to applications for the return of children to their country of habitual residence and for the recognition and enforcement of foreign court orders, applications may be made to the High Court for interim directions (1991 Act, ss. 12, 15) and for a stay on any other proceedings pending before the courts (1991 Act, s. 13).

Other Irish statutes which may interface with an abduction, removal or retention situation are the Guardianship of Infants Act 1964 (as amended), the Family Law Act 1995 and the Non-Fatal Offences Against the Person Act 1997. Of particular importance are the Guardianship of Infants Act 1964, s. 11 (as amended); the Family Law Act 1995, s. 47, which provides for the procurement of social reports; and the Non-Fatal Offences Against the Person Act 1997, s. 16 which creates a new criminal offence of abduction of children under 16 years of age.

14.4 Potential Situations with which Practitioners may be Presented

14.4.1 WHERE A CHILD IS ABOUT TO BE ABDUCTED

(a) Applications may be made to the *District Court, Circuit Court* or the *High Court* seeking:

    (i) orders pursuant to the Guardianship of Infants Act 1964, s. 11 (sole custody, passports, prohibiting removal of child from jurisdiction without consent of custodial parent or consent of court);

    (ii) orders pursuant to the Child Abduction and Enforcement of Custody Orders Act 1991, s. 37, which empowers members of An Garda Síochána to detain a child where he or she reasonably suspects that the child is about to be or is being removed from the State in breach of a court order regarding custody, access or wardship, a care order, an interim order under the 1991 Act or an order under the 1991 Act for the return of a child or the enforcement of decision relating to custody or access. A Garda can detain a child while proceedings for any such order 'are pending' or where an application for any of those orders is about to be made. Therefore, even before an order is formally granted, the Gardaí may act;

    (iii) if necessary, an application pursuant to the Guardianship of Infants Act 1964, as amended, appointing a natural father as a guardian of a child or granting him sole custody or access.

(b) An application may be made to the *Circuit Court* or the *High Court* for an injunction preventing the removal of the child, together with an order permitting notification of the Gardaí, the port authorities, airports, etc.

(c) A wardship application may be made to the *High Court*. This is particularly useful where the child may be removed to a non-Convention country.

14.4.2 WHERE A CHILD HAS BEEN ABDUCTED OUT OF THE JURISDICTION

(a) Establish the child's whereabouts: contact: Gardaí; Department of Justice; Irish Embassies in countries to which child may have been abducted; International Red Cross.

(b) If whereabouts ascertained establish whether child is within jurisdiction of Hague or Luxembourg Conventions; contact the Irish Central Authority.

(c) If the child is in a Luxembourg Convention country and if the dispossessed parent does not have an Irish court order confirming his or her rights, an application may be made for such an order, which should also contain a declaration that the removal was wrongful.

(d) If child has been abducted to a non-Convention country, it will usually be necessary to retain the services of a lawyer in that country; useful contacts include the relevant Irish Embassy and the Law Society for contact names.

14.4.3 HAGUE CONVENTION PROCEEDINGS: CHILD WRONGFULLY REMOVED TO OR RETAINED IN THIS JURISDICTION

Establish:

(a)   whether child is under 16;

(b)   whether wrongful removal or retention within meaning of Hague Convention, art. 3;

(c)   if confirm wrongful removal or retention, when it occurred;

(d)   where child's habitual residence is;

(e)   consent/acquiescence;

(f)   grave risk;

(g)   intolerable situation;

(h)   return of child would not be permitted by the fundamental principles of this State relating to the protection of human rights and fundamental freedoms;

(i)   note that even if the person who has abducted or retained a child can establish a grave risk etc., the court still has a discretion to return the child to the State of origin;

(j)   focus on building a case technical defences; substantive defences; apply to have information relating to the child's social background available to the court; apply to have a report prepared pursuant to the Family Law Act 1995, s. 47; consider necessity of obtaining a psychological assessment.

14.4.4 LUXEMBOURG CONVENTION PROCEEDINGS: CHILD IMPROPERLY OR WRONGFULLY REMOVED TO OR RETAINED IN THIS JURISDICTION

Establish:

(a)   whether child is under 16;

(b)   whether at the time of removal or retention the applicant had a custody or access order in his or her favour;

(c)   whether the child was removed to or retained in this State in breach of those custody or access rights, i.e. whether improper removal within meaning of Luxembourg Convention, art. 1(d);

(d)   that the request for the restoration was made to a Central Authority within six months from the date of the improper removal.

14.4.5 CHILD WRONGFULLY REMOVED TO THIS JURISDICTION FROM NON-CONVENTION COUNTRY

(a)   if applicable, consider obtaining orders or making a wardship application in this jurisdiction

(b)   focus on building a case in the same manner as in respect of a Hague Convention case identify: technical defences; substantive defences; apply to have a report prepared pursuant to the Family Law Act 1995, s. 47; consider the necessity of obtaining a psychological assessment.

14.5 Application under Hague Convention 1980 or Luxembourg Convention 1980

PROCEDURE

WHO MAY APPLY	*Hague Convention* Any person, institution or body who claims that a child has been wrongfully removed or retained in breach of custody or access rights	art. 3
	Luxembourg Convention Any person who has a court order giving them rights of custody and/or access	arts. 1, 8
WHICH COURT	High Court	1991 Act, s. 11
CONDITIONS PRECEDENT TO APPLICATION	*Hague Convention* Child must have been wrongfully removed or retained in breach of rights of custody or access which at the time of breach were actually exercised or would have been so exercised but for removal/retention	art. 3
	Child must have been habitually resident in a Contracting State immediately before his/her removal or retention or the breach of access rights	art. 4
	Child must have been under 16	art. 4
	Child must have been taken or retained after date on which Convention came into force between the two countries involved	
	Luxembourg Convention Child must be under 16	art. 1
	At the time of the removal the applicant must have a custody or access order made in his or her favour	art. 4
	The child must have been removed in breach of those custody or access rights to another Contracting State	art. 3
	If, at the time of the removal, there is no custody order in force, the Luxembourg Convention may apply to an order made after the removal if it also contains a declaration that the removal was wrongful	art. 12
APPLICATION PROCEDURE	By way of special summons, grounded upon affidavit and notice of motion, grounded upon affidavit; initiated by ex parte application before the High Court	

SERVICE By order of court /liberty sought at
ex parte stage

AFFIDAVIT IN ANSWER Defendant will usually seek time to
file affidavit(s)

May be appropriate to seek psychological
or psychiatric (or other medical) assessment

AFFIDAVITS OF LAWS May be necessary depending on jurisdiction involved

**NOTICES OF INTENTION
TO CROSS-EXAMINE** May be necessary depending on circumstances

FURTHER READING

Binchy, *A Casebook on Irish Family Law* (Professional Books, 1988).

Casey and Creaven, *Psychiatry and the Law* (Oak Tree Press, 1999).

Duncan and Scully, *Marriage Breakdown in Ireland* (Butterworths, 1990).

Irish Journal of Family Law (Round Hall).

O'Connor, *Key Issues in Family Law* (Round Hall, 1988).

Power, *Family Legislation Service* (Round Hall, 2000).

Shannon, *The Divorce Act in Practice* (Round Hall, 1999).

Shannon, *Family Law Practitioner* (Round Hall, 2000).

Shatter, *Family Law* (4th edn, Butterworths, 1997).

Walls and Bergin, *The Law of Divorce in Ireland* (Jordans, 1997).

Ward, *The Financial Consequences of Marital Breakdown* (Combat Poverty Agency, 1990).

INDEX

INDEX